Economic Resilience and Pandemic Response

I0888157

The COVID-19 pandemic upended our social and economic lives. Lockdowns forced firms to implement health and safety protocols, employees to work from home, and businesses of all sorts to close. Even as lockdowns eased, the landscape of work, commerce, leisure, and education was irrevocably transformed. While in many ways life has returned to normal, many of the changes wrought by the pandemic are here to stay. This book presents research on these transformations, examining how the economy and society were impacted. Organizing different aspects of the pandemic into individual chapters, this book examines issues such as financing structures, liquidity, profitmaking, investment, financial security, and market valuation, among other topics. Reflecting deep research as well as an extensive review of the literature, each chapter provides not just theoretical and empirical insight but also a set of policy recommendations to insure against similar crises in the future. Encompassing a range of case studies, it outlines strategies for dealing with the manifold challenges of today's business environment. This book showcases the development of particular sectors over the course of the pandemic, and as such, serves as a valuable study, enabling a comprehensive analysis of topics ranging from economics to social dynamics. It provides a deep understanding of this unique period's wide-ranging challenges and transformations, and underscores the central economic concern of the pandemic's effect on economic security, a topic discussed throughout several chapters. Furthermore, it includes a discussion on the broader scope of "polycrisis". This volume was designed to appeal to a wide range of readers interested in economics, management, regional studies, and related fields.

Agnieszka Rzepka is a Professor in the Department of Economics and Economic Management, Faculty of Management, Lublin University of Technology, Poland.

Artur Paździor is a Professor and Head of the Department of Finance and Accounting, Faculty of Management, Lublin University of Technology, Poland.

Routledge Advances in Regional Economics, Science and Policy

Smart Cities in Europe and Asia
Urban Planning and Management for a Sustainable Future
Edited by Prana Krishna Biswas and Robert Dygas

Sustainable Regional Development
Revitalizing Regions Through Innovation
Michael P. Clair

Governance and Leadership in Shrinking Cities
Strategies for Managing Urban Decline
Edited by Stanisław Mazur

Regional Policy in the Southern African Development Community
Edited by J. Ernst Drewes and Mariske van Aswegen

Regional Cooperation and Resilience in East Asia
Edited by Sebastian Bobowski

The Business of Affordable Housing
Case Studies of the Commercial Supply of Affordable Homes
Alexander Styhre

Spatial Planning and the European Union
Europeanisation from Within
Eva Purkarthofer

Economic Resilience and Pandemic Response
Edited by Agnieszka Rzepka and Artur Paździor

For more information about this series, please visit: www.routledge.com/series/RAIRESP

Economic Resilience and Pandemic Response

Edited by
Agnieszka Rzepka and Artur Paździor

Translated by Jakub Prachowski

Routledge
Taylor & Francis Group
LONDON AND NEW YORK

First published 2025
by Routledge
4 Park Square, Milton Park, Abingdon, Oxon OX14 4RN

and by Routledge
605 Third Avenue, New York, NY 10158

Routledge is an imprint of the Taylor & Francis Group, an informa business

© 2025 selection and editorial matter, Agnieszka Rzepka and Artur Paździor; individual chapters, the contributors

The right of Agnieszka Rzepka and Artur Paździor to be identified as the authors of the editorial material, and of the authors for their individual chapters, has been asserted in accordance with sections 77 and 78 of the Copyright, Designs and Patents Act 1988.

All rights reserved. No part of this book may be reprinted or reproduced or utilised in any form or by any electronic, mechanical, or other means, now known or hereafter invented, including photocopying and recording, or in any information storage or retrieval system, without permission in writing from the publishers.

Trademark notice: Product or corporate names may be trademarks or registered trademarks, and are used only for identification and explanation without intent to infringe.

British Library Cataloguing-in-Publication Data
A catalogue record for this book is available from the British Library

Library of Congress Cataloging-in-Publication Data
Names: Rzepka, Agnieszka, editor. | Paździor, Artur, editor. | Prachowski, Jakub, editor.
Title: Economic resilience and pandemic response / edied by Agnieszka Rzepka and Artur Paździor ; translated by Jakub Prachowski.
Description: Abingdon, Oxon ; New York, NY : Routledge, 2025. | Series: Routledge advances in regional economics, science and policy | Includes bibliographical references and index.
Identifiers: LCCN 2024007906 (print) | LCCN 2024007907 (ebook) | ISBN 9781032757728 (hardback) | ISBN 9781032757759 (paperback) | ISBN 9781003475583 (ebook)
Subjects: LCSH: Economic history—21st century. | Social history—21st century. | COVID-19 Pandemic, 2020—Influence.
Classification: LCC HC59.3 .E36 2025 (print) | LCC HC59.3 (ebook) | DDC 330.9—dc23/eng/20240329
LC record available at https://lccn.loc.gov/2024007906
LC ebook record available at https://lccn.loc.gov/2024007907

ISBN: 978-1-032-75772-8 (hbk)
ISBN: 978-1-032-75775-9 (pbk)
ISBN: 978-1-003-47558-3 (ebk)

DOI: 10.4324/9781003475583

Typeset in Sabon
by codeMantra

Contents

Figures

Tables

Contributors

Piotr Bolibok is an Assistant Professor at the Department of Economic Policy and Banking in the Faculty of Social Sciences at the John Paul II Catholic University of Lublin. He is also specialist in financial economics, banking, and macroprudential policy. His current research is focused on the value relevance of financial disclosures in the banking sector, the financial aspect of banks' CSR activities, and the macroeconomic consequences of consumer debt. He has authored or co-authored over 45 scientific papers and 4 monographs.

Wiesława Caputa is a Professor at Wyższa Szkoła Bankowa in Poznań, Scientific Institute of Finance and Economics. She specializes in creating and measuring customer capital and the controlling function. His current research focuses on customer digital awareness, inter-organizational and cross-sector relationship building, and CSR. In addition to 190 articles, she is the author or co-author of 14 monographs.

Adam Czarnecki is a sociologist who holds a Ph.D. in economic sciences. He is also a research fellow at the SGH in Warsaw and vice president of the ARC Rynek & Opinia Research Institute. He specializes in marketing, and social and epidemiological research. He has to his credit publications on communication and marketing research and epidemiology, including "Product placement: An unconventional marketing strategy" (2003). He is also the co-author of "Air Pollution Increases the Incidence of Upper Respiratory Tract Symptoms among Polish Children" (2021) and "Flattening the Curve of COVID-19 Vaccine Rejection – An International Overview" (2021).

Krystyna Gomółka is the Head of the Department of Eastern Studies at the Faculty of Management and Economics at the Gdańsk University of Technology. Her research interests include issues related to the eastern policy of the EU, economic and political cross-border cooperation, and economic aspects of the energy strategies of former USSR countries. She specializes in labor markets, employment, and wages, especially in the countries of Eastern Europe and Central Asia. She is also the author of numerous books and nearly 200 scientific articles in Polish, Russian, English, and Belarusian.

Piotr Kasprzak is an employee of the Department of Finance at the Faculty of Management and Economics at the Gdańsk University of Technology. He specializes in corporate and personal income taxation. His publications include papers on taxing energy sources and low-emission vehicles. He is also the author or co-author of more than 30 articles, monograph chapters, and one book.

Brygida Klemens is a Ph.D. at the Opole University of Technology in the Faculty of Economics and Management. She is a specialist in clusters, collaboration, social capital, regional and local development. Scientific interests include clusters, collaboration networks, social capital, broadly understood regional and local development, and the development of rural areas and the transfer of know-how or innovation. Her current research is focused on entrepreneurship and rural areas. In addition to 50 papers, she has contributed to 15 monographs. She is also the author or co-author of numerous papers, regional and local strategies, and expert opinions.

Izabela Krawczyk-Sokołowska is a Professor at the Faculty of Management at the Częstochowa University of Technology. Her scientific interests include innovation, business's potential for innovation, and the synergy between an innovative enterprise and its environment (including the transfer of knowledge, information, capital, human resources, and technology). Her research focuses on resilience to innovation, the culture of innovation, and factors shaping consumers' pro-innovation and pro-environmental attitudes. She is also the author or co-author of 148 publications, including 14 monographs.

Adrian Majek is a Lecturer at the Lublin University of Technology in the Faculty of Management. He is also a specialist in financial analysis, corporate finance, and financial accounting. His current research is focused on the impact of COVID-19 on managing corporate finance. His academic achievements include a publication in a monograph and three other publications.

Beata Milewska is a Lecturer at Wyższa Szkoła Bankowości in Poznań and the Faculty of Economics at the University of Szczecin. She is also a specialist in logistics, supply chains, quality management, and production management. She is the author of over 40 articles and co-author of 8 monographs. She has been conducting research on logistics and production in Polish clothing companies since mid-2017, and conducting observations and interviews with the management of clothing companies.

Andrzej Miszczuk is a Professor at the Faculty of Economics at Maria Curie-Skłodowska University. He received his Ph.D. in 1991 and a post-doctoral degree in social-economic geography in 2004. His research topics include local and regional development, EU regional policy, the functioning of local self-governments in Poland and the EU, trans-border cooperation, and NGOs. He is also the author and editor of 17 books and over 180 articles and chapters. He is the member of the Polish Academy of Science, an expert of the National Science Centre and the Ministry for Regional Development, and also a member of the editorial board of the "Regional Barometer" quarterly scientific journal.

Magdalena Miszczuk is a Professor at the Lublin University of Technology. She graduated from Maria Curie-Skłodowska University in Lublin with a degree in economics and received her Ph.D. in economics (finance) at the Faculty of Economics Maria Curie-Skłodowska University in Lublin. Her research interests include public finance, local and regional development, EU regional policy, functioning of local self-governments in Poland and the EU, and NGOs. She is also the author and editor of 5 books and over 80 articles and chapters.

Mieczysław Morawski is Professor of Management Science at the Warsaw University of Technology, Poland. His research focuses on knowledge management, human capital management, intelligent organizations, and innovative business models. He has published more than 145 scientific papers and 14 books, and has supervised a number of Ph.D. dissertations.

Kinga Ociesa is an assistant in the Department of Finance and Accounting at the Faculty of Management of the Lublin University of Technology. She holds a B.A. in Mathematics and Finance and an M.A. in Finance and Accounting from Maria Curie-Skłodowska University in Lublin. The subject of her research and her scientific interests include the management of sources of funding and the value of enterprises.

Artur Paździor is a Professor, head of the Department of Finance and Accounting at the Faculty of Management of the Lublin University of Technology, and vice president of the Management Board of the Polish Economic Society Branch in Lublin. He received his Ph.D. in 2006 and habilitation in finance in 2015. His scientific activity includes over 100 papers on major issues in financial management and value creation published nationally and internationally in monographs and scientific journals. His research interests focus on valuation and factors involved in assessing enterprise value or the operation of medical entities, measures used in the assessment of the effectiveness of decision-making in hospital controlling systems, and the effects of crises (including the COVID-19 pandemic) on the economic and financial conditions of businesses and individuals.

He has over 20 years of experience working with businesses, which resulted in over a hundred valuation reports and reorganization plans, economic and financial analyses, recovery programs, and more. He is a member of supervisory boards for various companies and academic bodies.

Radosław Piątek is an assistant at the Lublin University of Technology in the Faculty of Management in the Department of Strategy and Business Planning. He is also a specialist in quality management, brand management, strategy planning, and normalization. His research is focused on the automotive industry. Recently, he wrote a monograph on brand portfolio management in automotive firms (2021).

Przemysław Sałek holds a Master's degree in Economics (2012) and a degree in Political Science (2010). Currently, he is a Ph.D. student at Maria Curie-Skłodowska University. He is also the author of two scientific papers – "The presence of Ukrainian agricultural companies on the Stock Exchange in Warsaw" (2015) in Annals of Agricultural Economics and Rural Development, and "Examination of communication between Respect Index companies and their potential shareholders" (2015) in European Politics, Finance, and Marketing. His scientific interests focus on the capital market.

Magdalena Sobocińska is a Professor at the University of Economics in Wrocław and specializes in issues related to various aspects of culture, the use of the Internet in marketing, marketing research, the development of consumption, and sustainable development. She is the author or co-author of more than 200 publications including monographs (*Behaviours of Buyers in the Market of Cultural Goods and Services* (2008), *Conditions and Prospects for the Development of Market Orientation in Cultural Subjects* (2015)), monograph chapters, and articles. She is also the co-editor of three monographs on marketing research.

Marta Sokół is an assistant at the Department of Finance and Accounting at the Faculty of Management of the Lublin University of Technology and a member of the Audit Committee at the Polish Economic Society. She holds a B.A. in Finance and Accounting and an M.A. in Management. Her area of expertise includes the practical aspects of corporate finance where the current research concerns the impact of the COVID-19 pandemic on the financial and economic situation of entities from various industries.

Liubomyr Sozanskyi is a Senior Researcher in the Department of Problems of the Real Sector within Regional Economy at the Dolishniy Institute of Regional Research of NAS of Ukraine, taking part in various projects. His initiatives were widely implemented at the level of the Verkhovna Rada of Ukraine, the Cabinet of Ministers of Ukraine, the National Committee for Industrial Development of Ukraine, and state administrations of 22 regions of Ukraine. He is the author of 120 papers, including seven monographs and 70 articles.

Dobrochna Sztajerska holds a Ph.D. in Economics and a Master's degree in Psychology. She is the Head of the Institute of Computer Science at the Małopolska Uczelnia Państwowa in Oświęcim. In her academic work, she

deals with issues related to the Lean philosophy as well as topics related to the overlap between hard and soft competencies. Her work also includes national and international publications on tools for improving organizational performance, as well as the practical implementation of improvement concepts in businesses.

Katarzyna Turoń is an Assistant Professor at the Faculty of Transport and Aeronautical Engineering of the Silesian University of Technology. She has authored or co-authored more than 150 scientific publications, including publications from the JCR list, and TOP10 articles according to the Scopus database. She is the recipient of numerous scholarships, e.g., the Silesian Scientific Award or the Oxford University scholarship for her scientific and organizational activities. She is actively cooperating with leading scientific centers around the world while undertaking numerous international internships. Her research interests combine the issues of sustainable development in transport, specifically, the economy of sharing, mobility management, and open innovation.

Agnieszka Wójcik-Czerniawska is an Associate Professor in the Department of Finance and Management at Szkoła Główna Handlowa in Warsaw. She holds a Ph.D. in Economics and an M.B.A. in Spanish. She has lectured at international universities in Peru, Spain, Kenya, and Italy. Her research relates to modern finance, finance technology, digital currency, financial isolation, and innovation in finance, all of which are presented in her scientific publications. She is also an active participant in international conferences and international programs for academic staff members.

Aleksandra Zalewska is an Assistant in the Department of Finance and Accounting at the Lublin University of Technology and a member of the Polish Economic Society. She has majored in Finance and Accounting (B.A.) and Financial Management (M.A.). She is also the author of papers on practical aspects of financial management and enterprise value assessment.

Introduction

Understanding the Pandemic's Impact

Agnieszka Rzepka

In recent years, the global economy has been beset by a multitude of difficult and uncertain occurrences, which have had far-reaching consequences for ordinary citizens and entrepreneurs alike. Following a period of sustained economic growth, the year 2020 was marked by a global anxiety stemming from the coronavirus pandemic. Governments across the globe executed unprecedented measures by imposing mandatory [missing text]. Consequently, economic stagnation ensued, which in turn precipitated a worldwide recession. Millions of people worldwide passed away after becoming ill with the SARS-CoV-2 virus, and as a result of inadequate healthcare access, many entrepreneurs were forced to discontinue or suspend their business activities (World Health Organization, 2021).

The COVID-19 pandemic was one of the most significant socio-economic events of the 21st century. Considering the inability to forecast its occurrence, the capriciousness of its transmission, and the difficulties associated with ascertaining its economic, social, and medical ramifications, it could be categorized as one of the so-called Black Swans – occurrences of a global scale that are beyond prediction (Raikar, 2023).

The impact of the pandemic was widespread, reaching almost every corner of the world, including Poland, where the first case of SARS-CoV-2 virus infection was diagnosed on 4 March 2020 (Ministerstwo Zdrowia, 2020). The rapid spread of the virus and the global response through lockdown measures led to the freezing of economies in many countries. Consequently, access to various public services, including healthcare, was significantly limited or entirely halted.

The effects of the pandemic extended beyond the economic realm, affecting the social fabric as well. Citizens in numerous countries found themselves compelled to stay at home for extended periods, unable to utilize public infrastructure, such as state forests. This situation resulted in a myriad of negative mental health consequences, especially among children and adolescents (Shah et al., 2020).

It can be asserted that the COVID-19 pandemic and its associated events have significantly disrupted the functioning of many economies worldwide. The implementation of lockdowns resulted in a near-complete halt in the

DOI: 10.4324/9781003475583-1

health, transportation, tourism, and hospitality sectors. The crisis also led to a decline in household income and alterations in consumer behavior, triggering shocks in both supply and demand.

The impacts of the coronavirus crisis extended beyond the real economy to the financial sector, encompassing the banking industry, financial markets, as well as currency and commodity markets. It is important to note that during the first few weeks of the pandemic, stock exchange indices experienced significant drops, which were concurrent with a significant decline in the market value of particular raw materials. The price of crude oil futures contracts experienced its first negative price in history (Reed & Krauss, 2020), marking a momentous achievement.

To counteract the economic downturn, central banks implemented unprecedented interest rate cuts, resulting in the cost of money plummeting to nearly zero in many economic systems (Investing.com, 2023).

During the COVID-19 pandemic, on 24 February 2022, another crisis unfolded as Europe and the world were thrust into Russia's armed aggression against Ukraine. The magnitude of this conflict in its initial phase was staggering. Few anticipated an open armed conflict erupting in the heart of Europe, involving nearly the entire armed forces of the world's second-largest military power (Global Fire Power, n.d.). This unprecedented attack led to tragedy for millions and had significant repercussions on global capital, currency, and commodity markets. However, it appears that the most severe consequence across various market segments was global inflation, which reached several percent in many economies worldwide, including Poland (Trading Economics, 2023). Consequently, central banks were compelled to reverse the 100% interest rate reduction implemented during the coronavirus crisis. As a result, many economies in Europe and around the world faced an economic slowdown, with some entering recession (International Monetary Fund, 2021).

The year 2023 brought another tragic crisis to the world with the outbreak of war between Israel and Palestine. Presently, its consequences are confined to the regional scale, specifically in the Middle East. However, the trajectory and ultimate dimension of this tense situation remain uncertain.

Considering the aforementioned events, it is evident that recent years have transformed Europe and the world into the stage for not just one but multiple crises of social, humanitarian, and economic nature. A theoretical argument may be made regarding the phenomenon known as "polycrisis", which signifies the occurrence of numerous crises simultaneously (Cambridge Dictionary, n.d.). The interconnection of these crises is initiating a process of synergy, whereby they disrupt economies both practically and monetarily and, most notably, have an effect on both average citizens and business owners.

This book delves into the challenges arising from recent crises, focusing notably on the COVID-19 pandemic and its repercussions on the socio-economic landscape in Poland. It seeks to examine the influence of the

COVID-19 pandemic on the well-being of Polish citizens, the operations of businesses, and the dynamics of the public sector. The book is structured into five parts, each blending theoretical and empirical perspectives. Many sections include compelling case studies drawn from the Polish economy.

In the initial part of the monograph, the focus is directed toward the accessibility of public services and organizational commitment within companies amid the pandemic. This part also investigates digital transformation when confronted with uncertainty and disruptions in logistic chains during the spread of the SARS-CoV-2 virus.

The second part of the book unveils research findings on the economic and financial impacts of the coronavirus pandemic on the banking, insurance, and construction sectors in Poland. Additionally, this section explores the intricacies of process management under crisis conditions.

The third part of the book concentrates on social and organizational aspects of the pandemic. It delves into the relationship between organizational climate and employee trust amid the conditions of the COVID-19 pandemic. It also identifies changes in the enterprise sector in Poland and Ukraine. In addition, regional and consumer resistance to changes induced by the pandemic is analyzed.

The fourth part discusses issues related to the impact of the COVID-19 pandemic on the situation in various industries of the Polish economy, including the real estate market, biotechnology, and pharmaceutical industry. Tax strategies during periods of uncertainty are also given due consideration.

The authors devoted the final portion of the paper to intriguing subjects, including but not limited to those following: changes in productivity amidst the COVID-19 pandemic, consumer behavior in uncertain environments, the value management of streaming platforms, and enterprise investment activities.

The publication targets a broad spectrum of readers, including managers, business proprietors, public administration representatives, and students and postgraduates interested in understanding the effects of the COVID-19 pandemic on the socioeconomic landscape of Poland and its distinct sectors.

References

Cambridge Dictionary. (n.d.). *Polycrisis*. https://dictionary.cambridge.org/dictionary/english/polycrisis

Global Fire Power. (n.d.). *2023 military strength ranking*. Global Firepower – World Military Strength. https://www.globalfirepower.com/countries-listing.php

International Monetary Fund. (2021). *Real GPD growth*. IMF. https://www.imf.org/external/datamapper/NGDP_RPCH@WEO/OEMDC/ADVEC/WEOWORLD

Investing.com. (2023). *Central Bank interest rates*. https://www.investing.com/central-banks/

Ministerstwo Zdrowia. (2020). *Pierwszy Przypadek Koronawirusa w Polsce*. https://www.gov.pl/web/zdrowie/pierwszy-przypadek-koronawirusa-w-polsce

Raikar, S. P. (2023, October 26). *black swan event. Encyclopedia Britannica.* https://www.britannica.com/topic/black-swan-event

Reed, S., & Krauss, C. (2020, April 20). Too much oil: How a barrel came to be worth less than nothing. *The New York Times.* https://www.nytimes.com/2020/04/20/business/oil-prices.html

Shah, K., Mann, S., Singh, R., Bangar, R., & Kulkarni, R. (2020). Impact of covid-19 on the mental health of children and adolescents. *Cureus.* https://doi.org/10.7759/cureus.10051

Trading Economics. (2023, November 3). *Poland inflation rate.* https://tradingeconomics.com/poland/inflation-cpi

World Health Organization. (2021). *Coronavirus disease (COVID-19) pandemic.* https://www.who.int/emergencies/diseases/novel-coronavirus-2019

Part 1

Impact of COVID-19 on Public Services and Organizations

1 Impact of the COVID-19 Pandemic on Access to Public Services in Poland

Brygida Klemens

Introduction and Literature Review

Today, the COVID-19 pandemic has become one of the most serious socio-economic problems on a macro scale (Klemens & Solga, 2021). Baker et al. (2020) suggest that measures taken by numerous governments, such as lockdowns, have reduced the number of new cases reported in the population. Sadly, these measures have also contributed to economic turmoil, job losses, and economic uncertainty. Unlike ever before, we are observing a conflict in the way two competing priorities (public health and the economy) are addressed (Latemore, 2021).

Operating under the conditions of an ongoing pandemic has proven to be a challenge. In particular, the consequences associated with the pandemic have affected people living in areas traditionally associated with lower living standards and poor access to public services, i.e. residents of rural and remote areas. According to Shergold and Parkhurst (2010), one way to achieve this is to increase the availability and quality of public services.

According to Sánchez-Rivero et al. (2022), interruptions in product supply chains that occurred on a global scale meant that scarce resources were directed to more populated areas (cities) resulting in severe shortages for rural residents. Chang et al. (2020) point out that many companies have been limited in their activities affecting the labor market in significant ways and resulting in a decrease in full-time jobs, which has resulted in a decrease in incomes for many families, especially in rural areas where labor supply is scarce.

The closure of traditional sales channels has led consumers and sellers to move their trade to the digital domain. The solution proved convenient for urban dwellers but not so much for residents of rural regions with poor transportation infrastructure, poor accessibility (understood as distance and time), and poor access to the Internet.

For rural residents, changing from out-of-home consumption habits to home consumption has a negative impact on their quality of life. Sánchez-Rivero et al. (2022) believe that an insufficient quality of transportation and logistical infrastructure (or lack thereof) limits home delivery opportunities

DOI: 10.4324/9781003475583-3

in rural areas. However, paradoxically, such a situation may lead to positive changes regarding the environment and sustainability, leading to relative self-sufficiency in vegetable and fruit production, for example, reducing pollution from transportation, and promoting consumers' local ethnocentrism (Figiel, 2004; Sharma et al., 1987) through shopping for local produce.

Another major change caused by the COVID-19 pandemic is the shift from traditional work methods to remote work. In some industries, this change has been perceived positively and has been viewed as a way to increase work flexibility, save time, and reduce commute costs. However, this is only convenient in a situation where broadband Internet is available; for rural areas, such availability is limited or nonexistent.

When analyzing widely understood public services that have been impacted by the COVID-19 pandemic, they undoubtedly include administrative and social services, mainly those related to health, but also to welfare and education.

As rural areas lose population and age faster, residents need access to medical, rehabilitation, and welfare care that is readily available and of high quality. Zunyou and McGoogan (2020) showed that in the era of the COVID-19 pandemic, immunocompromised elderly individuals are more susceptible to Coronavirus infections and related deaths. Senior citizens who live in rural areas often have limited access to even basic medical care, while rehabilitation treatments or other medical services are only found in cities. As a result of a shortage of health care workers, reduced mobility of elderly people, and a lack of access to medical services, their situation is relatively worse than that of seniors who live in cities. The remedy could be a shift toward telemedicine services or video consultations but the essential requirement for a smooth operation of these services is Internet access and the capability to use the appropriate devices (e.g. computer, laptop, smartphone). It turns out that the scientific evidence supports the thesis that access to and understanding of Information and Communications Technologies (ICTs) in rural areas is definitely worse than it is in cities (Ohta et al., 2020, 2021).

Changing from a traditional classroom to a remote learning system, including higher education, has resulted in young people's ability to function in peer environments being heavily dependent on Internet access and mobile phone coverage, which is a problem in rural areas. On the one hand, alienation exacerbated frustration and loosened social ties, and on the other hand, for many young people, remote education opened up opportunities for taking up remote work and integrating it with higher education, for example.

There have been disparities related to access to ICT infrastructure before. As emphasized by Borda et al. (2022), the duration of the COVID-19 pandemic has contributed to digital inequalities. Van Deursen (2020) reported that research indicates that people who are relatively more privileged are more likely to use the information and communication opportunities available via the Internet, while less privileged people are less likely to utilize them. Moore and Hancock (2020) demonstrated that when it comes to age, digital inequality affects older people most severely. In addition, seniors who have used the Internet and social media platforms were often victims of misinformation and fraud related to COVID-19. Information such as this raises concerns in the context of rural residents who generally experience reduced access to information and information technology and whose average age is generally high. The COVID-19 pandemic has undoubtedly exacerbated existing disparities in this regard.

The Impact of COVID-19 on Rural Areas in Poland

Methodology and Research Scope

In this chapter, I have used desk research to analyze domestic and international publications on the impact of the COVID-19 pandemic on the condition of rural areas with special regard to access to public services. It includes a compilation of statistical data publicly available in Polish statistical publications, which mainly relate to aspects of the information society in rural areas compared to small and large cities in Poland. The aim was to provide an overview of the level of access to certain public services in rural areas in Poland during the COVID-19 pandemic and propose recommendations for the public sector in terms of public service management. In addition, considerations have been made about whether the COVID-19 pandemic might increase the disparity in development between cities and rural areas in Poland.

Two research hypotheses were defined:

H1: Access to public services for residents of rural areas is the same as access to the centers (usually urban) where these services are offered.

Considering the impact of the COVID-19 pandemic on changes in the way public services are delivered, a second research hypothesis was developed:

H2: Access to public services for residents of rural areas is becoming increasingly dependent on Internet access and the ability to use it.

The focus of the study was on rural areas in Poland, which account for more than 90% of the country's area and are inhabited by more than 15 million people, which accounts for about 40% of the country's population ("GUS – Bank Danych Lokalnych", n.d.). The large size of the area and the high share of rural residents in the country's population provide justification for conducting research related to access to public services and the quality of life in rural areas (see Michalska-Żyła & Marks-Krzyszkowska, 2018).

June 1989 marked the beginning of Poland's political transformation. During this period, rural areas were considered underdeveloped as a result of inadequate infrastructure, lack of equity, and a low level of qualifications among the population. At that time, life in the countryside was understood to be a form of social degradation. Factors such as unsubsidized agricultural activity, farmers' difficulties in repaying loans, and inadequate free-market activities provoked corrective measures to be taken by successive governments, which concentrated on developing non-agricultural functions for rural areas (Michalska-Żyła & Marks-Krzyszkowska, 2018). Poland's membership in the EU in 2004 opened up new opportunities for socio-economic and infrastructure activities in rural areas, increasing their quality in a significant way and becoming the subject of many studies (Bański, 2014).

Poland's Rural Areas with Regard to Access to Selected Public Services during the COVID-19 Pandemic

Heffner (2010, 2011) points out that rural living conditions are often subjectively perceived to be deteriorating due to the perceived difficulty of access to the provision of public services and their unsatisfactory quality. This is one of the factors contributing to a gradual decline of some of the rural zones with deteriorating development prospects, leading to a declining rural population in increasingly broader rural areas and their intensifying marginalization.

A very simple classification of public services divides them into three groups (Heffner & Klemens, 2016):

a municipal (infrastructure), which includes public transport services, the related infrastructure and networks, water supply management, drainage and disposal of sewage, waste management, and electricity supply;
b social, which includes health care (treatment and prevention), education, culture, sports and recreation, welfare, housing, or public safety;
c administrative, which includes various forms of legal and formal documentation services.

In Poland, a number of public services are provided by local (municipal) and supra-local (county) governments, but also regional or national ones. Some of the public services are only available in a limited number of locations across the region (e.g., teaching hospitals or specialist outpatient clinics), which emphasizes the need for public transport services and establishing a system that enables people to use and access these services easily (Heffner & Gibas, 2015).

Providing full access to public services requires ensuring their availability, which is particularly crucial for rural residents as well as the elderly and those without transport. Access to public services for these people is equivalent to access to places where the services are offered. Therefore, the key issue is a good quality of roads and reliable public transport (enabling quick connections from convenient locations, sufficient frequency of transport services at convenient times allowing for low-cost or free commutes via public and private services) connecting people with centers that provide such services, i.e. places where such services are provided or public office buildings (Klemens, 2020). In addition, the location of public services in urban centers is very important (Carbonaro et al., 2018; Heffner et al., 2019; Poot, 2007). Unfortunately, it often turns out that public services meant for rural residents are located unfavorably from a spatial standpoint – on the outskirts of local neighborhoods or in hard-to-reach urban districts (Heffner & Klemens, 2015).

Due to COVID-19, services are being provided through the Internet. It was found that a range of public services of social, administrative, and even health-related nature could be offered through ICT. Citizens were unable to access government offices, schools, universities, clinics, and so on for a considerable amount of time. Remote or hybrid operating models have been implemented in many places. There were many instances that could be handled via online platforms, as well. The pandemic has shown that accessing and using public services is equivalent to being able to access and use the Internet. However, how well is this tool accessed and used?

According to an analysis of the areas of Poland that are particularly vulnerable to digital deprivation as a result of infrastructure shortages over the period of the pandemic, 4% of Poles did not have Internet access, while 10% had Internet access that was too weak for effective learning or work (Kuc-Czarnecka, 2020).

In 2010, 56.2% of households in rural Poland used the Internet, compared with 82.0% in 2018. It is worth noting that in 2018 a total of 76.2% of rural households had access to the Internet via broadband (versus 80.8% in cities). In contrast to 2010, their numbers in the countryside increased by 29.3% and in the cities by 19.2% (GUS, 2020a). Among people aged 16–74 living in cities, the number of people who used the Internet was 65.1%, 72.9%, and 87.5% in 2010, 2015, and 2020, respectively; for rural areas, the rates were 48.1%, 60.0%, and 76.7%, respectively (GUS, 2021a). In either case, it is clear to see that this indicator is increasing rapidly, which is a positive phenomenon. However, the disparities between cities and rural areas are evident, and the gap is still significant (more than 11%).

As can be seen in Table 1.1, the disparity between rural residents and urban residents (towns and cities) is evident in almost every category. The most significant difference is observable when we compare rural areas and cities. In each of the areas analyzed, however, a positive development can be seen in which the share of households using ICT resources for communication or shopping has been increasing annually.

Only 38.3% of rural residents used Internet access for public administration services in 2021 compared to 60.9% of residents of large cities (Table 1.2). The disparity is caused, among other things, by varying familiarity with online tools, proficiency in their use, and Internet connection quality.

Poland's Ministry of Digital Affairs created the citizen.gov.pl website that provided information on how various official affairs can be handled through

Table 1.1 Use of Internet in Poland in 2016–2021 in rural areas, towns, and cities

Area/year	*2016*	*2017*	*2018*	*2019*	*2020*	*2021*
Percentage of households in a given group with Internet access						
Rural areas	**77.8**	**78.6**	**82.0**	**84.6**	**89.3**	**91.8**
Towns	80.6	81.4	82.7	85.6	89.7	91,6
Cities	82.9	85.6	87.8	90.0	92.1	93.8
A group's percentage of online voice or video calls						
Rural areas	**22.0**	**26.3**	**29.5**	**43.6**	**49.3**	50.8
Towns	31.3	32.5	34.4	48.0	56.4	57.9
Cities	33.2	38.5	40.1	51.8	61.5	62.9
The percentage of members of a group who send and receive emails						
Rural areas	**48.3**	**50.5**	**51.1**	**56.4**	**56.9**	**59.4**
Towns	58.7	59.8	61.4	64.4	66,8	70.4
Cities	69.8	72.6	73.2	77.0	77.6	79.2
The percentage of members of a group who use social networking sites						
Rural areas	**40.3**	**44.5**	**45.8**	**48.4**	**53.1**	**54.0**
Towns	44.6	49.0	50.6	53.6	54.0	57.6
Cities	49.2	51.8	54.7	58.8	58.0	60.0
A group's percentage of online purchases						
Rural areas	**33.8**	**39.4**	**41.9**	**48.1**	**54.5**	**56.2**
Towns	42.1	43.7	47.0	54.2	61,6	61.1
Cities	52.9	54.3	56.8	61.8	69.3	68.6

Source: Own elaboration on the basis of GUS's data (2020b, 2021b).

Table 1.2 Use of public administration services in Poland via Internet (% of the group's total)

Area	*Year*	*Using public administration services via the Internet*	*Searching for information on public administration websites*	*Downloading official forms*	*Submitting filled-out forms*
Rural areas	**2020**	**33.7**	**21.9**	**20.5**	**25.4**
	2021	**38.3**	**22.9**	**21.1**	**31.4**
Towns	2020	42.3	27.0	23.2	33.6
	2021	47.7	28.8	27,2	39.6
Cities	2020	53.4	35.0	35.0	44.9
	2021	60.9	39.6	37.0	52.7

Source: Own elaboration on the basis of GUS's data (2020b, 2021b).

e-services. The services were divided into various categories, and users could handle a wide range of administrative tasks through the ePUAP system. Figure 1.1 shows a breakdown of services by category which can be handled using e-administration (in red) and the hotline (in green). It was compiled in May 2020 when Poland was still under lockdown.

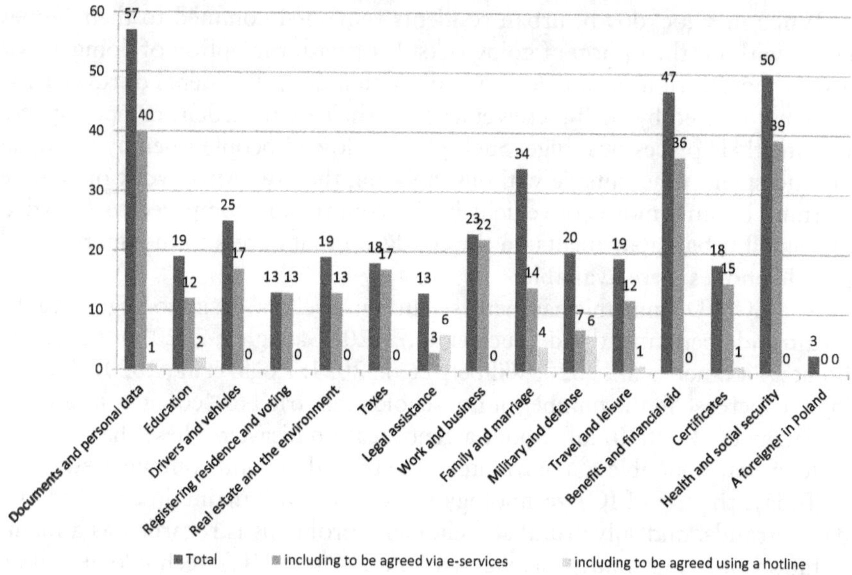

Figure 1.1 Catalog of public services available for processing through the citizen.gov.pl portal

Source: Own elaboration on the basis of data available at https://www.gov.pl/web/gov/uslugi-dla-obywatela/#dokumenty-i-dane-osobowe (retrieved 28 May 2021).

A number of other changes have been made in public services, including the introduction of e-prescriptions, telemedicine services, online patient accounts (through which one could apply to get vaccinated), etc. Purchasing habits have also changed and moved online (see Table 1.1). During the COVID-19 pandemic, courier and delivery companies flourished. For example, the number of parcel locker machines and parcel points operated by InPost in Poland as of 30 June 2022 is 24.743 ("Paczkomaty", n.d.). The machines are available in both urban and rural areas, making it easy for customers to pick up shipments at any time of the day. The company is not the only one offering similar services.

Discussion

In addition to the economic consequences of the pandemic, social changes have also occurred. Self-isolation, remote work, school closures, a ban on public events, and movement restrictions have led to changes in the way people work and their lifestyles. It seems that functioning in the so-called "new normal", which has caused many changes already continues to pose serious challenges to the economy, society, and administration for some time, and the long-term effects of the pandemic cannot be predicted yet (Klemens & Solga, 2021). However, the COVID-19 pandemic could have some benefits for rural residents.

While in a lockdown, urban residents remained confined to their homes either without the option of going outside or with the option of doing so for a very short period of time (e.g. a walk with a dog). Residents of rural areas were not limited by such inconveniences – their own gardens or open spaces became their places of refuge. Such places allowed people to enjoy the fresh air and spend time outside without violating the law. Also, work or remote learning became more convenient in the countryside compared to crowded and small urban apartments on the condition that access to the Internet and mobile phones were available.

The COVID pandemic has increased urban dwellers' desire to migrate to the countryside permanently (de Luca et al., 2020; Gallagher, 2020) or to second homes (Pitkänen et al., 2020; Willberg et al., 2021; Zoğal et al., 2020). Analyzing the increase in the number of households that tried to "counter-urbanize", Malatzky et al. (2020) talk about a gentrification disaster. These changes may be temporary but able to contribute to the revival of rural communities.

Today, the use of ICT technology to establish and maintain contacts, run daily errands, and solve rural stakeholders' problems is regarded as a manifestation of being *smart* – as well as an advantage. ICT technologies allow residents to take advantage of contactless services, ensure an efficient flow of information, and facilitate access to a wide range of services in spite of communication problems, thereby saving energy and resources. However, these opportunities appear to be limited for rural residents compared to urban residents whose infrastructure is more reliable.

In a way that has never been seen before, the COVID-19 pandemic has accelerated technological changes and the adoption and use of electronic systems. A significant number of administrative matters can be dealt with using remote technologies. As a result, access to administrative services has become easier, faster, and cheaper for people who have a good Internet connection and can make use of modern technology.

The operation of the public administration amid the COVID-19 pandemic has been a big challenge. Many offices reorganized their work models primarily through the introduction of remote or hybrid work, the introduction of scheduling and online registration for office visits, and more widespread use of electronic delivery boxes, e.g. ePUAP.

There is a growing consensus that broadband Internet access should be seen as a basic need rather than a privilege (Early & Hernandez, 2021). One of the arguments in favor of this, among other things, is the ability to be independent during lockdowns and have easier access to telemedicine, work, education, shopping, and interacting with others.

Due to the fact that the rural community is aging, it is unclear whether the pandemic could influence youth's decisions to stay in rural areas and commit to the countryside. As of the middle of 2022, when most restrictions in many states have been lifted or significantly scaled back, the majority of the public seems to expect a return to a similar "normality". Thus, young people will probably not be affected by the ending pandemic in their decision to stay in the countryside, and when infrastructure is lacking, it may be more motivating to seek out more urbanized, better-equipped, and accessible areas, i.e. in cities.

Conclusions and Recommendations

As a result of the COVID-19 pandemic, 90% of the world's population have been banned from moving and assembling (Gossling et al., 2020). The effects of the pandemic have not all been negative, however. It was possible to implement solutions very quickly and widely that would never have been possible otherwise, such as telemedicine, remote work, remote education, e-commerce, and e-administration.

The pandemic generated a number of problems faced by local governments in Poland, which included rotational shiftwork, staff shortages, increased demands on public office employees (e.g. their additional involvement in measures to improve public health), deteriorating material and living conditions of citizens, rapidly changing laws, etc.

For rural residents, access to public services was equated with access to centers (which are primarily urban) that provide them. However, the COVID-19 pandemic has partially verified this viewpoint, and today it can be pointed out that access to public services for rural residents is increasingly dependent on Internet access and the ability to use ICT tools. Thus, both research hypotheses have been positively verified.

The prerequisite for good access to administrative and social public services is sufficiently good access to public services that are technical in nature (primarily, public transportation and road accessibility). However, the COVID-19 pandemic has shown that the gap in accessibility for rural areas caused by the poorer quality technical infrastructure could be filled by providing broadband Internet access and increasing efforts aimed at educating rural residents (from different age groups) on the use of online tools. Having these skills will make using e-government tools easier and more efficient.

The development of rural areas might benefit from launching a craze for rural life in which we have nature at hand, our own workspace for remote work, and a less crowded place (and safer in the event of a pandemic). However, it is important to provide the conditions for a new way of life by ensuring the availability of convenient technical and social infrastructure, particularly broadband Internet access and a relatively high density of health centers.

When many areas of social life are shifted to the Internet, e.g. shopping, online banking, and public services, it is possible to change the way we perceive the countryside and shift it from an outdated to a safe place that is quiet and has a sophisticated infrastructure.

Recommendations for the public sector:

- widespread implementation of the idea of the *smart village*;
- providing access to broadband Internet in rural areas;

- educating rural residents on the use of computers, the Internet, and online tools in the context of e-administration (increasing digital competencies);
- making increased efforts to promote rural areas as a convenient place to live with good technical and social infrastructure;
- strengthening technical and social infrastructure;
- developing tools to encourage young rural residents to remain in their communities and stimulate local entrepreneurship;
- promoting remote work.

References

Baker, S., Bloom, N., & Davis S. (Eds.) (2020). COVID-Induced Economic Uncertainty. *Working Paper 26983*. Cambridge, MA: National Bureau of Economic Research. DOI 10.3386/w26983

Bański, J. (2014). Perspektywy rozwoju polskiej wsi-wybrane zagadnienia (Prospects for the Development of the Rural Areas of Poland—Selected Issues). *Wieś i Rolnictwo*, *4*, 13–25. Available online: http://kwartalnik.irwirpan.waw.pl/archive?year=2014 (accessed on 18 June 2022)

Borda, M., Grishchenko, N., & Kowalczyk-Rólczyńska, P. (2022). Impact of Digital Inequality on the COVID-19 Pandemic: Evidence from European Union Countries. *Sustainability*, *14*, 2850. https://doi.org/10.3390/su14052850

Carbonaro, G., Leanza, E., McCann, P., & Medda, F. (2018). Demographic Decline, Population Aging, and Modern Financial Approaches to Urban Policy. *International Regional Science Review*, *41*(2), 210–232. https://doi.org/10.1177/0160017616675916;

Chang, M., Rogers, J.H., & Zhou, S. (2020). Modern Pandemics: Recession and Recovery. *International Finance Discussion Papers 1295*. Washington: Board of Governors of the Federal Reserve System. https://doi.org/10.17016/IFDP.2020.1295.

van Deursen, A.J. (2020). Digital Inequality during a Pandemic: Quantitative Study of Differences in COVID-19—Related Internet Uses and Outcomes among the General Population. *Journal of Medical Internet Research*, 22, e20073. doi:10.2196/20073

Early, J., & Hernandez, A. (2021). Digital Disenfranchisement and COVID-19: Broadband Internet Access as a Social Determinant of Health. *Health Promotion Practice*, 22, 605–610. https://doi.org/10.1177/15248399211014490

Figiel, A. (2004). *Etnocentryzm konsumencki. Produkty krajowe czy zagraniczne.* Warszawa: Polskie Wydawnictwo Ekonomiczne.

Gallagher, S. (2020). Escape to the Country: Will People Leave Cities Behind Post-Pandemic? *The Independent*. 12.08.2020. Available online: https://www.independent.co.uk/life-style/people-leaving-cities-london-manchester-coronavirus-pandemic-lockdown-a9612116.html (accessed on 28 June 2022).

Gossling, S., Scott, D., & Hall, C. (2020). Pandemics, Tourism and Global Change: A Rapid Assessment of COVID-19. *Journal of Sustainable Tourism*, 1–20. https://doi.org/10.1080/09669582.2020.1758708

GUS (Główny Urząd Statystyczny). (2020a). Obszary wiejskie w Polsce. Warszawa.

GUS (2020b). Społeczeństwo informacyjne w Polsce w 2020r. Warszawa, Szczecin.

GUS (Główny Urząd Statystyczny). (2021a). Rocznik Statystyczny Rzeczpospolitej Polskiej. Warszawa.

GUS (2021b). Społeczeństwo informacyjne w Polsce w 2021r. Warszawa, Szczecin
GUS – Bank Danych Lokalnych. (n.d.). Retrieved 2 September 2022 from https://bdl.stat.gov.pl/bdl/start
Heffner, K. (2010). Regiony międzymetropolitalne a efekty polityki spójności w Polsce, [in:] M. Klamut, E. Szostak (eds.), *Jaka polityka spójności po roku 2013?*, Wyd. Uniwersytetu Ekonomicznego we Wrocławiu, Wrocław, 163–184.
Heffner, K. (2011). Wieś jako przedmiot badań w gospodarce przestrzennej. Procesy zagospodarowania przestrzeni wiejskiej w Polsce, [in:] M. Halamska (ed.), *Wieś jako przedmiot badań naukowych na początku XXI wieku*, Wydawnictwo Naukowe Scholar, Warszawa.
Heffner, K., & Gibas, P. (2015). Obszary funkcjonalne i ich związki z zasięgiem oddziaływania ośrodków subregionalnych (na przykładzie województwa opolskiego), *Studia Miejskie* 18, Wydawnictwo Uniwersytetu Opolskiego, Opole. https://doi.org/10.25167/sm.2422
Heffner, K., & Klemens, B. (2015). Wiejskie obszary funkcjonalne w kontekście dostępu do usług publicznych (przykład województwa opolskiego), [in:] Studia Obszarów Wiejskich, tom 38 *Wiejskie obszary funkcjonalne*, Komisja Obszarów Wiejskich PTG i IGIPZ PAN, Warszawa, 51–70. http://dx.doi.org/10.7163/SOW.37.3
Heffner, K., & Klemens, B. (2016). Potencjały i strefy problemowe w zakresie świadczenia usług publicznych na obszarach wiejskich w skali regionalnej, [in:] K. Heffner, B. Klemens (eds.) *Studia Obszarów Wiejskich*, *Przedsiębiorczy wymiar rozwoju obszarów wiejskich*, tom 42, Wydawnictwo PTG i iGIPZ PAN, http://dx.doi.org/10.7163/SOW.42.2
Heffner, K., Klemens, B., & Solga, B. (2019). Challenges of Regional Development in the Context of Population Ageing. Analysis Based on the Example of Opolskie Voivodeship. *Sustainability*, *11*(19), 5207. https://doi.org/10.3390/su11195207
Klemens, B. (2020). Obszary wiejskie w województwie opolskim w okresie przemian, [in:] B. Solga (ed.) *Województwo opolskie 1989–2019. Przemiany społeczno-gospodarcze i przestrzenne oraz wyzwania rozwojowe*, Politechnika Opolska, Opole.
Klemens, B., & Solga, B. (2021). Pandemia COVID-19 i jej wpływ na sytuację społeczno-gospodarczą kraju i regionów. *Studia Śląskie, 88–89.*
Kuc-Czarnecka, M. (2020). COVID-19 and Digital Deprivation in Poland. *Oeconomia Copernic*, *11*, 415–431. https://doi.org/10.24136/oc.2020.017
Latemore, G. (2021). COVID and the Common Good. *Philosophy of Management*, *20*. https://doi.org/10.1007/s40926-020-00154-w
de Luca, C., Tondelli, S., & Åberg, H.E. (2020). The COVID-19 Pandemic Effects in Rural Areas. *TEMA-Journal of Land Use, Mobility and Environment*; Laboratory of Land Use Mobility and Environmental: Naples, Italy. https://doi.org/10.6092/1970-9870/6844
Malatzky, C., Gillespie, J., Couch, D.L., & Cosgrave, C. (2020). Why Place Matters: A Rurally-Orientated Analysis of COVID-19's Differential Impacts. *Social Sciences & Humanities Open*, 2. https://doi.org/10.1016/j.ssaho.2020.100063
Michalska-Żyła, A., & Marks-Krzyszkowska, M. (2018). Quality of Life and Quality of Living in Rural Communes in Poland. *European Countryside*, *10*(2), 280–299. https://doi.org/10.2478/euco-2018-0017
Moore, R., & Hancock, J. (2020). Older Adults, Social Technologies, and the Coronavirus Pandemic: Challenges, Strengths, and Strategies for Support. *Social Media + Society*, *6*(3). https://doi.org/10.1177/2056305120948162

Ohta, R., Ueno, A., & Sano, C. (2021). Changes in the Comprehensiveness of Rural Medical Care for Older Japanese Patients during the COVID-19 Pandemic. *International Journal of Environmental Research and Public Health*, *18*(20), 10772. https://doi.org/10.3390/ijerph182010772

Ohta, R., Yoshinori, R., Sato, M., & Maeno, T. (2020). Challenges of using ICT regarding acute conditions in rural home care: A thematic analysis. *Journal of Interprofessional Education & Practice*, *20*, 100349. https://doi.org/10.1016/j.xjep.2020.100349

Paczkomaty. (n.d.). Retrieved 31 July 2022 from https://inpost.pl/znajdz-paczkomat

Pitkänen, K., Hannonen, O., Toso, S., Gallent, N., Hamiduddin, I., & Halseth, G. et al. (2020). Second Homes During Corona – Safe or Unsafe Haven and for Whom? Reflections from Researchers Around the World. *Matkailututkimus*, *16*(2), 20–39. https://doi.org/10.33351/mt.97559

Poot, J. (2007). Demographic Change and Regional Competitiveness: The Effects of Immigration and Ageing (*Population Studies Centre Discussion Paper* No.64). Hamilton, New Zealand: University of Waikato, Population Studies Centre. https://researchcommons.waikato.ac.nz/handle/10289/807

Sánchez-Rivero, M., Rodríguez-Rangel, M., Cerro, P., & García, A. (2022). Analysis of the Economic, Labour, and Management Effects of COVID-19 on Rural Accommodation: An Application to a Rural European Province (Cáceres, Spain). *Administrative Sciences*, *12*(2), 57. https://doi.org/10.3390/admsci12020057

Sharma, S., Shimp, T., & Shin, J. (1987). Consumer Ethnocentrism. Construction and Validation of the CETSCALE. *Journal of Marketing* Research, 24(3), 280–289. https://doi.org/10.2307/3151638.

Shergold, I., & Parkhurst, G. (2010). Operationalising "Sustainable Mobility": The Case of Transport Policy for Older Citizens in Rural Areas. *Journal of Transportation Geography*, *18*(2), 336–339. https://doi.org/10.1016/j.jtrangeo.2009.08.002

Willberg, E., Järv, O., Väisänen, T., & Toivonen, T. (2021). Escaping from Cities during the COVID-19 Crisis: Using Mobile Phone Data to Trace Mobility in Finland. *ISPRS International Journal of Geo-Information, 10*, 103. https://doi.org/10.3390/ijgi10020103

Zoğal, V., Domènech, A., & Emekli, G. (2020). Stay at (Which) Home: Second Homes during and After the COVID-19 Pandemic. *Journal of Tourism Futures*, *8*(1), 125–133. https://doi.org/10.1108/jtf-06-2020-0090

Zunyou, W., & McGoogan J.M. (2020). Characteristics of and Important Lessons from the Coronavirus Disease 2019 (COVID-19) Outbreak in China: Summary of a Report of 72 314 Cases from the Chinese Center for Disease Control and Prevention. *Cavity*, *323*, 1239–1242. https://doi.org/10.1001/jama.2020.2648

2 Digital Transformation of Organizations in Uncertain Conditions Using the Example of Selected Enterprises in Poland

Stages, Principles, and Effects

Mieczysław Morawski

Introduction

Modern civilization is about to undergo a fundamental change. We are on the brink of a technological breakthrough comparable to a new era. In much the same way that the Industrial Revolution transformed most of the world in the 18th and 19th centuries, many have pointed to the transformative power of an informational revolution today (Ojanpera et al., 2019).

In the reality of the Fourth Industrial Revolution, knowledge and the processes that optimize the management of it are becoming even more important because the ability to generate innovative knowledge, analyzing huge amounts of constantly incoming information effectively, and transferring knowledge inside and outside of the enterprise makes it possible for an enterprise to quickly adapt to changing conditions. Companies that respond quickly create never-before-seen business models based on innovative offerings, communication and distribution channels, and strategic partnerships. The main management mechanism is to ensure greater flexibility, agility, creativity, and innovation, but also to ensure social sensitivity to environmental, demographic, and sustainable development problems. The key elements that make up the new architecture of enterprise management include knowledgeable workers, strategies that incorporate long-term forecasts and spectacular plans for growth, flexible organizational structures, a work environment that encourages intellectual engagement, a work environment that utilizes mobile devices, and a culture based on collaboration and cooperation values. In response to changes, a new generation of intelligent organizations emerges. This new generation can be referred to as Intelligent Enterprise 4.0. The concept of an intelligent organization has always referred to companies that were exemplary during a given period of economic development, representing the best examples of well-run companies. Thus, theoretical generalizations were constructed that incorporated the distinctive features of this concept, emphasizing the utmost importance of intellect as the driving force behind an enterprise. Information, knowledge, competencies, technologies,

DOI: 10.4324/9781003475583-4

technical documentation, organizational methods, application procedures, specialized computer programs, and other intangible resources are the most important resources created and used by the intellect.

A question arises as to how companies that have been considered the best up to this point and whose management strategies have been models followed by other companies, cope with the inevitable technological revolution referred to as Industry 4.0. First of all, how does one implement digital transformation effectively, a process that involves implementing highly advanced technology solutions of Industry 4.0? There is a need to address these issues as we are already seeing significant disparities between leading companies and other organizations when it comes to adapting to a Fourth Industrial Revolution environment. According to the authors representing the Word Economic Forum,

> major gaps in performance are already emerging: there are increasing disparities in productivity, efficiency, and growth between the leaders and the rest of the pack; we may soon end up with a bipolar scenario, with only winners and losers. Delaying the Fourth Industrial Revolution transformation is no longer a viable option. Companies that wish to remain competitive must embark on this journey.
>
> (Betti & de Boer, 2019:6)

The main objective of this chapter is to identify patterns that occur in the digital transformation process (Digital Transformation Process: DTP) using enterprises located in Poland and to develop a model for organizational and managerial support for the DTP based on these patterns. The main part of the research was based on case studies of 35 companies of varying sizes and industries situated in Poland. The study of individual cases of the enterprises examined is centered on the progression of the DTP within an intelligent organization.

Results of the empirical study allow us to identify the existing regularities found in the DTP, including recurring stages in the process and principles used in its implementation, primarily in organizational, HR, and leadership contexts.

An additional aim of the study was to present the author's own research tools applied as part of the study, which the author recommends be used during the initial, conceptual stage of digital transformation.

The study also led to the development of a model describing organizational and managerial support for the DTP process, which includes recommendations for business managers seeking to engage in digital transformation.

It can be assumed that the implications of the study are relevant to the practice and theory of management of radical changes. It is recognized that technological change brings about other changes, and their interplay would seem relevant to management theorists and practitioners.

Due to the constrained size of this publication, emphasis has been placed on the findings and, above all, the resulting recommendations for decision-makers involved in DTPs.

The Concept of Digital Transformation in an Intelligent Enterprise in the Conditions of Industry 4.0: A Brief Review of the Literature

The concept known as Industry 4.0 in large part captures the essence of the Fourth Industrial Revolution (hereinafter referred to as 4IR). At its core is digitization which causes people and organizations to communicate and cooperate at a rapidly growing pace using wireless networks around the world (Schwab, 2016). The virtual world enters the real world of enterprises, segments of the market, products, financial and physical capital, and customers. The Internet is increasingly important to production processes, manufacturers must respond to the individual needs of customers who also purchase products online more frequently. At the same time, growing competition and the ability to choose from a virtually unlimited number of alternative offers force entrepreneurs to increase the speed and flexibility of their actions, resulting in substantial cost reductions on energy and resources, whereas environmental pressures force them to reduce the levels of harmful gas and substance emissions. The worlds of virtual and non-virtual social and economic networks penetrate one another, borders are clearly blurring, and new mechanisms are emerging to govern the flow of invisible resources. Inevitably, the business *status quo* is disappearing into history. Revolutionary technological changes occur in conjunction with other phenomena and processes (Deloitte Insights, 2019). The contemporary development of civilization is subject to the simultaneous influence of many different social, demographic, climatic, and economic factors. The new world is currently often described as the new normality of VUCA (Volatility-Uncertainty-Complexity-Ambiguity) (Morawski & Bąkowska-Morawska, 2021).

In these conditions, businesses face a huge challenge in maintaining a competitive edge and meeting the needs of quick-learning customers. Only the best who are able to view the business holistically, in a systemic manner, are able to cope with this situation. Intelligent organizations, which have high levels of intellectual capital, are capable of creating comprehensive and innovative management ideas. In the literature on the subject, the intelligent organization has long been known (Quinn, 1992; Prahalad & Hamel, 1994; Nonaka & Takeuchi, 1995; Christensen, 1997; Thannhuber, 2005). In today's world, the concept of an enterprise managed under the guiding influence of intellectual values assumes a special significance. Businesses that exhibit the characteristics of an intelligent organization are better prepared to make radical changes, including digital transformation, than other companies. Various studies have identified positive properties of intelligent enterprises. Intelligent enterprises are flexible, capable of adapting, and innovative; can cope with high complexity, a significant amount of information, and a broad range of expected services; and perform their operations with high precision in order to achieve a superior level of efficiency (Thannhuber, 2005). An intelligent organization has certain specific abilities that distinguish it from other organizations, e.g. the ability to adapt to changing reality, the ability to find new strategic fields, and the ability to influence and shape the environment (Schwaninger, 2009). In an intelligent enterprise, intellect is a key resource for production and service. It is an organization whose most valuable product is knowledge expressed as valuable services (Quinn, 1992). Intelligent organizations make use of a continuous learning process that is based on observations of the external and internal environment (Prahalad & Hamel, 1994). The concept of intelligent organizations is based on the way that members of the organization behave and the organizational culture where everyone is a knowledge worker (Nonaka & Takeuchi, 1995). The essence of an intelligent organization today is parameterized, with measurable characteristics (Fersht, 2018). They are also a means to compare companies, as well as an attempt to determine the preferences among individual companies. An important caesura for more precise identification of measurable criteria for intelligent organizations was the Strategic Innovation Symposium held in September 2016 by the Technology and Entrepreneurship Center at Harvard (TECH).

In 2018, Zebra Technologies conducted an end-user survey tracking these criteria, essentially 11 metrics designed to conceptually understand where companies are on the path to becoming an Intelligent Enterprise (Bowman, 2018). The online survey was fielded from August 6 to September 14, 2018, across a wide range of segments, including health care, manufacturing, retail, transportation, and logistics. In total, 918 IT decision-makers from nine countries were interviewed, including the U.S., Great Britain, France, Germany, Mexico, Brazil, China, India, and Japan (Zebra Technologies, 2018). The 11 criteria included: IT Vision (Driving transformational innovation starts with a vision), Technology Partner (Intelligent IoT solutions require a holistic perspective), Adoption (New user adoption is one of the most cited challenges), Change Management (the key to success is the end-user utilization), Deployment (Time to implementation is a key consideration), and Infrastructure (IoT execution requires a system to manage the technologies). It is important to note that all criteria/characteristics established as a result of international research are related to the challenges associated with digital transformation and associated specifically with a given stage in the process. In other words, the concept of an intelligent organization is now seen by managers as having a close relationship with technological progress. The link between digital transformation and the evolving way in which top businesses operate is clearly evident in a project undertaken by Word Economic Forum in collaboration with McKinsey & Co. Industry 4.0 leaders that were picked for the study were referred to as Lighthouses because of their importance in identifying the best way to achieve success with the adoption of 4IR solutions. Leveraging 4IR digital technologies, Lighthouses generate ever-increasing enterprise value in three ways: completely orienting the project toward the customer, breaking down organizational barriers, and maintaining continuous connectivity outside the organization with all the departments involved in the chain values, making data available to the outside world.

> The World Economic Forum, in collaboration with McKinsey & Company, launched the Global Lighthouse Network (GLN) in 2018. The network comprises a community of manufacturers showing leadership in using Fourth Industrial Revolution technologies to transform factories, value chains, and business models to generate compelling financial, operational, and environmental returns.
>
> (Betti & de Boer, 2019)

In 2020, the program included 54 companies that have achieved remarkable 4IR advancements within the four walls of factory sites or have effectively implemented end-to-end (E2E) digitization across the value chain (Betti et al., 2020:2). The gap between 4IR leaders and the rest of the companies was widening. The leaders' progress lies in the effective implementation of digitization across the entire E2E value chain.

Research Methodology

The idea is to carry out qualitative research through case studies involving enterprises with different business profiles, employment sizes, history, and operating as family businesses, other small businesses, or large enterprises (including branches of international companies). The companies surveyed are located in Poland, which is part of the EU and has experienced rapid economic growth in recent years, and is ranked 22nd globally for its economy size based on GDP.

The study aimed to identify the essential stages of the DTP and the established principles that were intended to effectively support the whole process. The initial assumption was made that the key guiding principles should address issues related to organization, personnel, and leadership. This assumption stems from the typical rules applied when organizations manage radical change. A major breakthrough in the existing operation of organizations is the need to establish strong leadership, adopt an appropriate approach to human resources, and implement necessary organizational changes in the arrangement of teams, organizational roles, authority, and responsibilities.

As a professor at the Faculty of Management, I asked Ph.D. students at all 19 faculties of the Warsaw University of Technology, one of Poland's largest and most prestigious technical universities, to participate in an interactive lecture entitled "Intelligent Enterprise Management in Economy 4.0. Transformation Support Model". More than 40 students, including engineers, architects, computer scientists, mechanics, and chemists who worked for a variety of companies enrolled for the lecture. For the most part, these were people who had a lot of professional experience and who were very familiar with the specifics of the sector in which their companies operated and with the specifics of the very organizations where they were employed. As professionals, they were at the top of their fields. Some members of this group held important managerial positions in their organization. All Ph.D. students agreed to be involved in the research (in the experiment).

As a result, a detailed structure describing enterprises' case studies was developed, as shown in the following section.

Structure of the case study

1 Enterprise characteristics: description of the company and the reason for choosing it

  1.1 Brief description of the enterprise: name, registered office, structure (legal and organizational), type of activity, timeline, scope of activity (domestic, international, customers, business partners), and employee competencies
  1.2 Reasons for being included in the intelligent enterprise category

2 The current state of the management system

  2.1 Description of basic elements of the management system
  2.2 Identification of digital transformation stages

3 Development prospects and recommendations

  3.1 Barriers to development: psychological, cultural, skills, organizational, financial, and other
  3.2 Enhancing the processes involved in managing digital transformation – necessary operational principles

The first step was to select a sample of enterprises to be included in the study using the knowledge obtained during the lecture, information gathered from the literature reviews they conducted, and a form containing a list of 25 control questions (Table 2.1) that was provided to them and which would allow them to evaluate whether a company is an intelligent organization or not.

Additionally, students could make use of a research form devoted to the management system in an intelligent organization (Table 2.2), in which management system components picked by respondents could be used to identify the essential features of management in each company studied.

The tools used in the research allowed the identification of which companies could be classified as intelligent enterprises and thus included in the target research sample.

Table 2.1 25-Question survey – assessing intelligent organization characteristics

A list of 25 questions: Has the enterprise become an intelligent organization?

1 Is the company guided by long-term goals for its development?
2 Does it have a business strategy and a business model that incorporates elements of knowledge management and human resources management? What do they entail?
3 Who are the stakeholders that make up an organization's ecosystem?
4 What factors contribute to a company's strategic advantage (tangible resources vs. intangible resources)?
5 Does the organization understand the importance of intellectual capital and how it is managed (identification, measurement, and development)?
6 Which areas of the company's strategy (e.g. production, technologies, marketing, logistics, and personnel) focus on rapid development and expansion?
7 Does the company analyze market trends, and recognize subtle signals emanating from the environment?
8 Does the organization initiate, design, and implement stages of digital transformation?
9 What kind of knowledge is contained in the company's products/services?
10 Is the organizational structure flat and does it have a low number of management levels?
11 Does the work organization dominate teams (problem, design, expert, and implementation) and decentralized business units?
12 What functions, organizational roles, and management styles do managers possess and apply?
13 Is there a dedicated knowledge management system (acquisition, codification, use, creation, and sharing) in the company?
14 Who in the organization is responsible for acquiring, collecting, disseminating, and using information and knowledge that comes from within the company and its environment?
15 How much autonomy do organizational positions have?
16 What is the company's expenditure on IT infrastructure, software, and knowledge management systems?
17 What ICT tools and programs assist the management of the knowledge flow process?
18 Are employees encouraged to come up with ideas, experiment, share knowledge, learn, and improve their skills?
19 Can employees communicate with each other? In what way?
20 How do employees develop their competencies, learn, and acquire knowledge?
21 How does organizational learning take place?
22 Does organizational culture rely on values such as trust, entrepreneurship, creativity, courage, and tolerance for uncertainty?
23 What are the ways in which key employees are selected in the company (special qualifications, unique practical skills, exceptional experience, responsibilities, and job position)?
24 In terms of the creation and exchange of information and knowledge, with which institutions and enterprises is the company involved?
25 How is relational capital created (e.g. internships in other companies, forming clusters, and joint business ventures)?

Source: Own elaboration

Table 2.2 Research survey for intelligent organization management system

Elements of a management system in an intelligent organization	*Guidelines for an intelligent organization*
Strategy + business model	Strategic management based on development aims, building competitive advantage on the basis of intangible resources, identifying and capturing market opportunities and chances, analyzing the external and the internal environment of the enterprise, focusing on accumulation, transferring and using knowledge and implementing innovative solutions, focusing on customers, web-based business models, and managing relationships with stakeholders
Organizational structure	Flat hierarchy, task teams, informal networks of experts connected by a common interest and passions, flexible organizational roles and functions, job rotation, processes and procedures that create added value for the customer
Policy on personnel	Acquiring employees with high potential and professional qualifications, identifying key groups of employees, rewarding creativity, competence management, talent management, facilitating knowledge management (acquisition, transfer, and use), encouraging and creating conditions for informal contacts between employees
Organizational culture	Open communication, informal contacts, openness to change, experimentation, absence of distance, sense of responsibility, a sense of partnership in creative action, professional ethos, key values: trust, dialogue, and commitment
Leadership/management style	Relationships between supervisors and subordinates based on partnership, substantive support, discussion and exchange of opinions, closeness among employees, expertise-based power, knowledge- and personality-based authority, digital transformation leadership
Key processes	information and knowledge management, intellectual capital, quality, competences, innovations, organizational learning processes, customer relationships, knowledge exchange with the environment, ICT design and implementation

Source: Own elaboration

Next, after eliminating companies that did not meet the requirements to be considered intelligent organizations, the students began the second stage of the study – creating case studies for 35 companies selected.

The case studies were developed according to the proposed structure, focusing specifically on the course of the DTP in an enterprise classified as an intelligent organization.

For the analysis of research material and the development of individual case studies, comprehensive source materials were used; after receiving consent from the companies, participants had access to selected source data and documents from the companies. Resources used by the students included corporate websites, reports on and summaries of individual departments' activities, brochures, descriptions of the enterprise's strategy and its strategic programs (including digital transformation concepts and plans), articles published in trade journals related to the company and the industry, advertising content, and product offerings. In addition, information gathered from interviews with senior management of the companies surveyed and the informal discussions with digital transformation participants was used. The empirical material collected is extensive and abundant, covering a wide range of content. Due to the limited size of this paper, only seven synthetic descriptions of the companies under study have been presented in Table 2.3. The companies that were studied were extremely diverse regarding employment, type of activity, history, and the length of time they had been operating. Each of them has entered the digital transformation journey to a varying degree.

Key Findings

1 Managers and employees in the surveyed enterprises recognize the need for significant change in how they manage the enterprise and its environment, including relationships with customers and other stakeholders within its business and public environment.
2 Even though they have enjoyed a generally good competitive position within their sectors, the companies are investing heavily in technologies, such as IoT, Virtual Reality, and Cloud Computing.
3 Activity has been initiated in selected areas of the companies' business operation and relates primarily to improving the efficiency of managing information that is used to establish relationships with customers, continuous customer service, service centers, and developing offers. In addition, various sources of information that are acquired by the companies need to be integrated and analyzed into synthetic reports.
4 Survey respondents believe digital transformation requires a holistic, strategic approach, including setting objectives, prioritizing, planning the steps to follow, and balancing costs and effects.
5 Groups comprising leaders of change, often young, well-educated, and knowledgeable in the Information and Communications Technologies (ICT) environment, have been gradually emerging during discussions among employees. Members of these groups propose specific solutions, defend them, are involved in various discussions, and become natural leaders and supporters of digital transformation.
6 The managers of the enterprises surveyed have proposed the idea to set up teams that would initiate change and be tasked with developing ideas for

Table 2.3 Featured intelligent enterprises

Name of company	*Sector*	*Type of activity*	*Number of employees*	*Change story — digital transformation*
PKP	Rail infrastructure	Assuring a high standard of services at railway stations by modernizing stations and adapting them to the needs of travelers and communities	68,000	Special systems are introduced with regard to the collaboration of employees at different levels in the hierarchy, data transmission and analysis, and contact with customers: SEDO, FIKOD, or Purchasing Platform. As a result of updates made, employees are able to communicate with each other more efficiently and transfer data securely. Along with the websites, there were also announcements for the railway community, initiatives aimed at employees, and courses for those who were interested
FESTO	Industrial automation and pneumatics	Production and sales of industrial automation equipment, including pneumatics and recently electrical appliances	20,000	The company focuses on digitization of interactions with customers; basic online services are used, e.g. catalogs of products and order processing
SYNTHOS	Chemical	Manufacturer and supplier of solutions for various industries. Its activity is the production of various semi-finished products and final products in a wide range of chemical products such as adhesives, rubbers, and latex	4,000	The organization is implementing the stages of digital transformation; two years ago, SAP was implemented, unified all departments, improving information flow, and improving all processes; The Enterprise Project Management system is responsible for overseeing projects. In addition, production support software has been greatly improved. All activities are supported by a digital system supervised by the IT department
UPONOR INFRA	Civil engineering	Finnish manufacturer and supplier of systems and solutions for delivering safe drinking water, and energy-efficient heating cooling systems, and reliable infrastructure solutions	200	Pipes, tanks, and wells can be calculated using a free multilingual computer program offered by the company. It is possible to select appropriate design solutions using the program

INSTYTUT BADAWCZY LEŚNICTWA (FOREST RESEARCH INSTITUTE)	Forest research	Researching and developing forest science-related topics. Providing forestry and forest management services is aimed at maintaining sustainable forestry in terms of production, conservation, and social benefits in the interest of current and future generations	179	Increasing digitization is aimed at increasing the speed and efficiency of communication between employees, the analysis of test results, and employee-to-employee or employee–customer communication
APPGO	IT	Designing and programming websites and mobile applications; e-commerce systems for platforms for trading and supply	20	Its activities have been extended by the implementation of machine learning systems used in e-commerce (recommendation systems ensuring safety by algorithms detecting anomalies in financial transactions). A cloud-based platform for managing intellectual resources, projects, and data, to increase the efficiency of working time
EMA Studio	Architecture and Urban Planning	Designing residential, office buildings, public utilities, and sports facilities, interior design, analysis of investment areas	A dozen employed	The company invests annually in licensing advanced BIM (Building Information Model) design software and has trained employees in the field of design using BIM technology via the cloud. Last year, the company also introduced VR (virtual reality) technology. The company is currently trying to obtain funding to develop both of these technologies on a number of additional workstations

Source: Own elaboration

solutions, analyzing their effects, and determining the necessary human, financial, and material resources.

7 Discussions that take place among employees are gradually breaking down barriers between different business areas. A growing desire can be seen to share experiences, proposals, and even doubts. Change is likely to result in a different approach to collaboration, which needs to be more spontaneous, informal, and open. The exchange of information, knowledge, and skills will foster a sense of partnership and participation in the change process.

8 The companies have proposed to hold meetings with external stakeholders. There are a variety of meetings and discussion forums, both online and offline. Contacts are established (or developed) with research units and universities and technology providers (suppliers of equipment, platforms, and computer software).

Recommendations: Organizational and Managerial Support Model for the Digital Transformation Process

The DTP in each enterprise looks somewhat different in terms of the identified stages, their chronological order, their detailed content regarding decisions, activities, and problems, how the process progressed during the research period, objectives chosen, resources employed, guidelines applied, partial effects obtained. Since this process has no end, it is hard to talk about its final effects. Rather, one can talk about the level of digital maturity achieved, which should be the subject of a separate study.

However, comparing DTPs in the 35 companies surveyed allows some careful conclusions to be drawn. An analysis of individual case studies reveals the presence of consistent patterns. In summary, the following outline of DTPs in the enterprises studied can be constructed:

- as a result of discussions about the challenges that the company faces in the 4IR context, a group of employees who are more than average engaged conceptually, emotionally, and intellectually in the DTP process can be identified;
- in the management's view, these individuals become partners in the change process. From among them, managers, coordinators, and proxies are selected to lead the changes according to their roles;
- a group of change leaders thus formed within the team (or teams) prepares reports on the potential, costs, and effects of digitizing the enterprise. Such reports identify personnel, organizational, and technological needs;
- meetings and discussions should be held between change leaders and the management of the enterprise, which would focus on setting digitization strategies, including goals, inputs, and outcomes;
- the use of test programs, evaluating new technological solutions along with solutions necessary in the organization of work, training, and development of new competencies, team collaboration, and exchange of

experiences. Selection of areas of the test program, such as relationships with a long-term supplier;

- the company is showing increasing interest in acquiring highly qualified Industry 4.0 specialists and developing the competence of its existing workforce who are talented, outstanding, and ready to participate in the DTP process;
- increasing the number of entities interested in cooperating and achieving common goals in digitization; using various channels such as social media, corporate websites, seminars, conferences, workshops, and clusters.

There aren't yet clearly defined stages, but instead a series of repeated actions that occur in different orders and with varying degrees of intensity.

As a result of the identified activities of each enterprise, we have developed a digital transformation support model. The recommended DTP protocol may consist of the following steps:

1 identifying strong leadership through discussions, evaluations, and assessments of the possible course of digital transformation;
2 building a culture of organizational collaboration and knowledge sharing;
3 developing a vision for the technological development of the enterprise and a DTP strategy;
4 identifying resource needs (human, organizational, technological), and acquiring suitable resources;
5 launching test programs, and testing various solutions;
6 acquiring and developing new 4.0 competencies;
7 creating a network of organizations involved in the DTP process: customers, research units, suppliers, partners, business services companies, financial institutions, and public institutions.

A critical aspect of the transformation is finding the right leadership among top managers and active, knowledgeable employees who can act as change agents. Their determination and belief in success must not only be strong, but they must also be well versed in the subject. The changes plunge businesses into uncertainty over outcomes, barriers, and problems. They require a lot of effort, the updating of qualifications, adjusting to new duties, and adjusting to new working rules. This raises concerns that must be resolved by relying on values based on mutual support, knowledge sharing, open communication, and trust. There will be times when it will require promoting an organizational culture that is different from the existing one. It is likely to be more challenging than implementing only technological solutions. In the companies studied, it seems that the so-called "soft" elements of management are not yet sufficiently understood. According to other studies (Pęczak, 2019), Polish companies show little interest in organizational culture or leadership issues.

Implementing each stage requires matching organizational and personnel solutions. As part of the next stages of enterprise digitization, Table 2.4 provides recommendations for supporting their implementation.

Table 2.4 Guidelines for the digitization process

Organizational principles – creating a work environment	*Regulations concerning personnel – education and training*	*Leadership principles – forming leaders*
Creating a position for a representative for the company's management responsible for digitization	Introduction of programs that evaluate employees' competence needs on an ongoing basis	The executive team is thoroughly versed in the latest concepts, trends, and technologies
Establishing teams of analysts, concept developers, and specialists to support DTP processes	Analyzing the level of employee satisfaction with the digitization process on a continuous basis	Creating conditions for open communication so that leaders of change can emerge
Establishing a new approach to organizational processes and procedures	Identifying employees with DTP key competencies	Developing student-teacher relationships through age management and mentoring
Creating new workstations for the exchange of information with the enterprise's environment	Identifying in-company talent, employees with high potential for growth in a digital environment	Enhancing access to knowledge (scholarships, conferences, and workshops) for independent implementation of digital solutions and revolutionary business models
Developing rules for accessing 4IR experts	Establishing a priority for knowledge sharing and competence development processes within the organization	Developing interpersonal, social, and psychological competences
Redesigning workstations for additional capabilities in information management	Maintaining workplace learning continuity	Creating sustainable collaboration networks within and outside the organization
Creating conditions and incentives to perform diverse organizational roles and functions: managerial, expert, and executive	Creating an Attractive Employer brand that promotes career development and growth in a 4IR environment	The possibility of developing casual, informal, personal relationships between employees through activities that promote integration and creating comfort zones in the company

Source: Own elaboration

Table 2.5 Digital transformation guidelines

Classical industrial enterprise	*Intelligent Enterprise 4.0*
Explicit knowledge	Continuous conversion of explicit and implicit knowledge
Management of manufacturing and service processes	Information and knowledge management based on 4IR technology
Staff at the executive level and narrow field specialists	Knowledge workers – leaders with high competencies who manage processes and teams
Routine, repetitive, and tangible work	Mental, creative, and analytical work
Culture of hierarchy, control, and exploitation	Culture of collaboration and knowledge sharing
Rivalry with the environment	Integration through 4IR technologies into the environment (suppliers, customers, companies in the industry, and business services companies)
Priority is given to the interests of owners/shareholders	Striving to reconcile the interests of all stakeholders
A profit-oriented approach	A value-oriented approach
Rewarding the performance of people, machines, and devices	Rewarding ingenuity, speed, and multidimensional efficiency

Source: Own elaboration

Based on individual case studies, assessing the kinds and levels of results obtained through the digitization processes is premature. It would be more useful to present the key outcomes of the transformation that are achievable through the implementation of an accepted vision and strategy for the advancement of digitization and the implementation of appropriate business models. The first stage of the DTP should include formulating guidelines for transforming an enterprise into Intelligent Enterprise 4.0. It should begin with the archetypal character of a classical industrial enterprise. The recommendations are presented in Table 2.5.

Conclusions

The author of this chapter is aware of the numerous limitations in the study's findings and the recommendations for managers responsible for digital transformation in enterprises presented in this chapter. The research used for the purposes of this chapter is not representative of the Polish business community. The selection of the sample was intentional. The scope of the study included only companies deemed intelligent. However, the goal of the study seems to have been achieved, and to a limited extent, the results have filled the void in the support for DTPs. This process is complex, and multidimensional, necessitating a holistic view of the concept of a company's operations. Each concept is therefore burdened with great risk and uncertainty.

References

Betti, F., & de Boer, E. (2019). Global Lighthouse Network: Insights from the Forefront of the Fourth Industrial Revolution, White Paper. World Economic Forum in Collaboration with McKinsey & Co. [online]. Available at: https://www.weforum.org/whitepapers/global-lighthouse-network-insights-from-the-forefront-of-the-fourth-industrial-revolution/ (Accessed: 04.11.2020).

Betti, F., de Boer, E., & Giraud, Y. (2020). *The Fourth Industrial Revolution and Manufacturing's Great Reset*. McKinsey & Co. [online]. Available at: www.mckinsey.com (Accessed: 04.11.2020).

Bowman, R. (2018). Zebra Technologies Assesses Progress Toward the 'Intelligent Enterprise'. Available at: https://www.supplychainbrain.com/articles/29159-zebra-technologies-assesses-progress-toward-the-intelligent-enterprise (Accessed 7.9.2022).

Christensen, C. (1997). Making Strategy: Learning by Doing. *Harvard Business Review, 75*(6), 141–146.

Deloitte Insights. (2019). *Success Personified in the Fourth Industrial Revolution. Four Leadership Personas for an Era of Change and Uncertainty*. Deloitte Insights. [online]. Available at www.deloitte.com/insights (Accessed: 1.10.2020).

Fersht, P. (2018). *Accenture's Intelligent Operations Research: The Future Belongs to Intelligent Operations*. HFS Research.

Morawski, M., & Bąkowska-Morawska, U. (2021). Open Innovations in the Hotel Chain. A New Value Chain Co-created with Clients: The Poland Case Study. In: Z. Macieła, M. Stuss, & R. Borowiecki (eds.), *Sustainability, Technology and Innovation 4.0*. New York: Routledge, pp. 161–189.

Nonaka, I., & Takeuchi, H. (1995). *The Knowledge-Creating Company*. Oxford: Oxford University Press.

Ojanpera, S., Graham, M., & Zook, M. (2019). The Digital Knowledge Economy Index: Mapping Content Production. *The Journal of Development Studies*, *55*(12), 2626–2643. https://doi.org/10.1080/00220388.2018.1554208

Pęczak, A. (2019). *W drodze ku Gospodarce 4.0. Wyniki badania Computerworlda*. Available at: https://www.computerworld.pl/news/W-drodze-ku-Gospodarce-4-0-Wyniki-badania-Computerworlda,412715.html (Accessed: 7.09.2022).

Prahalad, C.K., & Hamel, G. (1994). *Competing for the Future*. Cambridge: Harvard Business School Press.

Quinn, J. (1992). *Intelligent Enterprise*. New York: Free Press.

Schwab, K. (2016). *The Fourth Industrial Revolution*. Cologny, Switzerland: World Economic Forum.

Schwaninger, M. (2009). *Intelligent Organizations: Powerful Models for Systemic Management*. Berlin, Heidelberg: Springer-Verlag.

Thannhuber, M.J. (2005). *The Intelligent Enterprise: Theoretical Concepts and Practical Implications*. New York: Physica-Verlag, A Springer Company, p. 67.

Zebra Technologies. (2018). *The intelligent enterprise index*. www.zebra.com. https://www.zebra.com/content/dam/zebra_new_ia/en-us/campaigns/brand-campaign/harvard-symposium/how-intelligent-enterprise-survey-index-en-us.pdf

Part 2

Economic and Financial Implications

3 COVID-19 Pandemic and Financial Security of Blue Chips in Poland

Artur Paździor

Introduction

The perception of financial security has been radically altered by the COVID-19 pandemic and associated lockdowns mandates and restrictions, in relation to economic systems, individual countries, households, and businesses. Factors determining the security of businesses tend to be similar, though the type and extent of their impacts may vary depending on the business's size, profile, sales markets, relationship with external and internal environments, economic and financial conditions, economic situation, and other factors. Among publicly traded companies, financial security is additionally affected by their policies for dividend payouts, the efficiency with which shares and bonds are issued, exchange rate volatility, liquidity of stock exchange rates, finance source management, resistance to stock market crashes, and exposure to takeover attempts. The multitude and variety of determinants make the study of factors of financial security in public companies and their scope theoretically and empirically interesting. This applies to both the operational security related to liquidity (i.e., the ability to pay current liabilities on time) and the tactical security related to solvency (i.e., the ability to pay off financial obligations such as loans, leases, and bonds), as well as the strategic security related to the optimization of the capital structure, processes relating to mergers and acquisitions, and policies on increasing the market value of dividends.

The aim of this article is to analyze the factors and changes in the level of financial security in the largest public companies listed on the Warsaw Stock Exchange in the context of the pandemic and the related socioeconomic turmoil. Thus, a review of the literature, analysis of financial statements, analysis of changes in the price of shares, and statistical analysis were conducted. The impact of the COVID-19 pandemic on the economic and financial conditions of the companies surveyed, as well as their level of financial security, and changes in share prices, was assessed. Practical recommendations for those in charge of financial security under conditions of uncertainty were developed based on the findings.

DOI: 10.4324/9781003475583-6

Financial Security as an Element of Economic Security

There are many definitions of economic security in the literature. According to Księżopolski (2011:32), economic security is defined as "an undisturbed functioning of economies, which involves maintaining basic development indicators and ensuring a comparative balance with the economies of other countries". Żukrowska (2013:35) believes that economic security "means the conditions for harmonious development, allowing to build a sustainable well-being of the citizens of the state". Contrary to Księżopolski's definition, Żukrowska (2013:35–37) distinguished between macro- and microeconomic security:

> In macroeconomic terms, security is employment stability, low unemployment, predictable economic development prospects, characterized by financial liquidity. In microeconomic terms, it is the solvency of a household or enterprise. In both cases, it is about the possibility of balancing obligations against the needs in the medium term.

Raczkowski (2014:38) identified economic security with a non-inertial system of relative equilibrium

> to conduct free and regulated gainful activity, with the autonomy of the will of the parties, the need to maintain the existing risk volume by maintaining limited trust in economic and legal relations between the contracting parties, the internal environment and the environment, in which the given entity operates.

Stachowiak (2012) defines economic security as a result of economic development factors and the barriers limiting it. In his opinion, safe entities and economies have the ability to effectively counteract external stimuli that may negatively affect their stability, disrupting their development and limiting their potential.

Based on the definitions above, it can be concluded that economic security may refer to economic systems, individual economies, sectors within these economies, or specific enterprises. The definitions include undisturbed, harmonious development, which means maintaining basic development indicators and ensuring a comparative balance with other economies or enterprises. These definitions combine an economic element and political science. Therefore, it is possible to distinguish four dimensions of economic security, which are logically related and dependent. One of the most important areas, apart from raw materials and energy, food, and access to clean water, is financial security, which is analyzed in this chapter.

Although the COVID-19 pandemic is a relatively young phenomenon, and therefore not fully recognized, many scientific studies and practical analyses have been published. Research has been conducted by, among others, Song,

Yeon, and Lee (2021), who investigated the impact of pandemic phenomena on the American restaurant industry. Nicola et al. (2020) analyzed the socio-economic effects of the coronavirus pandemic in multiple sectors (agriculture, fuel industry, manufacturing companies, education, and the financial industry). Ellul, Erel, and Rajan (2020) examined the volatility of stock prices caused by the COVID-19 pandemic. Kostyk-Siekierska (2021) analyzed the impact of the COVID-19 pandemic on the financial situation and functioning of local government units. Spoz, Skibinska-Fabrowska, Kotlinski, and Zukowska (2021) attempted to determine the impact of the COVID-19 pandemic on the financial performance of public companies in Poland. Kraska (2022) tried to determine the impact of the pandemic on the financial conditions of companies in Poland using selected elements of index analysis. Paździor and Majek (2021) investigated the impact of the pandemic on the financial situation of households in Poland, and Paździor, Sokół, and Styk (2021) analyzed the impact of the COVID-19 pandemic on the economic and financial situation of micro- and small enterprises in Poland's construction and development industry.

These publications show that the COVID-19 pandemic has recently become a popular subject of scientific study and empirical analysis. Nevertheless, the subject seems topical and has not been fully investigated. Therefore, research on the impact of the COVID-19 pandemic on large capital companies, which is discussed in this chapter of the monograph, should continue.

Financial Security of Economic Entities in a Global Pandemic World

The continuous process of internationalization witnessed in various countries, driven by the third economic revolution (which is the computerization of life processes, including economic processes), results in an increasing economic dependence on the economies that make up the global market. International trade is now complemented by global capital flows of a different nature. In such conditions, the factor determining the position of enterprises in the modern world is their economic potential, which depends mainly on internal factors. However, external determinants also shape a company's competitive position. Such a situation takes place during periods of economic turmoil or, as recently, pandemic periods. In such conditions, the financial position of an enterprise largely depends on political decisions and the dynamics of the epidemic. An important issue is the current (pre-crisis) financial stability, the assortment and geographic structure of sales, the structure of financing sources, the industry and sector in which the company operates, etc. However, this does not mean that a company's financial security is solely the result of the impact of these factors. Even in such a turbulent environment, managers whose appropriate competencies can help reduce the negative effects caused by various types of shocks have a significant impact on the functioning of the organization.

One of the most serious shocks in the last few years has been the COVID-19 pandemic which began in late 2019 in Wuhan, China. First lockdown mandates were implemented there in the second half of January 2020. The virus spread rapidly throughout the globe, including Europe, within a few months. It was in March 2020 that the first patient in Poland was diagnosed with COVID. Within a week, a state of epidemic threat was announced across the country. It was accompanied by the introduction of a number of restrictions for the public. Poland's borders were closed, and the crossing of the border could only take place under certain conditions. The so-called social distancing – which restricted access to public places – was also introduced. As a result of a heightened risk of infection in large communities, restaurants were shut down, schools suspended classes, and companies implemented remote working. Although some restrictions were lifted over time, the final lifting of restrictions related to the pandemic took place only in March 2022 (Od marca łagodniejsze ..., 2022).

The pandemic also had a significant impact on the economy – initially, things were chaotic – there were restrictions on mass events and movements, and schools transitioned to online learning. The pandemic changed every aspect of human life and, as a result, the economy and entrepreneurs will be affected for years to come.

In the first months of the pandemic, even the world's largest economies were unable to cope with the negative effects of the lockdown mandates, and the overwhelmed health care systems in many countries turned out to be inefficient. In the first and second quarters of 2020, an economic downturn began in almost all countries. In the second half of 2020, as a result of the easing of the restrictions and as a result of favorable tax changes as well as significant interest rate reductions, and thanks to government aid, many countries started to recover from the recession, with positive GDP growth (Sheiner et al., 2021). As a consequence, at the end of 2021, the GDP per capita indicator in Poland exceeded its value from before the pandemic, i.e. the end of 2019 (Eurostat, 2022).

Contrary to what was originally believed, the consequences of the pandemic still reverberate today, i.e. in 2022, in broken supply chains and skyrocketing inflation. According to a microeconomic perspective, companies from many industries are still having trouble finding employees who, as a result of lockdowns, have changed their industries and found employment elsewhere. In industries such as tourism, gastronomy, and transportation, staff shortages are most prevalent.

As in other EU countries, Poland's situation is far from ideal. A major problem for the Polish economy is soaring inflation and the associated interest rate increases, leading to high credit and loan interest rates (Investing.com, n.d.). This makes it more and more difficult for potential loan borrowers to qualify for loans, and the existing customers of the banking sector's services will be adversely affected by the effects of interest rate increases on their loan installments. As a result, the symptoms of declining morale among consumers are becoming apparent (GUS, 2022), and the financial situation of many households and businesses, especially those that are heavily relying on leverage, is beginning to deteriorate. As a point of reference, an average installment for a 500k zlotys mortgage loan (approx. EUR 106k) was approx. 2,000 zlotys per month prior to a series of interest rate increases in Poland, and currently stands at 4,300 zlotys (an increase of 2,300 zlotys, that is 115%) (Kazimierski, 2022).

Moreover, the war in Ukraine that started in February 2022 has contributed to the high volatility of various elements of businesses' financial standing. The Russian invasion of Poland's eastern neighbor caused not only a great deal of anxiety for millions of people but also elevated volatility in the stock market, commodities (energy, precious metals, and agricultural products), and currency exchange rates.

Both the war in Ukraine and the freeing of many economies after the COVID-19 pandemic have become catalysts for price increases for commodities and agricultural products. As a result, inflation increased, resulting in a series of interest rate increases, which led to a drastic increase in monthly payments for both individuals and businesses.

Companies in Poland, as well as many other countries in Europe and the world, operate under such conditions. It would seem obvious to say that micro, small, and medium-sized enterprises are primarily affected by these events. Small businesses are the ones that are most exposed to various types of shocks and economic crises (Klein, 2014). For this reason, the study of change in the condition during the pandemic-caused turbulences, with particular emphasis on the level of financial security of large companies, seems to be academically intriguing and empirically underexplored.

Characteristics of Blue Chips in Poland and Research Methodology

The Warsaw Stock Exchange has been operating continuously since 1991. During the first session, there were only five companies listed, and the total turnover reached approximately USD 2,000. As of today, the Polish Stock Exchange is the largest stock exchange in Central and Eastern Europe and trades in one of the most dynamically developing capital markets in Europe (GWP, n.d.). One of the most important indices of the Warsaw Stock Exchange is WIG-30 which tracks the 30 largest and most liquid companies from the WSE main market (Czym jest indeks WIG20?, 2021).

Like the WIG20 index, the WIG30 index lists companies characterized by a stable financial situation and enjoying investor confidence. These types of companies are referred to as blue chips in the stock market terminology (PAP, 2013). At the end of May 2022, the WIG30 index comprised companies listed in Table 3.1.

The analysis presented in this chapter comprises companies listed in Table 3.1 apart from those in the financial sector (banks, insurance companies, etc.), raw materials sector (fuel, coal, and copper), chemical sector, and energy sector. The reason for this exclusion was the companies' ownership structure; a large proportion of the shares of companies in the

Table 3.1 An overview of the WIG-30 index (as of May 31, 2022)

No.	*Company*	*Sector/industry*	*No.*	*Company*	*Sector/industry*
1.	ALIOR	Banking	16.	AMREST	Hotels and restaurants
2.	MBANK	Banking	17.	ASSECOPOL	Information technology
3.	MILLENIUM	Banking	18.	CDPROJEKT	Information technology
4.	PEKAO	Banking	19.	TSGAMES	Information technology
5.	PKOBP	Banking	20.	GRUPAAZOTY	Chemical
6.	SANPL	Banking	21.	MERCATOR	Pharmaceutical
7.	ENEA	Energy	22.	KETY	Metal industry
8.	PGE	Energy	23.	LOTOS	Fuel industry
9.	TAURONPE	Energy	24.	PGNIG	Fuel industry
10.	KRUK	Financial, other types	25.	PKNORLEN	Fuel industry
11.	ALLEGRO	Retail	26.	JSW	Raw materials
12.	CCC	Retail	27.	KGHM	Raw materials
13.	DINOPL	Retail	28.	CYFRPOLSAT	Telecommunication
14.	LPP	The retail trade	29.	ORANGEPL	Telecommunication
15.	PEPCO	The retail trade	30.	PZU	Insurance

Source: Own study

above-mentioned sectors belong to the State Treasury. This means that those companies can count on government support during deep market downturns, which makes any comparison of the magnitude and nature of the effects of the pandemic on their financial standing misleading and unreliable.

The next selection criteria were the availability of reliable financial data and the company's stock market history. Therefore, the study includes only those companies whose IPO occurred no later than December 31, 2018. Among them are the following entities: AMREST, ASSECOPOL, CCC, CDPROJEKT, CYFRPOLSAT, DINOPL, KETY, LPP, MERCATOR, ORANGEPL, and TSGAMES, comprising the research group. For each of these companies, quarterly financial reports were obtained and financial security indicators were calculated for the periods before the pandemic (Q1 2018–Q4 2019) and during the pandemic (Q1 2020–Q4 2021). The indicators that were included in the evaluation are listed in Table 3.2.

Each of the indicators listed in Table 3.2 was calculated for each of the analyzed companies in each of the quarterly periods between 2018 and 2021. The results of this analysis are presented in the following section.

Analysis of the Financial Security of Blue Chips in Poland for Periods before and during the COVID-19 Pandemic

The empirical analysis conducted for the purpose of this chapter was based on quarterly financial statements and various analyses retrieved from financial

Table 3.2 Indicators used in study

No.	Description	Formula	Acronym	Preferred level
1.	Total debt ratio	Debt/total assets	DR	up to 80%
2.	Short-term debt Ratio	Short-term debt/total assets	STDR	up to 60%
3.	Interest coverage ratio	Operating profit/interest expence	ICR	at least 2
4.	Current ratio	Current assets/short-term debt	CR	1.2–2.0
5.	Altman Z-score	Altman Z-score	Z	at least 1.2

Source: Own study

websites. It was used to calculate the indicators listed in Table 3.2 and to verify the accuracy of calculations for 11 companies from the WIG-30 index.

The analysis allowed the following conclusions to be drawn:

- the financial condition of the companies improved significantly during the study period. This is evidenced by, among other things, growing financial security ratios and liquidity ratios. However, this does not imply that these positive trends can be observed across all periods examined;
- during the COVID-19 pandemic (Q2 2020), a deterioration in the financial standing could be observed, mainly among companies operating in the retail sector in the clothing and beauty industries. This is confirmed by the rising levels of debt ratios and declining financial liquidity indicators. Undoubtedly, this was caused by the temporary financial difficulties these companies faced as a result of pandemic-related lockdowns, due to which many shops and drugstores shut down. Similar negative consequences that stemmed from the restrictions related to the COVID-19 pandemic were observed by AMREST, a company that operates in the hotels and restaurants sector of the recreation and leisure industry; a significant drop in liquidity ratios, as well as an abrupt increase in short-term debt, was observed, resulting in a negative balance sheet;
- DINOPL, a company that deals mainly with food retail and represents the retail chain industry, made it through this pandemic remarkably well. Due to the fact that food stores continued to stay open despite the restrictions, the company could use this circumstance to expand its range of products and strengthen its geographic reach. Other beneficiaries of the pandemic included companies in the IT sector which saw their sales rise during the study period as a result of lockdown mandates and the consequent "transfer" of work and social life to the Internet. During the pandemic, there was a lot of interest in stock shares of companies in this sector, particularly in the gaming industry, which was confirmed by a rapid increase in their market value in a relatively short period. During the COVID-19 pandemic, the financial situation of the KETA steel company was also favorable. The reason for this is the fact that such plants continued to

operate during the pandemic, and the specificity of their activities meant that it was possible to effectively reduce the risk of SARS-CoV-2 infection by sanitary protocols;

- the events caused by the pandemic were of particular benefit to MERCATOR, which represents the pharmaceutical sector in the medical equipment and materials industry. Within just a few months of 2020, the company reduced its debt by over 70% and increased the levels of financial liquidity ratios by threefold. In just a year, specifically from Q4 of 2019 to Q4 of 2020, the company's sales value increased by 375%, its net profit increased by over 20,000%, its book value increased by 705%, and the market capitalization value increased by 4,147%;[1]
- changes in the financial condition of telecommunication companies should be assessed with caution. While CYFRPOLSAT showed signs of improvement in its financial situation during the pandemic, for ORANGEPL there was a noticeable deterioration in almost all of its financial security indicators. This may be due to the fact that the former company is a subscription-based TV service (Investing.com, n.d.) while the latter primarily provides access to telecommunication services via landline and mobile networks. This means that during the pandemic, CYFRPOLSAT could use the opportunities offered by the computerization of social and professional life to a greater extent.

Final Conclusions and Recommendations

The financial condition of most of the surveyed companies improved over the analyzed period, according to the empirical analysis, as evidenced by increasing financial security ratios and liquidity ratios, among other things. This outcome was achieved even though the COVID-19 pandemic initially had unfavorable effects. This was particularly evident for companies that operate in the retail sector in the clothing and cosmetics industry. AMREST, a company operating in the hotel and restaurant sector in the recreation and leisure industry, experienced particularly negative consequences of the pandemic restrictions.

DINOPL, which represents the retail industry and specializes in food retail, and KETY, which specializes in metallurgy, coped with the effects of the pandemic well. The reason for this was the fact that during the pandemic, such plants did not close, and the specific nature of their operations meant that they were capable of effectively reducing the risk of SARS-CoV-2 infection by following sanitary protocol measures.

A company representing the pharmaceutical industry, MERCATOR, turned out to be the biggest beneficiary of the pandemic events, with a fourfold increase in sales revenue and a significant, exceptionally dynamic increase in share prices in just one year.

As a result of the analysis and literature studies, as well as the author's business experience, recommendations can be made regarding how to handle shocks resulting from socioeconomic turmoil, which may be useful for managers of both large and smaller firms. Among the most important are:

- transferring part of business activities online;
- production relocation;
- increasing the flexibility of employment;
- increasing measures aimed to promote personal hygiene and improve working conditions, particularly for the production workforce;
- diversifying suppliers and recipients geographically;
- creating cooperation networks with other companies operating in the nearby area;
- diversifying of currencies used for financing sources;
- contracting all loans, loans, and leases at fixed interest rates;
- adjusting financial plans at shorter intervals;
- adopting more flexible operational and strategic goals;
- orienting strategic goals toward the optimization rather than the maximization of economic gains.

I believe that orienting the activities of high-level managers and directors of large public companies toward implementing the above-mentioned recommendations will contribute to reducing the level of operational and financial risk and will clearly limit the negative impact of future economic shocks. Suggested recommendations can also be successfully applied to smaller enterprises that often lack systemic measures to cope with crises. However, greater flexibility in the organizational structure and a more flattened decision-making process may positively affect the implementation of these recommendations, thanks to which negative consequences of any crisis may be mitigated.

Note

1 Own calculations based on the company's quarterly financial statements and an analysis of changes in market prices of shares.

References

Czym jest indeks WIG20? (2021). Retrieved 9 September 2022, from https://businessinsider.com.pl/gielda/indeksy/co-to-jest-indeks-wig20/eqden2s

Ellul, A., Erel, I., & Rajan, U. (2020). The COVID-19 Pandemic Crisis and Corporate Finance. *The Review of Corporate Finance Studies*, 9(3), 421–429. doi: 10.1093/rcfs/cfaa016

Eurostat. (2022). Main GDP aggregates per capita. Retrieved 9 September 2022, from https://ec.europa.eu/eurostat/databrowser/view/NAMQ_10_PC__custom_2943797/default/table?lang=en

GUS. (2022). Koniunktura konsumencka - maj 2022 roku. Retrieved 9 September 2022, from https://stat.gov.pl/obszary-tematyczne/koniunktura/koniunktura/koniunktura-konsumencka-maj-2022-roku,1,111.html

GWP. (n.d.). O spółce. Retrieved 9 September 2022, from https://www.gpw.pl/o-spolce

Investing.com. (n.d.). Informacje o spółce Cyfrowy Polsat SA - Investing.com. Retrieved 9 September 2022, from https://pl.investing.com/equities/cyfrowy-polsat-sa-company-profile

Kazimierski, M. (2022). Stopy procentowe znów w górę. Zobacz, o ile wzrośnie rata kredytu. Retrieved 9 September 2022, from https://www.money.pl/banki/stopy-procentowe-znow-w-gore-zobacz-o-ile-wzrosnie-rata-kredytu-6777574432528960a.html

Klein, N. (2014). Small and Medium Size Enterprises, Credit Supply Shocks, and Economic Recovery in Europe. *SSRN Electronic Journal*. doi: 10.2139/ssrn.2468025

Kostyk-Siekierska, K. (2021). Wpływ pandemii COVID-19 na sytuację finansową i funkcjonowanie jednostek samorządu terytorialnego. *Zeszyty Naukowe Małopolskiej Wyższej Szkoły Ekonomicznej W Tarnowie*, *51*(3), 29–45. doi: 10.25944/znmwse.2021.03.2945

Kraska, E. (2022). Wpływ pandemii COVID-19 na kondycję finansową przedsiębiorstw w Polsce. *Przegląd Prawno-Ekonomiczny*, (2), 79–96. doi: 10.31743/ppe.13241

Księżopolski, K. (2011). *Bezpieczeństwo ekonomiczne*. Warszawa: Dom Wydawniczy Elipsa.

Nicola, M., Alsafi, Z., Sohrabi, C., Kerwan, A., Al-Jabir, A., & Iosifidis, C. et al. (2020). The Socio-economic Implications of the Coronavirus Pandemic (COVID-19): A Review. *International Journal of Surgery*, *78*, 185–193. doi: 10.1016/j.ijsu.2020.04.018

Od marca łagodniejsze zasady bezpieczeństwa. (2022). Sprawdź, co się zmieni! - Koronawirus: informacje i zalecenia - Portal Gov.pl. Retrieved 9 September 2022, from https://www.gov.pl/web/koronawirus/od-marca-lagodniejsze-zasady-bezpieczenstwa-sprawdz-co-sie-zmieni

PAP. (2013). GPW podała skład nowego indeksu WIG30. Retrieved 9 September 2022, from https://www.bankier.pl/wiadomosc/GPW-podala-sklad-nowego-index-WIG30-2909097.html

PAP. (2022). Fitch podnosi prognozę inflacji w Polsce. Ceny jeszcze długo nie wyhamują. Retrieved 9 September 2022, from https://businessinsider.com.pl/gospodarka/inflacja-w-polsce-2022-fitch-podnosi-prognozy/q5clhy3

Paździor, A., & Majek, A. (2021). Impact of COVID-19 on Household's Financial Situation in Poland. *European Research Studies Journal*, *XXIV*(Special Issue 2), 492–502. doi: 10.35808/ersj/2279

Paździor, A., Sokół, M., & Styk, A. (2021). The Impact of the COVID-19 Pandemic on the Economic and Financial Situation of the Micro and Small Enterprises from the Construction and Development Industry in Poland. *European Research Studies Journal*, *XXIV*(Special Issue 2), 751–762. doi: 10.35808/ersj/2309

Raczkowski, K. (2014). Współczesny model tetrarchii zarządzania a bezpieczeństwo ekonomiczne obrotu gospodarczego. In K. Raczkowski (Ed.), *Bezpieczeństwo ekonomiczne obrotu gospodarczego. Ekonomia. Prawo. Zarządzanie* (p. 38). Wolters Kluwer.

Sheiner, L., Milstein, E., Campbell, S., & Kovalski, M. (2021). How pandemic-era fiscal policy affects the level of GDP. Retrieved 9 September 2022, from https://www.brookings.edu/blog/up-front/2021/10/19/how-pandemic-era-fiscal-policy-affects-the-level-of-gdp/

Song, H., Yeon, J., & Lee, S. (2021). Impact of the COVID-19 Pandemic: Evidence from the U.S. Restaurant Industry. *International Journal of Hospitality Management*, *92*, 102702. doi: 10.1016/j.ijhm.2020.102702

Spoz, A., Skibinska-Fabrowska, I., Kotlinski, G., & Zukowska, H. (2021). The Impact of the Covid-19 Pandemic on the Financial Performance of Public Companies in Poland. *European Research Studies Journal*, *XXIV*(Issue 4), 955–976. doi: 10.35808/ersj/2645

Stachowiak, Z. (2012). *Teoria i praktyka mechanizmu bezpieczeństwa ekonomicznego państwa*. Warszawa: Akademia Obrony Narodowej.

Żukrowska, K. (2013). Ekonomia jako sfera bezpieczeństwa państwa. In K. Raczkowski, K. Żukrowska & M. Żuber (Eds.), *Interdyscyplinarność nauk o bezpieczeństwie* (pp. 35–37). Warszawa: Difin.

4 The Importance of Process Owner Maturity in the Context of COVID-19 Pandemic Management – A Case Study

Dobrochna Sztajerska

Introduction

As a rule, organizations face numerous uncertainties resulting in diverse consequences. Challenges are handled by managers according to standards. However, in the event of a major crisis, uncertainty can reach extreme levels and traditional management models are rarely in line with market demands. Uncertainty can be measured by its size and duration. In both cases, the COVID-19 pandemic has created unique uncertainty regarding public health and economic damage. According to Brashers (2001), uncertainty management theory rejects the assumption that uncertainty is negative; instead, it is viewed as a neutral factor that can assist an organization in achieving its objectives. However, it should be remembered that the effects of uncertainty may be detrimental due to a failure of the process owner (PO) to adapt to the requirements of a dynamically changing market.

In addition to the so-called hard competencies related to specialist knowledge, the competencies of a modern manager include a number of soft competencies – social and psychological. Maturity is a complex construct, with regard to the organization, the process, and the PO (in this study, the PO is equivalent to the process manager). Therefore, it is extremely difficult to find a precise and consistent definition of the concept. Erikson (1950), one of the most famous developmental psychologists, skillfully described this concept, avoiding detailed descriptions and stating that

> each individual, to become a mature adult, must to a sufficient degree develop all of the ego qualities mentioned so that a wise Indian, a true gentleman, and a mature peasant may share and recognize them in one another the final stage of integrity.

It was demonstrated (Giberson et al., 2009; Hogan & Judge, 2012; Lord et al., 1986) that the personality of a manager is closely related to the way in which the process for which they are responsible is managed (Sztajerska, 2021a). If we treat the PO as the person who is ultimately responsible for the process and has the power and ability to make necessary changes in

DOI: 10.4324/9781003475583-7

order to achieve its goals, it seems rather obvious that the more integral the owner is, the better the process should be. This is especially true in uncertain circumstances when the need for flexibility and the ability to act swiftly when challenges arise is greater than ever. It has been shown in research that managers who pay special attention to information and show high trust in their employees can improve the efficiency of their company's business processes (Moormann & Grau, 2017). Poland, however, prefers to avoid uncertainty at all costs. In countries where such rigid beliefs and behaviors persist, unconventional ideas and behavior are not tolerated. In such cultures, there is an intrinsic need for rules (even if they don't always work), time is money, people work hard and are busy by nature, precision and punctuality are a norm, innovation is resisted, and safety is an important driver of motivation (Hofstede, 2011). Consequently, the maturity of managers appears to be a particularly promising research area related to process management in uncertain circumstances caused by the COVID-19 pandemic.

Research Methodology

The aim of the study was an attempt to create a profile of a mature manager and on its basis describe the importance of a manager's maturity as an aggregate measure for process management in uncertain circumstances related to the COVID-19 pandemic. To develop the manager maturity profile, I have incorporated my previous work (Sztajerska, 2021a, 2021b, 2020) and supplemented it with additional psychological concepts. Then, the profile was compared to the profile of the owner of an auxiliary process in a large production plant (Figure 4.2) and viewed in the context of a pandemic. The case study portrays a manager with 20 years of professional experience, who was elevated to the position by going up the ladder one step at a time and has been a PO for five years. The environment in which he works is masculinized and hierarchical.

The research was carried out according to the model presented in Figure 4.1.

As part of the preliminary phase, it was determined which features should be included in the model and according to which concepts they should be evaluated, i.e. which psychological tests should be used. The type of research methods to be used was also decided. Since the study was conducted with no standard timeframes, participant observations lasted for five days (breaks included) and were carried out after the most difficult pandemic period. In order to accurately interpret the test results, two interviews were conducted, i.e. before and after the results of the test were analyzed. In the proper phase of the study, research was carried out using a selection of tools, and the results were compared against the model of a mature manager, then conclusions were drawn through observation of the process and interviews.

Some authors claim that in order to become a mature manager, you have to be a mature person (Kozak, 2011). Thus, I supplemented Allport's description of human maturity (Allport, 1937) with a number of subjectively chosen

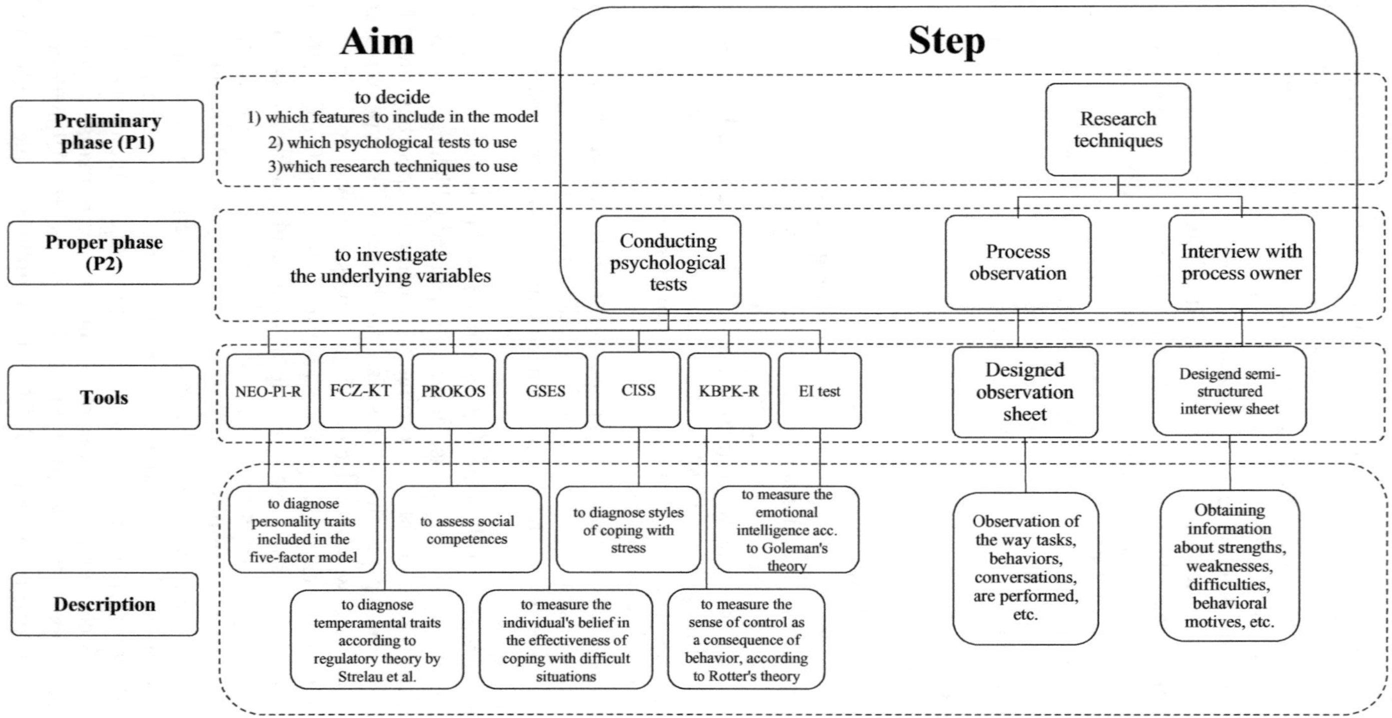

Figure 4.1 Research model

Source: Own elaboration

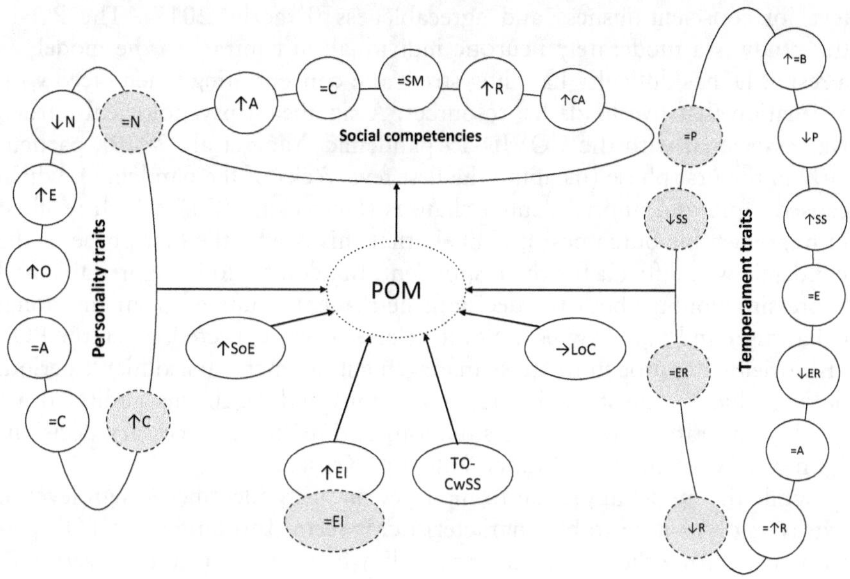

Figure 4.2 Model approach to process owner

Source: Own elaboration

detailed psychological concepts: personality traits (according to the Big 5 Personality Traits theory by Costa and McCrae (1992a, 1992b)) and temperament (as defined by Strelau (1996), the author of the Regulatory Theory of Temperament), and strategies for coping with stress (according to Endler and Parker's theory (Endler & Parker, 1990)). Also added to the manager's maturity construct were the concept of the locus of control (Rotter, 1966), the sense of agency (Bandura, 1977), social competencies (Matczak & Martowska, 2013), and emotional intelligence (Goleman, 1997). It should be mentioned that the concept of emotional intelligence is sometimes criticized, mainly due to the incorrect definition of the concept, which critics argue to be an idea describing a behavior, skill, or a form of knowledge, rather than specific intelligence (Brody, 2004; Fiori & Antonakis, 2012). However, it seems that whether it is considered intelligence or something else, it is an interesting element in maturity. Taking the above into account, I developed a model to describe a mature manager and compared it to the profile of the PO who took part in the study (Figure 4.2).

Note: Due to the short length of this work and the wide scope of the study, the interpretation of the results presented below is quite concise but comprehensive enough to achieve the intended outcome.

Results and Discussion – A Case Study

Based on personality traits, it can be concluded that mature managers possess low neuroticism, high extraversion, openness to experience, and a medium level of conscientiousness and agreeableness (Kraczla, 2017). The PO in this study is a moderately neurotic individual, in contrast to the model; as a result, he has difficulty handling stress and concentrating when faced with a situation that overloads his resources. A significant psychological burden was associated with the COVID-19 pandemic (Yang et al., 2020), particularly in the first phase (meaning the first few weeks of the pandemic), which caused rapid and unprecedented changes (Dymecka, 2021), which resulted in unpredictable outcomes. It is likely that this is why the first phase of the pandemic was difficult for the respondent. In addition to being irritable and expressing doubts about the decisions he made, he suffered from emotional exhaustion and mood swings. Nevertheless, as was expected, given the PO's task-oriented approach to stress management, after the first difficult period, he was able to adjust to the new conditions and regain his ability to act quickly and rationally in crisis situations and make the necessary decisions (James & Wooten, 2005; Muffet-Willett & Kruse, 2009).

While the model approach to manager maturity identifies a high level of extraversion as a desirable characteristic, it seemed to hinder the PO's performance during the pandemic, especially when it came to the transition to remote working. It manifested itself in procrastination, resulting in decreased efficiency and a depressed mood. Due to a lack of interpersonal contact and frequent exchange of ideas, the subject returned to working onsite, and his effectiveness improved.

By being open to experience, the PO demonstrated a higher level of creativity and flexibility in thinking and acting (DeYoung et al., 2005), which helped him solve non-standard problems in process management. After going through the first phase of the pandemic, the respondent felt comfortable in uncertain conditions, which translated into a more effective performance when faced with both organizational and environmental changes.

For process managers, agreeableness should be average, because it allows them to enforce tasks and reach compromises where necessary. Generally, autocratic management styles work best when uncertainty is present, while democratic management styles work best when normal conditions (non-crisis) prevail. Due to his average level of agreeableness, the subject had the ability to flexibly shift from the democratic style he normally prefers to a more centralized one.

Having a high level of conscientiousness (the second feature that distinguishes him from the model), the respondent had a harder time adapting to changes in the first phase of the pandemic because he prefers a well-organized and structured environment that is characteristic of highly conscientious people (Barrick & Mount, 1993). Thanks to his high conscientiousness and openness to experience, he was able to be a visionary and strategist after breaking through a weaker period. It was especially the latter that enabled him to focus on the long-term goal, survival, and holistic and multidimensional thinking. In addition to this, he displayed a keen sense of competence and a desire to succeed, both of which demonstrate a high level of conscientiousness. As a result, the PO in this study made decisions efficiently and was able to assume responsibility for them.

In terms of temperament traits, the PO has four subdimensions that differ from the model. The first is persistence. Due to its average level, the PO was more likely (at the beginning of the pandemic) to over-reflect on decisions made and to repeat unhealthy behaviors and reactions, such as over-analyzing decisions already made – focusing on past events at a particularly difficult time. As a result, the process stiffened and there was a lack of learning, resulting in the wrong conclusions being drawn, the causes not being analyzed, and appropriate corrective actions not being taken. This was also related to the average level of affective responsiveness, which hindered the PO's ability to interpret situations of crisis in a positive way and draw constructive conclusions after resources were exhausted. What also became apparent was a lack of long-term thinking (also characteristic of the organization the PO works for), which was exacerbated by a lack of rhythmicity in the respondent's activity, leading to chaotic behavior, particularly during anxiety. Because of the PO's low sensory sensitivity, which is associated with perceptiveness and vigilance, as well as his openness to the external environment, which is extremely important in situations of uncertainty, at first, the PO relied on reactive rather than proactive actions and didn't notice any disturbing signals from the process. It seems, however, that the rest of the traits that are consistent with the model allowed him to finally achieve a sense of control and focus on the tasks at hand.

The PO has a low level of perseverance, which is associated with accepting loss and failure without prolonged reflection and a tendency not to repeat the same behaviors under stress. Considering the many decisions that had to be made, often without detailed analysis and thus posing a considerable risk, the low level of perseverance was conducive to effective process management but only after the first phase had been completed. Initially, this trait was dominated by neuroticism and conscientiousness, with the resulting consequences described above.

Due to the PO's low level of affective responsiveness, even situations involving a significant stimulus value that are common during uncertainty periods in process management did not cause a meltdown. Instead, most of the time, decisions were made with accuracy despite the stress. Stress, as we know, threatens the immune system's responses (McEwen, 2008). As the Coronavirus attacks the immune system during a pandemic, this is a serious problem (Li et al., 2020). On the one hand, maintaining an average activity level provided the manager with sufficient professional, social, and physical engagement, even during lockdowns, but on the other hand, it limited impulsive and risky activities as well as a tendency to react negatively to monotony and absence of activity, which may have been exacerbated by the respondent's high level of extroversion.

In terms of resilience, it appears that its average level enabled the PO to accept hardships and inconveniences associated with pandemics, even under adverse circumstances and their high volatility. As a result of his average level of this trait, he was able to rest, as his body demanded. Process management styles, even authoritative ones, call for adapting to the team's capabilities. Due to the PO's understanding of the need for rest, it was easier. There is evidence that sleep enhances immunity, making this even more important (Gulia & Kumar, 2020).

My assessment of social competencies suggests that assertiveness, social resourcefulness, and social skills contributed to mature process management during the COVID-19 pandemic. This is due to the fact that an assertive manager is able to exert influence without seeking undue approval, which is of particular importance when trying to implement an authoritative management style. His high level of social resourcefulness gave the PO the ability to perform tasks that required other people's assistance efficiently. This was important because the pandemic required the acquisition of various unconventional resources such as disinfectants or protective measures (e.g. masks or rubber gloves), which, especially in the initial period of the pandemic, were unavailable and priced several times more than prior to the outbreak of the pandemic. From the standpoint of society's goals and values, Bowen described social responsibility as a very desirable pattern of behavior for managers as early as 1953. It is especially important in the context of a pandemic, as the interests of a wide range of stakeholders must be considered, not only employees but their families, the local community, and others. Therefore, it is necessary to be able to consider social needs and goals when considering the organization of work, including ensuring safety in a different way than previously, which the respondent managed to achieve.

The PO's cooperation and social competencies were only average, which gave him the opportunity to efficiently collaborate with other departments in this unique setting. On the other hand, the average level of these competencies prevented him from excessively bringing himself closer to others, which would significantly hinder his ability to perform tasks and issue orders, especially given the aforementioned authoritative management style. Therefore, the average level of both traits made it possible to achieve a balance.

Strong confidence in one's own ability (effectiveness) is important for every manager because a solid belief in one's own ability to succeed in a given situation allows one to focus and employ appropriate resources, including the skills necessary to cope with a given task, challenge, or problem (Bandura, 1977). It was particularly useful during the pandemic period when goals needed to be achieved. It was the PO's belief that despite many independent factors, he could still influence the process he was managing and the results he obtained. There was a substantive basis for this thanks to the belief that he was competent with knowledge and skills, resulting from a high level of conscientiousness and aiding him in feeling secure and thus reducing stress.

Research shows that emotional intelligence is beneficial to process management as it strengthens positive attitudes and work outcomes, as well as provides insight into individual and group emotions (Gardner & Stough,

2002; Srivastava & Nair, 2010). Despite his average emotional intelligence, it is evident from the PO's actions that at times he lacked the ability to alleviate stress resulting from having to manage under conditions of uncertainty, but also the ability to communicate effectively or empathize with others. It was particularly apparent in the first weeks of the pandemic during which the respondent had problems with overcoming challenges and resolving conflicts that occurred more often than usual, mainly as a result of the high level of stress and sometimes conflicting needs of all employees.

Managing stressful situations is an important competence for managers since they are almost constantly exposed to stress and its short- and long-term effects while managing the process. In the case of the pandemic, this was largely related to uncertainty regarding the dangerous situation in the external environment, therefore all the more difficult to control. Additionally, the situation was new, so it was unpredictable. For many people, elements of the physical environment interfered with their ability to accomplish their tasks and imposed additional demands on employees, leading to excessive stress and lower productivity (Saleem et al., 2021). As mentioned above, stress significantly reduces the body's immunity. As far as Endler and Parker's (1990) concepts of stress management are concerned, a task-oriented approach is not necessarily the most effective. There are situations where the remaining two styles may be a better fit, i.e. emotion-focused (e.g. mourning a colleague who has died from Coronavirus) or avoidant (e.g. avoiding excessive exposure to disease-related information about COVID-19 or the related mortality rates). It seems, however, that situations requiring a task-oriented approach are more likely to occur in the workplace. As for the PO, he is primarily task-oriented, which means that his process of coping with obstacles in the workplace often resulted in resolving the issue at hand that was the source of stress or relieving its unpleasant effects.

Certain personality traits, such as neuroticism, conscientiousness, and extraversion, have a particularly strong relationship with the feeling of stress (Afshar et al., 2015). People with a higher level of neuroticism, like the PO, tend to experience higher levels of stress than people with a higher level of conscientiousness and extraversion (Brebner, 2001; Lecic-Tosevski et al., 2011), both of which are also characteristics of the PO. As a result, it would seem that these are the main traits that made the respondent experience various difficulties in managing the process in the initial phase of the pandemic, but overcame them and managed the process efficiently in the subsequent period of the pandemic.

In the work of a manager, it is important to believe that the outcomes are determined by what we do (focus on internal control) rather than events beyond our control (focus on external control) (Zimbardo & Gerrig, 2012). Research has shown that people in senior positions in an organization tend to have an internal locus of control (Mamlin et al., 2001), and this is also the case with the PO surveyed. There is also evidence that locus of control is, at least to some extent, a response to circumstances (Hans, 2000). It should be noted, however, that internal orientation usually has to be accompanied by a strong sense of expertise and effectiveness in order for a person to be able to effectively experience a sense of self-control and responsibility (Ng et al., 2006). The PO is characterized by an internal locus of control, supported by a task-oriented style. Therefore, the PO is convinced that his actions have an impact on the outcome and, as a result, he understands that the actions he takes during the pandemic (which includes introducing safety measures) make sense. The respondent does not focus on conspiracy theories and negative propaganda but on actions and implementing them. His sense of control was also reinforced by his average resilience, which prompted him to rest and eat meals relatively regularly, which is a counterbalance to the low rhythmicity characterizing him.

Summary

Taking the conclusions presented in this chapter into account, I would like to offer the hypothesis that the PO's maturity has a major impact on the maturity of the management process under uncertainty. Therefore, it is recommended that organizations assess the maturity of their process managers, thereby enabling the identification of a PO's strengths and weaknesses regarding process management under uncertainty and, consequently, providing effective support. Therefore, the recommendation is to provide managers with effective training in soft skills in areas deemed as potentially needing improvement. This will not affect their personality or temperament but may increase their sense of effectiveness or social competence. A matrix for soft competencies should be created based on the results of the study for their measurement and understanding. Furthermore, employees involved in the process should be assessed for their maturity, allowing them to improve their competencies or have tasks assigned more effectively, as well as making it easier for POs to manage them.

Maturity is an aggregate measure and consists of many components. It should be taken into account that the presented model is open and in the course of subsequent research, it will probably be supplemented with further important variables. Research on a larger sample of process owners will likely reveal which components in the manager maturity model are most important for managing the process in uncertainty, and some may even prove irrelevant. It is important to keep in mind, however, that the manager's maturity is not the only factor to consider, but also the situational context, the PO's previous experiences, and the maturity level of his or her team. These factors have not been discussed here but may be important to coping with uncertainty and should be included in the study as well. Furthermore, professional knowledge contributes to one's sense of competence, and in the case described here, it plays a crucial role in supporting the sense of agency. All this implies the need to conduct much more advanced research than the one presented in this paper. It involves, for example, identifying variables that interfere with or change the outcome. Therefore, it would be advisable to conduct numerous interviews, pilot studies, and statistical analyses. It should be remembered that case analysis has the limitation of not being able to establish a causal relationship because it is not an experimental method and is used primarily to describe and possibly predict phenomena. Consequently, the results cannot be generalized to other individuals without consideration because the situational contexts as well as the characters of the individuals involved in the process may differ significantly. However, the studied case is one of the few, or perhaps the only one, that describes the importance of manager maturity in the uncertainty of the COVID-19 pandemic management comprehensively. In spite of the fact that it requires further research, I consider this to be an innovative approach to the topic.

References

Afshar, H., Roohafza, H., Keshteli, A., Mazaheri, M., Feizi, A., & Adibi, P. (2015). The association of personality traits and coping styles according to stress level. *Journal of Research in Medical Sciences: The Official Journal of Isfahan University of Medical Sciences, 20*(4), 353–358.

Allport, G. (1937). *Personality: A psychological interpretation.* Constable.

Bandura, A. (1977). Self-efficacy: Toward a unifying theory of behavioral change. *Psychological Review, 84*(2), 191–215. doi: 10.1037//0033-295x.84.2.191

Barrick, M., & Mount, M. (1993). Autonomy as a moderator of the relationships between the Big Five personality dimensions and job performance. *Journal of Applied Psychology, 78*(1), 111–118. doi: 10.1037/0021-9010.78.1.111

Brashers, D. E. (2001). Communication and uncertainty management. *Journal of Communication, 51*(3), 477–497. doi: 10.1111/j.1460-2466.2001.tb02892.x

Brebner, J. (2001). Personality and stress coping. *Personality and Individual Differences, 31*(3), 317–327. doi: 10.1016/s0191-8869(00)00138-0

Brody, N. (2004). What cognitive intelligence is and what emotional intelligence is not. *Psychological Inquiry, 15*(3), 234–238.

Costa, P., & McCrae, R. (1992a). *Revised NEO Personality Inventory (NEO-PI-R) and NEO Five-Factor Inventory (NEO-FFI) professional manual.* Odessa, FL: Psychological Assessment Resources.

Costa, P., & McCrae, R. (1992b). Four ways five factors are basic. *Personality and Individual Differences, 13*(6), 653–665. doi: 10.1016/0191-8869(92)90236-i

DeYoung, C., Peterson, J., & Higgins, D. (2005). Sources of openness/intellect: Cognitive and neuropsychological correlates of the fifth factor of personality. *Journal of Personality, 73*(4), 825–858. doi: 10.1111/j.1467-6494.2005.00330.x

Dymecka, J. (2021). Psychosocial effects of the COVID-19 pandemic. *Neuropsychiatry and Neuropsychology, 16*(1–2), 1–10. doi: 10.5114/nan.2021.108030

Endler, N., & Parker, J. (1990). The multidimensional assessment of coping: A critical evaluation. *Journal of Personality and Social Psychology, 58*, 844–854. doi: 10.1037/0022-3514.58.5.844

Erikson, E. H. (1950). *Childhood and society.* W W Norton & Co.

Fiori, M., & Antonakis, J. (2012). Selective attention to emotional stimuli: What IQ and openness do, and emotional intelligence does not. *Intelligence, 40*(3), 245–254. doi: 10.1016/j.intell.2012.02.004

Gardner, L., & Stough, C. (2002). Examining the relationship between leadership and emotional intelligence in senior level managers. *Leadership & Organization Development Journal*, *23*(2), 68–78. doi: 10.1108/01437730210419198

Giberson, T., Resick, C., Dickson, M., Mitchelson, J., Randall, K., & Clark, M. (2009). Leadership and organizational culture: Linking CEO characteristics to cultural values. *Journal of Business and Psychology*, *24*(2), 123–137. doi: 10.1007/s10869-009-9109-1

Goleman, D. (1997). *Inteligencja emocjonalna*, Poznań: Media Rodzina.

Gulia, K., & Kumar, V. (2020). Importance of sleep for health and wellbeing amidst COVID-19 pandemic. *Sleep and Vigilance*, *4*(1), 49–50. doi: 10.1007/s41782-020-00087-4

Hans, T. (2000) A meta-analysis of the effects of adventure programming on locus of control. *Journal of Contemporary Psychotherapy*, *30*, 33–60. doi: 10.1023/A:1003649031834

Hofstede, G. (2011). Dimensionalizing cultures: The Hofstede model in context. *Online Readings in Psychology and Culture*, *2*(1). doi: 10.9707/2307-0919.1014

Hogan, R., & Judge, T. A. (Eds.). (2012). Personality and leadership. *The Oxford handbook of leadership*. Oxford: Oxford University Press.

James, E., & Wooten, L. (2005). Leadership as (un)usual. *Organizational Dynamics*, *34*(2), 141–152. doi: 10.1016/j.orgdyn.2005.03.005

Kozak, A. (2011). *Dojrzałość menedżerska*. Warsaw: Difin.

Kraczla, M. (2017). Personality as a factor of managerial behavior in the light of the Big Five theory. *Scientific Papers of the Silesian University of Technology. Organization and Management Series*, *2017*(105), 195–208. doi: 10.29119/1641-3466.2017.105.14

Li, G., Fan, Y., Lai, Y., Han, T., Li, Z., Zhou, P., Pan, P., Wang, W., Hu, D., Liu, X., Zhang, Q., & Wu, J. (2020). Coronavirus infections and immune responses. *Journal of Medical Virology*, *92*(4), 424–432. doi: 10.1002/jmv.25685

Lecic-Tosevski, D., Vukovic, O., & Stepanovic, J. (2011). Stress and personality. *Psychiatry*, *22*(4), 290–297.

Lord, R., de Vader, C., & Alliger, G. (1986). A meta-analysis of the relation between personality traits and leadership perceptions: An application of validity generalization procedures. *Journal of Applied Psychology*, *71*(3), 402–410. doi: 10.1037/0021-9010.71.3.402

Mamlin, N., Harris, K., & Case, L. (2001). A methodological analysis of research on locus of control and learning disabilities. *The Journal of Special Education*, *34*(4), 214–225. doi: 10.1177/002246690103400404

Matczak, A., & Martowska, K. (2013). *Profil Kompetencji Społecznych. PROKOS. Podręcznik*. Warszawa: Pracownia Testów Psychologicznych Polskiego Towarzystwa Psychologicznego.

McEwen, B. (2008). Central effects of stress hormones in health and disease: Understanding the protective and damaging effects of stress and stress mediators. *European Journal of Pharmacology*, *583*(2–3), 174–185. doi: 10.1016/j.ejphar.2007.11.071

Moormann, J., & Grau, C. (2017). Impact of organizational culture on business process performance: An investigation in the financial services industry, extended abstract. In *Proceedings of the international conference on advanced technologies enhancing education (ICAT2E 2017)*, Amsterdam, Paris: Atlantis Press.

Muffet-Willett, S., & Kruse, S. (2009). Crisis leadership: Past research and future directions. *Journal of Business Continuity & Emergency Planning*, *3*(3), 248–258.

Ng, T., Sorensen, K., & Eby, L. (2006). Locus of control at work: A meta-analysis. *Journal of Organizational Behavior*, *27*(8), 1057–1087. doi: 10.1002/job.416

Rotter, J. (1966). Generalized expectancies for internal versus external control of reinforcement. *Psychological Monographs: General and Applied, 80*(1), 1–28.

Saleem, F., Malik, M., & Qureshi, S. (2021). Work stress hampering employee performance during COVID-19: Is safety culture needed? *Frontiers in Psychology*, *12*. doi: 10.3389/fpsyg.2021.655839

Srivastava, N., & Nair, S. K. (2010). Emotional intelligence & managerial effectiveness: Role of rational emotive behaviour. *Indian Journal of Industrial Relations*, *46*(2), 313–327.

Strelau, J. (1996). The regulative theory of temperament: Current status. *Personality and Individual Differences*, *20*(2), 131–142. doi: 10.1016/0191-8869(95)00159-x

Sztajerska, D. (2021a). Sylwetka Polskiego Menedżera w Świetle Narodowych Cech Osobowości i Kultury. In A. Jagodziński, B. Sypniewska, & S. Kowalski (Eds.), *Zarządzanie w warunkach niepewności*. Płock: Wydawnictwo Naukowe Mazowieckiej Uczelni Publicznej w Płocku.

Sztajerska, D. (2021b). Process owner's personality in creating pathologies within process. In J. Nesterak & B. Ziębicki (Eds.), *Business development in digital economy and COVID-19 crisis*. Cracow: Economic University, 267–278.

Sztajerska, D. (2020). Cechy Osobowości Współczesnego Menedżera – Systematyczny Przegląd Literatury. In A. Sawicki (Ed.), *Wybrane problemy zarządzania*. Pelplin: Bernardinum, 47–67.

Yang, Y., Li, W., Zhang, Q., Zhang, L., Cheung, T., & Xiang, Y.-T. (2020). Mental health services for older adults in China during the COVID-19 outbreak. *The Lancet Psychiatry*, 7(4). doi: 10.1016/s2215-0366(20)30079-1

Zimbardo, P. G., & Gerrig, R. J. (2012). *Psychologia i życie*. Warszawa: Wydawnictwo Naukowe PWN.

Part 3

Social and Organizational Aspects

5 Role of Corporate Social Responsibility in Driving Financial Performance, Risk, and Value Creation for Banks

Piotr Bolibok

Introduction

Financial stability and development opportunities of the modern banking industry are crucially dependent on public trust. Without it, commercial banks would not be able to attract deposits and transform them into profitable investments, such as loans. In comparison to other industries, banks are significantly more vulnerable to criticism from their stakeholders, and thus more exposed to reputational risk (Thompson & Cowton, 2004). Both trust in banks and their reputation were, however, significantly damaged in the aftermath of the global financial crisis of 2007–2008 (GFC). Not surprisingly, therefore, ever since then banks around the world have attempted to rebuild the public's trust in them, in particular by increasing their activity in the area of corporate social responsibility (CSR) (Viganò & Nicolai, 2009). Although the above change may seem an *ad hoc* solution to unexpected and supposedly temporary difficulties, it is also likely that just as in a multitude of other industries, banks have realized and appreciated the potential of CSR as a driver of their financial performance, risk, and market values.

First, engagement in CSR-related activities is supposed to enhance banks' economic, social, and environmental performance with respect to stakeholder expectations (Aguinis & Glavas, 2012). Second, by distinguishing themselves from competitors and improving public perception of the quality of their services, more socially responsible banks may attract new customers and enhance their growth opportunities (Gangi et al., 2018). Third, compliance with the principles of CSR enables banks to mitigate a wide range of Environmental, Social, and Governance (ESG)-related risks, allowing them to directly improve their financial performance (Ziolo, 2021), reduce the operational risk exposure (Koleśnik, 2018), lower the cost of equity (Gregory et al., 2014), and ultimately boost their market values. Fourth, more responsible banks are expected to be more prudent in managing the funds entrusted to them by the depositors, which should reduce their exposure to credit risk and improve the quality of loan portfolios, with all the related benefits for profitability, cost of equity, and market values (Gangi et al., 2018). Fifth, as CSR inherently involves an increased care for the reliability and transparency

DOI: 10.4324/9781003475583-9

of firms' communication with the market, responsible banks should provide their investors with more value-relevant reporting and be less likely to engage in earnings management practices (Bolibok, 2021).

Commitment to CSR and the related reporting requirements, however, inevitably involve increased administrative and overhead expenses. Therefore, the long-run impact of CSR on banks' financial performance, risk, and market values cannot be easily predicted, as it often depends on specific individual and systemic contextual factors (Carnevale & Mazzuca, 2014).

The existing empirical evidence on the impact of CSR on financial performance, risk, and market values in banks is relatively limited and largely mixed. Heterogeneous results of different studies conducted in various contextual settings and time frames suggest that our understanding of the linkages existing between those variables is still far from perfect. The complexity and multidimensionality of CSR make the assessment of such relationships a truly challenging task, while their still underdeveloped theoretical foundations suggest the need for their further scientific exploration. Therefore, this chapter aims to investigate the existing evidence on the impact of CSR on financial performance, risk, and value creation in banks in order to identify and portray the key channels of transmission of CSR impulses and their mutual interactions.

The remainder of this chapter is organized in three sections. The next section provides the review of the relevant international literature on the significance of CSR in banks and its impact on their financial soundness. The second section visualizes and discusses the structures and interactions between the identified channels of transmission of CSR-related impulses to financial performance, risk, and market values of banks. This chapter is closed with conclusions summarizing its key findings and the resultant recommendations for bank business practice.

The Role of CSR in Banks and Its Impact on Their Financial Soundness

The idea of CSR aims to extend the obligations of businesses beyond the interest of their owners in order to take into account the needs of other societal stakeholder groups (Carroll, 2018). Given the specificity of their key business activities and large exposure to reputational risk, banks should be inherently inclined to follow the path of social responsibility (Thompson & Cowton, 2004). Rational engagement in CSR need not cause any fundamental shift in the core economic role of banks, but rather it should allow them to improve the perceived quality of their services and differentiate themselves from the competitors (Gangi et al., 2018). A typically large scale of operations as leading financial intermediaries and their global interconnectedness considerably magnify banks' social impact. From that perspective, the responsibility of banks reaches far beyond the narrow interest of their owners. This regards not only banks' employees or customers but also the society and economy as a whole, due to the role of banks in accumulation and allocation of capital and the importance of their financial soundness for sustainable economic development. Social obligations of banks incorporate both the individual responsibility of each entity for the security of the deposits entrusted to them by the public and the collective responsibility of the whole sector for maintaining financial stability. From the perspective of both the public and the regulators, a true commitment of a given bank to CSR can be viewed as a way in which it may compensate the public for employing their resources to fulfill its obligations toward shareholders (Wu & Shen, 2013). At the same time, however, the reputational gains of banks likely depend on CSR awareness of the public (Bushman & Wittenberg-Moerman, 2012; Wu et al., 2017).

CSR has not attracted wide attention from banks until the outbreak of GFC. When it turned out that the crisis was brought upon largely by irresponsible business practices and moral hazard in the banking sector, banks around the world became more active in integrating the social dimension into their business strategies (Branco & Rodrigues, 2008). In this way, CSR has become an important tool both for restoring banks' reputation and augmenting the transparency of their business models. Today, banks seem to be more careful and more aware of ESG risks, as they are exposed to increasing CSR dynamics, both directly as business organizations and indirectly through financing activities of their clients (Viganò & Nicolai, 2009).

In contrast to non-financial enterprises, the evidence on the linkages between CSR, financial performance, risk, and value creation in the banking industry is relatively scarce (Wu & Shen, 2013). The review of the relevant literature indicates that although the majority of studies suggest that the impact of CSR is beneficial (see, e.g., Bolibok, 2021; Bolton, 2013; Carnevale & Mazzuca, 2014; Gangi et al., 2018, 2019; Neitzert & Petras, 2022; Shen et al., 2016; Taskin, 2015; Wu & Shen, 2013), some investigations are either inconclusive (see, e.g., Cheung & Mak, 2010; Chih et al., 2010; Soana, 2011), or report exactly opposite conclusions (see, e.g., Hamad et al., 2020; Oyewumi et al., 2018; Scholtens & Dam, 2007). This fact suggests the need for further exploration in this area. Mixed results of prior studies combined with the multidimensionality of CSR suggest that the above variables form a complex structure of interactions and feedback. The in-depth analysis of the methodologies and findings of prior studies allows us to identify five key channels of transmission of CSR-related impulses to financial performance, risk, and market values of banks, i.e., operating, pricing, loan portfolio quality, cost of equity, and reporting channel.

The details of the identified channels along with the supporting evidence available in the literature are discussed in the next section. Visualization of the internal structures, linkages, and feedbacks inherent in each channel (Figure 5.1), as well as their mutual interrelations (Figure 5.2), has been based on the method of conceptual modeling.

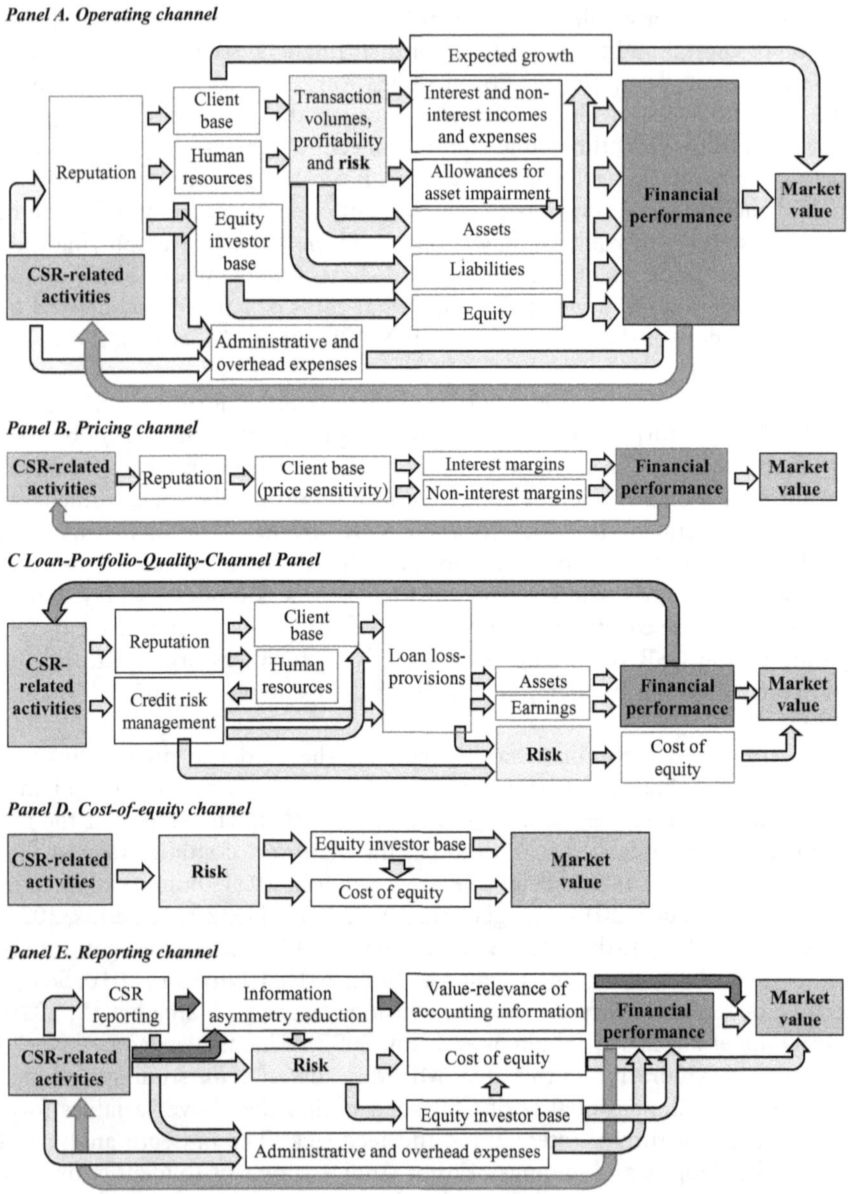

Figure 5.1 Channels of transmission of CSR-related impulses to financial performance, risk, and market values in banks

Source: Own elaboration

Transmission of CSR-Related Impulses to Financial Performance, Risk, and Market Value

Operating Channel

The operating channel captures the most fundamental interactions between CSR-related activities, financial performance, risk, and value creation in banks (Panel A in Figure 5.1). The most straightforward impact of CSR on a company's financial performance stems from the aspect of reputation. Within the operating channel, engagement in CSR-related activities improves customer trust, loyalty, and brand recognition, drawing banks' clients away from less socially responsible competitors. This, in turn, stimulates growth in volumes of transactions along with the related interest and non-interest incomes and expenses (Shen et al., 2016; Wu & Shen, 2013). Apart from the direct impact on current accounting items, enlargement and improved stability of the client base should increase the expected rates of growth, and hence the market values of banks. The ultimate benefits, however, are strongly dependent on the attitudes, motivations, and CSR awareness of their customers (Pérez & del Bosque, 2015).

Better reputation allows banks to attract, motivate, and retain more qualified employees, which should positively affect the volumes, profitability, and quality of their transactions (Gangi et al., 2018), in particular, due to better risk management and reduced impairment of asset portfolios. The reputational dimension of CSR might also affect the composition of banks' investor bases and the possibilities for their enlargement, and thus the conditions for raising additional equity which is often an inevitable prerequisite for further market expansion.

Increased engagement in CSR, however, unavoidably involves additional administrative and overhead expenses resulting from new or altered activities and processes launched to satisfy stakeholder requirements (Soana, 2011). As pointed out by Friedman (2007), such costs might likely exceed the corresponding increase in revenues and ultimately deteriorate a firm's financial performance and its competitive position. Indeed, some studies regarding the banking sector provide empirical evidence supporting such a view (Hamad et al., 2020; Scholtens & Dam, 2007). Additionally, as CSR investments are usually quite costly, they may become unsustainable for banks subject to financial constraints (Gangi et al., 2018), as the related financial benefits, if any, are likely to occur only in the long run. On the other hand, however, more socially responsible banks may be able to decrease the administrative expenses and overhead costs related to advertising, lawsuits, or employee turnover (Shen et al., 2016; Wu & Shen, 2013).

As demonstrated in Figure 5.1, CSR activities affect various aspects of bank financial performance, such as interest and non-interest margins, returns on assets and equity, or the quality of asset portfolios. In turn, the perception of this performance by the equity investors and their expectations regarding its future evolution drive banks' market values (Bolibok, 2017). In fact, a positive association between CSR and market values stems directly from the intermediate relationship between CSR and financial performance (Jo & Harjoto, 2012).

As suggested by the evidence in the relevant literature, however, the relationships between CSR activities and financial performance are not always unidirectional. In fact, there likely exists a strong feedback between banks' financial position and their social performance. In the long run, the key dimensions of the CSR framework, such as transparency of products and services, compliance with ethical and sustainability standards, or reliability of financial disclosures undoubtedly affect the foundations of banks' profitability and risk. On the other hand, given their role as financial intermediaries, banks' reputations and public trust in them are crucially dependent on their financial performance. Moreover, successful implementation of CSR principles is strongly conditional on banks' financial soundness (Lentner et al., 2015). It is, therefore, not surprising that banks in better financial positions often exhibit stronger social performance (Fijałkowska et al., 2018). In fact, the hope of creating a positive feedback loop between social and financial performance may be the very reason for the implementation of CSR in banks' strategies (Hamad et al., 2020). These bidirectional linkages may actually widen the array of CSR-related opportunities and threats that banks are exposed to. However, just as banks do not engage in CSR activities only because they are profitable, also such practices cannot simply guarantee banks' profitability (Taskin, 2015).

Pricing Channel

CSR-related impulses may also affect banks' financial performance and market values via the pricing channel (Panel B in Figure 5.1). Within this channel engagement in CSR activities allows banks to reduce the overall price sensitivity of their customers. This, in turn, affects positively both interest and non-interest margins (Hafez, 2015; Taskin, 2015). Higher margins improve banks' profitability and overall financial performance, and thus, also market values. Importantly, this effect may concern various types of bank products. CSR-sensitive customers may accept lower interest rates on their deposits kept in socially responsible banks, or be willing to borrow from them regardless of higher interest rates, fees, and commissions (Gangi et al., 2018). Hence, lower price responsiveness of customers enables banks to transfer some portion of the CSR costs onto their customers. In this way, the financial burden of banks' CSR engagement would actually be shared between them and the society (Taskin, 2015).

The efficiency of the pricing channel is, however, determined by the type of market structure dominating a given banking sector. The closer it is to an oligopoly, the easier it is for banks to employ various forms of price discrimination and use CSR branding to distinguish their offerings. In contrast, when the sector is closer to monopolistic competition, the efficiency of this channel subsides, as it is easier for the customers to find cheaper substitutes (Wu & Shen, 2013).

Loan Portfolio Quality Channel

Another important channel for transmitting CSR-related impulses in banks involves the quality of their loan portfolios (Panel C in Figure 5.1). Here, CSR affects not only banks' reputation, as in the case of operating and pricing channels but may also directly impact credit risk management processes by determining both the borrower selection criteria and the very assessment of credit risk (Shen et al., 2016). Apart from more rigorous requirements in terms of compliance with CSR principles, socially responsible banks are also expected to exhibit increased care for the safety of collected deposits, leading to more stringent credit policies.

The reputational dimension within the loan portfolio quality channel affects both the composition of client bases and the quality of banks' human resources. More reputable banks usually tend to attract more creditworthy and profitable borrowers (Bushman & Wittenberg-Moerman, 2012) and can afford to apply more rigorous borrower selection procedures (Gangi et al., 2018). In turn, attracting highly skilled human resources allows them to improve the efficiency of their credit risk management processes and to reinforce the related benefits for the quality of loan portfolios and profitability (Gangi et al., 2018).

The above factors should contribute to a higher quality of loan portfolios, lower loan-loss provisions, and more efficient allocation of funds (Gangi et al., 2018; Wu & Shen, 2013). Improvement in loan portfolio quality affects, in turn, banks' financial performance and market values. More stringent and selective credit risk management may also impact value creation by lowering the cost of equity due to reduced risk exposure.

Cost of Equity Channel

Within the cost of equity channel CSR becomes an important part of banks' risk management process, especially in the context of market discipline promoted by the Basel III Capital Accord (Basel Committee on Banking Supervision, 2022) (Panel D in Figure 5.1). The concept of market discipline assumes that banks, being exposed to the pressure from their stakeholders, have additional incentives to mitigate risks (Carnevale & Mazzuca, 2014). Compliance with the principles of CSR seems particularly useful in addressing operational (Koleśnik, 2018) and ESG risks (Gangi et al., 2019; Neitzert & Petras, 2022; Zioło, 2021). The benefits of CSR resulting from more sustainable business strategies, improved corporate governance, better quality and transparency of services, and strengthened loyalty of internal and external stakeholders may also reduce the unsystematic component of listed banks' risk (Orlitzky & Benjamin, 2001). Overall, banks with better CSR performance should generally be less risky than their less responsible counterparts (Bolton, 2013; Neitzert & Petras, 2022) and attract more risk-averse and CSR-sensitive investors, thus reducing the average required risk premium, and ultimately the cost of equity (El Ghoul et al., 2011; Gregory et al., 2014).

Socially responsible banks can also be expected to generate less volatile cash flows (Robinson et al., 2011) and to be more robust to unfavorable market developments (Soana, 2011), which should further reduce their riskiness and positively affect their market values.

Reporting Channel

The last of the discussed transmission channels focuses on the role of reporting and disclosure of CSR-related information (Panel E in Figure 5.1). Following the principles of CSR requires banks to provide the market with complete, timely, and reliable information on both the results of their core business activities and social performance (Bolibok, 2021). As banks' business models are typically opaque and complex (Koller et al., 2020), quality and accessibility of value-relevant information may become an important source of their competitive advantage.

In order to bring the desired effects for market value creation, investments in CSR require adequate information disclosure (Oyewumi et al., 2018). Efficient and reliable communication of banks' social performance reduces the information asymmetry between them and their key stakeholder groups (Wu & Shen, 2013). The access to additional information enables the stakeholders to assess banks' risk positions more accurately, lowering the required risk premium and, ultimately, the cost of equity (Cheng et al., 2014). Therefore, just as other industries with costly capital, banks may attempt to use CSR reporting to reduce this cost to boost their market values (Dhaliwal et al., 2011; Gregory et al., 2014). Given the above, CSR may become a crucial dimension of banks' business strategies aiming at sustainable value creation.

Reduced information asymmetry and improved transparency of communication with the market allow more socially responsible banks to enhance the value relevance of their accounting disclosures (Arraiano, 2020; Bolibok, 2021; Carnevale & Mazzuca, 2014). Such banks should also be more ethical and less likely to engage in earnings management practices and other kinds of data manipulation (Choi & Pae, 2011; Kim et al., 2012) which improves earnings persistence and predictability (Dimitropoulos & Koronios, 2021) and, ultimately, the overall quality and value relevance of their financial reporting.

Therefore, CSR reporting affects banks' market values both directly, by providing the equity investors with additional value-relevant information, and indirectly by affecting the assessment of banks' risk (and thus their cost of equity) and perception of their accounting disclosures by market participants.

Comprehensive and transparent communication facilitates risk assessment, thus attracting new investors to raise additional equity or reduce its cost.

Of course, additional organizational and data processing requirements related to CSR reporting involve a further increase in banks' administrative and overhead expenses, which adversely affects their financial performance. Just as in the case of operating, pricing, and loan portfolio quality channels, also the reporting channel encompasses the feedback between banks' financial performance and the intensity of their CSR activities.

Interactions and Feedback between CSR Transmission Channels

The investigation of CSR transmission channels suggests that the impact of socially responsible activities on banks' financial performance, risk, and value creation occurs within a compound system of mutually interrelated components. These interactions may also be analyzed at the level of the identified channels (Figure 5.2).

As demonstrated in Figure 5.2, CSR-related activities may directly influence a bank's financial performance through each of the identified channels, except the cost-of-equity one. In four channels (operating, cost of equity, loan portfolio quality, and reporting), CSR impulses affect a bank's market value indirectly through their impact on the risk perceived by the equity investors. Interestingly, the reporting channel turns out to be the most versatile one, as it enables the transmission of CSR-related impulses directly to banks' financial performance and risk, and indirectly to their market values by moderating the value relevance of accounting disclosures.

Three of the channels are also directly interrelated between themselves. Since both loan portfolio quality and reporting channels involve the impact of CSR on banks' risk, they are naturally linked to the cost-of-equity channel.

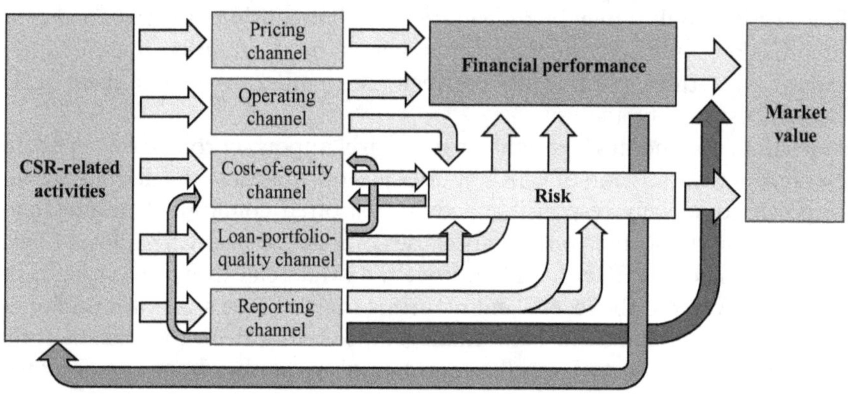

Figure 5.2 Interactions between CSR transmission channels in banks

Source: Own elaboration

Moreover, the feedback existing between banks' financial and social performance ultimately renders all the channels mutually interconnected.

Conclusions

The theoretical and empirical evidence available in the relevant literature allowed to identify five key channels through which CSR-related impulses may be transmitted to financial performance, risk, and market values of banks, i.e., operating, pricing, loan portfolio quality, cost of equity, and reporting channel. Detailed conceptual modeling of these channels revealed a complex system of interactions and feedback both within and between them.

The findings suggest that each of the channels, except the cost-of-equity one, enables transmission of CSR impulses to banks' financial performance, while three of them (cost of equity, loan portfolio quality, and reporting channel) are capable of transmitting such impulses to banks' risk and market values. The reporting channel appears to be the most versatile one, as it enables a parallel transmission of impulses to financial performance, risk, and market value both directly and indirectly through the impact on the value relevance of financial disclosures.

Additionally, a positive feedback loop that likely exists between bank social and financial performance renders all the identified CSR transmission channels mutually interrelated and interdependent. Moreover, three of them, i.e. cost of equity, loan portfolio quality, and reporting channel, are also directly interlinked through their impact on cost of equity.

The findings of the study offer some important lessons and recommendations for bank business practices. First, the results of conceptual modeling demonstrate that adoption of CSR-oriented strategies may affect the very pillars of banks' financial soundness (i.e. their financial performance, risk, and market values) through several distinct, yet mutually interrelated channels. Since CSR impulses may be transmitted simultaneously to several areas (and thus likely amplified), the decision-makers should carefully investigate the internal structures and linkages between the channels to include them in the related cost-benefit analysis.

Second, the findings highlight a particularly important role of the reporting channel in transmission of CSR impulses not only because the desired market response to socially responsible activities is often conditional on adequate information disclosures but also because compliance with CSR allows banks to reduce their overall risk and improve the value relevance of their financial reports. Given the above, efficient reporting may become a versatile and powerful tool in the hands of bank managers, enabling them to strengthen the beneficial impact of CSR on the foundations of banks' financial soundness and its perception by the market.

Third, the identified interrelations and feedbacks between the channels suggest that successful implementation of CSR principles may enable banks to create a "virtuous circle" between socially responsible behavior, financial soundness, and public trust in them, and thus to gain a uniqe competitive advantage over less responsible counterparts.

Fourth, following the above, CSR may play a key role in strengthening banks' resilience to various external shocks of both financial and real nature. This notion seems particularly important in the light of the increasing unpredictability of the global macroeconomic environment in the last decades, as demonstrated by the GFC, COVID-19 pandemic, or the recent Russian invasion in Ukraine. In times of soaring uncertainty, a true commitment to CSR may become the best solution to protect banks' most important "asset" – their reputation.

References

Aguinis, H., & Glavas, A. (2012). What We Know and Don't Know About Corporate Social Responsibility: A Review and Research Agenda. *Journal of Management, 38*(4), 932–968. https://doi.org/10.1177/0149206311436079

Arraiano, I. G. (2020). Is There Value Creation in the Banks Listed in the Dow Jones Sustainability Index Europe? In B. D. Diaz, N. Capaldi, S. O. Idowu, & R. Schmidpeter (Eds.), *Responsible Business in a Changing World. New Management Approaches for Sustainable Development* (pp. 53–68). Springer.

Basel Committee on Banking Supervision. (2022). *The Basel Framework*. Bank for International Settlements. https://www.bis.org/basel_framework/index.htm?export=pdf

Bolibok, P. (2017). The Role of Accounting Variables in Valuation of Banks. *Prace Naukowe Uniwersytetu Ekonomicznego We Wrocławiu, 479*, 23–33. https://doi.org/10.15611/pn.2017.479.02

Bolibok, P. (2021). The Impact of Social Responsibility Performance on the Value Relevance of Financial Data in the Banking Sector: Evidence from Poland. *Sustainability, 13*(21), 12006. https://doi.org/10.3390/su132112006

Bolton, B. J. (2013). Corporate Social Responsibility and Bank Performance. *SSRN Electronic Journal*. https://doi.org/10.2139/ssrn.2277912

Branco, M. C., & Rodrigues, L. L. (2008). Social Responsibility Disclosure: A Study of Proxies for the Public Visibility of Portuguese Banks. *The British Accounting Review, 40*(2), 161–181. https://doi.org/10.1016/j.bar.2008.02.004

Bushman, R. M., & Wittenberg-Moerman, R. (2012). The Role of Bank Reputation in "Certifying" Future Performance Implications of Borrowers' Accounting Numbers. *Journal of Accounting Research, 50*(4), 883–930. https://doi.org/10.1111/j.1475-679X.2012.00455.x

Carnevale, C., & Mazzuca, M. (2014). Sustainability Report and Bank Valuation: Evidence from European Stock Markets. *Business Ethics: A European Review, 23*(1), 69–90. https://doi.org/10.1111/beer.12038

Carroll, A. B. (2018). Corporate Social Responsibility (CSR) and Corporate Social Performance (CSP). In R. W. Kolb (Ed.), *The SAGE Encyclopedia of Business Ethics and Society* (Vol. 1–7, pp. 746–754). SAGE Publications, Inc. https://doi.org/10.4135/9781483381503

Cheng, B., Ioannou, I., & Serafeim, G. (2014). Corporate Social Responsibility and Access to Finance. *Strategic Management Journal, 35*(1), 1–23. https://doi.org/10.1002/smj.2131

Cheung, P., & Mak, W. (2010). *The Relation between Corporate Social Responsibility Disclosure and Financial Performance: Evidence from the Commercial Banking Industry* [Vancouver, Simon Fraser University, The University of British Columbia]. https://core.ac.uk/download/pdf/56366421.pdf

Chih, H.-L., Chih, H.-H., & Chen, T.-Y. (2010). On the Determinants of Corporate Social Responsibility: International Evidence on the Financial Industry. *Journal of Business Ethics*, *93*(1), 115–135. https://doi.org/10.1007/s10551-009-0186-x

Choi, T. H., & Pae, J. (2011). Business Ethics and Financial Reporting Quality: Evidence from Korea. *Journal of Business Ethics*, *103*(3), 403–427. https://doi.org/10.1007/s10551-011-0871-4

Dhaliwal, D. S., Li, O. Z., Tsang, A., & Yang, Y. G. (2011). Voluntary Nonfinancial Disclosure and the Cost of Equity Capital: The Initiation of Corporate Social Responsibility Reporting. *The Accounting Review*, *86*(1), 59–100.

Dimitropoulos, P., & Koronios, K. (2021). Corporate Environmental Responsibility and Earnings Value Relevance. In P. Dimitropoulos & K. Koronios (Eds.), *Corporate Environmental Responsibility, Accounting and Corporate Finance in the EU: A Quantitative Analysis Approach* (pp. 197–213). Springer International Publishing. https://doi.org/10.1007/978-3-030-72773-4_10

El Ghoul, S., Guedhami, O., Kwok, C. C. Y., & Mishra, D. R. (2011). Does Corporate Social Responsibility Affect the Cost of Capital? *Journal of Banking & Finance*, *35*(9), 2388–2406. https://doi.org/10.1016/j.jbankfin.2011.02.007

Fijałkowska, J., Zyznarska-Dworczak, B., & Garsztka, P. (2018). Corporate Social-Environmental Performance versus Financial Performance of Banks in Central and Eastern European Countries. *Sustainability*, *10*(3), 772. https://doi.org/10.3390/su10030772

Friedman, M. (2007). The Social Responsibility of Business Is to Increase Its Profits. In W. C. Zimmerli, M. Holzinger, & K. Richter (Eds.), *Corporate Ethics and Corporate Governance* (pp. 173–178). Springer. https://doi.org/10.1007/978-3-540-70818-6_14

Gangi, F., Meles, A., D'Angelo, E., & Daniele, L. M. (2019). Sustainable development and corporate governance in the financial system: Are environmentally friendly banks less risky? *Corporate Social Responsibility and Environmental Management*, *26*(3), 529–547. https://doi.org/10.1002/csr.1699

Gangi, F., Mustilli, M., Varrone, N., & Daniele, L. (2018). Corporate Social Responsibility and Banks' Financial Performance. *International Business Research*, *11*(10), 42–58. https://doi.org/10.5539/ibr.v11n10p42

Gregory, A., Tharyan, R., & Whittaker, J. (2014). Corporate Social Responsibility and Firm Value: Disaggregating the Effects on Cash Flow, Risk and Growth. *Journal of Business Ethics*, *124*(4), 633–657. https://doi.org/10.1007/s10551-013-1898-5

Hafez, H. M. (2015). Corporate Social Responsibility and Financial Performance: An Empirical Study on Egyptian Banks. *Corporate Ownership and Control*, *12*(2), 102–127. https://doi.org/10.22495/cocv12i2p9

Hamad, M. K., Jealo, K. A., & Ahmed, W. H. (2020). Impact of Corporate Social Responsibility on Financial Performance Applied Research in Iraqi Commercial Banks. *International Journal of Innovation*, *12*(1), 599–619.

Jo, H., & Harjoto, M. A. (2012). The Causal Effect of Corporate Governance on Corporate Social Responsibility. *Journal of Business Ethics*, *106*(1), 53–72. https://doi.org/10.1007/s10551-011-1052-1

Kim, Y., Park, M. S., & Wier, B. (2012). Is Earnings Quality Associated with Corporate Social Responsibility? *The Accounting Review*, *87*(3), 761–796. https://doi.org/10.2308/accr-10209

Koleśnik, J. (2018). Operational Risk in Banks – Revolution or Regulatory Evolution. *Research Papers of Wrocław University of Economics*, *509*, 168–178. https://doi.org/10.15611/pn.2018.509.14

Koller, T., Goedhart, M., & Wessels, D. (2020). *Valuation: Measuring and Managing the Value of Companies* (7th Edition). Wiley.

Lentner, C., Szegedi, K., & Tatay, T. (2015). Corporate Social Responsibility in the Banking Sector. *Public Finance Quarterly*, *60*(1), 95–103.

Neitzert, F., & Petras, M. (2022). Corporate Social Responsibility and Bank Risk. *Journal of Business Economics*, *92*(3), 397–428. https://doi.org/10.1007/s11573-021-01069-2

Orlitzky, M., & Benjamin, J. D. (2001). Corporate Social Performance and Firm Risk: A Meta-Analytic Review. *Business & Society*, *40*(4), 369–396. https://doi.org/10.1177/000765030104000402

Oyewumi, O. R., Ogunmeru, O. A., & Oboh, C. S. (2018). Investment in Corporate Social Responsibility, Disclosure Practices, and Financial Performance of Banks in Nigeria. *Future Business Journal*, *4*(2), 195–205. https://doi.org/10.1016/j.fbj.2018.06.004

Pérez, A., & del Bosque, I. R. (2015). How Customer Support for Corporate Social Responsibility Influences the Image of Companies: Evidence from the Banking Industry. *Corporate Social Responsibility and Environmental Management*, *22*(3), 155–168. https://doi.org/10.1002/csr.1331

Robinson, M., Kleffner, A., & Bertels, S. (2011). Signalling Sustainability Leadership: Empirical Evidence of the Value of DJSI Membership. *Journal of Business Ethics*, *101*(3), 493–505. https://doi.org/10.1007/s10551-011-0735-y

Scholtens, B., & Dam, L. (2007). Banking on the Equator. Are Banks that Adopted the Equator Principles Different from Non-Adopters? *World Development*, *35*(8), 1307–1328. https://doi.org/10.1016/j.worlddev.2006.10.013

Shen, C.-H., Wu, M.-W., Chen, T.-H., & Fang, H. (2016). To Engage or not to Engage in Corporate Social Responsibility: Empirical Evidence from Global Banking Sector. *Economic Modelling*, *C*(55), 207–225. https://doi.org/10.1016/j.econmod.2016.02.007

Soana, M.-G. (2011). The Relationship between Corporate Social Performance and Corporate Financial Performance in the Banking Sector. *Journal of Business Ethics*, *104*(1), 133. https://doi.org/10.1007/s10551-011-0894-x

Taskin, D. (2015). The Relationship between CSR and Banks' Financial Performance: Evidence from Turkey. *Yaşar Üniversitesi E-Dergisi*, *10*(39), 21–30.

Thompson, P., & Cowton, C. J. (2004). Bringing the Environment into Bank Lending: Implications for Environmental Reporting. *The British Accounting Review*, *36*(2), 197–218. https://doi.org/10.1016/j.bar.2003.11.005

Viganò, F., & Nicolai, D. (2009). CSR in the European Banking Sector: Evidence from a Survey. In R. Barth & F. Wolff (Eds.), *Corporate Social Responsibility in Europe. Rhetoric and Realities* (pp. 95–108). Edward Elgar Publishing. https://www.elgaronline.com/view/9781847207647.00017.xml

Wu, M.-W., & Shen, C.-H. (2013). Corporate Social Responsibility in the Banking Industry: Motives and Financial Performance. *Journal of Banking & Finance*, *37*(9), 3529–3547. https://doi.org/10.1016/j.jbankfin.2013.04.023

Wu, M.-W., Shen, C.-H., & Chen, T.-H. (2017). Application of Multi-level Matching between Financial Performance and Corporate Social Responsibility in the Banking Industry. *Review of Quantitative Finance and Accounting*, *49*(1), 29–63. https://doi.org/10.1007/s11156-016-0582-0

Ziolo, M. (2021). Business Models of Banks toward Sustainability and ESG Risk. In M. Ziolo, B. Z. Filipiak, & B. Tundys (Eds.), *Sustainability in Bank and Corporate Business Models. The Link between ESG Risk Assessment and Corporate Sustainability* (pp. 185–209). Palgrave Macmillan.

6 Organizational Commitment and Organizational Climate in the Context of COVID-19

Jacek Dziwulski and Krystyna Wojciechowska

Introduction

The COVID-19 pandemic has significantly affected the functioning of virtually all organizations in the world, including Poland. Sanitary protocols and social distancing began to reshape the social environment at work in an unprecedented way. The unique effects of COVID-19 on organizations and enterprises, as well as the fact that they are omnipresent, point to the need for research into the functioning of human capital under pandemic conditions. Organizational climate and employee commitment are key aspects of the social dimension of organizations. The relationship between the organizational climate and commitment shapes an organization's human capital, affecting its added value as well as its position within the market in its attempt to gain a competitive advantage. Getting to know how organizational climate and commitment change as well as how they are related during times of crisis such as the COVID-19 pandemic have become important issues.

Von Rosenstiel and Boegel, two German psychologists, have developed their own concept of organizational climate, which is based on a definition that defines organizational climate as a set of shared perceptions and assessments among employees regarding objective and important factors and organizational behavior (Rosenstiel & Boegel, 1992). They referred to the psychological field theory of Kurt Lewin (Lewin, 1951) who had drawn attention to the role of subjective interpretation of environmental stimuli in human behavior. Rosenstiel and Boegel argued that there exists a relationship between its formal features as well as elements of its culture and its employees in every organization (Rosenstiel, 2003). The nature of these relationships determines the unique atmosphere and climate of the organization. Hence, the organizational climate that can be examined with the help of a questionnaire constructed by the two authors is a concept that refers to a set of features of the entire internal environment of the organization that is perceived and evaluated by employee groups (Rosenstiel & Boegel, 1992). Steers identified the interdependence between climate and employee commitment (McMurray, Scott, & Pace, 2004). Richardson and Vandenberg, drawing on Bowen and Ostroff's research, saw employee group engagement as the basis

DOI: 10.4324/9781003475583-10

for its analysis according to the dimensions identified by Lawler, i.e., motivation, communication, rewards, and knowledge. Richardson and Vandenberg also pointed out that the climate of commitment had a positive impact on absence rates as well as on the manifestation of desirable socio-organizational attitudes. The researchers emphasized the need to explore variables and their interrelationships in order to understand this problem better (Richardson & Vandenberg, 2005).

Employee organizational commitment is considered one of the key factors contributing to the effective performance of an organization (Ahmad & Bakar, 2003). Studies have shown that commitment positively affects the amount of effort and productivity put into work (Sager & Johnston 1989). Employees who are committed are more satisfied with their work (Rose, Kumar, & Pak, 2009). According to Blau and Boal (1987), organizational commitment and job involvement are key factors that negatively affect the level of staff absenteeism and turnover (Csikszentmihalyi & LeFevre, 1989). Researchers point to the relationship between employee organizational commitment and the intensity of their involvement in civic activities (Meyer & Allen, 1991). As Ogilvie (1986) stated, the belief in the fairness of the promotion process accounts for a higher level of organizational commitment than the relationship with the superior (Ogilvie, 1986; Meyer & Smith, 2000). According to the theory of expectations and the theory of social exchange, an engaged worker who contributes more than average to the success of the company generally expects greater rewards; for instance, he or she may expect that the organization will provide them with greater opportunities for career development, salary increases, and bonuses (i.e. an opportunity for objective professional success) in exchange for their loyalty and additional efforts.

In this study, we have relied on Schaufeli's concept of job involvement (Schaufeli et al., 2002). Work engagement, in his view, is understood as "a positive, fulfilling, work-related state of mind that is characterized by vigor, dedication, and absorption" (Schaufeli et al., 2002). Vigor is understood as experiencing high levels of energy and mental resilience during work and being able to resist distractions. In addition, it is associated with a desire to accomplish tasks in spite of difficulties and adversities. Dedication to work means doing it enthusiastically as well as experiencing its meaning, and being proud to be able to do it. Absorption with work means being fully absorbed and immersed in one's work, which may be accompanied by the feeling that time flies (Baka & Cieślak, 2010)."

Work engagement is defined as

> a positive, fulfilling, work-related state of mind that is characterized by vigor, dedication, and absorption. Rather than a momentary and specific state, engagement refers to a more persistent and pervasive affective-cognitive state that is not focused on any particular object, event, individual, or behavior. Vigor is characterized by high levels of

> energy and mental resilience while working, the willingness to invest effort in one's work, and persistence even in the face of difficulties. Dedication refers to being strongly involved in one's work and experiencing a sense of significance, enthusiasm, inspiration, pride, and challenge. Absorption is characterized by being fully concentrated and happily engrossed in one's work, whereby time passes quickly and one has difficulties with detaching oneself from work.
>
> (Schaufeli et al., 2002; Schaufeli & Bakker, 2004a)

The research presented herein is focused on organizational climate and employee involvement, with the study group consisting of private SMEs. Due to the small number of employees in the SME sector, the organizational climate has a particular impact on increasing employee activity. It is expected that they will perform professional duties with a wide range of specialization, making their full involvement essential. The research problem concerns the development of human capital in the SME sector in the context of a crisis induced by the COVID-19 pandemic. In order to address it, it is necessary to determine how the organizational climate and employee engagement in private SMEs have been developing during COVID-19. As per Lewin's (1951) concept, pandemic circumstances, the related changes to the way work is done, the restriction of social contact, as well as concerns about health, can play a part in shaping both the level of organizational climate and employee commitment. The following questions must, therefore, be answered: What is the level at which these phenomena manifest themselves? In what ways does the way work is organized and how the enterprise operates influence the organizational climate and employee commitment? What is the relationship between organizational climate and employee engagement during COVID-19?

In order to answer these questions, the following hypotheses were proposed:

H1: In a crisis that is caused by the COVID-19 pandemic, the level of the organizational climate in private enterprises in the SME sector is low;

H2: In a crisis that is caused by the COVID-19 pandemic, the level of work engagement among employees at enterprises in the private SME sector is low;

H3: In a crisis that is caused by the COVID-19 pandemic, the organizational climate and employee engagement are positively correlated (cf. Durniat, 2018).

Methodology

In order to collect data, an indirect survey was used (Kaczmarczyk, 2014). Questions and answers were provided in writing without direct contact between the respondents and the researcher. A translational approach was used, in which a classic questionnaire was digitized and uploaded to the Internet (Skitka & Sargis, 2006). The data was collected using the *e-mail survey* technique (Kaczmarczyk, 2014). Although the manner in which the data was collected was dictated by the Chief Sanitary Inspector's instructions on social distancing (Article 3. 1. Announcement of the Marshal of the Sejm of the Republic of Poland of 29 October 2021 on the publication of a uniform text of the Act on special solutions related to the prevention, counteracting, and combating COVID-19, other infectious diseases and crisis situations caused by them), it is worth noting that it offers many advantages such as asynchronicity; a low degree of bias due to a lack of interaction between research subjects and researchers (Dodou & de Winter, 2014) and a low tendency to place oneself in a good light on the part of the respondents (Lelkes et al., 2012). These advantages increase the reliability of responses. However, some authors argue that an online study does not meet standardization requirements (Reips, 2000), since every participant responds under different circumstances, e.g., at different times of the day, in different places; everyone has different hardware and software, etc. Due to the social distancing requirement of the COVID-19 pandemic, we have chosen the Computer Assisted Web Interview (CAWI) method for the collection of empirical data.

In order to collect data on organizational climate, the Polish version of the German questionnaire for measuring organizational climate by Rosenstiel & Boegel was used in this study (version II, Durniat, 2005/6; $N = 367$; validation and normalization: Durniat, 2015; $N = 976$) (Durniat, 2018). As far as the so-called psychometric goodness is concerned, the questionnaire version meets all the criteria (Hornowska, 2007). As a result of this adaptation, a shortened questionnaire was created, consisting of 55 test items. The questionnaire uses a 5-point Likert scale. Based on the normalization of the organizational climate questionnaire (Durniat, 2018), the raw results were expressed using a sten score and expressed in this format for statistical calculations. The scales used in the questionnaire include the following dimensions of organizational climate (Durniat, 2018): introductory (general), which is used to study generalized observations and climate assessments in a given organization; collaborators, which is based on the Blake & Mouton management style concept (Blake & Mouton, 1985); organization of work; information and communication; representation of employee interests; career development and professional development – based on Maslow's hierarchy of needs concept (Maslow, 1954). The organizational climate questionnaire can be used to study organizational climate, its dimensions, and the relationship between the climate and other socio-organizational factors such as engagement (Durniat, 2018).

In order to collect data on engagement, the Utrecht Work Engagement Scale (UWES) questionnaire that comprised 17 items was used (Schaufeli & Bakker, 2004b), which in its original version contained three subscales: vigor, absorption, and dedication. In studies that were conducted using the UWES scale, the α-Cronbach consistency factors for each scale were usually between

0.80 and 0.90. In addition, it has been shown that the correlations between the three scales in the UWES questionnaire are usually equal to 0.65, which indicates the one-factor nature of the tool (Schaufeli & Bakker, 2004a). The Polish version of the UWES questionnaire was obtained from Schaufeli's website. The questionnaire uses a seven-point Likert scale (from 1 – "I've never felt this way" to 7 – "Every day I felt this way").

The study group consisted of 599 employees from private SME enterprises. There were 257 men (43%) and 342 women (57%). Those surveyed were aged 18–63 (average age of 33) and had been working in the enterprises for 1 month to 39 years (average of 7 years), earning a net income ranging from 2000 to 7000 Polish zlotys (average of 2,600). Because of the way work was organized, most employees polled were employed on a permanent basis (76%), most employees held non-managerial positions (81%), and most employees worked in enterprises that employed Polish workers only (60%). In terms of the type of work respondents performed, half did physical work (299 people) and half did mental work (300 people). The pandemic period led to more than half of the surveyed employees working as they had before (53%); 28% of respondents worked remotely from home, and 19% of respondents did not do so but remained at the employer's disposal as a result of GIS regulations suspending the company's operations. As for the nature of the organization, nearly half of the respondents worked in small enterprises (49%), slightly more than half worked at one location (52%), service enterprises (57%), and most of the respondents were employed by Polish companies (76%).

Results

The results of the study into the perception of the organizational climate in private enterprises of the SME sector are characterized by good reliability – the α-Cronbach coefficient for climate as a whole is 0.93, and for its individual dimensions, it varies from 0.63 to 0.78; for engagement, it is 0.93 (see Table 6.1). Data analysis revealed that, in addition to engagement, climate and its dimensions do not follow a normal distribution – the results of the Kolmogorov–Smirnov test values are $p<0.01$; they have skewed to the right apart from the climate as a whole and engagement, which means that most of the respondents' responses are below average; the standard skew error for all climate dimensions is 0.01 and for the involvement, it is 0.1. In addition, the data obtained are platykurtic apart from the climate, which means that the respondents were unlikely to provide extreme responses; there is a standard error of kurtosis of 0.2 for all climate dimensions and commitment dimensions.

All respondents considered the entire organizational climate to be at a lower average level of M=4.00. Career development and professional development were found to be at a higher average level of M=6.17 (Table 6.2); organization of work at an average level of M=5.02; and overall organizational

Table 6.1 Organizational climate and engagement in private enterprises in the SME sector during COVID-19 – distribution parameters and reliability ($N = 599$)

Organizational climate – dimensions (weighted averages on a Sten score scale)	*Number of positions on a scale*	*Weighted average M*	*Standard deviation SD*	*Median*	*Skewness*	*Kurtosis*	*Test K – S (d)*	*α-Cronbacha (p<0.05)*	*α-Cronbach (p<0.05) 2nd Polish version*
Organizational climate (as a whole)	55	4.00	2.47	3.00	–0.07	–0.67	0.109*	0.93	–
Overall climate	5	4.21	2.39	3.00	0.63	–0.78	0.207*	0.71	0.85
Colleagues	9	4.76	2.09	4.00	0.83	–0.18	0.199*	0.68	0.86
Supervisors	12	3.76	2.51	3.00	0.73	0.05	0.197*	0.78	0.92
Organization of work	7	5.02	2.65	5.00	0.78	–0.41	0.201*	0.68	0.81
Information and Communication	10	4.40	2.43	4.00	0.33	–0.94	0.136*	0.78	0.90
Representation of interests of employees	5	4.68	2.36	4.00	0.50	–0.62	0.138*	0.63	0.81
Promotion and professional development	7	6.17	2.35	6.00	0.64	–0.35	0.170*	0.74	0.85
									Original version
Involvement (weighted averages on a scale of 1.00–7.00)	17	4.70	1.20	4.65	–0.12	–0.26	0.054**	0.93	0.70

*$p<0.01$; **$p<0.1$.

Source: Own elaboration based on empirical research; α-Cronbach II values of the Polish adaptation of the scale based on Durniat, K., Polish adaptation of L. Rosenstiel and R. Boegel's organizational climate diagnosis questionnaire. *Polish Journal of Applied Psychology*, 2012, 10 (1), 163; α-Cronbach values for the engagement factor based on: Schaufeli W.B., Bakker A.B. and Salanova M., The measurement of work engagement with a short questionnaire. Educational and Psychological Measurement, 2006, 66(4), 701–716.

climate, collaborators, information and communication, and representation of employees' interests at a level below the average level of M=4.21–4.76. On the other hand, the management style was perceived to be at a low level of M=3.76. Due to the conditions governing the organization of work and the enterprise, the organizational climate as a whole was generally average or above average (M=5.64–6.77) (see Table 6.2). The organizational climate was given the highest ratings by the supervisors (M=6.77), which was significantly different from the ratings given by subordinates (M=6.03) (U Mann–Whitney test Z=2.82 for p<0.01); the ratings given by employees in branch offices (M=6.56) differed significantly from the ones given by those working in companies with only one location (M=5.00) (Z=2.62 for p<0.05). The organizational climate as a whole was perceived as the worst by employees who were at the employer's disposal, who suspended operations of the company due to the pandemic (M=5.65) differing significantly from those continuing to work as usual (M=6.25) (H=2.68 for p<0.05) and working remotely from home (M=6.38) (H=3.04 for p<0.01). Those working for foreign-owned companies M=5.73 and temporary employees M=5.76 also rated the climate as poor, differing significantly from the ratings given by permanent employees M=6.30 (Z = 2.59 for p<0.01).

The results indicate that the most highly rated dimensions of organizational climate were information and communication which were rated by respondents at an average and below-average level. They were rated highest – at a level above average – by employees of branch offices M=6.01 (Table 6.2), differing significantly from employees of network companies M=4.84 (Kruskal–Wallis test results of H=3.52 for p<0.01) and those working in companies with one location M=4.63 (H=5.02 for p<0.001). They were rated highest – at an average level – by supervisors M=5.80, contrasting significantly with subordinates M=4.84 (Z=3.24 for p<0.01) and employees of companies that employed more than 250 people M=5.45. Most employees saw career development and professional development and the way the company was managed to be at a lower-than-average level. Career development and professional development were best perceived by employees in office branches M=5.54, differing significantly from those working for companies with only one location M=4.33 (H=4.48 for p<0.001) and for network companies M=4.53 (H=2.77 for p<0.05) as well as supervisors M=5.38, differing significantly from subordinates (Z = 2.75 for p<0.01). The management style was rated the highest by employees of companies with mixed capital M=5.19, differing significantly from those in companies with foreign capital M=4.20 (H=2.95 for p<0.01) as well as supervisors M=5.15.

Representation of employees' interests and relationships among employees were also rated mostly at a below-average level, with some low ratings. Representation of employees' interests was rated highest by employees working in companies located in branch offices M=5.02, differing significantly from those working in companies with only one location M=4.23 (H=3.16 for p<0.01) and in network organizations M=4.11 (H=3.03 for p<0.01).

Table 6.2 Organizational climate in private enterprises in the SME sector during COVID-19 (N=599, weighted averages on a Sten score scale)

Factors work organization		N	*Organizational climate (as a whole)*	*Overall climate*	*Coworkers*	*Supervisors*	*Organization of work*	*Information and communication*	*Representation the interests of employees*	*Promotion and professional development*
			M	*M*	*M*	*M*	*M*	*M*	*M*	*M*
Type of employment	Permanent	455	6.30	4.10	4.28	4.87	3.88	5.19	4.56	4.81
	Temporary	144	5.76	3.67	3.98	4.42	3.36	4.48	3.90	4.24
Type of work during the pandemic	No change	317	6.25	4.04	4.24	4.79	3.70	5.18	4.38	4.67
	Remote (from home)	168	6.38	4.15	4.42	4.95	4.34	5.22	4.83	5.12
	At company's disposal	114	5.65	3.66	3.81	4.41	3.17	4.30	3.81	4.04
Job type	Physical workers	299	5.98	3.83	4.04	4.55	3.31	4.79	4.17	4.47
	White-collar workers	300	6.37	4.17	4.38	4.98	4.20	5.25	4.62	4.88
Position hierarchy	Supervisors	116	6.77	4.56	4.27	5.15	4.09	5.80	4.95	5.38
	Subordinates	483	6.03	3.87	4.19	4.67	3.68	4.84	4.27	4.51
Nationality	Polish	361	6.07	3.90	4.24	4.84	3.68	4.94	4.40	4.53
	International	238	6.33	4.15	4.16	4.65	3.88	5.15	4.40	4.90

Organizational factors of the enterprise										
Enterprise's size	10–50 employees	138	6.16	4.05	4.22	4.83	3.81	4.87	4.33	4.61
	50–250 employees	167	6.03	3.90	4.23	4.79	3.53	4.94	4.37	4.41
	Over 250 employees	294	6.38	4.02	4.15	4.59	3.92	5.45	4.58	5.13
Type of company	Production	101	5.86	3.02	3.32	4.08	3.18	5.17	4.76	4.93
	Commercial	94	5.96	3.56	4.15	4.64	3.12	4.58	4.03	4.17
	Service	341	6.39	4.46	4.55	5.04	4.14	5.16	4.45	4.77
Location type	One location	310	5.99	3.85	4.26	4.91	3.65	4.63	4.23	4.33
	Branch offices	149	6.56	4.15	3.88	4.51	4.27	6.01	5.02	5.54
	Network of outlets	140	6.18	4.17	4.44	4.71	3.44	4.84	4.11	4.53
Capital type	Polish	454	6.18	3.94	4.15	4.75	3.79	5.15	4.55	4.79
	Mixed	90	6.44	4.43	4.65	5.19	4.08	4.79	3.98	4.25
	Foreign	55	5.73	3.76	3.98	4.20	2.96	4.33	3.85	4.38

Legend: 1.00–2.99 – climate level very low; 3.00–3.99 – low level; 4.00–4.99 – average lower level; 5.00–5.99 – average level; 6.00–6.99 – average higher level; 7.00–8.99 – high level; 9.00–9.99 – very high level; 10.00 – the highest level.

Source: Own elaboration based on empirical research.

It was considered the worst by employees who remained at the employer's disposal M=3.81, differing significantly from those working remotely from home M=4.83 (H=2.93 for p<0.05) as well as by those working in companies with foreign capital M=3.85. Relationships among employees were rated at the lowest level by those working in production companies M=3.32, differing significantly from those working in service companies M=4.55 (H=3.63 for p<0.001) as well as by those who were at the employer's disposal M=3.81. The overall climate illustrating the atmosphere in the company was also rated at a low and below-average level. It was rated the lowest by workers in production companies M=3.02 and commercial companies M=3.56, differing significantly from employees of service companies M=4.46 (H=4.65 for p<0.001 for production companies; H=3.65 for p<0.01 for commercial); those at the employer's disposal M=3.66 and those employed temporarily. The climate-related aspect of the organization of work was given the lowest rating by respondents. The most negative perception of the organization of work was expressed by those working for enterprises with foreign capital M=2.96, differing significantly from those working for enterprises with mixed capital M=4.08 (H=2.95 for p<0.01); those working for production companies M=3.18 and commercial companies M=3.12, differing significantly from employees of service companies M=4.46 (H=3.58 for p<0.01 for production companies; H=3.07 for p<0.01 for commercial ones); employees who were at the employer's disposal following the closing of the company due to the pandemic M=3.17, differing significantly from those working remotely M=4.34 (Z = 3.66 for p<0.001); physical workers M=3.31 differing significantly from white-collar workers M=4.20 (Z=–3.95 for p<0.01); temporary employees M=3.36; and employees in network companies M=3.44, differing significantly from employees in office branches M=4.27 (H=2.53 for p<0.05).

According to the research, respondents engaged in work more frequently than the average, i.e. several times a week M=4.70. Due to the conditions governing the organization of work, people working remotely from home were the most actively engaged as a result of the pandemic M=5.10, differing significantly from those remaining at the employer's disposal M=4.42 (H=4.46 for p<0.001); supervisors M=5.03 differing from subordinates M=4.61 (Z=3.23 for p<0.01); white-collar workers M=4.97 differing from physical workers M=4.40 (Z=–6.11 for p<0.001); and permanent workers M=4.82 as opposed to temporary employees M=4.24 (Z=4.75 for p<0.001). Due to the way the operation of the companies were organized, branch office employees were the most engaged M=4.84, differing from those working in a network M=4.49 (H=2.09 for p<0.05); employees of companies that employed more than 250 people M=4.81; and employees of companies that provided services M=4.79 as opposed to commercial companies M=4.43 (H=3.07 for p<0.01).

The results show a positive correlation between commitment and organizational climate as well as its dimensions in the first months of the COVID-19 pandemic. The correlation between the entire organizational climate and engagement for all respondents was low with Spearman's coefficient p=0.21

($p<0.001$). The strongest correlation between organizational climate and engagement was found for the overall climate with $\rho=0.23$ ($p<0.001$), the organization of work with $\rho=0.21$ ($p<0.001$), and career development and professional development with $\rho=0.21$ ($p<0.001$), while the weakest correlation was found for inter-employee relationships with $\rho=0.09$ ($p<0.05$). Due to the conditions governing the organization of the company, the strongest correlation between the overall climate and engagement occurred among employees working in branch offices with $\rho=0.43$ ($p<0.001$), and in companies employing 10–50 people with $\rho=0.31$ ($p<0.001$) (Table 6.3); while the weakest was found among employees in companies with only one location $\rho=0.19$ ($p<0.01$), while in network companies such a correlation did not occur. The results indicate that engagement is most correlated with climate in the overall dimension. Branches employees exhibited it most strongly $\rho=0.43$ ($p<0.001$), as opposed to network employees for whom it did not occur; employees working for production companies $\rho=0.41$ ($p<0.001$), as opposed to commercial ones, where it did not occur; in companies employing 10–50 people $\rho=0.40$ ($p<0.001$) and over 250 people $\rho=0.31$ ($p<0.001$), as opposed to entities employing 50–250 people, where it did not occur; and supervisors $\rho=0.34$ ($p<0.001$). The weakest and least significant correlation was shown between commitment and employee relationships with $\rho=0.13$ ($p<0.01$)–0.21 ($p<0.05$). As a result of the organization of the company, the strongest correlation between climate and engagement was found among employees of branches $\rho=0.48$ ($p<0.001$)–0.17 ($p<0.05$), as opposed to network employees, companies employing from 50 to 250 people, trading companies, and companies with mixed and foreign capital, where such a correlation did not occur. Because of the conditions surrounding the organization of work, the correlation between commitment and climate was most noticeable among people working in managerial positions $\rho=0.34$ ($p<0.001$)–0.22 ($p<0.05$), in contrast to temporary employees and those working remotely from home because of the pandemic for whom it did not occur.

Discussion

A survey of employees of private small and medium-sized businesses during the COVID-19 pandemic found that the overall organizational climate was above average, information and communication were average, while employee relationships, management methods, representation of employee interests, career development opportunities, and professional development opportunities were all below average, and the organization of work was the worst. The high rating given to the climate with respect to information and communication indicates a relation between structural empowerment understood as a psychological construct (Conger & Kanungo, 1988) and commitment (Demerouti et al., 2001). As long as employees are informed or subjectively convinced that the organization's resources are readily available, empowerment can be generated, resulting in increased engagement.

Table 6.3 Relationships between organizational climate and commitment in private SME enterprises during COVID-19 (N=599; p-Spearman coefficient values)

Factors affecting the organization of work		N	*Organizational climate (as a whole)*	*Overallclimate*	*Coworkers*	*Supervisors*	*Organization of work*	*Information and communication*	*Representation of employe interests*	*Promotion and professional development*
Type of employment	Permanent	455	0.22***	0.24***	0.08	0.17***	0.21***	0.17***	0.20***	0.22***
	Temporary	144	0.14	0.15	0.08	0.07	0.14	0.09	0.15	0.13
Type of work during the pandemic	No change	317	0.23***	0.28***	0.04	0.16**	0.24***	0.19***	0.16**	0.18***
	Remote (from home)	168	0.13	0.1	0.06	0.10	0.12	0.10	0.14	0.17*
	At company's disposal	114	0.21*	0.24*	0.21*	0.27**	0.13	0.07	0.28**	0.23*
Job type	Physical workers	299	0.18**	0.19***	0.07	0.18**	0.12*	0.18**	0.14*	0.20***
	White-collar workers	300	0.19***	0.23***	0.07	0.12*	0.20***	0.12*	0.19**	0.19**
Position hierarchy	Supervisors	116	0.30**	0.34***	–0.06	0.11	0.22*	0.27**	0.32***	0.25**
	Subordinates	483	0.18***	0.18***	0.13**	0.17***	0.21***	0.12**	0.15**	0.18***
Nationality	Polish	361	0.20***	0.23***	0.14**	0.18***	0.21***	0.15**	0.18***	0.18***
	International	238	0.24***	0.23***	0.01	0.14*	0.21**	0.20**	0.22**	0.25***
Organizational factors of the enterprise										
Enterprise's size	10–50 employees	138	0.31***	0.40***	0.18**	0.26***	0.27***	0.30***	0.28***	0.30***
	50–250 employees	167	0.01	–0.01	–0.001	0.02	0.09	–0.002	0.01	0.08
	Over 250 employees	294	0.24**	0.31***	0.01	0.18*	0.25**	0.10	0.22**	0.18*

Type of company	Production	101	0.28**	0.41***	–0.18	0.20*	0.17	0.26**	0.25*	0.25*
	Commercial	94	0.15	0.19	0.08	0.12	0.11	0.04	0.05	0.09
	Service	341	0.22***	0.22***	0.18**	0.23***	0.25***	0.16**	0.22***	0.24***
Location type	One location	310	0.19**	0.23***	0.16**	0.24***	0.21***	0.10	0.15*	0.16**
	Branch offices	149	0.43***	0.43***	0.17*	0.26**	0.38***	0.41***	0.42***	0.48***
	Network of outlets	140	0.009	0.07	–0.08	–0.03	0.01	0.003	0.04	0.005
Capital type	Polish	454	0.26***	0.27***	0.14**	0.19***	0.27***	0.21***	0.22***	0.25***
	Mixed	90	–0.05	0.07	–0.19	0.004	–0.11	–0.01	–0.05	0.18
	Foreign	55	0.12	0.2	0.02	0.18	0.12	0.00	0.29*	0.08

*p<0.05; **p<0.01; ***p<0.001.

Source: Own elaboration based on empirical research.

In the context of the enterprise's organization, the organizational climate was most highly evaluated by employees of network companies and companies located in branches, and especially by those working in manufacturing firms and companies with foreign capital.

Due to the way work was organized, on the other hand, employees in managerial positions rated the organizational climate as the highest, while employees at the employer's disposal because the company was closed due to COVID-19 along with those who were on temporary contracts rated it as the lowest.

The study has shown that employees working for private companies in the first months of the COVID-19 pandemic committed to working more than the average. Due to the organization of the workplace, people working remotely from home, supervisors, white-collar workers, and permanent employees were most engaged. These results confirmed that committed employees are willing to give up personal goals for the sake of organization and professional work, while also showing responsibility and independence in non-schematic situations (Żurek, 2015). Employee independence is very important in difficult, unique, and unpredictable situations, especially when it is consistent with the interests of the company or their own interests within the company (Boshoff & Mels, 2000; Bugdol, 2006). Due to the conditions governing the organization of the companies, employees working in branch offices, employees in companies employing more than 250 people, and employees of companies providing services were the most engaged in their work. These results confirmed the fact that people engage in work as a result of a sense of belonging to the team and loyalty to colleagues and supervisors (Boshoff & Mels, 2000).

The results of the study indicated a low-level positive correlation between commitment and the organizational climate along with its dimensions. The strongest correlation was found between engagement and the overall climate, while the weakest one could be found in the organization of work and relationships among employees. In the context of the enterprise's organization, the strongest correlation between the organization's overall climate and commitment was observed among people working in branch offices and in companies that employed 10–50 people, confirming the fact that people work because they are loyal and part of a team (Boshoff & Mels 2000) that involves a mutual exchange of experiences between themselves and the organization (Juchnowicz, 2010); however, such a correlation did not occur in network companies. Due to the organization of work, the strongest correlation between engagement and climate could be found among people in managerial positions. Results showing a low but statistically significant correlation between engagement and climate regarding career development opportunities, professional development, and management style have been confirmed in research by Schaufeli and Bakker (2004a) demonstrating that employee engagement is influenced by available resources in the work environment, such as supervision and professional development.

References

Ahmad, K., & Bakar, R. (2003). The association between training and organizational commitment among white-collar workers in Malaysia. *International Journal of Training and Development*, *7*(3), 166–185. doi: 10.1111/1468-2419.00179

Baka, Ł., & Cieślak, R. (2010). Zależności między stresorami w pracy a wypaleniem zawodowym i zaangażowaniem w pracę w grupie nauczycieli: pośrednicząca rola przekonań o własnej skuteczności i wsparcia społecznego. *Studia Psychologiczne*, *48*, 5–19.

Blake, R., & Mouton, J. (1985). *The managerial grid*. Houston: Gulf Pub.

Blau, G., & Boal, K. (1987). Conceptualizing how job involvement and organizational commitment affect turnover and absenteeism. *Academy of Management Review*, *12*(2), 288–300. doi: 10.5465/amr.1987.4307844

Boshoff, C., & Mels, G. (2000). The impact of multiple commitments on intentions to resign: An empirical assessment. *British Journal of Management*, *11*(3), 255–272. doi: 10.1111/1467-8551.00165

Bugdol, M. (2006). *Wartości organizacyjne*. Kraków: Wydawnictwo Uniwersytetu Jagiellońskiego.

Conger, J., & Kanungo, R. (1988). The empowerment process: Integrating theory and practice. *Academy of Management Review*, *13*(3), 471–482. doi: 10.5465/amr.1988.4306983

Csikszentmihalyi, M., & LeFevre, J. (1989). Optimal experience in work and leisure. *Journal of Personality and Social Psychology*, *56*(5), 815–822. doi: 10.1037/0022-3514.56.5.815

Demerouti, E., Bakker, A., de Jonge, J., Janssen, P., & Schaufeli, W. (2001). Burnout and engagement at work as a function of demands and control. *Scandinavian Journal of Work, Environment & Health*, *27*(4), 279–286. doi: 10.5271/sjweh.615

Dodou, D., & de Winter, J. (2014). Social desirability is the same in offline, online, and paper surveys: A meta-analysis. *Computers in Human Behavior*, *36*, 487–495. doi: 10.1016/j.chb.2014.04.005

Durniat, K. (2018). Kwestionariusz do pomiaru klimatu organizacyjnego Rosenstiela i Boegela - polska adaptacja i normalizacja. *Studia Oeconomica Posnaniensia*, *6*(3), 48–72.

Hornowska, E. (2007). *Testy psychologiczne: teoria i praktyka*. Warszawa: Wydawnictwo Naukowe "Scholar".

Juchnowicz, M. (2010). *Zarządzanie przez zaangażowanie*. Warszawa: Polskie Wydawnictwo Ekonomiczne.

Kaczmarczyk, S. (2014). Metody zbierania danych ze źródeł pierwotnych przez internet w badaniach marketingowych. *Studia Ekonomiczne. Metody Ilościowe W Badaniach Marketingowych*, *195*. doi: 10.15584/nsawg.2016.1.31

Lelkes, Y., Krosnick, J., Marx, D., Judd, C., & Park, B. (2012). Complete anonymity compromises the accuracy of self-reports. *Journal of Experimental Social Psychology*, *48*(6), 1291–1299. doi: 10.1016/j.jesp.2012.07.002

Lewin, K. (1951). *Field theory in social science*. London: Harper & Raw.

Maslow, A. H. (1954). The instinctoid nature of basic needs. *Journal of Personality*, *22*, 326–347. https://doi.org/10.1111/j.1467-6494.1954.tb01136.x

McMurray, A., Scott, D., & Pace, R. (2004). The relationship between organizational commitment and organizational climate in manufacturing. *Human Resource Development Quarterly*, *15*(4), 473–488. doi: 10.1002/hrdq.1116

Meyer, J., & Allen, N. (1991). A three-component conceptualization of organizational commitment. *Human Resource Management Review*, *1*(1), 61–89. doi: 10.1016/1053-4822(91)90011-z

Meyer, J., & Smith, C. (2000). HRM practices and organizational commitment: Test of a mediation model. *Canadian Journal of Administrative Sciences/Revue Canadienne Des Sciences De L'administration*, *17*(4), 319–331. doi: 10.1111/j.1936-4490.2000.tb00231.x

Ogilvie, J. (1986). The role of human resource management practices in predicting organizational commitment. *Group & Organization Studies*, *11*(4), 335–359. doi: 10.1177/0364108286114003

Reips, U. D. (2000). The web experiment method: Advantages, disadvantages, and solutions. In: M. H. Birnbaum (Ed.), *Psychological experiments on the Internet.* San Diego, CA: Academic Press, 89–118.

Richardson, H., & Vandenberg, R. (2005). Integrating managerial perceptions and transformational leadership into a work-unit level model of employee involvement. *Journal of Organizational Behavior*, *26*(5), 561–589. doi: 10.1002/job.329

Rose, R., Kumar, N., & Pak, O. (2009). The effect of organizational learning on organizational commitment, job satisfaction and work performance. *Journal of Applied Business Research (JABR)*, *25*(6). doi: 10.19030/jabr.v25i6.995

Rosenstiel, L. (2003). *Grundlagen der Organisationspsychologie.* Stuttgart: Schäffer-Poeschel Verlag.

Rosenstiel, L., & Boegel, R. (1992). *Betriebsklima geht jeden an!.* München: Bayer. Staatsministerium für Arbeit, Familie u. Sozialordnung.

Sager, J. K., & Johnston, M. W. (1989). Antecedents and outcomes of organizational commitment: A study of salespeople. *The Journal of Personal Selling and Sales Management*, *9*(1), 30–41. http://www.jstor.org/stable/40428341

Schaufeli, W., & Bakker, A. (2004a). Job demands, job resources, and their relationship with burnout and engagement: A multi-sample study. *Journal of Organizational Behavior*, *25*(3), 293–315. doi: 10.1002/job.248

Schaufeli, W., & Bakker, A. (2004b). *UWES Utrecht work engagement scale preliminary manual.* Utrecht: Occupational Health Psychology Unit Utrecht University.

Schaufeli, W., Salanova, M., Gonzalez-Roma, V., & Bakker, A. (2002). The measurement of engagement and burnout: A two sample confirmatory factor analytic approach. *Journal of Happiness Studies*, *3*, 71–92. doi: 10.1023/A:1015630930326

Skitka, L., & Sargis, E. (2006). The Internet as psychological laboratory. *Annual Review of Psychology*, *57*(1), 529–555. doi: 10.1146/annurev.psych.57.102904.190048

Żurek, A. (2015). *Zarządzanie przez zaangażowanie. Jak bezinwestycyjnie poprawić wyniki firmy.* Gliwice: Helion.

7 Changes in Enterprise Markets in Poland and Ukraine during the COVID-19 Pandemic

Krystyna Gomółka and Piotr Kasprzak

Introduction

Only some Asian countries that had faced local epidemics like SARS in the past had procedures in place to combat the COVID-19 virus when it struck in late 2019 and early 2020. The necessary measures to prevent the spread of the virus, such as social distancing, altered work conditions, and changes to the way in which organizations operate, were not something European countries (including Poland and Ukraine) had prepared for. There have been a number of measures taken by governments around the world in order to rescue economies, mainly through fiscal and monetary policy measures that were mainly theoretical. At the start of the pandemic campaign, Poland and Ukraine took measures to prevent unfavorable economic phenomena from occurring and mitigate the effects of the recession that developed as a result of socioeconomic lockdowns. The Polish government has proposed a set of policies and instruments dubbed the Anti-Crisis Shield and Financial Shield. Similar measures were also implemented by Ukrainian authorities, albeit on a smaller scale.

Because the COVID-19 pandemic is still in progress and the economy is still recovering, it is too early to determine the effectiveness of the aid and the fiscal and administrative measures. Despite this, it is possible to estimate how the pandemic has affected a number of companies.

The purpose of this chapter is to present an analysis of changes in the enterprise market in Poland and Ukraine during the COVID-19 pandemic between 2019 and 2021. This chapter presents a monthly breakdown of the frequency with which enterprises were suspended or closed between 2020 and 2021. This chapter also attempts to characterize and evaluate the assistance provided by the governments of Poland and Ukraine in 2020 and 2021 to owners of micro-, small-, and medium-sized enterprises, as well as their employees. Among the sources of information were reviews of the literature and macroeconomic data collected by Poland's Central Statistical Office (GUS) and the Ukrainian Statistical Service. The data collected were analyzed using descriptive, tabular, and graphical methods, as well as dynamic indicators and variation coefficients.

DOI: 10.4324/9781003475583-11

Research Progress

The first Ukrainian monograph dedicated to the economic impact of the pandemic entitled "Impact of COVID-19 and quarantine restrictions on the economy of Ukraine Office study" was released in July 2020 and only provided recommendations for the Ukrainian government. The same is true when it comes to the assessment of the impact of the COVID-19 pandemic on Ukraine's economy in a monograph edited by Sergey Kulitsky (2020), which does not fully reflect the effects of the pandemic. The most comprehensive analysis has been done by the collective paper entitled "The impact of the COVID-19 pandemic on the socio-economic situation in Ukraine". The article by Adelina Konskaya shows that forced isolation led to restrictions on production, trade, and consumption, reduced solvency of legal and natural persons, extended debt repayment periods, loss of key markets or customers, services, and deterioration of entrepreneurs' situation. Many small businesses have been forced to shut down due to a lack of financial assistance. Government-proposed aid measures were insufficient to prevent their failure.

A number of priorities should be taken into consideration when supporting small businesses, including reducing the role of the government in the operations of small businesses, eliminating administrative barriers to conducting business, decreasing corruption, modernizing the tax system, timely reimbursement of VAT, easing the wage burden by lowering social insurance rates or Personal Income Tax rates, increasing the accessibility of financing for small businesses provided by banks by reducing the requirements for borrowers, accelerating the digitization of public services, and developing e-commerce.

In the aftermath of the COVID-19 pandemic, the GDP declined, unemployment rose, and goods and services production declined. According to Jana Tverskaya, quarantine restrictions extended to shopping and entertainment centers, cinemas, event venues, postal operators, banks, gas stations, privately-owned laboratories, logistic services, supermarkets, pharmacies, and schools. Airlines, the travel industry, and restaurants suffered the most (Tverska & Litvinenko, 2021). Analysts estimate that 50%–90% of restaurateurs have exhausted their financial savings, and cinemas and theaters have laid off almost 1/3 of their employees (Patrash, 2022). Revenues will take several years to return to pre-pandemic levels (Roik, 2022). The most significant impact of the pandemic has been on services. The European Business Association reported that one in five small businesses in Ukraine was at risk of closing in 2021 (Ero, 2020). This is confirmed by Krasota and Kirev's research that in 2020, quarantines and social distancing policies led to an increase in bankruptcies among small business entities (Krasota & Kirev, 2021; Fedyuk, 2022).

COVID-19 affected entrepreneurs in non-food products, real estate, consulting, and legal services to a lesser extent (Belitski et al., 2021). As per official Ukrstat data, 58% of large enterprises had a greater chance of survival due to their larger inventories, access to bank loans, and financial reserves (Ukrstat, 2021). Medium-sized companies (59%) reduced production, lost some partners, and flexibility provided them with less production downtime (7%). Small and micro companies, however, accounted for the majority of companies that discontinued their operations (35%), and they were the most affected by COVID-19 (Shevchenko-Perepelkina, 2021). The programs implemented by the Ukrainian government aimed to mitigate the effects of COVID-19 among SMEs included such measures as support for agricultural businesses, preferential tax rates, and grace periods (Ukraine, 2020d). According to Horashchuk (2022), the easing of restrictions at the end of 2020 resulted in a revival of economic activity. Ukraine's GDP fell by 4% in 2020, which was less than most experts had predicted. Low external demand for commodities (ferrous metals, grains, and fertilizers) and protectionist policies introduced by some partners were responsible for disruptions in foreign trade. Compared to 2019, imports of goods and services decreased by 17.9% (Ukrinform, 2021).

The gradual easing of restrictions and the return of tourism was not a cure-all for the industry as 40%–50% of (mostly small) businesses in the tourism industry could not resume work (Angolyuk, 2021; ShiStrategies, 2021). Ukraine's tourism industry profit in 2021 was 60%–80% of that in 2019 ("Impact of COVID-19 and quarantine restrictions on the economy of Ukraine", 2020), and experts expect it to take at least two years before such results are achieved (Polinkevych, 2020).

According to Melnychenko (2022), foreign investment is one of the instruments used to stimulate the economy after the pandemic. Foreign investments were supposed to lead to technological changes, boost production and product assortment structure, increase product quality, increase revenues, or reduce costs. Ukrainian experts have confirmed that the COVID-19 pandemic caused a much deeper drop in economic indicators in Ukraine than elsewhere around the world because of the state of the country's economy while returning to pre-pandemic levels such as the one in 2019 will require at least three years and could take until 2024 (Ukraine, 2020a).

Several scientific papers have been written in Poland and Ukraine to assess the economic effects of COVID-19 in 2020. The results of a survey conducted in July 2020 indicated that companies with 50–249 employees, service providers in the finance and insurance sectors (90.1%), the largest entities involved in wholesale (80.7%), services (77.6%), and construction (76.6%) had the longest survival periods (of more than 6 months) (Główny Urząd Statystyczny, 2020). Smaller companies struggled to cope with the pandemic and its effects threatened their stability as costs soared, sales and revenues declined, and supply chains were disrupted. The most common measures used by these companies were job cuts, missed social security payments, and bank loans (Janecki, 2022). A particularly difficult situation was noted in service companies in the accommodation and catering sector, retailers of fabrics, clothing, and footwear, and those engaged in specialized construction. Results of a subsequent survey by Devire revealed that 69% of entrepreneurs felt COVID-19 negatively impacted the company. Entrepreneurs from Łódzkie, Wielkopolskie and Ślaskie regions in Poland suffered the most as they reported the most cases of COVID-19 (Devire, 2020). Ligaj and Pawlos (2021) emphasized that many companies remain affected by the crisis, despite the "unfreezing". These include businesses in tourism and hospitality, food service, and mining (Ligaj & Pawlos, 2021).

The pandemic has also had a negative impact on the agricultural market in Poland. In 2020, the greatest difficulties were observed in the poultry and dairy sectors, which faced export challenges, leading to a rise in stocks. Measures introduced by the government, e.g., subsidies for goods storage in private facilities have stabilized the market in the short term. The decline in household incomes and the economic difficulties of the businesses in the sector can negatively impact demand in the domestic market (Szajner, 2020).

An attempt to assess the effectiveness of the Polish government's efforts to stabilize the macroeconomic situation in the Polish economy was presented by Barczyk and Urbanowicz (2021). Research by Stawasz (2021) revealed that government support did not improve the company's financial performance, so it was seen by many companies as a means of sustaining their operations on a daily basis. A survey carried out by Kunz (2021) among companies from Pomerania found that 90% of entrepreneurs felt that the government had failed to provide assistance for entrepreneurs, 83% of respondents said this assistance did not reach all those affected by the pandemic, and those whose PKD (Polish Classification of Activity) number made them eligible for such assistance did not always receive it due to complicated legal and bureaucratic procedures. According to Werner (2021), the size of government aid in 2020 totaled 43,000,000 euros. Interest rate subsidies, guarantees, and warranties predominated. Polski Fundusz Rozwoju S.A., Bank Gospodarstwa Krajowego, and Minister Funduszy i Polityki Regionalnej were responsible for the disposition of these funds. There was no plan to determine which sectors should be supported, and the decision was made on an ad hoc basis. Research by Kraska (2022) shows that companies began cutting operational costs during the COVID-19 pandemic. A large decrease in the net return on current assets can be observed in the first half of 2021 compared to earlier years. Though the financial situation of the surveyed companies may appear to be good, the late payment gap during the first six months of 2021 stood at 92 days, whereas inventory turnover was twice as long.

Pawłos (Ligaj & Pawlos, 2021) examined how COVID-19 affected the business sector. Despite the "unfreezing", many companies are still experiencing the effects of the crisis. Industry sectors such as tourism, hotels, catering, and mining were hit hardest by the crisis. However, during the pandemic period, e-commerce grew significantly. Szarucki, Noga, and Kosch (2021) found that the most common change during the COVID-19 pandemic was digitization. Many companies introduced websites and started using social media for marketing purposes. Customers were able to combine online and in-store shopping, and businesses introduced flexible working hours. A study conducted by Chomicki and Mierzejewska (2020) found that Polish employers have quickly gotten used to working remotely, and private firms outperformed public companies and those with foreign capital in this respect (Ligaj & Pawlos, 2021).

Stabilization Programs of Ukraine and Poland

In Ukraine, the first sick patients were reported on 3 March 2020, a day earlier than in Poland. Border closures caused many people who worked in Poland to leave after businesses shut down. On 13 March 2020, just like in Poland, schools were closed, restrictions on border crossings were introduced, and self-isolation was recommended. On March 17, foreigners were prohibited from entering the country. On March 25, the government imposed a state of emergency (Ukraine, 2020b) but it was not until March 30 that a mandatory quarantine was imposed on all foreign visitors (Ukraine, 2020c), i.e. 15 days later than Poland. However, government efforts were being hindered by local authorities. Opposition leaders who also served as mayors in many cities boycotted the government's measures and introduced their own solutions, regardless of what the central government was trying to impose. Nevertheless, in March 2020, the Ukrainian government announced a stabilization program that consisted of four components (Ukraine, 2020c) (Table 7.1).

In 2020, the Polish government prepared and enacted an aid package consisting of six Anti-crisis Shields – 1.0, 2.0, 3.0, 4.0, and additionally 5.0 (Shield for Tourism) and 6.0 (Shield for Industry), as well as Financial Shield 1.0. Assistance was provided to entrepreneurs through various institutions such as Polski Fundusz Rozwoju (total amount of support PLN 62.6 billion the number of entities supported totaled 348,100, the number of jobs supported totaled 2,800,000, and main beneficiaries included 25% trade industry, 16% construction industry, 11% scientific and technical industry); Bank Gospodarstwa Krajowego (total amount of support – PLN 54.2 billion, the number of entities that received support – 38,900, main beneficiaries – trade 32%, industrial processing 23%, construction 11%; most of the companies supported included microenterprises – 60%); Zakład Ubezpieczeń Społecznych (total amount of support – PLN 18.6 billion the number of entities and jobs supported – 5,100,000, main beneficiaries – trade 18%, construction 11%, scientific and technical activities 10%); Ministerstwo Rozwoju, Pracy i Technologii (total amount of support – PLN 27.4 billion, the number of employees supported – 4,300,000, of which 2,900,000 were supported by the job protection scheme aimed to subsidize employee wages within the framework of the FGŚP, and 1,400,000 were supported by subsidizing wages, and social security contributions due thereon) and Agencja Rozwoju Przemysłu (PLN 152,000,000 the total number of entities that benefited from support – 87, the aid was mainly intended for medium and large enterprises) (Dębkowska et al., 2021).

Table 7.1 Ukraine's stabilization program in 2020

Name of the measure	*Scope*
"Credit holidays" 26 March 2020	1 Introduction of a special grace period for loan repayment 2 Ability to restructure the loan in agreement with the bank 3 Allowing clients to be exempt from the repayment of the principal for a period equal to or longer than the lockdown and restrictions imposed because of the pandemic 4 Exemption from fees and interest for late loan repayment
Tax preferences 17 March 2020	1 Exemptions from fees and taxes on real estate used for business purposes and property tax on housing units in March 2020. 2 Limiting the majority of penalties for tax violations 3 Moratorium on tax audits until 30 June 2020 4 Temporary exemption from paying integrated social security contributions, for the periods from 1 to 31 March and 1 to 30 April 2020 5 Postponement of the introduction of cash registers for all categories of taxpayers submitting tax returns under simplified procedures 6 Increase annual income thresholds for sole proprietors[1] 7 VAT exemption for the importation of goods used to combat Coronavirus, as well as medicine and disinfectants 8 Simplify the system of accounting for products and introduce a tax-free regime for state-owned enterprises producing alcohol-based disinfectants
Support for the SME sector 30 March 2020	1 Financial support for employers and small and medium-sized enterprises that have reduced or ceased operations due to the COVID-19 pandemic 2 Introduce the status of "temporarily unemployed" for the duration of the pandemic. Owners of small and medium-sized businesses with employees were able to declare them as temporarily unemployed so that those employees could receive benefits[2]
Agribusiness support January, March 2020.	1 4,700,000 UAH to support the agro-industrial sector – subsidizing the purchase of agricultural machinery and equipment, cheaper bank loans, and development of farms, supporting and developing private drainage systems, and providing government subsidies for the development of state drainage systems

It should be noted that the primary objective of the various governments' actions during the so-called first wave of the pandemic (i.e., the first and second quarter of 2020) was to ensure the basic financial and economic security of citizens. In Poland, the first attempts to implement aid mechanisms began as early as March 2020. The government divided its goals and priorities into five elements, including (1) protecting jobs and worker security, (2) financing corporate liquidity, (3) health care, (4) improving the financial system, and (5) public investments.

As part of mitigating the effects of the economic crisis caused by the COVID-19 pandemic, a series of protective measures using business support tools (Anti-Crisis Shield) was important for entrepreneurs. In order to maintain the liquidity of the enterprises, an additional mechanism was introduced as part of the assistance provided by Polski Fundusz Rozwoju, the so-called PFR Financial Shield, which complemented the Anti-Crisis Shield. The program offered low-interest, easily accessible loans, and non-refundable and partially non-refundable grants for all types of enterprises. Initially, government aid was provided on an ad hoc basis; in subsequent months, more systematic aid was provided.

The primary goal of the measures was to protect jobs and the economic and financial security of employees. These instruments aimed to subsidize wages and cover social security contributions paid by the employer. For the self-employed and those working under a contract of mandate or contract for work, the government has decided to fund a one-time allowance from Zakładu Ubezpieczeń Społecznych (the Social Insurance Institution). The benefit was equal to 80% of Poland's minimum wage. As part of the assistance, the government also decided to pay benefits to parents of children aged 1–8 who had to look after them when nurseries, kindergartens, and schools were closed. What's more, as part of these measures, it was decided to suspend loan repayment for individuals and entrepreneurs who provided a valid reason for deferring repayment in light of their economic circumstances caused by the pandemic. In addition, as part of the various measures, the government introduced a number of specific incentives, such as those related to accounting business expenses, including, for example, the possibility of more favorable loss deductions in tax returns. Table 7.2 shows the detailed implementation of the aid.

Grants, loan subsidies, guarantees, loans, contribution exemptions, and wage subsidies were offered to entrepreneurs. In a survey conducted by the Polish Economic Institute, 86% of surveyed entrepreneurs used the Anti-Crisis Shield. More than one support mechanism was used by the vast majority (92%). Companies rated government aid with an average rating of 3.5 (on a scale of 1–5). Among the most popular and frequently used are exemptions from social security contributions (average rating of 3.63; beneficiaries – 73%), Financial Shield (3.59; 65%, respectively), subsidized wages, and social security contributions (3.53; 65%, respectively), reduced working hours or working remotely (3.53; 66%, respectively).

When comparing the measures introduced by the Ukrainian and Polish governments that were aimed at reducing the economic impact of the COVID-19 pandemic, it should be emphasized that the stabilization program proposed by the Polish government was much broader than the Ukrainian one. The Ukrainian program was announced mostly in March, and the Polish program was announced at the end of December 2020.

The Polish authorities did not inform Polish entrepreneurs of their next steps. Both Polish and Ukrainian entrepreneurs complained about the lack of

Table 7.2 The scope of the Polish government's efforts to support businesses during the COVID-19 pandemic in 2020

Name of the measure	*Date of entry*	*Scope of the measure*
1.0	31 March 2020	1 Wage subsidies 2 Introduction of flexible working hours 3 Idle time benefit for the self-employed 4 Grants of up to PLN 5,000 for entrepreneurs 5 Tax relief measures (possibility of retroactive settlement of PIT and CIT tax losses, longer time to file PIT returns, deferred filing of JPK_VAT declaration for high-income taxpayers; waiving sanctions for errors in JPK_VAT records)
2.0	18 April 2020	1 Reducing eligibility criteria for idle time benefits (maintaining only the income decrease criterion) 2 Extending eligibility for idle time benefits to civil law contracts concluded before 1 April 2020 3 Introducing loans to cover any out-of-pocket costs incurred in connection with running a business, including for entrepreneurs who do not have employees 4 Introducing exemptions from social security contributions
PFR Financial Shield	18 April 2020	1 Supporting operational liquidity of large enterprises through: loans, guarantees, or warranties, and through leasing or other instruments related to the financing of operations
3.0	16 May 2020	1 Broadened and extended possibility of exemption from social security contributions 2 Support for the passenger rail industry 3 Support for the cultural sector 4 Subsequent steps in simplifying administrative regulations, including tax regulations
4.0	24 June 2020	1 Allocating PLN 560 million for subsidized loans for companies negatively affected by the pandemic 2 Temporary protection from takeovers by non-EU investors for Polish companies 3 Making public procurement easier
5.0	October 15, 2020	1 Idle time benefits for enterprises that have not previously benefited from this form of support (a benefit equal to 80% of the minimum wage entrepreneurs can receive three times) 2 Introducing idle time benefits for companies that have experienced a decline in revenue of at least 75% in the month preceding the application date 3 continued exemption from social security contributions

(*Continued*)

Table 7.2 (Continued)

Name of the measure	*Date of entry*	*Scope of the measure*
Industry Shield 6.0	19 and 30 December 2020	1 Exemptions from social security contributions for specific industries (education, cultural and entertainment, catering, food service, sports, tourism, transportation, retail, laundry services) 2 Extending the deadline for applying for idle time benefits - a grant of PLN 5,000 to those who have never used this form of assistance 3 Support for job maintenance from Fundusz Gwarantowanych Świadczeń Pracowniczych (the Guaranteed Employee Benefits Fund) (up to PLN 2,000)

Source: Own compilation based on the PIE report (Dębkowska et al., 2021).

comprehensive information on aid programs and the difficulty in completing the necessary forms.

Enterprises during the COVID-19 Pandemic

Lockdowns introduced during the COVID-19 pandemic had many negative effects on the functioning of businesses. Isolation, temporary suspension of operations, and the poor financial condition of a number of companies, mainly small businesses, became reasons for their suspension or liquidation (Table 7.3).

A total of 22,000 to almost 32,000 new businesses were established between 1 December 2019 and 31 December 2021, with the majority being established in May, June, and July 2021. The largest number of enterprises suspended or liquidated their operations at the beginning of the lockdown in March 2022 and at the end of the period under study (in December 2021). The number of suspended or liquidated enterprises decreased until November 2020 and increased again in December and January, and then decreased from February 2021 onward. Suspensions numbers were highest in the accommodation and food service sector, retail trade in textiles, clothing, and footwear, and specialized construction. As a result, these companies had to lay off the most workers (Ligaj & Pawlos, 2021) (Table 7.4).

In Ukraine, the number of start-ups remained similar. The smallest number of enterprises were established in April 2020 a month after the lockdown began, and the largest in January 2019, i.e. prior to the pandemic, and in May, June, and December 2021. Most of them were set up in the retail, small catering, and new technology sectors (Ukraine, 2020a). In December and January 2020, before the pandemic, the number of liquidated and suspended enterprises in Ukraine reached its highest point. During the pandemic, far fewer businesses were closed or suspended, most often in the tourism, hospitality,

Table 7.3 Number of enterprises newly established and suspended, and liquidated from December 2019 to December 2021 in Poland

Date	*Newly created entities*	*Suspended/ liquidated entities*	*Total number of enterprises*
12.2019	22,651	24,300	4,509,916
01.2020	33,747	48,818	
02.2020	28,180	32,046	
03.2020	23,249	60,538	4,534,908
04.2020	13,521	30,609	
05.2020	22,274	18,655	
06.2020	29,454	22,277	4,573,499
07.2020	30,264	20,326	
08.2020	26,838	29,490	
09.2020	31,296	38,897	4,628,534
10.2020	29,758	38,020	
11.2020	22,592	36,167	
12.2020	25,082	47,440	4,663,378
01.2021	27,601	40,460	
02.2021	26,078	31,180	
03.2021	31,734	34,022	4,694,912
04.2021	30,703	29,378	
05.2021	31,997	28,772	
06.2021	31,499	34,232	4,747,966
07.2021	31,752	31,959	
08.2021	27,323	39,808	
09.2021	29,481	39,872	4,796,388
10.2021	30,502	36,263	
11.2021	28,923	38,250	
12.2021	30,699	67,965	4,836,214

Source: Own compilation based on CSO (https://bdl.stat.gov.pl/bdl/dane/podgrup/wymiary/25/439/2613) and Central Economic Information Center (https://www.coig.com.pl/) data.

Table 7.4 Number of enterprises newly established and suspended, and liquidated from December 2019 to December 2021 in Ukraine

Period	*Newly created entities*	*Suspended/ liquidated entities*	*Total number of enterprises*
12.2019	23,789	44,225	1,346,174
01.2020	35,178	45,548	1,350,627
02.2020	29,770	21,966	1,354,069
03.2020	24,337	31,752	1,358,597
04.2020	14,026	29,021	1,361,632
05.2020	22,836	–8,061	1,363,612
06.2020	30,683	–4,368	1,365,876
07.2020	31,478	–1,218	1,369,162
08.2020	27,870	8,796	1,373,510
09.2020	33,138	24,119	1,375,919
10.2020	30,635	24,804	1,382,099

(*Continued*)

Table 7.4 (Continued)

Period	*Newly created entities*	*Suspended/ liquidated entities*	*Total number of enterprises*
11.2020	23,429	27,710	1,386,272
12.2020	25,710	28,025	1,390,292
01.2021	28,698	38,775	1,395,448
02.2021	27,126	19,102	1,399,336
03.2021	32,908	15,330	1,403,364
04.2021	31,203	13,461	1,407,405
05.2021	32,762	7,393	1,411,578
06.2021	32,509	9,414	1,414,175
07.2021	30,553	17,059	1,417,488
08.2021	28,446	18,423	1,420,514
09.2021	31,147	21,434	1,423,677
10.2021	31,758	22,536	1,427,141
11.2021	29,755	25,753	1,430,124
12.2021	31,412	29,956	1,433,833

Source: Own compilation based on Ukrstat data, (http://www.ukrstat.gov.ua/edrpoy/ukr/EDRPU_2021/ks_opfg/arh_ks_opfg_21.htm)

Table 7.5 Share of suspensions and bankruptcies in the total number of enterprises

Rok	*Quarter*	*Share in Poland (%)*	*Share in Ukraine (%)*
2020	Q1	3.12	2.44
2020	Q2	1.56	0.41
2020	Q3	1.92	0.77
2020	Q4	2.61	1.94
2021	Q1	2.25	1.75
2021	Q2	1.96	0.72
2021	Q3	2.33	1.34
2021	Q4	2.95	1.82

Source: Own compilation based on data from CSO (https://bdl.stat.gov.pl/bdl/dane/podgrup/wymiary/25/439/2613), COIG (https://www.coig.com.pl) and Ukrstat (http://www.ukrstat.gov.ua/edrpoy/ukr/EDRPU_2021/ks_opfg/arh_ks_opfg_21.htm)

food service, entertainment and sports, and non-food retail sectors (Konska, 2022). Ukrainian government estimates that as a result of operating during COVID-19, Ukraine's hotel and carrier sectors lost 1.5 billion USD in 2020. Closed borders and the suspension of flights caused travel agencies to halt operations, sending staff on leave without pay. Due to quarantines, outbound tourism in Ukraine decreased by 90%, and 35%–40% of hotels in Ukraine closed while the rest operated on a very limited basis. Those that continued to operate (7,000–8,000 facilities) lost 60%–90% of their income (Lozova, 2022). Tour operators and travel agencies were experiencing a decline in the dynamics of their travel services from 2019 to 2021. The number of tourists decreased by 48.2% (Ukrstat, 2021) (Table 7.5).

If we compare the number of suspended or liquidated enterprises in Poland and Ukraine over eight quarters, i.e. 2020–2021, it can be observed that the numbers were significantly higher in Poland than in Ukraine. Perhaps, this can be explained by the relatively simple procedures for suspending or liquidating a company in Poland compared to those in Ukraine. Furthermore, it should be noted that in Poland there were 3.5 times more enterprises operating in this period than in Ukraine.

Summary

The COVID-19 pandemic had an impact on changing the macroeconomic environment of Poland and Ukraine, which subsequently affected the functioning of businesses. The governments of both countries have taken measures to prevent the pandemic, including closing the borders, imposing quarantine upon entering the country, restricting the operation of shopping malls, shutting down international air and rail connections, restricting public gatherings, closing food outlets and other entertainment venues, temporarily restricted the businesses' operations and limited the supply of certain types of items. In addition, the authorities restricted access to certain places and facilities. This resulted in the suspension or liquidation of operations for many companies. The tourism, hospitality, food service, entertainment and sports, and non-food retail sectors closed the most businesses in both countries. More companies were suspended or liquidated in Poland than in Ukraine. Procedures for suspending or resuming a business are much simpler than those in Ukraine. In addition, Poland had 3.5 times more operating companies than Ukraine in 2020–2021. As a result of their efforts to combat the COVID-19 pandemic, both countries were able to mitigate its effects. The government's aid benefited some entrepreneurs in Poland and Ukraine. Ukrainian entrepreneurs lacked access to relevant information on state aid, which accounts for this state of affairs. Some Polish Classification of Activity (PKDs) were not covered by the shields in Poland, and once a PKD was eligible, access to the proposed assistance was hindered by complicated procedures. Therefore, only a few companies have benefited from state assistance.

Recommendations

1 The situation in both countries could be improved by solutions that would prevent businesses from having to lay off workers. There are a number of suggestions, including interest-free loans, longer tax grace periods, compensating labor costs (social security, health insurance contributions) over a longer period;
2 Financial support for entrepreneurs who use remote work solutions wherever possible;
3 Reducing the financial cost of borrowing by companies from banks and financial institutions;

4 It seems necessary to study the short- and long-term consequences of the aid and its impact on the operation of enterprises;
5 Introduction of targeted tools in the future aimed at specific companies and industries, so that assistance is not directed to every entity but only to those that really need the help;
6 Introduction of government designated funds and financing mechanisms (e.g., treasury bonds) for similar situations (e.g. in the event of war), which would provide funds for systemic and strategic measures to rescue economies;
7 Introduction of tax measures that would not reduce the level of consumption but lower the risk of inflation (i.e. reducing VAT along with introducing a progressive income tax).

Notes

1 Tax authorities adopted the following method for calculating the amount of income for "sole proprietors " for groups 1 to 3 in 2020 (effective as of April 2, 2020): Group 1 - 1,000,000 UAH (until April 2 the threshold was 300,000 UAH); Group 2 - 5,000,000 UAH (until April 2 the threshold was 1,500,000 UAH); Group 3 - 7,000,000 UAH (until April 2 the threshold was 5,000,000 UAH).
2 Unemployment benefits are partially paid during the quarantine period if the insured, who is the employer or sole proprietor, pays a one-time contribution to the compulsory social security system for the six months preceding the date of termination of employment or operation.

References

Angolyuk, M. A. (2021). Restorannyy biznes v Ukrayini ta sviti [Restaurant business in Ukraine and the world]. In: *Hotel'no-Restorannyy Ta Turystychnyy Biznes: Realiyi i Perspektyvy, Tezy dopovidey VII Vseukrayins'koyi Student·s'koyi Naukovoyi Konferentsiyi* [Hotel-Restaurant and Tourist Business: Realities and Prospects, the Abstract of the Reports of the VII All-Ukrainian Student Scientific Conference], 24–27.

Barczyk, R., & Urbanowicz, Z. (2021). Działania stabilizacyjne w gospodarce polskiej w okresie pandemii COVID-19. *Prace Naukowe Uniwersytetu Ekonomicznego we Wrocławiu*, *65*(3), 23–39.

Belitski, M., Guenther, Ch., Kritikos, A., & Thurik, R. (2021). Economic Effects of the COVID-19 Pandemic on Entrepreneurship and Small Businesses, DIWBerlin. Retrieved 26 September 2022, from https://d-nb.info/1239652372/34.

Board of the National Bank of Ukraine. (2020). POSTANOVA 26 bereznya 2020 rokum. INFORMATSIYNYY LYST №9 Karantynni novov vedennya dlya biznesu Chastyna 2. Podatok na dokhody fizychnykh osib, mistsevi podatky, YESV, administruvannya [RESOLUTION March 26, 2020 Kyiv, INFORMATION LETTER №9 Quarantine innovations for business Part 2. Personal income tax, local taxes, SSC, administration]. Retrieved 26 September 2022, from https://www.tax.gov.ua/data/material/000/324/414815/Informaciyniy_list_9.pdf.

Chomicki, M., & Mierzejewska, K. (2020). Przygotowanie polskich przedsiębiorstw do świadczenia pracy zdalnej. *E-mentor*, *5*(87). https://www.e-mentor.edu.pl/artykul/index/numer/87/id/1492.

Diyu podatkovykh preferentsiy prodovzheno do zakinchennya karantynu. [Tax preferences are extended until the end of quarantine] (2020). Press Service of the State Tax Service of Ukraine. Retrieved 26 September 2022, from https://tax.gov.ua/nove-pro-podatki--novini-/419011.html.

Devire. (2020). Wpływy koronowirusa na polskie przedsiębiorstwa. Wyniki badań Devire. Retrieved 26 September 2022, from https://www.devire.pl/wp-content/uploads/2020/03/Raport_Devire_Wp%C5%82yw_koronawirusa_na_polskie_przedsi%C4%99biorstwa.pdf.

Dębkowska, K., Kłosiewicz-Górecka, U., Szymańska, A., Ważniewski, P., & Zybertowicz, K. (2021). Tarcza Antykryzysowa... Koło ratunkowe dla firm i gospodarki? Gniazdowski, M., Kubisiak, A., Kutwa, K., Rybacki, J. (współpr.), Polski Instytut Ekonomiczny, Warszawa.

Ero, O. (2020). Yak vryatuvaty malyy biznes v umovakh karantynu? [How to save small business in quarantine?]. Retrieved 26 September 2022, from https://delo.ua/opinions/jakvrjatuvati-malijbiznes-v-umovah-karantinu-367890/.

Fedyuk, B. (2022). Osoblyvosti Formuvannya Finansovykh Rezul'tativ Pidpryyemstv Maloho Biznesu V Umovakh Pandemiyi Covid-19. [Peculiarities of Formation of Financial Results of Small Business Enterprises in the Conditions of Covid-19 Pandemic]. In: *Vplyv Pandemiyi Na Sotsial'noekonomichni Protsesy V Ukrayini Ta Sviti* [The Impact of The Pandemic on Socio-Economic Processes in Ukraine and the World], 16–18.

Główny Urząd Statystyczny. (2020). Wpływ pandemii COVID-19 na koniunkturę gospodarczą – oceny i oczekiwania (dane szczegółowe), Aneks do publikacji „Koniunktura w przetwórstwie przemysłowym, budownictwie, handlu i usługach 2000-2020 (lipiec 2020). Retrieved 26 September 2022, from https://stat.gov.pl/files/gfx/portalinformacyjny/pl/defaultaktualnosci/5516/4/39/1/aneks_do_publikacji_koniunktura_w_przetworstwie_przemyslowym_budownictwie_handlu_i_uslugach_2000-2020_lipiec_2020.pdf.

Horashchuk, I. (2022). Sotsial'no – Ekonomichnyy Rozvytok Ukrayiny V Umovakh Pandemiyi [Socio - Economic Development of Ukraine in the Condition of a Pandemic]. In: *Vplyv Pandemiyi Na Sotsial'no ekonomichni Protsesy V Ukrayini Ta Sviti* [The Impact of the Pandemic on Socio-Economic Processes in Ukraine and the World], 34–36.

Janecki, J. (2022). Ocena konsekwencji kryzysu pandemicznego COVID-19 w sektorze polskich przedsiębiorstw. *Studia BAS, 1*(69), 41–67.

Kraska, E. (2022). Wpływ pandemii COVID-19 na kondycję finansową przedsiębiorstw w Polsce. *Przegląd Prawno Ekonomiczny*, 2, 79–95. Retrieved 26 September 2022, from https://czasopisma.kul.pl/index.php/ppe/article/view/13241/12331.

Konska, A. (2022). Priorytety pidtrymky maloho pidpryyemnytstva dlya podolannya naslidkiv pandemiyi Covid-19 [Priorities of small business support to overcome the consequences of the Covid-19 pandemic]. Vplyv Pandemiyi Na Sotsial'no ekonomichni Protsesy V Ukrayini Ta Sviti [The Impact of the Pandemic on Socio-Economic Processes in Ukraine and the World], 7–9.

Krasota, O., & Kirev, I. (2021). Osoblyvosti rozvytku maloho pidpryyemnytstva v umovakh porushennya makroekonomichnoyi stabil'nosti. [Peculiarities of small business development in the conditions of macroeconomic stability violation].

Elektronne Naukove Fakhove Vydannya "Efektyvna Ekonomika" [Electronic Scientific Professional Publication "Effective Economics"] 2021/2, 5–6.

Kulitsky, S. (2020). Problemy rozvytku ekonomiky Ukrayiny, obumovleni pandemiyeyu koronavirusu COVID-19 u sviti, ta poshuk shlyakhiv yikh rozv"yazannya [Problems of economic development of Ukraine caused by the pandemic of coronavirus COVID-19 in the world, and the search for ways to solve them].

Kunz, W. (2021). Identyfikacja wpływu rządowego programu tarcz antykryzysowych na funkcjonowanie przedsiębiorstw w czasie pandemii COVID-19. Podejście propagandowe czy pomocowe? In: P. Walentynowicz & A. Sałek-Iwińska (Eds.), *Zarzdzanie i rynek pracy w warunkach pandemii Covid 19*. Peplin, 47–61.

Ligaj, M., & Pawlos, W. (2021). Wpływ COVID-19 na funkcjonowanie przedsiębiorstw w Polsce. *Gospodarka Materiałowa I Logistyka, 03*(2021), 60–65. doi: 10.33226/1231-2037.2021.3.6

Lozova, M. (2022). Rehional'ni aspekty rozvytku turyzmu v postpandemichnyy period [Regional aspects of tourism development in the post-pandemic period]. In: *Vplyv Pandemiyi Na Sotsial'no ekonomichni Protsesy V Ukrayini Ta Sviti* [The Influence of the Pandemic on Socio-Economic Processes in Ukraine and the World], 52–54.

Melnychenko, G. (2022). Investytsiyi, Yak Odna Z Vazhlyvykh Sfer Pidpryyemnytstva V Postpandemichnyy Period [Investment as One of The Important Areas of Entrepreneurship in the Postpandemic Period]. In: *Vplyv Pandemiyi Na Sotsial'no ekonomichni Protsesy V Ukrayini Ta Sviti* [The Impact of the Pandemic on Socio-Economic Processes in Ukraine and the World], 9–11.

Patrash, K. (2022). Vplyv Pandemiyi Covid-19 Na Ekonomiku Ukrayiny [The Impact of the Covid-19 Pandemic on the Economy of Ukraine]. In: *Vplyv Pandemiyi Na Sotsial'no ekonomichni Protsesy V Ukrayini Ta Sviti* [The Impact of the Pandemic on Socio-Economic Processes in Ukraine and the World], 13–14.

Polinkevych, O. (2020). Stratehiyi Rozvytku Hotel'no-Restorannoho Biznesu V Ukrayini [Strategies of Hotel and Restaurant Business Development in Ukraine]. *Economic Journal of Lesya Ukrainka Eastern European National University*, 4, 24–29. Retrieved 26 September 2022, from https://echas.vnu.edu.ua/index.php/echas/article/view/630/511.

Roik, D. (2022). Problemy Ta Perspektyvy Rozvytku Turyzmu V Period Pandemiyi [Problems and Prospects of Tourism Development during the Pandemic Period]. In: *Vplyv Pandemiyi Na Sotsial'no ekonomichni Protsesy V Ukrayini Ta Sviti* [The Impact of the Pandemic on Socio-Economic Processes in Ukraine and the World], 56–58.

Shevchenko-Perepelkina, P. (2021). Shlyakhy Rozvytku Maloho Biznesu V Umovakh Covid-19. [Ways of Small Business Development in Covid-19]. *Ekonomika Ta Upravlinnya Pidpryyemstvamy [Economics and Enterprise Management]*, 147–151.

ShiStrategies. (2021). Turyzm V Ukrayini narodzhenyy kryzoyu. [Tourism in Ukraine was born of the crisis] Retrieved 26 September 2022, from https://strategi.com.ua/turyzm-v-ukraini-narodzhenyy-kryzoiu/

Stawasz, E. (2021). Wpływ kryzysu COVID-19 na zachowania mikro- i małych przedsiębiorstw w Polsce – studia przypadków. In: P. Walentynowicz & A. Sałek-Iwińska (Eds.), *Zarzdzanie i rynek pracy w warunkach pandemii Covid 19*. Peplin, 11–27.

Szajner, P. (2020). Wpływ pandemii COVID-19 na sytuację na rynkach rolnych w Polsce, Ubezpieczenia w Rolnictwie – Materiały i Studia, *1* (73), 73–93.

doi: 10.48058/urms/73.2020.2. Retrieved 26 September 2022, from https://www.krus.gov.pl/fileadmin/moje_dokumenty/obrazki/kwartalnik/nr_73/73_Szajner_n.pdf.

Szarucki, M., Noga, G., & Kosch, O. (2021). Wpływ pandemii COVID-19 na modele biznesu przedsiębiorstw sektora MŚP w Polsce. *Horyzonty Polityki, 12*(10), 95–114.

Tverska, Y., & Litvinenko, M. (2021). Zminy V Stratehiyi Rozvytku Maloho Pidpryyemnytstva U Zv'yazku Zi Svitovoyu Pandemiyeyu Covid-19. [Changes in the Small Entrepreneurship Development Strategy in Connection with the World Covid-19 Pandemic]. Bulletin of NTU 2021 t. HPI, 43–47. Retrieved 26 September 2022, from http://es.khpi.edu.ua/article/view/243634/241629.

Ukraine. (2020a). Deyaki pytannya za bezpechennya trudov y khprav derzhavnykh sluzhbovtsiv, pratsivnykiv derzhavny khorhaniv, pidpryyemstv, ustanovta orhanizatsiy na chas vstanov lennya karantynu u zv"yazku iz zahostrennyam sytuatsiyi, pov"ya zanoyi zposhyrennya mvypadki vhost royirespiratornoyi khvoroby COVID-19, sprychynenoyi koronavirusom SARS-CoV-2, vid 25 bereznya 2020 r. № 256. [Some issues of ensuring the laborrights of civilservants, employees of statebodies, enterprises, institutions and organizationsduring the quarantine in connection with the aggravation of the situationrelated to the spread of cases of acute respiratory disease COVID-19 caused by coronavirus SARS-CoV-2, of March 25, 2020 № 256]. https://ukurier.gov.ua/media/files/2020-4/256-p.pdf.

Ukraine. (March 30th, 2020b). Pro vnesennya zmin do deyakykh zakonodavchykh aktiv Ukrayiny, spryamovanykh na zabezpechennya dodatkovykh sotsial'nykh ta ekonomichnykhharantiy u zv"yazku z poshyrennyam koronavirusnoyi khvoroby (COVID-19), 30 bereznya 2020 roku № 540-IX. [On Amendments to Certain Legislative Acts of Ukraine Aimed at Providing Additional Social and Economic Guarantees in Connection with the Spread of Coronavirus Disease (COVID-19) March 30, 2020 № 540-IX]. https://ukurier.gov.ua/media/files/2020-4/256-p.pdf.

Ukraine. (June 2020c). Pro vstanovlennya karantynu ta zaprovadzhennya posylenykh protyepidemichnykh zakhodiv na terytoriyiiz znachnym poshyrennyam hostroyi respiratornoyi khvoroby COVID-19, sprychynenoyi koronavirusom SARSCoV-2: Postanova Kabinetu Ministriv Ukrayiny vid 22 lypnya 2020 r. № 641. [About establishment of quarantine and introduction of the strengthened anti-epidemic measures in the territorywith a significant spread of acute respiratory disease COVID-19 caused by coronavirus SARSCoV-2: Resolution of the Cabinet of Ministers of Ukraine of July 22, 2020 № 641]. https://zakon.rada.gov.ua/laws/show/641-2020-%D0%BF#Text.

Ukraine. (August 2020d), Vplyv COVID-19 na ekonomiku i suspil'stvo (bachennya postpandemichnoho rozvytku u 2020-2024 rr. ochyma ekspertiv ta molodi). [The impact of COVID-19 on the economy and society (vision of post-pandemic development in 2020--2024 through the eyes of experts and youth].

Ukrinform. (2021), Eksport Ta Import Tovariv Ta Posluh. [Export and import of goods and services]. https://www.ukrinform.ua/rubric-economy/3403805-eksport-tovariv-zbilsivsa-na-384-aimport-poslug-majze-na-tretinu-derzstat.html.

Ukrstat. (2021). Kolektyvni Zasoby Rozmishchuvannya. [Collective accommodation facilities]. Retrieved 26 September 2022, from http://www.ukrstat.gov.ua/metaopus/2021/2_03_12_02_2021.htm.

Ukrstat. (2022). Kil'kist' Yurydychnykh Osib Za Orhanizatsiyno-pravovymy formamy hospodaryuvannya. [Number of legal entities by organizational and legal forms of management]. Archive 2019, 2020, 2021. Retrieved 26 September 2022, from https://ukrstat.gov.ua/edrpoy/ukr/EDRPU_2019/ks_opfg/arh_ks_opfg_19.htm.

Vplyv COVID-19 ta karantynnykh obmezhen' na ekonomiku Ukrayiny Kabinetne doslidzhennya [Impact of COVID-19 and quarantine restrictions on the economy of Ukraine Office study]. (2020). Kiev. Retrieved 26 September 2022, from https://www.kas.de/documents/270026/8703904.

Werner, A. (2021). Pomoc państwa w obliczu Covid 19 na przekładzie instrumentów wykorzystanych w Polsce. *Kwartalnik Nauk o Przedsiębiorstwie*, *5*, 63–75.

8 Regional Resilience during COVID-19 Pandemic

Magdalena Miszczuk and Andrzej Miszczuk

Introduction

In the 21st century, we are faced with a number of rapid events and phenomena that require a change of perspective on the functioning of countries, their regions, cities, local units, or enterprises. A particularly difficult situation has arisen as a result of the outbreak of COVID-19, which originated in Wuhan, China, but has spread worldwide due to global connectivity and cross-continental travel. By 2022, it had affected more than 0.5 billion people, and more than 6 million had died as a result of Coronavirus infection. As part of efforts to contain the pandemic, lockdowns were introduced and economic activity was halted. The disruption also affected previously overstretched supply chains. The security of national health also posed a challenge. All this raises the question of how vulnerable countries, regions, cities, local units, and business entities are to the threat of a pandemic as well as how to adapt and recover. Answers to these questions revolve around the increasingly popular notion of resilience, which is examined across different spatial dimensions, i.e.: global, international, national, regional, and local.

The purpose of this chapter is to provide a theoretical and methodological discussion about regional resilience to the COVID-19 pandemic. In particular, the focus is on identifying the determinants of regional resilience to a pandemic in comparison with other shocks, i.e. climate challenges, the financial crisis of 2008–2009, or Russia's military aggression against Ukraine. This chapter focuses on regional resilience recognizing that it is one of the most important factors affecting the operation and resilience of economic actors but, at the same time, the resilience of economic actors affects the resilience of the region. This chapter examines the category of territorial capital, emphasizing that its size, quality, and structure determine the threat-response capability. It also identifies determinants that can affect territorial capital both negatively (increased vulnerability) and positively (increased adaptability). It also attempts to quantify regional resilience by proposing appropriate measures.

Today, in 2022, the problem of the COVID-19 pandemic has not yet been finally resolved and seasonal recurrences (or outbreaks of new pandemics)

DOI: 10.4324/9781003475583-12

are to be expected resulting in possible economic perturbations internationally, nationally, regionally, and locally.

An Overview of Regional Resilience

For those living in politically and economically uncertain times, the concept of regional resilience is becoming increasingly popular when it comes to economic geography and regional studies, and among regional policymakers. Its fuzzy nature, however, has been criticized, as it lacks a clear definition. Although resilience has its origins in ecology and psychopathology, today it plays an important role in many scientific disciplines.

It is possible to distinguish four lines of research and define the concept of resilience (Fröhlich & Hassink, 2018). The first assumes that there are one or more equilibriums to which things return once the shock has been dealt with. This means that a region is resilient when, following a shock, it returns to its original equilibrium or does not get pushed to an alternative equilibrium. The second approach considers the system (which could also be a region, for instance) as a whole, taking both internal and external factors that affect it into account. Internal and external factors can either strengthen the system or weaken it; external factors are generally seen as shock producing, and internal factors are seen as ones that strengthen the system. The third line of reasoning assumes that the observed equilibria are a manifestation of path-dependent development, which is a consequence of successive decisions made over a long period of time. The fourth strand of research emphasizes a long-term view of building resilience.

Regional resilience can be defined as the ability of the regional economy to survive or recover from economic, competitive, and environmental shocks through adjustments in economic structures and social or institutional arrangements aimed at maintaining or restoring the previous path of development or moving to a new, sustainable path that is characterized by fuller and more productive use of physical, human, and environmental resources (Martin & Sunley, 2014).

Three types of regional resilience can be distinguished, namely (Giannakis & Bruggeman, 2017):

- engineering resilience, which refers to the ability to regain a pre-shock state of equilibrium;
- ecological resilience, which determines the scale of disruption that a regional system can absorb before it changes its structure and moves to a new state of equilibrium;
- evolutionary resilience, which refers to a region's ability to "bounce back", that is, to respond to shocks by adapting and transforming its functions.

Regional (but also local, national, international, or global) resilience is thus a kind of balance of vulnerability (susceptibility) to threats (shocks), and capacity to adapt (Zaucha et al., 2014). It can also be described as a process that includes the following interrelated elements (Giannakis & Bruggeman, 2017):

- the vulnerability of the regional economy to economic disruption;
- recovery demonstrating how quickly the regional economy responds to disruptions;
- structural reorientation of production and employment in the region;
- a recovery that involves a return to the pre-recession growth path.

When analyzing regional resilience, it is important to determine the scale, nature, and duration of the shock, and then to analyze the regional economic structure, resources, capabilities, and competencies that affect the region's resilience. The reason for varying resilience between regions may be rooted in the fact that the structure of the regional economy is comprised of important entities that are resistant to shocks to a lesser or greater extent (Gong et al., 2020). The Financial Crisis of 2008–2009, for example, had less impact in regions whose economies were not too closely linked to international financial markets. In contrast, climate change is less likely to affect regions that have previously taken measures to adapt to it. As for the Ukraine war, it is also acknowledged that one of the elements of the country's resilience to Russian aggression was the decentralization reform of public administration that started in 2014 and aimed at strengthening local governments while also decentralizing fiscal authority and reducing the number of the smallest local units, which improved the availability and standard of public services provided (Romanova, 2022).

Other important factors include corporate culture, trust, and expectations of business players as well as regional and local communities, national and regional institutions (including the norms and values they follow), and experience with dealing with previous shocks (the so-called institutional learning). Institutions are associated with the policies they implement and the tools used according to the policies' framework to deal with new shocks and evaluate their effectiveness (Gong et al., 2020).

In the case of the COVID-19 pandemic, however, the problem is that the previous global pandemic of the Spanish flu occurred about 100 years earlier, so the currently living generations have not had a chance to learn how to handle a pandemic. Another issue is the problem of how much of this knowledge – in light of the dynamic progress in medicine over the last 100 years – would have been useful today. The lessons learned from World War II, which ended nearly 80 years ago, are also of little use in responding to the Russian-instigated war in Ukraine. In contrast, climate change has been dynamically accelerating but relatively long-lasting, which promotes the emergence of the so-called Giddens paradox that rests on the fact that a lack of a tangible, immediate threat posed by climate change ensures that most communities will take no action. However, by the time the danger becomes clearly observable, it will be too late to act since greenhouse gas emissions take time to warm up the planet (Gong et al., 2020). In such circumstances, various institutions learn how to respond best when confronted with cyclical economic and financial crises, although the causes of these crises may also vary.

A general measure of resilience, without going into its specifics, consists of synthetic macroeconomic indicators related to (Drobniak, 2017; Giannakis & Bruggeman, 2017):

- regional accounts, especially with GDP, GDP per capita, and their dynamics;[1]
- labor market, and in particular – the resilience index expressed by the following formula[2]:

$$\beta_{EU}res = [(ERt - ERt - 1) / ERt - 1 - (EEUt - EEUt - 1) / EEUt - 1] / \\ |(EEUt - EEUt - 1) / EEUt - 1|,$$

where

ER – employment rate at regional level (persons);
EEU – employment rate at EU-28 level (persons);
$t - 1$ – the initial period of the analysis (year);
t – the end period of the analysis (year).

According to the regional resilience index, if a region shows a relatively smaller decline in employment (or a relatively higher growth) than the basis of comparison (in this case, the EU) the region is said to be resilient. On the other hand, if a region shows a relatively larger decline in employment (or relatively smaller growth), it is described as non-resilient. The dynamics of GDP and GDP per capita are interpreted in a similar way. However, we have also found great cognitive value in subindices that measure regional vulnerability and adaptability. These topics will be discussed in more detail in the subsequent section of this chapter.

Territorial Capital vs. Regional Vulnerability and Adaptability

The literature on regional resilience highlights the importance of human capital (Giannakis & Bruggeman, 2017) and social capital (Gong et al., 2020). It seems that the concept that best illustrates resources and internal factors affecting vulnerability and regional adaptability is referred to as territorial capital. It is defined as a set of resources (assets) of various kinds that characterize a given territory (Camagni et al., 2011). In particular, this applies to unique and irreplaceable resources, the use of which creates a competitive advantage for the territory (Przygodzki, 2016). This structure is determined by the state, transformation, and impact of fundamental development factors that determine its relational structure (Przygodzki, 2016). Ekins' model of four capitals is the prototype of territorial capital, which consists of (Ekins, 1992; Ekins, Dresner, and Dahlström, 2008):

- economic capital, including man-made resources that are used to produce other goods and provide services (machinery, tools, buildings, and infrastructure);

- natural (ecological, environmental) capital, including natural resources that are directly and indirectly related to social well-being; includes ecosystems and their biodiversity, providing water, energy, minerals, wood, air, and other things;
- human capital, which is related mainly to the health, well-being, and potential for productivity, including but not limited to physical and mental health, education, motivation, skills, determining the quantity and quality of labor resources;
- social capital – which, like human capital, relates to societal well-being, but on a community-wide rather than individual basis; it involves a network of social ties that support an efficient, cohesive society; facilitates social and intellectual relationships among its members; refers to those resources of social trust, norms, and relationships that people can use to solve common problems and create social cohesion; its manifestations include civic organizations, neighborhood associations, cooperatives, political and legal structures that foster political stability, democracy, effective governance, and social justice.

A study by the World Bank has shown that 20% of the world's wealth can be attributed to natural capital, 16% to economic capital, and the remaining 64% to human and social capital combined (Gorzelak, Płoszaj, & Smętkowski, 2006). Without denying these proportions, it seems natural capital will become more important in the face of progressive climate change.

A more complete systematization of the components of territorial capital was proposed in a model by Camagni (Camagni et al., 2011) that distinguishes between bonding (i.e. social capital) and bridging (i.e. relational capital). He also used two criteria for dividing the components of territorial capital, i.e.: the type of competition for goods (private, club-owned, quasi-public, and public) and their nature (tangible, mixed, and intangible). Thus, tangible private goods include private fixed capital and the so-called hard externalities, club-owned and quasi-public goods include private networks, resources, and common goods (landscape, cultural heritage), and public goods include natural resources, cultural resources, and resources relating to infrastructure. Intangible private goods comprise human capital (entrepreneurship, creativity, knowledge, and experience) and the so-called soft externalities, club-owned and quasi-public goods comprise relational capital (willingness to associate, ability to cooperate, capacity for collective action, and collective competence), and public goods are composed of social capital (institutions, behavioral patterns, values, trust, and reputation). On the other hand, mixed private goods include market services in the following areas: establishing relationships among companies and transferring technology, club-owned and quasi-public relate to cooperation networks (strategic alliances in R&D, public-private partnerships, space management, and cultural resources), while public includes R&D agencies, agglomeration benefits, clusters, and various ties.

As Churski et al. (2019) emphasize, innovation plays an important role in the formation of territorial capital and is the result of the phenomenon (process) of innovation and the innovation environment. According to Zaucha et al. (2014), territorial capital should also include political capital, namely public management models, leadership and its legitimacy, participation, decentralization, management potential, sovereignty, and development monitoring systems (using specific configurations of territorial capital components in spatial arrangements).

In summary, there are three dimensions of territorial capital, i.e. (Nowakowska, 2017):

- geographical, defined by the availability of common and classic resources of a physical nature, specific resources (tangible and intangible) that determine the competitive advantage of the territory, and the spatial proximity within its framework that strengthens the closeness and intensity of relationships among entities and contributes to the exchange of information and the creation of knowledge and innovation, among other things;
- relational, which shows how embedded economic activity, as well as its effects, are in the social environment and is created by social structures and relationships (trust, bonding, identity, and belonging), as well as economic, cultural, and historical norms and values;
- institutional, which shows the way in which a territory is organized and the ways in which the behavior of its actors is coordinated; it includes informal organizations and institutional proximity (shared customs, rules, and cooperation procedures), and fosters the exchange of information, cooperative processes, interactive and collective learning, and reduces risks and transaction costs.

The aforementioned authors emphasize that the most important components of territorial capital are social capital, including bonding capital, bridging (relational) capital, as well as human capital. Undoubtedly, regional resilience depends on the quality of these capitals. What proved particularly important in the case of the COVID-19 pandemic was the solidarity of local and regional communities aimed at minimizing the spread of the virus and helping those who are most vulnerable. Innovation and entrepreneurship, which are characteristics of both human and social capital, influenced the search for effective remedies such as vaccines and drugs. Implementation of such innovations would not be possible without economic (economic-financial) capital. The importance of bridging social capital can also be seen when there is a massive influx of migrants from a neighboring country at war, as is the case with Poland (especially its border areas) and Ukraine. Particularly in the context of climate change, there is great importance given to environmental capital and all material, financial, and infrastructural resources.

According to the principles of the new institutional economics, attention is drawn to the role of institutions and decision-making procedures as means of stimulating development. By analogy with game theory, these factors increase social benefits as a result of long-term cooperation. Development is based on adjusting to changing circumstances and changing institutional structures. Unless institutions evolve in a way that meets the expectations of local communities and private investors, they become a barrier to a region's development. The main problem caused by institutions includes rising transaction costs and a preference for local political and economic elites to make quick profits by providing incentives for them, which will discourage outside investors (Dawkins, 2003).

To summarize, territorial capital consists of many elements that are in multi-directional interactions and feedback with one another. The quality of the components of this capital, shaped as a result of processes involving civilization, history, geopolitics, technology, socioeconomics, demographics, and natural resources, among other factors, determine vulnerability and resilience. The essence of resilience lies in the efficiency of institutions operating in a decentralized state and civil society.

Measurement of Regional Vulnerability and Adaptability

With reference to the concept of territorial capital, the aforementioned authors (Zaucha et al., 2014) proposed a set of sub-measures for regional resilience expressed in terms of vulnerability (susceptibility) of the region:

- foreign direct investment (FDI): FDI inflow per capita, the share of accumulated FDI in GDP, the number of companies with foreign capital;
- the openness of the economy (measured as the share of exports and imports in GDP);
- the share of employment in the finance and construction industries;
- the share of employment in industry and agriculture;
- diversification of the region's economic structure (measured by the Herfindahl–Hirschman Index (HHI), which is the sum of the squares of the individual market shares among all companies in the region);
- the efficiency of the economy (measured by gross value added per worker compared to the national average; nominal wages compared to the national average; employment-related costs compared to the national average);
- the share of BERD (business sector R&D spending) in GDP compared to the national average;
- structural (long-term) unemployment compared to the national average;
- agglomeration index (expressed as the share of the population in the agglomeration compared to the region's total population).

The set of measures listed above is particularly useful in analyzing regional vulnerability during economic and financial crises. When we interpret these measures, we can see that regions with more internationally open economies (which increase the risk that a crisis will be transmitted from one part of the world to another) are more susceptible to shocks than others. Such regions have a large share of foreign players operating in an undiversified economic structure that is mainly composed of crisis-prone industries (i.e. the finance and construction sectors), with high labor costs and persistently high structural unemployment. Regions with low vulnerability to shocks are those whose economic structure is diversified, their industry and agriculture are relatively important, they have high productivity and high wages, and BERD shares in GDP and agglomeration indexes are high.

The experience of the COVID-19 pandemic shows that regions structured by large foreign entities based on global supply chains experienced difficulties in maintaining their operations. Regions with a high share of tourism (which was restricted and did not offer frontline services) suffered similar difficulties. Restrictions placed on a range of tangible services were also severe, while intangible services evolved through the use of the Internet. Agricultural areas (characterized by dispersed production and relatively rigid demand) with scattered settlements (no large cities), i.e. those considered peripheral and underdeveloped, were less susceptible to COVID-19.

In terms of regional adaptability, the proposed measures include (Zaucha et al., 2014):

- quality of institutions, which is reflected in the region's high investment attractiveness;
- social capital, as measured by civilization competencies (the share of citizens using the Internet), social activity (participation in elections, the number of NGOs per 1,000 residents), entrepreneurship (the number of businesses per 1,000 residents);
- human capital, as measured by GDP per capita;
- total and own revenues of regional and local governments per capita compared to the national average;
- EU funds raised per capita in comparison to the national average;
- average annual migration balance per 1,000 residents.

Regions with higher quality institutions, higher social capital, higher GDP per capita, higher local government income per capita, greater involvement with raising external funding, and lower migration rates are more equipped to implement adaptation measures. As for adaptation measures, the above criteria are generally suitable in the event of a financial and economic crisis like that associated with a pandemic. Some of these measures (in addition to migration rates) are also useful in assessing a migration crisis brought about by war refugees. Only in the case of climate change is it necessary to use measurements related to the reduction of greenhouse gas emissions, the energy production structure, or carbon footprint as an element of competitiveness of economic entities.

It is also worth noting the external conditions that may affect the region's resilience, geopolitical considerations in particular. On the one hand, integration processes strengthen the resilience of countries and regions. In economic terms, integration involves the gradual removal of barriers between economies and the establishment of common institutions among the countries that make up an integration group. It is a process that involves successive phases, such as (Haliżak, 2006): preferential trade zones, free trade zones, customs unions, common markets (ensuring free movement of labor, capital resources, and technology), economic unions (including a common currency, unified monetary and fiscal policies) and political unions (which include not only full economic integration but also the unification of legal systems of member countries, which can make them function under a federation). Far-reaching integration makes it possible to strengthen (complement) the territorial capital of individual regions. The situation of border areas seems particularly, especially that of a group's external borders (Prokkola, 2019). Such regions' resilience depends on the nature and function of the border, as demonstrated by the war in Ukraine.

Summary

Resilience is a relatively new research category in social science. The term refers to resilience to external shocks such as pandemics, financial crises, climate change, or war. In general, we generally distinguish vulnerability (sensitivity) to shocks and the ability to adapt to them. Resilience exists both globally and locally. According to the authors, its regional aspect is important for the operation of business entities, and it is possible to see bilateral correlations, i.e. a resilient region influences the resilience of business entities and, vice versa, strong business entities contribute to the resilience of the region. The source of resilience lies in the right quality of territorial capital, including social capital and human capital that foster cooperative attitudes, innovation, and entrepreneurship. In a decentralized (regional) state and civil society, well-functioning institutions are the essence of territorial capital. Paradoxically, the experience with COVID-19 shows that regions that were less developed proved to be more resistant.

Notes

1 It's worth mentioning that economists are beginning to question the usefulness of GDP as a measure of shocks to economies (cf: Stiglitz, Fitoussi, & Durand, 2018).
2 This version of the index is used to show the resilience of a specific region in comparison with the EU. However, the basis for such comparison may be different, e.g. a country.

References

Camagni, R., Caragliu, A., & Perucca, G., (2011). *Territorial capital. Relational and human capital*. Milano: Politecnico di Milano.

Churski P., Herodowicz T., Konecka-Szydłowska B., & Perdał R. (2019). Czynniki rozwoju w praktyce polityki spójności zorientowanej terytorialnie. In J. Danielewicz & D. Sikora-Fernandez (Eds.), *Zarządzanie rozwojem współczesnych miast*. Łódź: Wydawnictwo Uniwersytetu Łódzkiego, 141–164.

Dawkins, C. (2003). Regional Development Theory: Conceptual Foundations, Classic Works, and Recent Developments. *Journal of Planning Literature*, *18*(2), 131–172. doi: 10.1177/0885412203254706

Drobniak, A. (2017). Economic Resilience of Wroclaw in the Context of European Cities. *Prace Naukowe Uniwersytetu Ekonomicznego We Wrocławiu*, *490*, 123–133. doi: 10.15611/pn.2017.490.11

Ekins, P. (1992). A Four-capital Model of Wealth Creation. In P. Ekins & M. Max-Neef (Eds.), *Real-life economics. Understanding wealth creation*. London, New York: Routledge, 147–155.

Ekins, P., Dresner, S., & Dahlström, K. (2008). The four-capital method of sustainable development evaluation. *European Environment*, *18*(2), 63–80. doi: 10.1002/eet.471

Fröhlich, K., & Hassink, R. (2018). Regional Resilience: A Stretched Concept? *European Planning Studies*, *26*(9), 1763–1778. doi: 10.1080/09654313.2018.1494137

Giannakis, E., & Bruggeman, A. (2017). Determinants of Regional Resilience to Economic Crisis: A European Perspective. *European Planning Studies*, *25*(8), 1394–1415. doi: 10.1080/09654313.2017.1319464

Gong, H., Hassink, R., Tan, J., & Huang, D. (2020). Regional Resilience in Times of a Pandemic Crisis: The Case of COVID-19 in China. *Tijdschrift Voor Economische En Sociale Geografie*, *111*(3), 497–512. doi: 10.1111/tesg.12447

Gorzelak, G., Płoszaj, A., & Smętkowski, M. (2006). Ocena strategii rozwoju regionu – wykorzystanie modelu czterech kapitałów na przykładzie województwa lubuskiego. *Studia Regionalne i Lokalne*, 6, 67–82.

Haliżak, E. (2006). Regionalizm w stosunkach międzynarodowych. In E. Haliżak & R. Kuźniar (Eds.), *Stosunki międzynarodowe. Geneza, struktura, dynamika*, Warszawa: Wydawnictwo Uniwersytetu Warszawskiego, 269–296.

Martin, R., & Sunley, P. (2014). On the Notion of Regional Economic Resilience: Conceptualization and Explanation. *Journal of Economic Geography*, *15*(1), 1–42. doi: 10.1093/jeg/lbu015

Nowakowska, A. (2017). Terytorializacja rozwoju i polityki regionalnej. *Biuletyn KPZK PAN*, *268*, 26–38.

Prokkola, E. (2019). Border-Regional Resilience in EU Internal and External Border Areas in Finland. *European Planning Studies*, *27*(8), 1587–1606. doi: 10.1080/09654313.2019.1595531

Przygodzki, Z. (2016). Kapitał terytorialny w rozwoju regionów. *Acta Universitatis Lodziensis – Folia Oeconomica, 2(319)*, 83–97.

Romanova, V. (2022). Ukraine's resilience to Russia's military invasion in the context of the decentralisation reform. Retrieved 17 September 2022, from https://www.batory.org.pl/wp-content/uploads/2022/05/Ukraines-resilience-to-Russias-military-invasion.pdf

Stiglitz, J., Fitoussi, J., & Durand, M. (2018). *Beyond GDP. Measuring what counts for economic and social performance*. OECD Publishing.

Zaucha, J, Ciołek, D., Brodzicki, T., & Głazek, E. (2014). Wrażliwość polskich regionów na wyzwania gospodarki globalnej. In K. Gawlikowska-Hueckel & J. Szlachta (Eds.), *Wrażliwość polskich regionów na wyzwania współczesnej gospodarki. Implications for Regional Development Policy*, Warszawa: Oficyna a Wolters Kluwer Business, 206–244.

9 Shared Mobility in the Uncertain Conditions of the COVID-19 Pandemic

Operation, Management, Business Models, Opportunities, Risks, and Challenges

Katarzyna Turoń

Introduction

The social and cultural processes taking place in the development of cities, such as the increase in their numbers, the expansion of urban areas, and the share of the urban population, that is, urbanization, are becoming a global phenomenon year after year. Statistics indicate that 55% of the world's population currently resides in urban areas (United Nations, 2019). The figure is expected to rise to 68% by 2050 (United Nations, 2019). The growing population has influenced many of the problems facing modern cities. Among these is ensuring a properly functioning system of transportation, because it is responsible for meeting one of society's basic needs, mobility (Mattioli, 2016). It also plays a role in the quality of the economy and the accessibility to other services, and it is a factor that directly affects the levels of various types of investments by cities, including the speed of digitization (Banister & Bowling, 2004; Kauf, 2019; Mattson et al., 2021). To fulfill these needs, a number of new transportation services are emerging in modern cities, and they are created with sustainability in mind. Shared mobility systems are an excellent example of this type of service.

Shared mobility services provide short-term rentals of vehicles, such as bicycles, scooters, electric scooters, and cars in cities (Hu & Creutzig, 2022; Zhu et al., 2022). They are commonly referred to as "vehicles for minutes" (Alharthi et al., 2021) because their functionality is based on the principle of automated rentals, the main goal of which is to provide an alternative form of mobility to transportation by a privately owned vehicle in accordance with the concept of the sharing economy (McKenzie, 2020). Because they make it easy for drivers to get where they need to go in comparison with other forms of public transportation and do not require expenditures for maintenance on the part of users, and the systems have been gaining popularity in recent years (Krauss et al., 2022). This is evidenced by the steadily growing value of the market, which was $85.8 billion in 2021 (Research and Markets Reports, 2021). As the systems continued to develop, more and more operators began to appear in the market offering ride-sharing services (Turoń et al., 2018). Unfortunately, as of 2020, the good fortune of developing shared mobility

DOI: 10.4324/9781003475583-13

Figure 9.1 A timeline of shared mobility services in Poland

Source: Own compilation

services worldwide was halted by the sudden onset of the COVID-19 pandemic (Alonso-Almeida, 2022). Many restrictions and prohibitions were imposed by the administrative bodies of various countries on transport services, and this led in some cases to total or temporary restrictions on the operation of the systems. This situation caused quite a bit of chaos in global transportation markets. Vehicles from shared mobility systems may have posed an increased risk of COVID-19 contagion, but they had also become an alternative to public transportation for people who did not have their own vehicles (Turoń, 2022). The gradual restoration of services of transport systems had to involve adjusting services to meet pandemic requirements and customer expectations that had been changed because of the outbreak. In order to survive the hard times of uncertainty and pandemonium, shared mobility service providers had to make changes to the services they offered.

The research included analyses of foundational data and an expert survey of shared mobility service operators in Poland. The selection of the Polish market was not without purpose, since, despite the fact that shared mobility services appeared in Poland relatively late, on a European scale it is considered one of the more interesting sites in terms of development dynamics (Turoń & Czech, 2019). A detailed timeline of the development of the shared mobility market in Poland is presented in Figure 9.1.

Significant growth in shared mobility services in Poland has been observed since 2017 (Research and Markets Reports, 2021). At that time, there were 17 car-sharing operators in the market (Research and Markets Reports, 2021). The systems were available in 250 cities (Research and Markets Reports, 2021). In addition to car-sharing services, users also had 14 scooter-sharing systems at their disposal (Research and Markets Reports,

2021). Currently, in 2022, after the main COVID-19 pandemic, there are 10 car-sharing systems, 5 scooter-sharing systems, 8 bicycle-sharing systems, and 12 scooter-sharing systems in the market (Research and Markets Reports, 2021). This brings the total to 35 different shared mobility systems available to users in Polish cities.

The purpose of this chapter in the monograph was to analyze the principles of operation and management of shared mobility service enterprises during the pandemic period. This chapter demonstrates the main changes and business practices implemented by operators. Moreover, the main challenges they faced are also pointed out. The work is divided into four parts. The first characterizes the research problem and provides information about the shared mobility market under study. The second section indicates the methodology used in conducting the study and describes the questionnaire used for the expert survey. The third part outlines the results obtained. The fourth section presents a discussion of the results obtained and a summary of the work.

Methodology

In order to get an idea of the changes that have been made in companies offering shared mobility services, a self-study in the form of an expert survey was proposed. Expert research is one of the key methods of investigation (Wright et al., 2020). It assesses various types of changes taking place in companies and involves specialists in the selected business field (Loveridge, 2004).

The survey was conducted among Polish operators offering bike-, car-, moped-, and scooter-sharing services. It relied on a diverse sample of 20 experts who were representatives of individual shared mobility companies, with the following composition: 4 representatives of bike-sharing services, 6 representatives of moped-sharing services, 6 representatives of car-sharing services, and 4 representatives of scooter-sharing services. The companies considered in the survey offered their services in Poland's four leading urban centers in terms of transportation, namely, Gdansk, Katowice, Warsaw, and Wroclaw. The research was conducted between March and May 2022.

A purposive sample was used for the study due to the need to obtain responses from a specified group of respondents who had specific knowledge of shared mobility services and the rules of their operation during the pandemic period (Etikan et al., 2016). The sample size for the expert survey was determined based on Mishin's guidelines for constructing expert surveys (Mishin, 2003). The minimum number of experts needed for the study was determined by equation (1):

$$Experts_{min} = 0.5\left(\frac{3}{\vartheta} + 5\right) \tag{1}$$

where:

ϑ = statistical compliance of 10%.

$$Experts_{min} = 18 \rightarrow 20 \ experts \tag{1}$$

The survey was conducted via the Internet using computer-assisted online interviewing technology. The survey questionnaire developed as part of the study included the following ten questions:

Question 1. Has your company been forced to implement new business practices as a result of the COVID-19 pandemic?
Question 2. What areas of your company's operations were affected by the practices implemented from a COVID-19 pandemic perspective?
Question 3. Define what practices have been put in place at your company because of the COVID-19 pandemic?
Question 4. Can you describe the implemented practices as innovative?
Question 5. Would you have implemented the indicated practices if the COVID-19 pandemic had not occurred?
Question 6. Did the practices introduced during the COVID-19 pandemic translate into a positive financial outcome for your company?
Question 7. Did the implemented practices also include changes to your company's business model?
Question 8. In your opinion, will the implemented practices be the standard provided in the post-pandemic period as well? Will any of these practices be abolished?
Question 9. In your opinion, can your process of implementing new business practices be described as challenging?
Question 10. In your opinion, would failure to implement new business practices risk a temporary or complete closure of operations?

Analyses of respondents' answers were conducted in a quantitative and qualitative manner. Detailed results and a discussion of them are presented in the following sections of the chapter.

Results

Twenty representatives of shared mobility companies took part in the survey, and the companies constituted 58% of the companies operating in the market. From the standpoint of implementing new business practices due to the COVID-19 pandemic, all respondents answered that their companies were forced to implement new business practices.

In their responses, respondents identified two main activities to which their implemented practices were related, describing them as the area related to the operation of systems and the area related to user safety. Referring to

Figure 9.2 Areas of implemented practices during the COVID-19 pandemic in the Polish shared mobility services market

Source: Own compilation

the entire shared mobility market analyzed, results indicated an advantage of the operation of the systems (75%) over user security (25%). The detailed distribution of results is presented in Figure 9.2.

Next, respondents identified specific practices that were implemented at their companies in the wake of the COVID-19 pandemic. A detailed summary of practices is presented in Table 9.1.

From the point of view of the innovativeness of the implemented solutions, 75% of respondents said that the practices introduced during the pandemic period were innovative.

In contrast, 80% of those surveyed stressed that they would not have introduced new solutions into their enterprise if the pandemic had not occurred. Interestingly, for 75% of respondents, the implemented solutions translated into a positive financial result.

It is noteworthy that despite the new practices introduced, only 5% of the surveyed companies had not included the change in their business models.

According to the majority of respondents (70%), the practices introduced will remain in place at the company even after the pandemic period. Detailed results are presented in Figure 9.3.

According to respondents, the practices of having to wear masks and protective gloves when using vehicles will be abolished.

More than half of the respondents (60%) believed that the practices introduced during the pandemic were challenging for them, but, importantly,

Table 9.1 Practices implemented in Polish shared mobility enterprises due to the COVID-19 pandemic

L.p.	*Practice characteristics*	*Practice type*	*Type of services provided*			
			Bike-sharing	*Car-sharing*	*Moped-sharing*	*Scooter-sharing*
1.	Implementation of additional service operation zones	Maintenance	+		+	+
2.	Implementation of additional parking spaces or docking stations	Maintenance	+	+		
3.	Introduction of new tariffs for the use of the system (bundled services)	Maintenance	+	+	+	+
4.	Introduction of the possibility of multiday rentals	Maintenance	+	+	+	+
5.	Introduction of the requirement to wear a mask when using a vehicle	Security		+	+	+
6.	Introduction of a requirement to wear protective gloves when using the vehicle	Security		+		
7.	Introduction of a requirement that hand disinfection be done before using the vehicle	Security	+	+	+	+

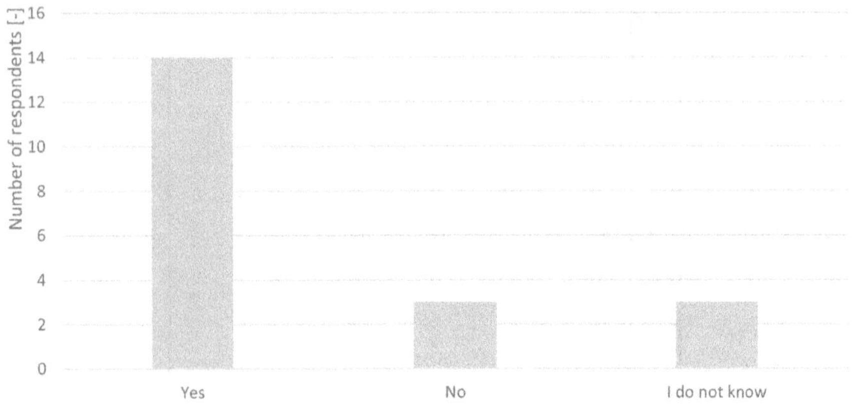

Figure 9.3 Respondents' feedback on the application of practices implemented during the pandemic, including the post-pandemic period

Source: Own compilation

according to 90% of the respondents, failure to implement them would have risked a total or temporary closure of services.

Discussion and Summary

The study shows that the Polish shared mobility services industry made changes in the operation of its systems during the difficult and fluid time of the COVID-19 pandemic. The practices implemented were related to two main areas of activity: ensuring user security and maintaining systems. Interestingly, the leading practices appeared to be related to the maintenance of systems, and this may have been associated with the search for solutions to survive in the market during a pandemic. Most practices were implemented by operators offering short-term car rentals. The other forms of vehicle sharing (i.e., bike-, moped-, and scooter-sharing services) followed. Each of the shared mobility service providers, in an effort to improve the availability of their services, implemented new tariffs for the use of the systems, as well as long-term rental options. Also importantly, for each of the operators of the services provided, there was a requirement that hands be disinfected before using the vehicle.

It is worth noting the operators' approaches to implementing the practices. The results indicated that for more than half of the respondents, this was a challenge, and in the absence of a pandemic, new business practices would not have been introduced. This meant that companies were reluctant to make changes to their services, even though they noted that such improvements had contributed to the profitability of their systems.

Based on the results, it is recommended that operators in the shared mobility industry who would like to benefit from the experience of the Polish market should monitor the services they offer and not be skeptical about the possibility of implementing changes, because as the research indicates, the changes were likely to translate into financial gain. What's more, when researchers are monitoring the current state, it is also worth paying attention to direct user feedback about the services offered. The results indicated that operators focused mainly on operational issues, because for them, this was associated with the potential for a good financial result. It is also worth noting that users of the systems could turn their attention to different areas of operation of the businesses, and this could lead to many contradictions in the services offered. Therefore, a holistic approach was particularly helpful, especially when deciding how to function properly in uncertain pandemic conditions. One should also mention that zones of availability of the systems were modified during the time studied. In the future, the zones might be varied further and adjusted according to service demand.

Like any study, this chapter in the monograph also carries certain limitations. The main limitation due to General Data Protection Regulation (GDPR) privacy issues is that it is not possible to provide the specific names of the companies that took part in the survey or to present detailed results for each type of shared mobility. Therefore, most of the study refers to the overall shared mobility industry in Poland. In addition, due to the limited willingness of shared mobility service operators to share data on the authorized company, it was not possible to receive responses from all service representatives in the Polish market.

In further research, the author plans to conduct a study on the changes introduced in shared mobility systems in other European countries in order to be able to make comparisons with the results obtained for the Polish market.

References

Alharthi, M., Alamoudi, H., Shaikh, A. A., Bhutto, M. H. (2021). "Your ride has arrived" – Exploring the nexus between subjective well-being, socio-cultural beliefs, COVID-19, and the sharing economy. *Telematics and Informatics*, 63, 101663. https://doi.org/10.1016/j.tele.2021.101663.

Alonso-Almeida, M. D. M. (2022). To use or not use car sharing mobility in the ongoing COVID-19 pandemic? Identifying sharing mobility behaviour in times of crisis. *International Journal of Environmental Research and Public Health*, 19(5), 3127. 10.3390/ijerph19053127.

Banister, D., Bowling, A. (2004). Quality of life for the elderly: The transport dimension. *Transport Policy*, 11(2), 105–115. https://doi.org/10.1016/S0967-070X(03)00052-0.

Etikan, I., Musa, S. A., Alkassim. R. S. (2016). Comparison of convenience sampling and purposive sampling. *American Journal of Theoretical and Applied Statistics*, 5(1), 1–4. 10.11648/j.ajtas.20160501.11

Hu, J.-W., Creutzig, F. (2022). A systematic review on shared mobility in China. *International Journal of Sustainable Transportation*, 16(4), 374–389. doi: 10.1080/15568318.2021.1879974.

Kauf, S. (2019). Smart logistics as a basis for the development of the smart city. *Transportation Research Procedia*, 39, 143–149. https://doi.org/10.1016/j.trpro.2019.06.016.

Krauss, K., Krail, M., Axhausen, K. W. (2022). What drives the utility of shared transport services for urban travellers? A stated preference survey in German cities. *Travel Behaviour and Society*, 26, 206–220. https://doi.org/10.1016/j.tbs.2021.09.010.

Loveridge, D. (2004). Experts and foresight: Review and experience. *International Journal of Foresight and Innovation* Policy, 1, 33–69.

Mattioli, G. (2016). Transport needs in a climate-constrained world. A novel framework to reconcile social and environmental sustainability in transport. *Energy Research & Social Science*, 18, 118–128. https://doi.org/10.1016/j.erss.2016.03.025.

Mattson, J., Brooks, J., Godavarthy, R., Quadrifoglio, L., Jain, J., Simek, Ch., Sener, I. (2021). Transportation, community quality of life, and life satisfaction in metro and non-metro areas of the United States. *Wellbeing, Space and Society*, 2, 100056. https://doi.org/10.1016/j.wss.2021.100056.

McKenzie, G. (2020). Urban mobility in the sharing economy: A spatiotemporal comparison of shared mobility services. *Computers, Environment and Urban Systems*, 79, 101418. https://doi.org/10.1016/j.compenvurbsys.2019.101418.

Mishin, V. M. (2003). *Research of Control Systems*: Textbook for Universities. Moscow, Russia: Unity-Dana.

Research and Markets Reports. (2021). Ride sharing market by type (E-hailing, station-based, car sharing & rental), car sharing (P2P, corporate), service (navigation, payment, information), micro-mobility (bicycle, scooter), vehicle type, and region – global forecast to 2026. Available online: https://www.researchandmarkets.com/reports/5351549/ride-sharing-market-by-type-e-hailing-station?utm_source=GNOM&utm_medium=PressRelease&utm_code=lsqc47&utm_campaign=1554819+-+Global+Ride+Sharing+Market+Report+2021%3a+Market+is+Projected+to+Grow+from+%2485.8+Billion+in+2021+and+Reach+%24185.1+Billion+in+2026&utm_exec=chdo54prd (accessed 7 May 2022).

Turoń, K. (2022). Open innovation business model as an opportunity to enhance the development of sustainable shared mobility industry. *Journal of Open Innovation: Technology, Market, and Complexity*, 8, 37. https://doi.org/10.3390/joitmc8010037.

Turoń, K., Czech, P. (2019). The concept of rules and recommendations for riding shared and private E-scooters in the road network in the light of global problems. In: Macioszek, E., Sierpiński, G. (Eds.), *Modern Traffic Engineering in the System Approach to the Development of Traffic Networks*. TSTP 2019. Advances in Intelligent Systems and Computing, vol. 1083. Cham: Springer. https://doi.org/10.1007/978-3-030-34069-8_21.

Turoń, K, Kubik, A., Łazarz, B., Czech, P., Stanik, Z. (2018). Car-sharing in the context of car operation. In: Brzezanski, M., Mitianiec, W. (Eds.), *IOP Conference Series-Materials Science and Engineering. International Scientific Automotive Conference on Automotive Vehicles and Combustion Engines (KONMOT)/ Scientific Conference on Automotive Progress*. 13–14.09.2018. doi: 10.1088/1757-899X/421/3/032027.

United Nations, Department of Economic and Social Affairs & Population Division. (2019). World Urbanization Prospects: Highlights (St/Esa/Ser.A/421).

Wright, G., O'Brien, F., Meadows, M., Tapinos, E., Pyper, N. (2020). Scenario planning and foresight: Advancing theory and improving practice. *Technological Forecasting and Social Change*, 159, 120220. doi: 10.1016/j.techfore.2020.120220.

Zhu, J., Xie, N., Cai, Z., Tang, W., Chen, X. (2022). A comprehensive review of shared mobility for sustainable transportation systems. *International Journal of Sustainable Transportation*. doi: 10.1080/15568318.2022.2054390.

Part 4

Industry-Specific Insights

10 Supply Chain Disruptions and Adaptations

Beata Milewska

Introduction

Many companies in the modern world operate globally, especially the larger ones. Production is bought or outsourced in the most profitable parts of the world – typically those with low production costs, e.g. the Far East. Additionally, they frequently sell their products in multiple countries across continents. Their global operation often allows them to achieve a leading position in terms of costs, however, the response time to customer needs is usually longer, which can take many months with goods produced, for example, in Southeast Asia and transported to Europe by sea.

Many companies choose regionalization over globalization, which is an acceptable compromise. Supplies are bought or production is outsourced to a nearby country whose production costs are lower. For example, many Polish and Western European companies have commissioned production in Eastern Europe, for instance in Ukraine or Belarus. It seemed to be a good solution as production costs were lower than, for example, in Poland and significantly lower than in Western European countries, and the delivery time was much shorter than it would have been from the Far East. Companies from Poland or Western Europe were also attracted to the markets of Eastern European countries.

For several years, however, the economic environment has been extremely unstable, which has had a negative impact on supply chains. Frequently, they broke, disrupting production, distribution, and sales. As a result of the COVID-19 pandemic, many commodities and finished goods, especially those produced in geographically remote areas, did not reach their destinations or were delayed. Additionally, the start of the war in Ukraine broke many regional supply chains. Specifically, this included both the acquisition of goods produced in Eastern European countries, as well as the distribution and sale of finished products in these countries. The war in Ukraine meant that many companies from Central and Western Europe stopped selling their products to customers in Ukraine and Russia.

Supply chain disruptions under conditions of uncertainty and how companies responded to these disruptions have been at the center of my research

DOI: 10.4324/9781003475583-15

presented in this paper. The research also includes a comparison of the impact of the COVID-19 pandemic and the war in Ukraine on supply chains. Using a sample of Polish clothing companies, this chapter presents disruptions and their implications on global, regional, and local supply chains under conditions of uncertainty, and uses this information to make recommendations for companies. This is a highly timely issue that fills a research gap. No studies have yet compared the impact of the COVID-19 pandemic and the war in Ukraine on supply chains divided into global, regional, and local ones. The chapter's hypothesis is as follows: When under conditions of uncertainty (e.g. the COVID-19 pandemic, the war in Ukraine), disruptions in global and regional supply chains are generally greater than in local supply chains; therefore, diversification, especially in supply and production, is safer – besides global or regional suppliers and producers, it is safe to use local ones as well.

Review of the Literature

In recent months, publications have begun to appear on the effects of the COVID-19 pandemic on supply chains and globalization. For example, a study by Hohenstein (2022) provided evidence of the serious impact of the COVID-19 pandemic on supply chains. According to Kanwal (2022), the COVID-19 pandemic threatens globalization because it has limited the movement of people, decreased global trade, and disrupted international supply chains. According to Zhuoyan (2022), the COVID-19 pandemic intensified the trend of deglobalization, which began in 2008 with the global financial crisis. On the other hand, Drelich-Skulska et al. (2021) believe that although international trade growth has slowed down, there is little evidence that the global economy is already in the era of deglobalization and the current slowdown in globalization is a natural consequence of the earlier unsustainable expansion of globalization. According to Milewski (2021), the COVID-19 pandemic has had a large impact on the prices of transportation services and their quality but is unlikely to have an impact on supply chain strategies, including the decisions concerning locations. Milewski (2022) also believes that opinions regarding the ineffectiveness of the Lean Management concept, including the Just-In-Time system, were premature. Research by Roth et al. (2022) shows that companies that experienced difficulties in obtaining semi-finished products as a result of the COVID-19 pandemic are much more likely to switch to a supplier who is nearer, although the changes appear to be temporary. According to Vargas-Hernández (2022), despite being economically efficient, global supply, production, and value chains are not secure. According to Kersan-Škabić (2021), it is imperative to strike a balance between performance and resilience when developing global value chains. Furthermore, I have discussed the impact of the COVID-19 pandemic on supply chains, focusing on the impact of the pandemic on the clothing distribution system which was based on the change in how deliveries to online customers are organized according to sustainability principles (Milewska, 2022) as well as on the energy efficiency of the last mile in e-commerce distribution in the context of the COVID-19 pandemic (Milewski & Milewska, 2021).

The impact of the Ukrainian war on supply chains is rarely discussed in published articles. Simchi-Levi and Haren (2022) state that the war in Ukraine also influences the growing interest in local supply chain strategies. Korn and Stemmler (2022) believe that both Ukraine and Russia will struggle to regain their pre-conflict international economic positions if the war in Ukraine lasts long enough. Ganeshan and Boone (2022) have presented the effects the war has had on electronic device supply; they believe that governments should adopt policies to increase the resilience of critical supply chains and support local production of key materials and components, whereas manufacturers should reduce the risk by identifying a number of sources of critical components and building up reserve stocks, for instance.

In light of the research presented above, there is a research gap regarding the resilience (or lack of resilience) of global, regional, and local supply chains to disruptions caused by the COVID-19 pandemic and the war in Ukraine, as well as a comparison of supply chain disruptions resulting from these two factors. In particular, there is a lack of research on how these issues have affected the clothing industry, which has been adversely affected by the effects of the COVID-19 pandemic and whose production is highly globalized.

Research Methods

I have studied the impact of the COVID-19 pandemic on the supply chains of clothing companies starting in March 2020, and the disruptions caused by the war in Ukraine starting in March 2022. I conducted a similar study on Polish clothing companies in mid-2017; therefore, the subject matter presented in this chapter represents a fragment of a larger study that encompasses logistics, production, supply chains, and quality management in clothing companies.

Observations and interviews with company management have been used as research methods since mid-2017. As of March 2020, however, due to the pandemic, telephone interviews took over as the primary method of research.

A secondary research method involved the analysis of periodic and current reports from clothing companies that were listed on the stock exchange. Choosing interviews with company management for the main research method was determined by the advantages associated with this method which involve obtaining accurate, detailed information, ensuring that respondents understand the questions well and that the researcher understands the answers well, as well as the opportunity to ask additional questions. A general list of questions was prepared by me beforehand; however, depending on the answers given, I asked follow-up questions to each of the questions from the list.

The study was conducted among Polish clothing companies which can be divided according to the following criteria:

- depending on their place in the supply chain – manufacturing companies (sewing factories) and distribution companies (e.g. chains of retail stores);
- depending on the role in the supply chain – supply chain leaders and supply chain actors. A supply chain leader is a company that creates and manages a given chain. It is very common for clothing distribution companies to be the industry leaders as they hire sewing factories to produce their own clothing under their own brands which they then sell in their own stores. A supply chain leader can also be a production company (sewing factory) that manufactures clothing according to their own designs and under their own brand, which they then sell to various distribution companies or online customers;
- depending on the type of supply chain; considering the location of the three links in the supply chain: production (sewing factories), distribution (distribution center), and sales (retail stores), I divided supply chains into:
  - global – involving links on at least two continents (for instance, companies that outsource production to Southeast Asia, and distribute and sell their products in Europe and the Middle East);
  - regional – involving links in at least two European countries (for instance, companies that produce in Central and Eastern Europe, and distribute and sell their products throughout Europe);
  - local – companies whose production, distribution, and sales units are located only in Poland;
  - mixed – involving companies whose supply chains are a combination of global, regional, and local. For example, companies outsource the production of typical clothing to sewing factories located in Southeast Asia (due to very low production costs). However, the production of expensive high-quality clothing with unpredictable demand is outsourced to sewing factories in Eastern Europe and Poland. An example of such a supply chain is shown in Figure 10.1.

The survey included Polish sewing factories that are not leaders in the supply chain, but merely participants (i.e. they sew garments commissioned by other companies according to their designs and under their brand). They are usually included in the local supply chains (when the client is Polish) or regional ones (when the client is from Western Europe).

Research Findings

First, disruptions and their effects on the supply chains of Polish clothing companies caused by the COVID-19 pandemic will be presented, followed by those caused by the war in Ukraine.

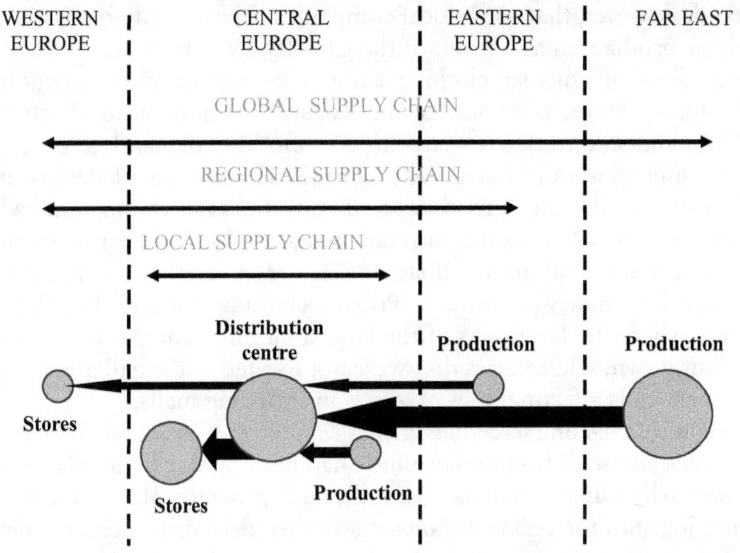

Figure 10.1 Global, regional, and local supply chains (including production, distribution, and sale links)

Source: Own compilation

Supply and production of clothing, as well as distribution and sales, have been disrupted by the COVID-19 pandemic. Companies operating globally experienced more disruptions to supply and production than those operating locally. Polish companies purchasing or outsourcing production in countries with low production costs have periodically experienced disruptions in the supply of clothing commissioned in the Far East in addition to intermediate products, such as packaging and materials. These delays resulted, for example, from quarantines in ports or on the vessels that carried the products and disruptions at the producers' facilities. As an example, at the beginning of the pandemic, sewing factories in Bangladesh and India that produced clothes for the largest Polish clothing company – LPP SA, were shut down even though sewing factories in other Southeast Asian countries continued to produce, albeit under some restrictions or under normal conditions. Companies operating globally were also affected by an increase in shipping rates as a result of the pandemic and the increase in the price of such items as fabric, yarn, and packaging. Due to the disruptions, many of these companies began stockpiling due to the risk of delays in deliveries and the fear of further increases in the prices of intermediate goods. Despite these difficulties, many Polish clothing companies still outsource a large portion of their production to Southeast Asia, even though this strategy is not as effective as it once was. There were also problems affecting companies operating regionally or locally, but generally to a lesser degree, such as price increases for intermediate goods, quarantines of employees, or reduced production orders. It should be noted, however, that some local companies experienced no disruptions to supply or production as a result of the COVID-19 pandemic.

Regardless of whether clothing companies rely on global, regional, or local supply chains, distribution and sales disruptions have affected them all. The pandemic caused a sharp drop in clothing demand, affecting companies selling clothes in Poland and abroad. The severity of the disruptions in distribution and sales varied depending on the sales channel, i.e. whether companies were selling goods in retail stores or via the Internet. During the pandemic, many clothing retail stores were temporarily closed or operated under a strict sanitary protocol. In Poland, clothing stores in shopping malls, which is where the boutiques of the largest clothing companies are located, were shut down, while stores that were not located in the galleries continued to be open, thus affecting sales of goods in shopping malls.

Despite this, e-commerce has grown rapidly as a result of the pandemic. Companies whose distribution channels had been diverse before the pandemic (i.e., they sell online as well as in stores), were generally able to arrange their delivery logistics for online customers so as to meet their increased demand, although at the beginning of the pandemic, the quality of deliveries declined. For example, LPP SA would sell about 10% of its products online before the pandemic. A sharp surge of online sales, during the first lockdown, disrupted deliveries to online customers. The company, however, expedited the investments that it had been planning to make which involved developing a network of warehouses for e-commerce deliveries. This allowed them to improve the quality of delivery provided to their customers. Currently, the sale of LPP clothing via the Internet has increased to about 30%. Some clothing companies, however, either failed to develop online sales or didn't attempt it at all, believing that e-commerce would become less important after the pandemic ran its course. However, it appears that the online clothing market will continue to grow, though not as rapidly as it did at the beginning of the pandemic. This distribution channel is greatly appreciated by customers.

Apart from expanding their online sales and developing their logistics infrastructure intended to handle deliveries to online customers, companies tried to mitigate the effects of the pandemic by reducing costs, for example by terminating their lease agreements with shopping malls or renegotiating the rent, cutting orders for the next season, or reducing investment expenses. In response to shortages, however, many companies began to build up stockpiles fearing further disruptions, failure to meet customer needs, and further increases in the prices of intermediate goods and finished goods.

The war in Ukraine also affected Polish clothing companies. Many of them, which have been leaders in supply chains, outsourced the production of clothes to sewing factories in Eastern Europe, especially Ukraine. The reasons for this were both logistical and cost-related. Eastern European sewing factories have lower production costs than Polish factories. In contrast, production costs in Eastern Europe are higher, but transport costs are lower and delivery times are shorter compared with sewing factories in the Far East.

Furthermore, quality-related reasons could also be attributed – the ability to frequently visit contractors located in countries not too far from Poland makes it easier to control the quality of clothes made there. The sewing plants in Eastern Europe, where the Polish companies commissioned production, made clothes according to their own design and under their brands, using fabrics provided by the Polish companies.

The outbreak of the war came as a surprise to many Polish clothing companies which outsourced their production to Ukrainian sewing factories. Since operating in this region was dangerous for employees and risky from an economic perspective, Polish companies had to suspend their collaboration with sewing factories there. Due to the war, some Polish companies were not able to receive the clothes they had ordered or the fabrics they had sent to Ukraine. In particular, this was a problem for companies that had agreements with distribution firms, and which, due to the war in Ukraine, were unable to have their orders delivered on time. As a result of suspending collaboration with Ukrainian companies, Polish sewing factories began to outsource production. Generally, companies that commissioned sewing clothes in both Ukraine and Poland were more flexible in responding to the changing environment. For some companies, however, finding a suitable Polish sewing factory was a problem since, following the outbreak of the war in Ukraine, clothing companies from Western Europe, such as those from Italy and France, began to outsource sewing work to Polish sewing factories, whose production capacity is limited. Thus, the war in Ukraine has disrupted the supply chains of Polish companies that had commissioned production there and which, by moving this link to local factories, will incur higher sewing costs. On the other hand, the situation of Polish sewing factories that manufacture clothing for contractors has improved now that they are working with more contractors and can utilize their full production capabilities.

However, the war in Ukraine affected both production and sales of clothing. In Eastern Europe, the largest Polish clothing company, LPP SA, had a large market for its clothing. In addition to its showrooms in Russia and Ukraine, the company also operated a distribution center in Russia that supplied retail stores and a supply center that handled deliveries to online customers. As a result of the war, retail and online sales in Russia were suspended and clothing deliveries were halted. Later, the company decided to withdraw from the Russian market and sell its stores and distribution centers to a Chinese consortium without the right to use the clothing brand's name or logo. Despite the Russian market's significant share of LPP SA's sales, the development of both retail and e-commerce in European Union countries allowed the company to continue to grow. LPP SA also had stores in Ukraine but they have been closed due to the war until conditions ensuring employees' safety had been restored. The company also took steps to provide support to employees in Ukraine and their families (LPP SA, 2022). Polish clothing companies, especially those with business connections with Ukraine, became involved in helping Ukrainian refugees as well.

Conclusions and Recommendations for Companies

The research described above demonstrated the impact of the conditions of uncertainty caused by the COVID-19 pandemic and the war in Ukraine on the global, regional, and local supply chains of Polish clothing companies. The hypothesis that in times of uncertainty (caused by the COVID-19 pandemic and the war in Ukraine), disruptions to global and regional supply chains are typically more severe than those to local supply chains, which was confirmed. It has also been confirmed that diversifying makes sense, i.e. in addition to working with global and regional suppliers and producers, it is also safe to work with the local ones. For example, before the pandemic, LPP SA diversified its production locations, commissioning production in several countries of the Far East, and also manufacturing approximately 10% of its clothing locally, in Polish factories.

The COVID-19 pandemic disrupted clothing companies' global supply chains more than local ones. In addition to disruptions in sewing factories in the Far East, global supply chains suffered noticeable disruptions related to the transportation of goods, increased transportation costs, and increased prices of goods purchased in the Far East. On the other hand, disruptions to regional and local supplies also occurred but were generally milder, while some local businesses did not experience the disruption at all. Due to the pandemic, the efficiency of global supply chains has decreased but in the companies surveyed, purchasing policies have not changed because of this; still, many Polish clothing companies outsource a large part of their production to countries with low production costs. The COVID-19 pandemic also affected the distribution and sale of clothing, no matter whether the supply chain was local, regional, or global. It was generally observed that sales declined in retail stores while online sales increased sharply and consistently.

The war in Ukraine affected the supply chains of those clothing firms that outsourced production to sewing factories in Ukraine or that sold their products in Ukraine or Russia. In many cases, there was a change in the production link (from Ukrainian sewing plants to Polish ones), which increased the costs associated with the production of clothing but was beneficial to sewing factories in Poland. Suspending operations or withdrawing completely from the Eastern European market exposed Polish companies to losses.

The impact of the COVID-19 pandemic is fundamentally different from that of the war in Ukraine. There was no significant impact of the COVID-19 pandemic on the reallocation of clothing production. The Polish clothing industry continues to outsource sewing garments to the Far East despite supply disruptions and rising costs. Meanwhile, the war in Ukraine did contribute to the reallocation of production – companies suspended their collaboration with sewing factories in Ukraine because these partnerships were too risky and began to outsource production to the Polish sewing factories.

The research has shown the significance of flexibility in the operation of companies and supply chains. Companies that were able to adapt quickly to the new situation did better by increasing their online sales, finding new sources of supply, and transferring production from Ukrainian sewing factories to Polish ones. Adaptability to changes in the environment was generally greater if companies prepared for different scenarios before disruptions occurred and diversified their activities. For example, during the pandemic, LPP SA was able to expand its e-commerce sales quickly and significantly having already invested in the development of this sales channel and making significant progress toward doing so. Similarly, many Polish clothing companies were able to quickly transfer production from sewing factories in Ukraine to those located in Poland thanks to having established contacts with Polish sewing factories or having diversified their production by utilizing both Polish and Ukrainian sewing factories.

The research presented above focused on Polish clothing companies. It is also possible, however, to formulate conclusions and recommendations on the basis of these findings for other companies:

- if disturbances occur in the environment, a diversified strategy is less risky than focusing on one supply or sales market, or one sales channel;
- local producers and suppliers are also safe to rely on in addition to global and regional ones;
- It is essential to find an alternative in case of disruptions before they arise, e.g. if you outsource production globally or regionally, you should also reach out to local counterparts;
- to flexibly adapt to changing conditions in the environment, scenarios covering various disturbances need to be examined;
- it is necessary to recalculate the profitability of overseas production and purchase strategies (e.g. in the Far East), taking not only the increase in transport and storage costs into account but also the increased risk of supply chain disruptions, i.e. the cost of lost sales;
- you should monitor the company's environment, including political circumstances so that you are prepared for potential disruptions, e.g. caused by a war in a particular geographical region.

Accordingly, the current economic climate is more unstable than previously appeared, so companies should be prepared for a variety of scenarios and diversify their activities. A flexible approach is essential to adapting to changing conditions in the environment, especially in uncertain times.

References

Drelich-Skulska, B., Bobowski, S., & Gola, J. (2021). Global value chains in the era of the COVID-19 pandemic: Symptoms of deglobalization. *European Research Studies Journal*, *XXIV*(Special Issue 3), 905–913. https://doi.org/10.35808/ersj/2532

Ganeshan, R., & Boone, T. (2022). How the war in Ukraine impacts global supply chains. Retrieved 8 September 2022, from https://www.ips-journal.eu/topics/economy-and-ecology/how-the-war-in-ukraine-impacts-global-suppy-chains-5894

Hohenstein, N. (2022). Supply chain risk management in the COVID-19 pandemic: Strategies and empirical lessons for improving global logistics service providers' performance. *The International Journal of Logistics Management*. Ahead-of-print. https://doi.org/10.1108/IJLM-02-2021-0109

Kanwal, M. (2022). Death of globalization during COVID-19 era. Available at SSRN. https://doi.org/10.2139/ssrn.4101253

Kersan-Škabić, I. (2021). The COVID-19 pandemic and the internationalization of production: A review of the literature. *Development Policy Review*, *40*. https://doi.org/10.1111/dpr.12560

Korn, T., & Stemmler, H. (2022). Russia's war against Ukraine might persistently shift global supply chains. Retrieved 8 September 2022, from https://voxeu.org/article/russias-war-against-ukraine-might-persistently-shift-global-supply-chains

Milewska, B. (2022). The Impact of the COVID-19 pandemic on supply chains in the example of Polish clothing companies in the context of sustainable development. *Sustainability*, *14*, 1899. https://doi.org/10.3390/su14031899

Milewski, D. (2021). Impact of demand characteristics on the profitability of a purchasing strategy. *Scientific Journal of the Maritime University*, *67*, 1–10. https://doi.org/10.17402/478

Milewski, D. (2022). Managerial and economical aspects of the just-in-time system "lean management in the time of pandemic". *Sustainability*, *14*, 1204. https://doi.org/10.3390/su14031204

Milewski, D., & Milewska, B. (2021). The energy efficiency of the last mile in the E-commerce distribution in the context the COVID-19 pandemic. *Energies*, *14*(23), 7863. https://doi.org/10.3390/en14237863

Raporty – Oficjalna strona LPP SA. (2022). Retrieved 8 September 2022, from https://www.lppsa.com/relacje-inwestorskie/raporty

Roth, D., Kleifgen, E., & Stepanok, I. (2022). The Covid-19 pandemic and international supply chains. https://doi.org/10.2139/ssrn.4051422

Simchi-Levi, D., & Haren, P. (2022). How the war in Ukraine is further disrupting global supply chains. Retrieved 8 September 2022, from https://hbr.org/2022/03/how-the-war-in-ukraine-is-further-disrupting-global-supply-chains

Vargas-Hernández, J. (2022). Relocation strategy of production, global supply, and value chains. *Frameworks and Cases on Evolutional Supply Chain*. https://doi.org/10.4018/978-1-7998-9800-9.ch013

Zhuoyan, H. (2022). Research on the trend of deglobalization under the COVID-19 pandemic advances in social science. *Education and Humanities Research*, *653*. https://doi.org/10.2991/assehr.k.220401.194

11 The COVID-19 Pandemic and Financial Situation of Companies in the Construction Industry in Poland

Aleksandra Zalewska

Introduction

According to Polish law, an enterprise is an organized set of intangible and tangible assets intended for conducting business activity. A correct selection of these elements is conducive to the functioning and development of the individual. Clear and precise goals are equally important since they sometimes determine a company's existence and future (Buczkowska, 2012). Defining goals carefully and verifying them allows an individual to adapt to changes effectively. Both entrepreneurs and participants in the market economy should strive to accomplish their goals.

Any modern enterprise should strive to maximize its profits while effectively and sustainably using its resources (Paździor, 2015). It is often emphasized that value is a long-term perspective for generating cash flows (Sosińska-Wit & Gałązka, 2019). Value creation is a complex process as it requires a thorough analysis of external and internal factors affecting the individual. A conscious entrepreneur, taking into account his financial gains and his desire to develop, is compelled to conduct operational activities effectively while actively responding to dynamically changing circumstances. The literature on the subject often emphasizes the notion that in order to gain a competitive advantage, owners should consider the environment in which they operate (Jaska & Werenowska, 2017).

The environment can act as both a positive and a negative stimulus, affecting the company's functioning, and thus be a source of opportunities and threats for its current and future activities. The ability to turn a positive change from the environment into added value is crucial for entrepreneurs in achieving their goals when it comes to creating value or gaining a competitive advantage. However, the way managers deal with crises and the way they respond to environmental risks may prove crucial for the continuation of a company's operation. In today's socioeconomic environment, an unprecedented crisis on a global scale caused by the coronavirus pandemic could be considered to be the biggest threat to business.

On 11 March 2020, the World Health Organization (WHO) declared the coronavirus pandemic. The aggressive and rapidly spreading virus has

DOI: 10.4324/9781003475583-16

destroyed the established order, not only health-wise but also economically. The implementation of preventive measures and sanitary protocols triggered significant changes in society (Blau, Koebe, & Meyerhofer, 2020). A partial shutdown of the economy and recommendations to maintain social distance increased mental health problems and negatively impacted the labor market (Coibion, Gorodnichenko, & Weber, 2020). As a consequence of the pandemic and government decisions, production and consumption have slowed or halted in many sectors (Yu et al., 2020). These changes have affected the economic and financial climate of the most affected industries. Radlińska (2021) argues that the socioeconomic effects caused by COVID-19 resulted from a choice between a more severe recession and an increased pandemic scale. A freeze in the economy in the most affected industries has resulted in the suspension or even the closure of a number of businesses involved in trade, tourism, hotels, transport, catering, and services, which in the future will have an impact on individuals' lives. It is a natural consequence of restrictions that imposed social distancing, however.

Due to the challenges associated with the pandemic, business risks are increasing in many sectors of the economy, not only in those most affected by the pandemic but also in the construction industry. The construction industry is considered one of the key industries to the economy, and at the same time, it is not separated from the current macro- and microeconomic conditions. Therefore, it seems reasonable to analyze the impact that global economic fluctuations have on the activities of companies in the construction industry.

The purpose of this study was to assess changes in the financial status of companies in the construction industry between 2019 and 2021, i.e. before and during the COVID-19 pandemic. The research was carried out for companies from the construction industry listed on the Warsaw Stock Exchange on the basis of an analysis of quarterly financial statements. The empirical study examined and evaluated changes in financial analysis indicators related to the areas of financial risk and return on capital. Additionally, descriptive statistics were used, and the empirical research was supplemented with a review of the literature pertaining to economics and finance as well as publications related to the industry. Based on the analysis, we created a set of recommendations for decision-makers and recipients of financial statements from the industry under study concerning the broadly understood state and effectiveness of the company's operations.

Risk analysis as a Tool for Assessing the Financial Condition of a Business

The improvement of management processes entails the utilization of appropriate tools, including financial analysis indicators and risk analysis. The functioning of enterprises in a free market economy depends on recognizing and responding to changes in the environment and within the business in a timely manner. As Bartkowiak, Jaki, and Kaczmarek (2018) point out, the point and goal of an organization is to improve the efficiency and rationality of the way resources and production factors are managed. This implies the necessity of clearly defining a company's goals and constantly monitoring its environment and internal factors. Indicator analysis is used to assess risk with a view to improving the management processes of an entity and predicting possible directions of development or bankruptcy risk. Conducting a thorough analysis of the achieved economic results is a crucial part of efficient operations, and if there is a crisis, it is a prerequisite for the survival of an organization in the market (Kuciński, 2018).

Running a business is therefore associated with exposure to some kind of uncertainty and risk. Risk is a broad concept that is difficult to define. In psychological terms, it refers to a specific state of mind in which the course of the decision-making process is influenced by factors related to the outcome of one's actions (Monkiewicz & Gąsiorowski, 2010). This concept is also used in economics and finance, referring to the risk of incurring a loss. Risk can also refer to undesirable consequences associated with decisions entrepreneurs make in response to events beyond his or her control. Risk can be attributed to macroeconomic and microeconomic factors.

At present, COVID-19's consequences are the most significant source of uncertainty and risk. Entrepreneurs need to consider the negative effects of situations in which access to necessary information is significantly restricted or it is impossible to predict the direction in which the environment will develop. A decision based on past and speculative data can result in inaccurate predictions about future conditions of doing business, as Nowak (2010) highlights. As a result of the pandemic, uncertainty and risk have significantly affected business operations and become integral aspects of a company's reality (Sosińska-Wit, 2020). The situation in question affects all areas of business activity and is an unavoidable phenomenon, which is why special attention should be paid to this issue in business management. According to Smithson, Smith, and Wilford (2000), a company's balance sheet, consolidated profit and loss account, and cash flow statement can reflect risk.

It is possible to estimate an entity's financial condition based on the quarterly reports, and thus determine its level of risk. A way to determine uncertainty in an organization is to determine its liquidity and solvency. According to the literature on the subject, the assumption is that certain index values reflect whether liquidity is maintained on the basis of operating, investment, and financial activity flows (Kuciński & Byczkowska, 2018); any index values that deviate significantly from the norm may indicate risk, and future payment problems or excessive capital freezing (Janik & Paździor, 2011).

Another problem entrepreneurs face is the issue of financing and determining the right structure of the company's capital and assets. Today, companies have many alternative sources of capital to choose from. It is important to select the right kind of financing according to the level of financial risk, both during periods of relative stability and during periods of economic fluctuation. Conducting business is complex, which makes it difficult to determine the best property and capital structure based on the industry or scale of activity. Obtaining and allocating capital depends on many factors, so an ideal level of foreign capital participation (which results in increased foreign capital profitability) is not constant. In terms of risk, it is equally important to look at the profitability of capitals as well as their debt. By using indicators of return on equity, it is possible to determine the rate of return on the funds used by the entity, which directly impacts its financial condition and level of risk (Janik & Paździor, 2010a, 2010b).

Poland's Construction Industry Characteristics

As has been repeatedly emphasized, there is a close relationship between the functioning of businesses and the nation's and world's economic situation. This relationship is unbreakable and reinforced by the laws that govern the market. It is widely acknowledged that the construction sector is crucial for the functioning of any developed economy. The economic situation in the construction industry affects related industries, such as the metals and chemical industries, trade, logistics and transportation, or the broadly understood financial sector. In this study, the construction industry, which is a segment of the industrial sector, was given special attention. It includes all civil engineering activities, such as general construction works related to the construction of new buildings and modernization or repair work on existing facilities. In Poland, these issues are regulated by the Construction Law, according to which construction activity may include activities involving the design, construction, maintenance, and demolition of building objects. The range of activities within the construction industry is quite wide because it is associated with all stages of work – from erecting through improvements or repairs to the demolition of various types of constructions. In addition, this sector is a kind of network of interconnected links that consists of contractors, subcontractors, manufacturers of materials, and suppliers, in which some entities provide services on behalf of others, all of whom remain in mutual relation with one another.

The coronavirus pandemic meant that managers had to take immediate steps to adapt their organization's plans and goals to the new reality in order to minimize the risks involved. Having to prepare for the impending crisis and the economic downturn seemed inevitable for companies. Since government regulations implemented after 11 March 2020 did not explicitly prohibit construction works, it was predicted that the decrease in investments would not occur immediately. Therefore, cyclical crises have affected the industry with a certain delay.

Research Methodology

The aim of the study was to assess changes in the financial condition of companies operating in the construction industry between 2019 and 2021, i.e. before and during the COVID-19 pandemic. Therefore, it was of particular interest to analyze a sample of companies listed on the Warsaw Stock Exchange. The study covered the period of 12 quarters, i.e. from 2019 to 2021, providing information on the economic and financial situation before and after the pandemic. In this way, the data could be analyzed and compared for each time interval in a more detailed manner. A total of seven companies from the WIG construction index were selected for the study. This index comprises businesses that provide services in general construction, industrial construction, other construction services, telecommunications and construction installations, civil engineering, and the distribution of building materials. As a selection criterion, the value of sales revenues above PLN 1,000,000 in 2021 was chosen. Among the research participants were three companies engaged in industrial construction (ERBUD, MOSTOSTAL, POLIMEX), three companies engaged in general construction (BUDMEX, MIRBUD, and UNIBEP), and one company engaged in the sector in another capacity (DEKPOL).

A financial analysis was conducted using past financial data. In the planning process and setting goals, this method offers the unquestionable advantage of being able to predict, draw conclusions, and make recommendations. By analyzing the past, emerging threats can be detected and eliminated in a timely manner so that management can be improved. By using it, it is possible to identify dependencies and trends in development (Paździor, 2015). In Polish reality, early warning systems are of particular importance. As Grzegorzewska (2016) argues, Polish enterprises do not use modern tools for forecasting bankruptcy. An economic downturn caused by external factors, such as a pandemic, may result in the company ceasing to operate. With the use of appropriate tools, you can not only detect problems early but also improve your long-term strategy, since their effectiveness doesn't diminish over time (Lichota, 2020).

Additionally, elements of descriptive statistics were used in the analysis, including arithmetic means, medians, and standard deviations. The empirical research was also supplemented by a review of literature in the fields of economics and finance as well as industry-related publications. Based on the findings, a set of recommendations regarding the broadly understood condition and effectiveness of enterprise operations has been developed for decision-makers and recipients of financial statements from the industry under study.

Research Results and Recommendations

The indicator analysis conducted made it possible to examine the financial condition of companies in the construction industry and determine the level of financial risk. In addition, thanks to the quarterly data format, changes in the phenomena under study in the period before the pandemic (2019), during the first wave (2020), and in subsequent periods of its duration could be observed.

As has been expected, the study confirmed a decline in investment activity and a slowdown in the economy, both of which were delayed in time. The financial condition of the entities surveyed did not deteriorate as a result of the COVID-19 pandemic. There was also no increase in the level of risk related to debt, liquidity, or the structure of property and capital. To better illustrate the data in question, the results of the analysis are summarized in Table 11.1.

The average total debt of the surveyed companies was 76%. The values of the ratio for POLIMEX and DEKPOL were below the median, indicating their exceptionally favorable situation. Thus, the firms have a reduced financial risk due to the relatively low debt level. Overall, there is a predominance of short-term debt in all of these entities, which is confirmed by the relatively low long-term debt ratio in the group – 18%. MOSTOSTAL WARSZAWA has an interesting situation, as its debt-to-equity ratio is more than five times higher than the average. The situation may indicate an increased financial risk, which is why further analysis is reasonable. In all surveyed companies, the overall financial situation is very satisfactory, based on debt and asset information. There are slight fluctuations in the ratios during the period under study, which may or may not be due to pandemic-related challenges. Liquidity analysis confirms this situation at all levels with companies able to settle their liabilities in a timely manner and provide adequate collateral in the event of an accelerated repayment.

Table 11.1 Indicator analysis

Average value	*B*	*P*	*E*	*M*	*U*	*D*	*MW*	*G*
Total debt ratio	0.85	0.61	0.74	0.68	0.76	0.72	0.93	0.76
Long-term debt ratio	0.15	0.13	0.10	0.32	0.17	0.20	0.17	0.18
Debt-to-equity ratio	6.11	1.59	3.14	2.19	3.41	2.74	18.82	5.43
Equity to fixed assets ratio (Balance sheet golden rule)	0.69	1.03	1.43	0.73	0.98	1.12	0.45	0.92
Equity to foreign capital ratio (Golden rule of finance)	1.41	1.38	2.05	1.49	1.72	1.94	1.85	1.69
Working capital to circulating capital ratio	0.11	0.23	0.21	0.35	0.21	0.30	0.11	0.22
Variable capital to circulating capital ratio	0.89	0.77	0.77	0.62	0.76	0.70	0.87	0.77
Financial condition indicator	1.60	1.78	2.72	2.43	2.27	2.86	2.22	2.27
Current liquidity ratio	1.13	1.29	1.31	1.62	1.31	1.45	1.16	1.33
Quick ratio (I)	0.43	0.47	0.27	0.30	0.31	0.22	0.20	0.31
Quick ratio (II)	0.78	1.11	1.25	1.04	0.87	0.87	0.69	0.95
ROE	0.13	0.02	0.03	0.04	0.03	0.06	0.06	0.05
ROA	0.14	0.03	0.04	0.05	0.04	0.07	0.14	0.07
EDF	-0.01	-0.01	-0.01	-0.01	-0.01	-0.01	-0.08	-0.02

(*Continued*)

Table 11.1 (Continued)

Median	*B*	*P*	*E*	*M*	*U*	*D*	*MW*	*G*
Total debt ratio	0.86	0.62	0.77	0.67	0.75	0.71	0.93	0.75
Long-term debt ratio	0.15	0.12	0.11	0.31	0.17	0.21	0.13	0.15
Debt-to-equity ratio	6.27	1.63	3.35	2.11	3.38	2.54	16.91	3.24
Equity to fixed assets ratio (Balance sheet golden rule)	0.70	1.04	1.42	0.74	0.97	1.16	0.39	0.90
Equity to foreign capital ratio (Golden rule of finance)	1.38	1.36	2.08	1.50	1.70	2.00	1.34	1.56
Working capital to circulating capital ratio	0.11	0.22	0.21	0.38	0.21	0.33	0.05	0.21
Variable capital to circulating capital ratio	0.89	0.78	0.78	0.62	0.74	0.66	0.92	0.77
Financial condition indicator	1.57	1.77	2.62	2.41	2.31	3.03	1.45	2.19
Current liquidity ratio	1.13	1.27	1.28	1.62	1.34	1.51	1.08	1.29
Quick ratio (I)	0.43	0.41	0.22	0.24	0.31	0.23	0.20	0.29
Quick ratio (II)	0.69	1.10	1.19	0.99	0.88	0.85	0.68	0.92
ROE	0.10	0.02	0.04	0.03	0.03	0.04	0.05	0.04
ROA	0.12	0.03	0.05	0.04	0.04	0.05	0.12	0.05
EDF	–0.01	–0.01	–0.01	–0.01	-0.01	–0.01	–0.04	-0.01
Standard deviation	*B*	*P*	*E*	*M*	*U*	*D*	*MW*	*G*
Total debt ratio	0.03	0.02	0.05	0.03	0.01	0.04	0.01	0.10
Long-term debt ratio	0.01	0.04	0.02	0.05	0.02	0.07	0.07	0.08
Debt-to-equity ratio	1.35	0.12	0.57	0.25	0.31	0.63	5.39	6.01
Equity to fixed assets ratio (Balance sheet golden rule)	0.12	0.12	0.19	0.06	0.09	0.13	0.16	0.33
Equity to foreign capital ratio (Golden rule of finance)	0.12	0.10	0.25	0.17	0.19	0.28	0.75	0.42
Working capital to circulating capital ratio	0.03	0.03	0.05	0.10	0.05	0.07	0.09	0.11
Variable capital to circulating capital ratio	0.03	0.03	0.07	0.06	0.04	0.08	0.09	0.10
Financial condition indicator	0.20	0.17	0.61	0.48	0.35	0.67	1.14	0.74
Current liquidity ratio	0.04	0.05	0.14	0.16	0.07	0.15	0.12	0.19
Quick ratio (I)	0.16	0.12	0.12	0.20	0.06	0.05	0.07	0.15
Quick ratio (II)	0.17	0.05	0.14	0.19	0.06	0.18	0.05	0.23
ROE	0.12	0.02	0.04	0.02	0.02	0.03	0.12	0.08
ROA	0.12	0.02	0.04	0.02	0.02	0.03	0.11	0.08
EDF	0.00	0.00	0.00	0.00	0.00	0.01	0.10	0.04

B, BUDIMEX; P, POLIMEX; E, ERBUD; M, MIRBUD; U, UNIBEP; D, DEKPOL; M, MOSTOSTAL WARSZAWA; G, GROUP

Source: Own elaboration

The return on equity of the surveyed firms fluctuated around the average, which is confirmed by the standard deviation values. The negative effect of financial leverage may indicate an increased risk but given the fact that the ratio values remained at a constant level throughout, it is more likely that the ratio values reflect a policy choice than a high risk.

The ratio values derived from the fundamental analysis may lead to several important conclusions, which can serve as recommendations for decision-makers and financial statement recipients:

1. When setting company objectives, both operational and long-term, managers must maintain an appropriate level of caution. The construction industry has not been affected by the pandemic as much as the service sector, direct trade, or tourism generally, as evidenced by the assessment of the financial condition. It is crucial to consider, however, the possibility of future negative effects of economic fluctuations. Thus, managers of companies operating in the construction industry should pay special attention to the level of debt associated with it financial risk;
2. A constant monitoring of a company's financial situation is necessary. To ensure a high level of security characteristic of the construction industry, indicators like liquidity, debt, and profitability must be maintained at appropriate levels. Whenever deviations occur in relation to planned standards, they should be investigated;
3. Early warning systems can ensure a company's survival and functioning. When increased risk is detected early, appropriate preventive measures can be implemented. It is possible to minimize risk by observing the basic indicators of fundamental analysis;
4. Finance structures should be structured carefully, keeping both debt costs and operating costs in mind, while aiming to maximize leverage. It is imperative that managers in the construction industry approach the subject of external financing with extreme caution, keeping in mind that the ability to repay liabilities may deteriorate over time.

References

Bartkowiak, P., Jaki, A., & Kaczmarek, J. (2018). Kształtowanie przewagi konkurencyjnej w procesie restrukturyzacji i kreowania wartości przedsiębiorstwa. *Przegląd Organizacji*, 3–8. doi: 10.33141/po.2018.02.01

Blau, F., Koebe, J., & Meyerhofer, P. (2020). Who are the Essential and Frontline Workers? IZA Discussion Paper No. 13650. Available at: https://ssrn.com/abstract=3687126, DOI: http://dx.doi.org/10.2139/ssrn.3687126

Buczkowska, A. (2012). Cele przedsiębiorstwa a pomiar jego dokonań. *Zeszyty Naukowe Uniwersytetu Szczecińskiego*, *45*, 5. https://doi.org/10.18276/frfu

Coibion, O., Gorodnichenko, Y., & Weber, M. (2020). Labor markets during the covid-19 crisis: A preliminary view. *National Bureau of Economic Research*, *27017*, 8–10. https://doi.org/10.3386/w27017

Grzegorzewska, E. (2016). Predictive bankruptcy models as a tool in evaluating the economic situation of furniture market in Poland. *Annals of Warsaw University of Life Sciences – SGGW, Forestry and Wood Technology*, 261–267. https://doi.org/10.5604/18985912

Janik, W., & Paździor, A. (2010a). *Zarządzanie finansami spółki kapitałowej*. Polskie Wydawnictwo Ekonomiczne, p. 126.

Janik, W., & Paździor, A. (2010b). *Zarządzanie finansami spółki kapitałowej*. Polskie Wydawnictwo Ekonomiczne, p. 128.

Janik, W., & Paździor, A. (2011). *Zarządzanie finansowe w przedsiębiorstwie*. Politechnika Lubelska, pp. 77–78.

Jaska, E., & Werenowska, A. (2017). *Komunikacja przedsiębiorstwa z otoczeniem w gospodarce opartej na wiedzy*. Wydawnictwo SGGW, p. 5.

Kuciński, A. (2018). *Analiza finansowa jako narzędzie oceny kondycji finansowej przedsiębiorstwa*. Akademia im. Jakuba z Paradyża w Gorzowie Wielkopolskim, p. 129.

Kuciński, A., & Byczkowska, M. (2018). Ocena płynności finansowej przedsiębiorstw na podstawie analizy rachunku przepływów pieniężnych. *Zeszyty Naukowe Małopolskiej Wyższej Szkoły Ekonomicznej w Tarnowie*, 2(38), 90.

Lichota, W. (2020). The comparative analysis of the prediction effectiveness of selected discriminant analysis models. *Zeszyty Naukowe Małopolskiej Wyższej Szkoły Ekonomicznej w Tarnowie*, 4, 27–36.

Monkiewicz J., & Gąsiorowski, L. (2010). *Zarządzanie ryzykiem działalności organizacji*. Wydawnictwo C.H. Beck, p. 34.

Nowak, E. (2010). Zarządzenie ryzykiem w działalności przedsiębiorstwa w Nowak E. (red.) *Rachunkowość w zarządzaniu ryzykiem w przedsiębiorstwie*. Polskie Wydawnictwo Ekonomiczne, p. 11.

Paździor, A. (2015). *Zarządzanie wartością współczesnego przedsiębiorstwa*. Politechnika Lubelska, p. 7.

Poland. Sejm. (1994). Ustawa z dnia 7 lipca 1994 r. - Prawo budowlane [Building Law Act of July 7, 1994] (No. 89, item 414). as amended.

Radlińska, K. (2021). Pandemia COVID-19 Implikacje Dla Polskiego Rynku Pracy. *Zeszyty Naukowe Wydziału Nauk Ekonomicznych*, *1*(24), 113–126.

Smithson, C. W., Smith, C. W., & Wilford, D. S. (1998). *Managing financial risk: a guide to derivative products, financial engineering, and value maximization* (pp. 160–190). New York: McGraw-Hill.

Sosińska-Wit, M., & Gałązka, K. (2019). *The role of social capital in the development of MMP of the Lublin Voivodeship*, In W. Janik & A. Paździor (Eds.), *Przedsiębiorstwo i rynek*. Wydawnictwo Politechniki Lubelskiej, p. 106.

Sosińska-Wit, M. (2020). *Cost accounting in the management of a micro and small enterprise on the example of own research*. In M. Miszczuk & M. Sosińska Wit (Ed.), *Financial management problems of efficiency*. Wydawnictwo Politechniki Lubelskiej, p. 51.

Yu, X., Liu, C., Wang, H., & Feil, J. (2020). The impact of COVID-19 on food prices in China: Evidence of four major food products from Beijing, Shandong and Hubei Provinces. *China Agricultural Economic Review*, *12*(3), 445–458. doi: 10.1108/caer-04-2020-0054

12 Consumer Resistance to Product Innovation in Conditions of Uncertainty

Izabela Krawczyk-Sokołowska

Introduction

Despite efforts to increase the chances of creating consumer-oriented product innovations that would meet their expectations and deliver satisfactory value, a large number of innovative companies face difficulties in doing so, which arise from failures regarding the diffusion of product innovations. Research suggests that innovation failure rates are around 40%–55% (Castellion & Markham, 2013; Rutkowski, 2021; Urbanowska-Sojkin, 2012). It should be recognized that the limited adoption of innovation by consumers or the complete lack thereof may be caused by their resistance to innovation (Ram & Sheth, 1989). The reasons for such resistance are varied and relatively unexplored due to the fact that numerous studies have only been concerned with factors conducive to a consumer's affirmative decision to accept and adopt a product innovation (Lennon et al., 2007). Researchers are increasingly seeking to identify consumer resistance factors to understand why product innovations have had limited success in spreading. In light of this, I present a few points in which I try to answer the questions of what factors influence consumer resistance to product innovation, and what causes a lack of acceptance or interest in product innovations. The analysis was carried out from two perspectives – innovative product characteristics and consumer characteristics.

The COVID-19 pandemic and the war in Ukraine also contribute to our need to pay attention to this area of socioeconomic activity. In these circumstances, it is necessary to develop new behaviors to stimulate creativity and commitment, i.e. all those intangible elements of strategic resources (Caputa, 2010; Pierscieniak & Stelmaszczyk, 2020) that can contribute to a successful business operation in conditions of restrictions related to the pandemic or the war in Ukraine.

The aim of this chapter was to identify (diagnose) the reasons for consumer resistance to product innovation. A particular focus was placed on two research areas. The first area was an overview of the idea of consumer resistance to product innovation. The second one was the search for and evaluation of key consumer characteristics and product innovation characteristics

DOI: 10.4324/9781003475583-17

in relation to innovation resistance. The first part of this chapter offers definitions of basic concepts such as product innovation or consumer resistance and establishes their essence and meaning in order to clarify what they describe and what processes they may be associated with. The second part of this chapter is an outline of the methodology and the steps used in evaluating consumer resistance to product innovation. The following sections present research results, conclusions, and recommendations.

Consumer Resistance to Product Innovation – Literature Review

Product innovation is the development of a new or significantly improved product or service (GUS, 2021; Rennings & Zwick, 2002). It has always been associated with altering and endangering existing product characteristics and uses, which tends to evoke resistance in most potential consumers. A product's external image is one of the most important signals to consumers when they evaluate new products as it affects their choice to purchase or reject the product.

A concept such as consumer resistance to innovation can be understood in several different ways; it is not only linked to business practice but also represents an important area for social science analysis (Garcia, Bardhi, & Friedrich, 2007; Gourville, 2006; Heidenreich & Handrich, 2014; Huang et al., 2021). According to Ram and Sheth (1989), the resistance consumers exhibit comes from the fact that it creates a change from a satisfactory status quo or because it conflicts with their belief structure. It consists of abandoning the attempt to innovate in one of three ways: rejection (strong opposition to innovation), deferral (delaying acceptance of innovation), and dissent (active rebellion against innovation) (Hauser, Tellis, & Griffin, 2006; Rogers, 2003). Consumer resistance theory requires an understanding of what influences consumer resistance. As per consumer resistance theory, it is important to distinguish the contradiction between traditions and norms that have a social dimension and conflicts that relate to consumers' personal habits (Garcia & Atkin, 2002; Kleijnen, Lee, & Wetzels, 2009). Research into factors has been conducted by various authors (Antioco & Kleijnen, 2010; Heidenreich & Kraemer, 2015; Talke & Heidenreich, 2014; Tornatzky & Klein, 1982;). Consistently with the review of the literature (Heidenreich & Handrich, 2014), two types of consumer resistance to innovation stand out – active and passive. Active resistance to innovation involves the formation of a negative attitude toward innovation driven by innovation-specific factors (Kleijnenet al., 2009; Laukkanen et al., 2008). Consumers shape their attitudes toward product innovation based on the attributes of the product. When some aspects of innovation do not meet consumer expectations, resistance to innovation occurs (Heidenreich & Spieth, 2013). In passive resistance to innovation, the consumer develops a predisposition to resist a new product before evaluating it (Talke & Heidenreich, 2014). Products that are perceived as new threaten the status quo of consumers, which in turn provokes resistance (Laukkanen et al., 2008; Talke & Heidenreich, 2014).

The assumption in this analysis is that consumer resistance to innovation, i.e. an explicit rejection or resistance to innovation, can be described as a negative response to innovation and to innovation-related changes that occur in the process of accepting innovation. In this study, nine areas were identified, which were divided into two groups of characteristics: innovative product characteristics (five areas) and consumer characteristics (four areas). The innovative product characteristics that affect consumer resistance include the advantages associated with the product innovation that is being offered, the risks associated with the product, the complexity of innovation, the reactions to changes in the price, and the social impact affecting whether the innovation is adopted. Consumer-related characteristics include motivation for adopting the innovation, self-efficacy, negative emotions associated with the innovation, and one's attitude toward the existing product.

Research Methodology

A survey was used to determine the factors contributing to product innovation resistance, and to collect empirical data, a Paper and Pen Personal Interview (PAPI) was used. It was conducted in May 2022, and the response rate was 100%. The research sample consisted of 414 respondents (174 students at public universities and 240 University of Third Age participants). The study used a non-random sample selection. Sample characteristics are not homogeneous, but it is possible to identify their characteristics based on the sample's structure. The study included 77% women and 23% men. The majority (58% of respondents) were over 60 years old. As for education, most respondents had a Bachelor's degree (43%), Master's degree (25%), or high school diploma (27%), while the smallest number of respondents was vocationally trained (5%). The research tool used in this study was a questionnaire that asked 21 questions about consumer resistance to product innovation. The Likert scale was used to evaluate individual resistance factors from 1 minimum to 5 maximum. Based on the quantitative analysis, we were able to determine the position of factors in the ranking and interpret them as elements of consumer resistance. We used Spearman's rank correlation coefficient along with Kruskal–Wallis's non-parametric ANOVA test as well as the Mann–Whitney *U*-tests.

Study Results

As a result of the assessment, respondents assigned each factor a value between 1 minute and 5 maximum, allowing us to calculate the average for each factor. Among the features of an innovative product that affects consumer resistance are its advantages, namely quality (51% of respondents said "yes" and 39% said "rather yes") and usability (40% answered "yes" and 41% said "rather yes"). The response to price change also received high ratings, with 46% of respondents stating that the price of an innovative product affects their decision to purchase it (46% answered "yes" and 42% said "rather yes") and that respondents weigh the costs and advantages when deciding to purchase an innovative product (51% answered "yes" and 31% "rather yes"). The complexity of product innovation proved important in terms of consumer resistance and purchase decisions (28% answered "yes" and 42% "rather yes"). The impact of innovation-related risks on consumer resistance to innovation was less clear (22% said "yes" and 34% said "rather yes"). A relatively small number of respondents (about 40% answered "yes" and "rather yes") acknowledged the importance of social influence on their adoption of product innovation and admitted to trusting the opinion of others about innovative products.

As part of the study of consumer characteristics and resistance to innovation, it is important to consider the motivation behind the adoption of innovative products which is expressed as an understanding that innovative products are needed, as the survey confirmed (31% of respondents said "yes" and 50% said "rather yes"), as well as openness and interest in product innovation (28% of respondents said "yes" and 52% "rather yes"). Consumer resistance to product innovation is influenced by self-efficacy, i.e. ability to use innovative products (17% of respondents said "yes" and 41% "rather yes") and new technologies (11% of respondents said "yes" and 29% "rather yes"). In terms of negative emotions related to product innovations, incentives are least likely to arouse interest in product innovations among respondents (3% said "yes" and 28% said "rather yes"); however, the tendency for respondents to put in additional effort into the acquisition of innovative products is also limited (12% said "yes" and 24% said "rather yes"), and the tendency to resist failure when disappointed with innovative products (8% of respondents said "yes" and 24% "rather yes"). Consumer resistance to product innovation may be related to their attitude toward the existing product, i.e. the belief that the current product meets expectations (19% of respondents said "yes" and 52% "rather yes") and the belief that there is no need to change the current product (15% of respondents said "yes" and 24% "rather yes").

Based on an analysis of dependencies, individual areas were assessed according to gender. According to the study, women were more likely than men to agree that improved functionality influences their choice of an innovative product, with $p<\alpha$ ($p=0.0132$). Furthermore, women were more likely to trust the opinions of others when it came to innovative products, with $p<\alpha$ ($p=0.0177$), and existing products were more likely to meet their expectations, with $p<\alpha$ ($p=0.0050$). In contrast, men were more likely to be willing to take on the risks associated with acquiring a new product, with $p<\alpha$ ($p=0.0186$), while the complexity of the innovative product had a greater impact on their decision to purchase, with $p<\alpha$ ($p=0.0458$).

Education was also analyzed as a factor in the assessment of innovation in particular fields. The study showed that education also influenced the decision to choose an innovative product based on its improved functionality. Those with a bachelor's degree (an average rating of 4.51) and with a vocational degree at the least (an average score of 3.40) agreed with this statement. Education also had to do with the assessment of whether the improvement in quality affects the choice of an innovative product, with $p<\alpha$ ($p=0.0087$). Most respondents who agreed with this statement held a bachelor's degree (an average rating of 4.55), while those with vocational training scored the lowest (3.60). Education was related to how respondents assessed their knowledge about innovations, with $p<\alpha$ ($p=0.0304$). Those with a bachelor's degree reported having the greatest amount of knowledge on this subject (3.17) and those with a high school diploma (2.61) had the least amount of knowledge. Education was also associated with how respondents assessed their willingness to take risks in a decision to acquire an innovative product, with $p<\alpha$ ($p=0.0129$). It was highest among those with a bachelor's degree (3.67) and lowest among those with a high school diploma (3.11) or those with a college degree (3.12). A correlation was found between education and how respondents judged whether their opinions were the only factors contributing to their decision to purchase an innovative product, with $p<\alpha$ ($p=0.0000$). In most cases, university graduates (3.5) and high school graduates (3.46) agreed with this statement, and bachelor's degree holders (2.53%) were the least likely to agree. Education was also correlated with respondents' assessment of how much they trusted other people's opinions about innovative products, with $p<\alpha$ ($p=0.0002$). People with a bachelor's degree (3.57) were the most likely to trust other people's opinions, while those with vocational education were the least likely to do so. Education was also correlated with the evaluation of one's own skills in new technologies, with $p<\alpha$ ($p=0.0004$). Bachelor's degree holders rated it the highest (3.56) while those with a college degree rated it the lowest (2.73). Education also influenced the assessment of respondents' ability to use innovative products, with $p<\alpha$ ($p=0.0002$). The highest rating was given by those with a bachelor's degree (3.94) and the lowest by those with higher education (3.17). Education was also associated with responding to incentives used to arouse interest in product innovations, with $p<\alpha$ ($p=0.0083$). Those with a high school diploma were the least likely to respond to such incentives (2.58) and those with a bachelor's degree were most likely to respond (3.19).

The study results were also analyzed as to whether age affected how each area was assessed. Again, the Kruskal–Wallis analysis of variance test was used for it. There are four age categories: under 25 years old, 26–65, 66–70, and over 70 years old. There are nine areas related to innovation resistance that were also affected by age, according to the research.

Age played a role in the assessment of whether improvements in a product's functionality affected the decision to buy an innovative product. The older the respondents were, the less likely they were to agree with the statements. People under 25 were the most likely to agree with the statements, while those over 70 were the least likely to do so. Age also influenced the assessment of risk associated with the decision to acquire an innovative product, with $p<\alpha$ (p=0.0019). Similar to the previous trend, the older the respondents were, the less willing they were to take the risks associated with acquiring innovative products. Age played a role in deciding whether respondents were only influenced by their own opinions to purchase an innovative product, with $p<\alpha$ (p=0.0003). Those aged under 25 agreed the least with this statement, while those aged 66–70 agreed the most. There was also an association between age and trust in others' opinions about the innovative product, with $p<\alpha$ (p=0.0000). The youngest respondents (those under the age of 25) were the most likely to trust the opinion of others, whereas the oldest respondents reported the least amount of trust. Age also had an impact on respondents' understanding of the need for innovative products, with $p<\alpha$ (p=0.0062). The study showed that those under the age of 25 exhibited the greatest level of such recognition, whereas the least amount of it was found among respondents aged 26–65. Age was also associated with the assessment of their skills in the field of new technologies, with $p<\alpha$ (p=0.0031). A downward trend can be seen here with age – the older one gets, the lower the assessment of one's own skills in terms of new technologies. Skill ratings are highest among the youngest under 25 years of age, while the lowest are among those aged 70 and older. Age also influenced the assessment of the ability to use innovative products, with $p<\alpha$ (p=00036). A person's ability to use innovative products decreased with age. Respondents' age was also associated with their response to incentives used to arouse interest in product innovations, with $p<\alpha$ (p=0.0005). Incentives are most effective among people under the age of 25 and least effective among people between 26 and 65. There was a relationship between the respondents' age and their satisfaction with existing products, with $p<\alpha$ (p=0.0211). The most satisfied with existing products are those over 70 years old, and the least satisfied are those between 26 and 65 years old.

Conclusions, Recommendations, and Research Limitations

For the creators of innovative products, entrepreneurs, as well as customers, these difficult times characterized by uncertainty and greater risk have posed special challenges to creativity and adaptability. The synergy between these relationships and the co-creation of innovative products depends on the ability to utilize new technologies and intellectual capital as well as meet creators' and consumers' expectations. Existing business models and consumption models must be modified on a continuous basis.

In analyzing factors contributing to consumer resistance to product innovations, it is apparent that product characteristics, such as quality, price, benefits, and functionality are the most significant factors. According to the analysis, it is difficult to assess the strength of their impact, but the ranking of the aforementioned factors indicates that innovation features contribute to resistance to product innovation. In general, resistance to innovation decreases as consumers perceive more benefits from innovation; the greater the benefits, the lower the resistance. There is a risk associated with innovation, and consumer resistance to innovation is a negative reaction to risk; the greater the risk, the greater the resistance. A consumer's ability to use an innovative product is also taken into consideration when deciding whether to buy an innovative product. The complexity of innovative products and modern technologies that require additional effort on behalf of consumers can lead to negative emotions and consumer resistance. Based on the results of this study, it is necessary to draw attention to ways of reducing consumer resistance by enhancing incentives used to increase the appeal of product innovations, highlighting their benefits, and creating practical means to discover and understand innovative products (free testing).

The world of consumers is characterized by constant and ever-faster changes that require constant and endless innovation. Consumer resistance to product innovation is prevalent in various innovation contexts, so managers must identify the source and improve their strategies to overcome it. Understanding consumer resistance to product innovation should help managers develop more effective strategies to market innovative products.

This study is significant because it identifies factors that influence consumer resistance to product innovation and sheds light on the reasons why innovative product acceptance is lower than expected. In addition, this study is of academic significance as it focuses on factors of consumer resistance to product innovation, which traditionally have been studied mainly from the perspective of the effectiveness of innovation product diffusion. Consumers can benefit from this study by developing new knowledge, particularly in relation to the development of innovation and ethics.

While the study contributes to the dissemination of literature on product innovation, it has limitations that need to be addressed in future research. In future studies, the sample size should be widened to make the results more generalizable. Yet another limitation is the use of a single research method, namely a survey, indicating the possibility of expanding the study. Furthermore, the study can be expanded to include empirical data from different cultural and geographical regions.

Identifying differences in consumer resistance to product innovation and to innovation related to services can provide an important foundation for further research. Furthermore, quantitative and qualitative studies of consumer resistance to product innovations are necessary to deepen and broaden theoretical and practical perspectives.

References

Antioco, M., & Kleijnen, M. (2010). Consumer adoption of technological innovations. *European Journal of Marketing*, *44*(11/12), 1700–1724. doi: 10.1108/03090561011079846

Caputa, W. (2010). Innovativeness in the process of creating customer value. *Forum Statisticum Slovacum*, 6, 23–28.

Castellion, G., & Markham, S. (2013). Perspective: New product failure rates: Influence of argumentum ad populum and self-interest. *Journal of Product Innovation Management, 30*(5), 976–979.

Garcia, R., & Atkin, T. (2002). Co-petition for the diffusion of resistant innovations: A case study in the global wine industry. In *25th International Conference of the System Dynamics Society*, 3.

Garcia, R., Bardhi, F., & Friedrich, C. (2007). Overcoming consumer resistance to innovation. *MIT Sloan Management Review, 48*(4), 82–88.

Gourville, J. (2006). Eager sellers and stony buyers: Understanding the psychology of new-product adoption. Retrieved 18 September 2022, from https://hbr.org/2006/06/eager-sellers-and-stony-buyers-understanding-the-psychology-of-new-product-adoption

GUS. (2021). Działalność innowacyjna przedsiębiorstw w Polsce. Retrieved 18 September 2022, from https://stat.gov.pl/obszary-tematyczne/nauka-i-technika-spoleczenstwo-informacyjne/nauka-i-technika/dzialalnosc-innowacyjna-przedsiebiorstw-w-polsce-w-latach-2018-2020,14,8.html

Hauser, J., Tellis, G., & Griffin, A. (2006). Research on innovation: A review and agenda for marketing science. *Marketing Science*, *25*(6), 687–717. doi: 10.1287/mksc.1050.0144

Heidenreich, S., & Handrich, M. (2014). What about passive innovation resistance? Investigating adoption-related behavior from a resistance perspective. *Journal of Product Innovation Management*, *32*(6), 878–903. https://doi.org/10.1111/jpim.12161

Heidenreich, S., & Kraemer, T. (2015). Innovations-doomed to fail? Investigating strategies to overcome passive innovation resistance. *Journal of Product Innovation Management*, *33*(3), 277–297. https://doi.org/10.1111/jpim.12273

Heidenreich, S., & Spieth, P. (2013). Why innovations fail. The case of passive and active innovation resistance. *International Journal of Innovation Management*, *17*(05), 1350021. doi: 10.1142/s1363919613500217

Huang, D., Jin, X., & Coghlan, A. (2021). Advances in consumer innovation resistance research: A review and research agenda. *Technological Forecasting and Social Change*, *166*, 120594. doi: 10.1016/j.techfore.2021.120594

Kleijnen, M., Lee, N., & Wetzels, M. (2009). An exploration of consumer resistance to innovation and its antecedents. *Journal of Economic Psychology*, *30*(3), 344–357. doi: 10.1016/j.joep.2009.02.004

Laukkanen, P., Sinkkonen, S., & Laukkanen, T. (2008). Consumer resistance to internet banking: Postponers, opponents and rejectors. *International Journal of Bank Marketing*, *26*(6), 440–455. doi: 10.1108/02652320810902451

Lennon, S., Kim, M., Johnson, K., Jolly, L., Damhorst, M., & Jasper, C. (2007). A longitudinal look at rural consumer adoption of online shopping. *Psychology and Marketing*, *24*(4), 375–401. doi: 10.1002/mar.20165

Pierscieniak, A., & Stelmaszczyk, M. (2020). Organizational wisdom: The impact of organizational learning on the absorptive capacity of an enterprise. *European Research Studies Journal*, *XXIII*(Special Issue 2), 271–281. doi: 10.35808/ersj/1823

Ram, S., & Sheth, J. (1989). Consumer resistance to innovations: The marketing problem and its solutions. *The Journal of Consumer Marketing*, *6*(4), 5–14. doi: 10.1016/0737-6782(89)90083-0

Rennings, K., & Zwick, T. (2002). The employment impact of cleaner production on the firm level—empirical evidence from a survey in five European countries.

International Journal of Innovation Management, 06(03), 319–342. doi: 10.1142/s1363919602000604

Rogers, E. M. (2003). *Diffusion of innovations* (5th ed.). New York: Free Press.

Rutkowski, I. (2021). Wskaźniki powodzenia oraz niepowodzenia nowych produktów wprowadzonych na rynek — fakty i mity. *Marketing I Rynek, 08*(2021), 3–11. doi: 10.33226/1231-7853.2021.8.1

Talke, K., & Heidenreich, S. (2014). How to overcome pro-change bias: incorporating passive and active innovation resistance in innovation decision models. *Journal of Product Innovation Management, 31*(5), 894–907.

Tornatzky, L., & Klein, K. (1982). Innovation characteristics and innovation adoption-implementation: A meta-analysis of findings. *IEEE Transactions on Engineering Management, 29*(1), 28–45.

Urbanowska-Sojkin, E. (2012). Ryzyko w procesie wyborów strategicznych przedsiębiorstwa, *Organizacja i Kierowanie, 149*(1A), 165–176.

13 Assessing the Impact of the COVID-19 Pandemic on Real Estate Development Companies in Poland

Marta Sokół

Introduction

The outbreak of the COVID-19 pandemic in March 2020 caused a serious drop in economic activity in Poland and around the world. In an effort to prevent the spread of the coronavirus, the government introduced a number of restrictions affecting the entire socioeconomic landscape. Executives were faced with the challenge of maintaining efficiency in their operations by responding proactively to changing business circumstances. Skillful management and the ability to react quickly to external stimuli are key to value creation even in a turbulent environment (Miszczuk & Sosińska-Wit, 2017). For businesses, changes in their environment (with which all entities are constantly interacting) can be a source of risks and opportunities for their operations.

Changes caused by the pandemic in the values of macroeconomic indicators and, consequently, in the state of the economy have had a significant impact on the level of real estate prices and, consequently, on the development of supply and demand in the real estate market and the mutual needs and opportunities for investors and buyers. In light of this, it is worthwhile to analyze the change in the situation of the development industry caused by the outbreak of the pandemic.

The aim of this chapter was to assess the financial condition and market valuation of real estate development companies between 2019 and 2021, that is, before and during the COVID-19 pandemic, and to evaluate the impact of the pandemic on their financial performance. This allowed us to answer the question of whether and to what extent the financial performance of the surveyed companies affected their value.

Enterprise Value Creation: The Goal of Business Operations

Every business activity is designed to yield financial gains through the use of its resources. A company's results are heavily influenced by the quality of its management processes. Under the same conditions and with the same resources, it is possible to achieve completely different economic results (Czekaj & Dresler, 2001). The effective management of resources and a

DOI: 10.4324/9781003475583-18

quick response to external stimuli are keys to the efficient operation of a business.

At present, the value-based management concept is considered the most effective management concept. It is based on the assumption that the primary goal in the operation of modern enterprises should be to strive to increase their value over the long term. Maximizing the enterprise value is the starting point for a number of specific goals and brings together the expectations of owners and other stakeholders (Paździor, 2015).

Because the concept of enterprise value is multidimensional and the factors that shape it are numerous, many categories of it can be differentiated; this chapter, however, focuses on the book value and the market value of businesses.

The book value of a company is the difference between the value of its assets and the value of its liabilities. It is therefore calculated on the basis of balance sheet components. In contrast, a company's market value is determined during a purchase-sale transaction and represents the price a buyer is likely to pay for the business and the price the seller is likely to accept. It is quite common for the market value to differ significantly from the book value. The reason for this is that certain factors that cannot be valued using current accounting principles can influence the valuation of shares that deviate from the book value (Paździor, 2015). These include, for example, such aspects as a well-known brand, intellectual capital, or an extensive distribution network. No less crucial to the value of shares are the skills of a company's management and, consequently, the decisions they make, or the economic risks involved in running a particular business. It is also worth noting that the value of shares is influenced not only by pure economic calculations but just as much by current market trends at a given time that may be related to certain moods, preferences, economic fluctuations, or political changes.

The success of an organization, as measured by increasing its value, is therefore determined by a diverse set of factors involving its internal resources, both those of a financial and nonfinancial nature, and the environment in which it operates.

The internal value drivers related to finances include

- sales growth rate;
- operating profit margin;
- investments in fixed assets;
- investments in current assets;
- income tax rate;
- cost of capital;
- and value payback period.

A change in the value of any of these factors results in a change in the value of the company. The company's management can determine strategic actions that will create value by considering the aforementioned factors in operational, investment, and financial decisions (Bielecki & Pawłowicz, 2015).

In addition to financial factors, nonfinancial factors also have a significant impact on the value creation process. This impact is particularly important when market conditions are changing dynamically. The answer to these changes lies in intangible assets because they can significantly increase a company's market value relative to its book value (Rzemieniak, 2013).

Intangible resources are referred to as intellectual capital, and they include human, organizational, and relational capital. Human capital represents employees' potential and employees' ability to utilize it based on their motivation (Bombiak, 2016). In essence, it is the sum of all of a company's knowledge, experience, abilities, and aptitudes. Organizational capital refers to all the systems, procedures, and mechanisms of an enterprise that accelerate the flow of knowledge and information within it, as well as patents, copyrights, and know-how. Relational capital, on the other hand, refers to human interactions and the company's relationship with its stakeholders. It includes, among other things, customer loyalty, strategic partnerships, reputation, and good relationships with the environment, as well as intelligence about competitors.

Intellectual capital is reflected in the difference between a company's market value and its book value. When intellectual capital is effectively utilized, it enhances an organization's competitive advantage, thereby contributing to its long-term goal of value creation with a focus on pro-development policies (Janik & Paździor, 2011).

The value of an enterprise is also affected by the factors related to the environment in which it operates. These include the unique characteristics of a given sector, the level and trajectory of changes in the inflation rate, and the government's fiscal and economic policies (Szczepankowski, 2013); the reason for this is that every enterprise interacts constantly with its environment. An organization's efficiency is largely determined by the degree of adaptation to its various elements. In the current economic scenario, the environment is changing dynamically. This necessitates constant development and an active response to changes in a volatile economy. It is also possible for the environment to influence the operation of an enterprise in both positive and negative ways, and thus be a source of opportunities and dangers to its current and future operations (Zastempowski et al., 2018).

A significant factor that affected the Polish economy and that of the rest of the world was the COVID-19 pandemic. Pandemic-induced economic changes have had a significant impact on many aspects of the economy, including the development of the real estate supply and demand and of the needs and opportunities for investors and buyers.

COVID-19 Pandemic and the Development Industry

The outbreak of the COVID-19 pandemic in March 2020 caused sharp declines in financial markets, both in Poland and around the world. Government-imposed restrictions aimed at reducing infection rates triggered a severe drop in economic activity. In Poland in the second quarter of 2020, the gross domestic product (GDP) decreased by 8.9% from the previous quarter and was 7.9% lower than a year earlier (Główny Urząd Statystyczny [GUS], 2020a). In the third and fourth quarters of 2020, the value of the GDP improved slightly relative to the second quarter, but it was still lower than a year earlier by 2%–3% (GUS, 2020b). In an effort to protect the economy from the effects of the pandemic, the Monetary Policy Council decided to cut interest rates three times, in March, April, and May. This reduced the cost of loans and, at the same time, lowered deposit rates. Increased access to cheaper money and the desire to safeguard capital already accumulated may therefore have provided the impetus for investors to seek more lucrative investments than deposits or bonds. Real estate may have appeared to be a relatively safe investment solution to protect capital from inflation. Real estate values increase over time, plus they allow one to create passive income. The increased interest in real estate may also have been influenced by the lockdowns that were introduced, which reinforced the public's preference for settling on the outskirts of cities.

The socioeconomic turmoil caused by the pandemic was reflected in real estate prices. Compared with 2019, the pre-pandemic period, in 2020 housing prices increased by 8.9%; the increase in the primary market was 6.0% and in the secondary market 11.2% (GUS, 2020d). In contrast, in 2021 prices of residential units increased by 12.1% compared with 2020; in the primary market the increase was 11.9% and in the secondary market 12.2% (GUS, 2021).

The number of completed housing units also increased in 2020 compared with the previous year. According to GUS data, developers handed over 9.4% more housing units than in the same period of 2019. The number of building permits issued to developers also increased by 2.5% year-on-year. On the other hand, the number of construction starts by developers decreased by 8.3% compared with those in 2019 (GUS, 2020e).

In 2021, the number of housing units completed by developers fell slightly, by 0.7%, from 2020. On the other hand, the number of construction permits issued increased significantly. Developers received as much as 23.9% more than in 2020. In addition, in contrast to the previous year, significant increases were recorded regarding the number of construction starts. In 2021, developers started as much as 27.7% more housing constructions than in 2020 (GUS, 2022).

In view of the data cited, it seems interesting to analyze whether companies in the development industry were positively valued by the market and whether they managed to create market value added.

Research Methodology

The purpose of this chapter was to analyze the financial conditions and market valuations of real estate development companies from 2019 to 2021, that is, before and during the COVID-19 pandemic, and to assess the impact of the pandemic on their financial performances.

The research in question was conducted for selected companies in the real estate development industry listed on the Warsaw Stock Exchange and included in the WIG-real estate index. The criterion for selecting companies for the study was based on the value of their total assets. Out of 33 entities in the WSE Developers sector, 5 Polish companies were selected whose minimum asset values at the end of 2021 oscillated around 1 billion euros. The selected developers, in order of highest asset value, were:

1 Globe Trade Centre S.A. (GTC);
2 Echo Investment S.A.;
3 Polski Holding Nieruchomości S.A. (PHN);
4 MLG Group S.A.;
5 Dom Development S.A.

Research methods including literature studies, financial statement analyses, ratio analyses, and stock price analyses were used to achieve the goal. The analyses were based on data contained in the consolidated financial statements of the surveyed companies and data published on online portals, particularly BusinessRadar. The study was conducted for the years from 2019 to 2021, a period before and during the COVID-19 pandemic. Due to the dynamically changing pandemic situation, quarterly data were relied upon. First, the financial conditions of the selected companies were diagnosed by using the ratios of current liquidity, total debt, and return on sales, equity, total capital, and leverage. Next, share price quotations were analyzed. Value creation was assessed using the market value added (MVA) index by comparing each company's book valuation with its market valuation. This allowed for the verification of whether, despite the economic turmoil caused by the pandemic, development companies managed creating added value.

The value of the MVA ratio represents a kind of premium added in the market to the capital committed to the company (Szczepankowski, 2013). If the company's market value is positive, it means that it is viewed positively by potential investors. MVA reflects investors' attitudes toward a company's growth prospects (Paździor, 2015). Because the calculation of the MVA indicator takes into account the share price, it should be borne in mind that its value can be distorted regardless of the company's actions, or it may be distorted as a result of the prevailing market situation.

Results

Among the determinants of investors' decisions to buy shares are the financial conditions of companies. Hence, an analysis of the audited companies' financial performances and an assessment of their financial positions will be made first.

In 2019 and the first quarter of 2020, all of the surveyed companies achieved positive financial results, both operating and net results. In the second quarter of 2020, that is, after the World Health Organization had announced the pandemic, the companies' financial performances deteriorated significantly, with only Dom Development managing to achieve double the profits of the previous quarter. GTC and PHN, on the other hand, suffered a loss. No clear trends were observed in the subsequent quarters of the period under review, either in comparison with subsequent quarters or with the corresponding periods of the previous year. Significantly, only GTC closed 2020 with a net loss, while in 2021 all of the surveyed companies made a positive net profit in each of the quarters studied.

Making a profit for a company is the essence of its profitability. However, since the objective measure of a company's profitability is the relative amount of profit, the profitability analysis was based on sales and capital profitability ratios. Table 13.1 summarizes the obtained results of the indicator analysis.

Dom Development had the lowest operating profit margin and net profit margin in 2019, while MLG Group had the highest. Also during the pandemic period, that is, the following quarters in 2020 and 2021, the highest operating and net profit margins were observed at MLG Group (except for Q2 2020). For the other companies surveyed, there were no clear trends in the performances of the indicators in question.

Another important aspect in assessing financial health is the return on capital. The return on equity ratio was positive at all the surveyed companies in 2019, with the highest value (9.05%) at GTC and the lowest value (0.90%) at PNH. In the following year, the return on equity declined at all of the companies except Dom Development. The largest decline in profitability was observed at GTC (down 181%). In 2021, the value of the index increased at all of the companies except Dom Development, although it should be noted that this developer showed the most stable profitability in the period under review at 5.5%–7%. The profitability of total capital showed trends similar to those of the profitability of equity. By comparing the values of the return on equity and return on assets ratios and calculating the leverage effect, the profitability of the company's debt was evaluated. During the period under review, debt in companies positively affected returns on equity (except for GTC in 2021). The highest profitability of debt was observed at MLG Group and Dom Development and the lowest at GTC and PHN.

In order to assess the financial health of the companies, the level of total debt was also examined. GTC had the highest debt at around 90% but showed a decreasing trend. Debt, on the other hand, was on the rise at PHN. In contrast, Echo Investment (70%), MLG Group (54%), and Dom Development (64%) remained at similar levels.

Liquidity plays a key role in the smooth operation of any entity. An entity is considered capable of the timely repayment of liabilities when the value of the indicator is 1, while the optimal level is 1.2–1.5. According to the survey, only GTC could have liquidity problems in 2019, while PHN was on

Table 13.1 Results of indicator analysis

Indicators	*Name*	2019				2020				2021			
		Q1	*Q2*	*Q3*	*Q4*	*Q1*	*Q2*	*Q3*	*Q4*	*Q1*	*Q2*	*Q3*	*Q4*
Operating profit margin	GTC	0.79	0.87	0.82	0.52	0.53	–0.96	0.71	–1.43	0.57	0.70	0.64	0.41
	ECHO	0.75	0.86	0.35	0.52	0.66	0.18	0.22	0.25	0.47	–0.05	0.31	0.18
	PHN	0.46	0.48	0.66	0.69	0.22	–0.54	0.26	0.23	0.28	0.06	0.51	0.53
	MLP GROUP	0.66	2.15	1.70	0.74	4.49	0.07	1.00	0.93	0.73	3.55	1.63	6.35
	DOMDEV	0.20	0.16	0.18	0.21	0.16	0.23	0.20	0.23	0.27	0.22	0.21	0.13
Net profit margin	GTC	0.50	0.55	0.46	0.28	0.07	–0.97	0.40	–1.45	0.23	0.31	0.25	0.20
	ECHO	0.46	0.59	0.20	0.37	0.26	0.04	0.11	0.07	0.16	0.08	0.18	0.12
	PHN	0.29	0.34	0.34	0.39	0.18	–0.55	0.09	0.17	0.20	0.01	0.10	0.25
	MLP GROUP	0.37	1.72	0.82	0.84	2.63	0.20	0.54	0.39	0.32	3.16	0.74	5.07
	DOMDEV	0.16	0.13	0.14	0.17	0.12	0.17	0.16	0.19	0.22	0.17	0.16	0.09
Return on equity	GTC	–	0.12	0.10	0.06	0.01	–0.16	0.07	–0.22	0.03	0.04	0.03	0.03
	ECHO	–	0.02	0.03	0.12	0.03	0.01	0.02	0.02	0.01	0.01	0.04	0.05
	PHN	–	0.01	0.01	0.01	0.01	–0.02	0.00	0.03	0.01	0.00	0.00	0.01
	MLP GROUP	–	0.07	0.03	0.03	0.11	0.01	0.03	0.02	0.01	0.11	0.02	0.17
	DOMDEV	–	0.03	0.06	0.08	0.03	0.07	0.05	0.12	0.14	0.05	0.05	0.03
Profitability of total capitals	GTC	–	0.01	0.01	0.01	0.00	–0.01	0.01	–0.02	0.01	0.01	0.01	0.01
	ECHO	–	0.01	0.01	0.04	0.01	0.00	0.01	0.01	0.01	0.01	0.01	0.02
	PHN	–	0.01	0.01	0.01	0.01	–0.01	0.01	0.02	0.01	0.00	0.01	0.01
	MLP GROUP	–	0.03	0.02	0.01	0.07	0.00	0.02	0.02	0.01	0.05	0.01	0.08
	DOMDEV	–	0.01	0.02	0.03	0.01	0.03	0.02	0.04	0.06	0.02	0.02	0.01
Current liquidity	GTC	1.07	0.79	0.84	0.85	1.22	0.74	1.39	1.36	3.15	2.47	1.87	2.27
	ECHO	2.06	2.29	1.72	1.6	1.41	1.33	2.28	1.43	1.60	1.42	1.56	1.60
	PHN	0.84	1.03	0.99	1.06	1.13	1.00	0.98	2.05	1.77	1.00	0.93	0.93
	MLP GROUP	0.96	1.98	2.04	1.43	1.60	1.80	1.67	3.01	2.15	1.89	1.35	1.38
	DOMDEV	2.60	2.53	3.01	2.78	2.47	2.10	2.01	2.11	2.03	1.96	2.38	2.14
Total debt	GTC	0.92	0.92	0.92	0.91	0.91	0.90	0.90	0.89	0.89	0.88	0.88	0.86
	ECHO	0.66	0.66	0.70	0.68	0.68	0.69	0.69	0.70	0.70	0.77	0.75	0.74
	PHN	0.34	0.38	0.40	0.41	0.41	0.42	0.44	0.45	0.44	0.44	0.44	0.45
	MLP GROUP	0.51	0.54	0.54	0.55	0.56	0.56	0.56	0.55	0.55	0.52	0.52	0.52
	DOMDEV	0.58	0.66	0.65	0.63	0.67	0.64	0.68	0.64	0.57	0.65	0.68	0.68

Source: Own compilation based on the data in financial statements.

Table 13.2 Market value added (MVA) per share

Period		*Name of the entity*				
Year	*Quarter*	*GTC*	*Echo investment*	*PHN*	*MLG group*	*Dom development*
2019	Q1	7.31	0.51	–30.88	–1.88	35.75
	Q2	7.47	0.28	–30.53	–4.43	39.33
	Q3	7.64	1.36	–32.28	–0.60	43.11
	Q4	7.75	0.88	–36.47	–1.68	51.35
2020	Q1	4.19	0.01	–35.11	–5.04	27.27
	Q2	4.37	–0.16	–30.88	21.92	45.50
	Q3	3.90	0.12	–31.88	14.36	61.28
	Q4	4.70	–0.04	–33.08	21.55	68.10
2021	Q1	4.37	0.24	–32.38	10.14	81.68
	Q2	3.61	0.65	–30.20	6.72	92.00
	Q3	4.02	0.32	–31.01	3.43	86.57
	Q4	3.23	0.00	–34.17	–6.56	71.16

Source: Own compilation based on quarterly financial statements for 2019–2021 of selected companies and their share price quotations

the verge of liquidity. In the period of 2020 to 2021, liquidity was preserved at all of the surveyed entities, with the highest value at 2 recorded at Dom Development.

In an analysis of share prices in the first quarter of 2020, all companies surveyed saw a decline in share prices compared with the previous quarter as a result of the pandemic outbreak. Starting in the second quarter, GTC's share price continued on a horizontal trend, while the others were on an upward trend. This meant that the shares of Echo Investment, PHN, MLG Group, and Dom Development rose steadily during the pandemic period.

The final stage of the research conducted was an analysis of value creation using the MVA ratio, which is the difference between an entity's market value and its book value. The results obtained are summarized in Table 13.2.

In the pre-pandemic period, market value was created by three developers. Dom Development had the highest MVA per share. Its value in 2019 increased in successive quarters but then decreased as a result of the outbreak of the pandemic, while it increased from the second quarter of 2021. The highest market value was created in Q2 2021 at PLN 92/share. It should be noted in particular that Dom Development had the lowest operating profit and net profit margins among the surveyed entities in 2019. However, the entity was characterized by a stable financial condition. Throughout the pandemic period, the return on equity was at similar levels (5.5% to 7%), as was the level of total debt (64%). In addition, there was a current liquidity level of 2, which could even be considered overliquidity.

In 2019, market value was also created at GTC. With the outbreak of the pandemic, the value per share declined; it remained at similar levels throughout 2020 and 2021 but did not return to its pre-pandemic value.

Echo Investment also showed a positive market value before the pandemic, but at only a few tens of pennies per share. The company's performance did not improve during the pandemic period, unlike that of MLG Group. This developer did not achieve market value added before the pandemic, while from Q2 2020 to Q3 2021 the value of its MVA index was positive. This shows that during the pandemic, MLG Group created MVA in contrast to the pre-pandemic period. The weakest results were obtained with the PHN study. This developer did not create MVA throughout the period under review, either before or during the pandemic. It should be noted that this developer was characterized by its relatively weakest financial condition, and in addition, the ratio analysis indicated liquidity problems.

Summary and Recommendations

The theory of value creation, which emerged as a result of progressive economic growth and growing financial awareness among investors, is a response to the search for methods and tools to effectively activate capital allocated in companies.

Profit is undoubtedly an important and necessary outcome of any enterprise, but it has certain shortcomings as a measure of value creation, stemming from the fact that investors expect to be compensated for their contributed capital at a level commensurate with the risks they have incurred. If the accounting profit exceeds the level of expected profit, then there will be an economic profit, which is, as Paździor (2015) notes, the real source of the increase in the value of the enterprise and the wealth of its owners, which is the long-term goal of enterprises in a market economy.

Based on the study, the following conclusions and recommendations could be made:

1 The results confirm the fact that achieving a positive accounting financial result does not guarantee the creation of added value in an enterprise;
2 Entities with relatively lower book profits are able to create more MVA;
3 Although the COVID-19 pandemic negatively affected the value creation of real estate development entities in the initial period, it could have been a factor in enhancing the MVA due to changes in socioeconomic trends in subsequent periods;
4 As a result of the aforementioned changes in socioeconomic trends caused by the pandemic, companies that had created market value before the pandemic were also able to maintain it at similar or even higher levels during the pandemic;
5 Companies with a stable financial standing that are able to steadily improve their performance are regarded more favorably by investors, and their share prices are rising as a result;
6 Considering the uncertain environment in which real estate developers operate today, it is necessary to continually monitor both their performance and the socioeconomic events affecting them.

References

Bielecki, K., & Pawłowicz, L. (2015). *Managing the value of a capital company.* Warsaw: CeDeWu, p. 38.

Bombiak, E. (2016). Kapitał intelektualny jako specyficzny zasób współczesnych organizacji. *Zeszyty Naukowe Uniwersytetu Przyrodniczo-Humanistycznego w Siedlcach nr 109*, 109.

Czekaj, J., & Dresler, Z. (2001). *Zarządzanie finansami przedsiębiorstw: podstawy teorii.* Warsaw: PWN. s.14.

GUS. (2020a). Wstępny szacunek produktu krajowego brutto w 1 kwartale 2022 roku. Retrieved 26 September 2022, from https://stat.gov.pl/obszary-tematyczne/rachunki-narodowe/kwartalne-rachunki-narodowe/wstepny-szacunek-produktu-krajowego-brutto-w-1-kwartale-2022-roku,3,79.html

GUS. (2020b). Rachunki narodowe. Retrieved 26 September 2022, from https://stat.gov.pl/obszary-tematyczne/rachunki-narodowe/

GUS. (2020c). Wstępny szacunek produktu krajowego brutto w czwartym kwartale 2020 roku. Retrieved 26 September 2022, from https://stat.gov.pl/obszary-tematyczne/rachunki-narodowe/kwartalne-rachunki-narodowe/wstepny-szacunek-produktu-krajowego-brutto-w-czwartym-kwartale-2020-roku,3,74.html

GUS. (2020d). Wskaźniki cen lokali mieszkalnych w IV kwartale 2020 roku. Retrieved 26 September 2022, from https://stat.gov.pl/obszary-tematyczne/ceny-handel/wskazniki-cen/wskazniki-cen-lokali-mieszkalnych-w-iv-kwartale-2020-roku,12,10.html

GUS. (2020e). Budownictwo mieszkaniowe w okresie styczeń-maj 2022 roku. Retrieved 26 September 2022, from https://stat.gov.pl/obszary-tematyczne/przemysl-budownictwo-srodki-trwale/budownictwo/budownictwo-mieszkaniowe-w-okresie-styczen-maj-2022-roku,5,127.html

GUS. (2021). Wskaźniki cen lokali mieszkalnych w IV kwartale 2020 roku. Retrieved 26 September 2022, from https://stat.gov.pl/obszary-tematyczne/ceny-handel/wskazniki-cen/wskazniki-cen-lokali-mieszkalnych-w-iv-kwartale-2020-roku,12,10.html

GUS. (2022). Budownictwo mieszkaniowe w okresie styczeń-maj 2022 roku. Retrieved 26 September 2022, from https://stat.gov.pl/obszary-tematyczne/przemysl-budownictwo-srodki-trwale/budownictwo/budownictwo-mieszkaniowe-w-okresie-styczen-maj-2022-roku,5,127.html

Janik, W., & Paździor, A. (2011). *Financial management in the enterprise.* Lublin: Politechnika Lubelska, pp. 235, 239.

Miszczuk, M., & Sosińska-Wit, M. (2017). *Otoczenie a wartość biznesu.* Lublin: Politechnika Lubelska, p. 7.

Paździor, A. (2015). *Zarządzanie wartością współczesnego przedsiębiorstwa.* Lublin: Politechnika Lubelska, pp. 9, 22, 101.

Rzemieniak, M. (2013). *Zarządzanie niematerialnymi wartościami przedsiębiorstw.* Toruń: Dom Organizatora, p. 11.

Szczepankowski, P. (2013). *Determinanty wartości rynkowej spółek kapitałowych wczesnej fazy rozwoju.* Warsaw: Vizja Press & IT Warsaw, pp. 39, 99.

Zastempowski, M., Glabiszewski, W., & Liczmańska-Kopcewicz, K. (2018). Makrootoczenie polskich MŚP w kontekście ich innowacyjności. *Organizacja i Kierowanie*, 2, 119–134.

14 Import Dependence and Machine Industry

Liubomyr Sozanskyi and Wiesława Caputa

Introduction

Mechanical engineering is one of the basic and strategic sectors of the Polish economy. According to the data (CSOP, 2021), mechanical engineering accounted for 41% of the exports and 43.4% of the imports of Poland's processing industry in 2020. The vast majority of the country's machine-building products are exported throughout the EU; in 2020, 76.5% of the country's machine-building products were exported to other EU countries. Among machine-building industries, motor vehicles, trailers, and semi-trailers (code NACE C29) were the most exported to EU countries; in 2020, this figure stood at 83.8%. At the same time, EU countries account for 49.8% of this country's machine-building imports. In the structure of the export and import of mechanical engineering in Poland, the share of manufactured motor vehicle, trailer, and semi-trailer products prevails; in 2020, this production accounted for 47.1% of the exports and 39.9% of the imports of the machine-building products of the country. Among all of the EU countries, Poland occupies a high position in terms of the export and import of machine-building products; in particular, Poland ranked seventh in the EU in its volume of exports of machine-building products and fourth in terms of its volume of corresponding imports in 2019 according to the data (Eurostat, 2022).

The activity of this sector plays a decisive role in the innovative and socio-economic development of the country. The importance of mechanical engineering is determined by the following aspects: *first*, mechanical engineering is the sector with the greatest potential for creating and implementing all kinds of innovations; *second*, mechanical engineering is potentially the center of cross-sectoral connections of the economic system – this is due to the fact that mechanical engineering is connected with almost all of sectors of the economy through the consumption of each other's intermediate consumption products; *third*, mechanical engineering is the only sector of the economy that produces production assets (machines, equipment, tools, etc.) for all sectors of the economy (as is widely known, no sector of the economy will be able to achieve technological advantages in foreign and domestic markets without modern basic means of production); and *fourth*, close cross-sectoral connections and the innovative potential of mechanical

DOI: 10.4324/9781003475583-19

engineering can potentially have the greatest multiplier effect on the adjacent sectors and the socio-economic development of the country in general (Ishchuk & Sozanskyy, 2021).

However, only large industrial economies can achieve significant success in machine building under the conditions of economic globalization and instability (and the Polish economy can be considered to be one of them) therefore. First of all, this can be explained by the fact that Poland is an industrial country with considerable experience and potential in mechanical engineering. The first enterprises for producing electric machines in the territory of modern Poland arose during the 70s and 80s of the 19th century. The oldest enterprise for producing electric machines (the Roberta factory Roberta Gülchera in Białej) began operation in 1876 and was engaged in the repair and manufacture of textile machinery (Hickiewicz, 2021). However, Polish mechanical engineering has functioned and developed under the influence of many complex systemic factors during the recent decades that have significantly weakened the technological and innovative prospects of Polish mechanical engineering. First of all, this is about the transformation of the state and economic system in 1989, the accession of Poland into the EU in 2004, the consequences of the global financial and economic crisis of 2008, the European recession of 2015, and the pandemic that was caused by COVID-19. The impact of these processes on the functioning of Poland's mechanical engineering is a multifaceted issue that requires a more detailed study from the standpoint of the role of Polish mechanical engineering in the innovativeness of Poland's economy and security.

Research Results

Trends in Polish Mechanical Engineering

One of the largest and most important sectors of Polish engineering is the automobile industry; however, significant transformations have taken place in this engineering sector in recent decades. In particular, the automotive industry of Poland was reoriented from the production of full-cycle cars to the supplier of individual services or parts. As a result, the production of once-famous brands of passenger cars (the Polonez, Fiat 126p, and FSO 1300 and 1500) disappeared, and the number of cars that were manufactured in Poland decreased sharply. According to the data (CSOP, 2021), 279,000 passenger cars were manufactured in Poland in 2020; this was more than three times fewer than in 2008 (842,000 units). On the other hand, Poland ranks fifth in the EU in terms of the volume of the production of various parts and spare parts for cars. In 2018, 59% of the Polish automotive industry's production was spare parts and accessories for cars (as compared to 41% in 2005). At the same time, about 80%–85% of the Polish automotive industry's products are exported to the European country's markets or businesses (accounting for 32 billion euros). The main place in the development of the

Polish automobile industry is occupied by foreign companies; these account for 95% of the largest firms in this sector (Zduniuk, 2019). Polish companies that are involved in the automotive industry have increasingly become specialized in the production of metal products, electrical devices, and various parts, and they are gradually increasing their involvement in product design and development. At the same time, experts believe that Poland needs to start producing its own cars in order to rise above the level of a supplier of spare parts and accessories (Raporty Specjalne, 2018). On the other hand, national Polish automobile enterprises suffer from a lack of investment, low innovation, technology and the digitization of their production processes (Ostrowski, 2021), high competition, the overproduction of cars, and profit reductions due to increases in the costs of materials (Włodarczyk & Janczewski, 2014).

Poland is a maritime country that is located at the crossroads of trade routes, and it has potential and experience in shipbuilding; however, 7,300 GTs of seagoing ships were produced in 2020 as compared to 722,000 in 2005 (CSOP, 2021). Marine engineering in a maritime state is a strategic sector of its economy; therefore, a country should be provided with national products as much as possible for the purposes of its economic security. In addition, it should be taken into account that the multiplier effect on the economy of shipbuilding may even exceed that of automobile production. The ship-production process is interconnected with almost all sectors of industry, science, and the IT sphere and has very high potential for producing and implementing all kinds of innovations. In this regard, the decrease in the number of manufactured high-tech engineering products (passenger cars and sea ships) can be considered one of the important factors that restrains production and product innovations in Poland.

At the same time, the production of some less-technological and -innovative types of machine-building products has grown recently. In particular, the production of vehicles for public transport increased to 6,000 units in 2020 (as opposed to 1,800 units in 2003). The number of cargo semi-trailers produced in Poland increased to 166,000 units in 2020 (as compared to 55,400 units in 2009). It follows from this that there has been a decrease in the technological level of Polish mechanical engineering over the last 20–30 years.

Most machine-building products in Poland are produced in four regions of the country: the Silesian, Mazovian, Greater Poland, and Lower Silesian voivodeships. In particular, more than 66% of Poland's machine-building industrial products were produced in these voivodeships in 2020 (CSOP, 2021). On the other hand, more than 75% of the country's machine-building industrial products were produced in these same regions in 2010. It follows that the regional structure of Poland's mechanical engineering industry has undergone a transformation over the past ten years. First of all, this has been due to the significant decrease in the shares of two old industrial regions (the Silesian and Lower Silesian voivodeships). The share of the former decreased by 10.1 p.p. (percentage points) over the ten years, and the share of the latter decreased by 5.1 p.p.

At the same time, there were noticeable increases in the shares of the Lódz, Lesser Poland, Mazovian, Subcarpathian, and Greater Poland voivodeships.

Low Innovation and Import Dependance

A decrease in manufacturability also causes a decrease in the innovativeness of products in mechanical engineering. In particular, the share of enterprises that introduced product innovations out of the total number of innovative machine-building enterprises in Poland was almost the lowest in the EU in 2018 according to the data (Eurostat, 2022). The value of this indicator for the most important machine-building industry in Poland (the production of motor vehicles, trailers, and semi-trailers) was 23.9%; in Germany, this was 47.0%, in France – 45.5%, and in Italy – 48.0%. According to this indicator, Poland was ahead of only Romania, Slovakia, Latvia, and Greece among the EU countries.

One of the most important indicators of product efficiency and competitiveness is the share of new or significantly improved products that are new to the market out of the total volume of innovative products. According to this indicator, Poland's mechanical engineering was also among the outsiders of the EU. In particular, this indicator for the production of motor vehicles, trailers, and semi-trailers in Poland was 4.7% in 2018, while the same indicator was 12.8% in Germany, 15.1% in Italy, 27.2% in Belgium, and 36.9% in Portugal. It is important to note that, according to the data (CSOP, 2021), the same indicator was 13% for Poland in 2006. It follows that, during the period of 2006–2018, the share of products that were new to the market out of the volume of innovative products of the production of motor vehicles, trailers, and semi-trailers in Poland experienced a nearly threefold decrease.

A similar situation was observed by the indicator of the share of costs for innovation in the amount of new or significantly improved products. In Poland's mechanical engineering, this indicator was 11.2% in 2018, while it was 25.1% in Germany and 23.9% in France.

Innovative activity in mechanical engineering is one of the main indicators of the competitiveness of products and activities of this industry sector. The low innovative activity and innovativeness of products as well as insufficient costs for innovations indirectly testify to the low multiplier effect of machine building on the socio-economic sphere of the country.

The considered processes (transformational trends and low innovativeness) can be interconnected (being a cause and effect at the same time) with one more extremely important feature – excessively high control by foreign companies and TNCs of machine-building activities in Poland. Thus, 77.4% of the mechanical engineering products that were produced in Poland were controlled by foreign enterprises in 2018 according to the data (Eurostat, 2022); this accounted for 70.7% in 2008. Most of Poland's machine-building products are controlled by German enterprises and EU countries in general. In particular, 50.7% of Poland's mechanical engineering production was controlled by enterprises from other EU countries in 2018. At the same time,

German enterprises controlled 21.4% of Poland's machine-building products. The described situation gives us reason to believe that Polish mechanical engineering (which is the foundation of the economy, the key base of the production and implementation of innovations, and the main strategic sector of the economy) is controlled by foreign enterprises in the vast majority. In addition to mechanical engineering, the economy of Poland is generally under the significant control of foreign enterprises. According to the data (Eurostat, 2022), 36.97% of the added value of enterprises in the Polish economy was controlled by foreign enterprises in 2018 (as opposed to 32.98% in 2009); this was 9.01 p.p. higher than the EU-27 indicator (which was 23.97% in 2018). On the other hand, this figure was 18.52% in Germany, 16.97% in France, and 16.12% in Italy. At the same time, the same indicators were within a range of 40%–50% in such countries as the Czech Republic, Estonia, Luxembourg, Hungary, Romania, and Slovakia. Under conditions of instability, increased control of Poland's economy by foreign enterprises is a threat to the country's economic security.

Under the influence of economic globalization, Polish mechanical engineering has joined global value chains over the past 20 years; this has contributed to increases in employment as well as the output and export of mechanical engineering. At the same time, the other side of economic globalization is the increased dependence of machine-building industries on the import of intermediate consumption products. In order to determine the dependence of Polish engineering on the import of intermediate consumption products in terms of the types of economic activity, Ishchuk, Caputa, and Sozansky *created an indicator of the share of imports in the costs of engineering production* (Ishchuk et al., 2020). According to the calculated data of this indicator, the share of imports out of the costs of the general mechanical engineering of Poland (code NACE D26–D30) is 48.3%; in Germany, this is 31.3%. These figures can be considered to be high (but not critical) levels of import dependence of the machine-building in these countries. However, if we consider the dependence of machine-building on the import of products of individual sectors (the products of which are used by machine-building industries), then this situation is significantly different. Fossil energy resources are one of the most important sectors – the products of which are used in machine-building and significantly affect the price competitiveness of machine-building products. As a result of many factors (including political ones), Polish and German mechanical engineering is critically and dangerously dependent on the import of fossil energy resources, the mining sector, and quarrying, energy producing products (D05T06), mining and quarrying, non-energy-producing products (D07T08), and mining support service activities (D09). In particular, the shares of imports in the mining sector product support service activities (D09) that are consumed by machine building in Poland and Germany are 100%. The production of the D05T06 and D07T08 sectors that is used in mechanical engineering (D26–D30) in Poland is supplied by 73.0% imports; in Germany, this level is 92.2% (Table 14.1).

Table 14.1 Share of imports in costs of mechanical engineering in Poland and Germany in 2018 (%)

Industry/Sector	D26		D27		D28		D29		D30		D26–D30	
	Pol	*Ger*	*Pol*	*Ger*	*Pol*	*Ger*	*Pol*	*Ger*	*Pol*	*Ger*	*Pol*	*Ger*
D01T02: Agriculture, hunting, and forestry	21.3	38.3	13.5	40.1	14.4	40.3	19.0	27.6	9.6	46.7	15.6	35.0
D03: Fishing and aquaculture	0.0	100.0	0.0	66.7	50.0	70.6	66.7	70.6		100.0	42.9	70.8
D05T06: Mining and quarrying, energy producing products	90.0	92.9	78.7	93.2	62.7	93.5	54.4	92.2	56.4	93.1	73.0	93.2
D07T08: Mining and quarrying, non-energy-producing products	16.0	87.4	9.5	92.2	6.0	95.9	4.2	86.8	3.5	85.3	7.3	92.2
D09: Mining support service activities	100	100	100	100	100	97.06	100	100		100	100	98.8
D10T12: Food products, beverages, and tobacco	14.5	22.4	16.7	26.1	16.8	27.9	19.2	26.4	17.5	28.8	17.2	26.5
D13T15: Textiles, textile products, leather, and footwear	45.2	53.9	57.2	49.4	63.9	55.7	65.8	63.1	69.8	63.3	65.1	60.7
D16: Wood and products of wood and cork	19.0	26.3	18.6	27.5	18.4	27.0	19.4	28.9	17.6	24.1	18.7	26.4
D17T18: Paper products and printing	35.6	28.9	33.3	29.1	34.0	24.8	32.8	20.3	33.5	24.8	33.4	25.7
D19: Coke and refined petroleum products	24.8	43.7	28.4	43.1	27.4	45.8	27.0	47.6	26.4	44.0	27.2	45.8
D20: Chemical and chemical products	69.0	60.0	71.3	55.6	70.5	58.4	69.7	60.7	70.5	58.0	70.4	59.3
D21: Pharmaceuticals, medicinal chemical, and botanical products	49.5	21.2	46.7	16.6	53.7	22.1	69.3	19.1	48.8	24.0	58.6	20.2
D22: Rubber and plastic products	43.6	30.9	42.9	31.9	40.9	31.5	42.7	32.0	40.8	32.0	42.6	31.8
D23: Other non-metallic mineral products	21.8	20.6	20.6	21.1	21.0	22.0	21.5	22.9	20.1	19.9	21.0	22.0
D24: Basic metals	70.9	53.5	69.1	49.8	59.0	42.3	57.6	40.6	58.3	42.5	62.0	43.5
D25: Fabricated metal products	32.1	19.3	30.7	21.4	30.8	20.4	31.2	20.7	29.1	18.2	30.9	20.3
D26: Computer, electronics, and optical equipment	**87.5**	**80.2**	**78.1**	**77.4**	**76.5**	**73.5**	**80.4**	**63.1**	**77.7**	**53.2**	**85.6**	**76.4**
D27: Electrical equipment	**72.4**	**42.9**	**72.5**	**46.8**	**70.4**	**42.0**	**65.9**	**43.1**	**68.6**	**34.7**	**71.2**	**44.3**
D28: Machinery and equipment	**79.4**	**26.5**	**78.5**	**30.2**	**85.6**	**31.1**	**77.9**	**29.1**	**80.6**	**28.5**	**81.2**	**30.4**

D29: Motor vehicles, trailers, and semi-trailers	**50.8**	**39.7**	**46.6**	**43.3**	**61.0**	**36.5**	**75.7**	**35.1**	**68.3**	**17.7**	**74.7**	**35.2**
D30: Other transport equipment	**44.0**	**32.5**	**23.9**	**47.7**	**25.2**	**35.6**	**33.8**	**35.9**	**66.3**	**61.5**	**62.2**	**60.3**
D31T33: Manufacturing nec.; repair and installation of machinery and equipment	34.6	24.0	18.1	14.9	12.3	13.3	17.5	13.0	12.5	22.5	16.4	15.2
D35: Electricity, gas, steam, and air conditioning supply	8.9	2.2	6.7	2.9	3.9	2.7	3.8	2.3	3.3	2.7	4.7	2.5
D36T39: Water supply – sewerage, waste management, and remediation activities	6.9	6.0	5.9	9.0	3.3	7.1	5.5	5.1	3.3	14.5	4.9	6.6
D41T43: Construction	8.0	4.3	2.0	7.1	2.9	6.4	5.2	5.1	2.8	13.8	3,4	6.0
D45T47: Wholesale and retail trade – repair of motor vehicles	33.5	28.4	27.8	28.5	29.0	29.1	28.4	30.3	28.8	32.1	29.1	29.7
D49: Land transport and transport via pipelines	24.3	37.5	20.8	36.7	21.7	36.6	18.8	37.9	20.8	36.0	20.9	37.1
D50: Water transport	68.7	35.6	65.7	35.6	66.9	30.6	68.8	69.1	85.9	27.7	69.4	48.5
D51: Air transport	51.1	95.9	45.8	94.6	46.1	95.2	44.9	91.7	52.9	92.8	47.3	94.4
D52: Warehousing and support activities for transportation	27.6	14.0	21.4	17.9	24.6	14.7	21.5	11.0	25.0	27.7	23.1	13.8
D53: Postal and courier activities	21.9	7.4	18.5	7.5	18.8	7.5	22.1	8.0	16.7	10.4	20.0	7.6
D55T56: Accommodation and food service activities	18.0	2.6	3.5	3.6	3.0	1.7	10.0	4.1	3.4	8.8	5.7	2.8
D58T60: Publishing, audiovisual, and broadcasting activities	31.6	32.8	29.4	35.4	31.5	35.6	32.1	36.5	30.0	27.6	30.9	34.7
D61: Telecommunications	50.0	8,9	15.5	8.4	17.1	8.0	17.3	7.2	17.2	7.6	19.5	8.0
D62T63: IT and other information services	48.1	32.0	38.6	31.9	38.0	32.1	42.0	30.9	37.7	31.2	41.2	31.6
D64T66: Financial and insurance activities	12.2	12.7	11.4	14.1	10.3	12.6	13.3	12.4	11.0	12.9	11.9	12.7

(Continued)

Table 14.1 (Continued)

Industry/Sector	D26		D27		D28		D29		D30		D26–D30	
	Pol	*Ger*	*Pol*	*Ger*	*Pol*	*Ger*	*Pol*	*Ger*	*Pol*	*Ger*	*Pol*	*Ger*
D68: Real estate activities	4.1	1.3	2.7	1.3	2.9	1.2	4.4	1.2	2.3	1.6	3.2	1,2
D69T75: Professional, scientific, and technical activities	20.9	16.0	17.4	14.9	19.3	12.2	21.7	12.6	18.9	17.2	19.5	13.4
D77T82: Administrative and support services	5.4	6.0	6.5	6.2	8.2	5.8	7.7	5.9	7.6	5.8	7.1	5.9
D84: Public administration and defense – compulsory social security	5,6	3.7	8.3	3.3	9.4	6.3	14.9	3.5	7.5	7.6	9.3	4.3
D85: Education	4.1	5.0	2.5	2.5	4.3	4.5	5.7	1.5	4.2	3.2	3.7	2.4
D86T88: Human health and social work activities	31.6	21.0	10.0	27.0	7.7	23.5	14.3	10.1	6.9	23.8	12.5	16.9
D90T93: Arts, entertainment, and recreation	37.5	29.2	28.6	27.5	21.1	22.5	38.5	16.7	11.7	26.2	26.7	20.9
D94T96: Other service activities	9.4	3.1	3.8	3.9	2.6	4.7	8.1	4.7	3.3	7.1	5.1	4.3
For all sectors of economy	59.9	39.3	43.6	34.2	42.0	28.8	50.2	29.9	42.2	37.5	48.3	31.3

Source: Author's calculations based on data (OECD, 2022).

Note: The bold text emphasizes the data relevant to the topic covered in this chapter.

Chemical is also an important sector – the products of which are consumed in mechanical engineering and chemical products (D20). However, these products are covered by 70.4% imports in Poland and 59.3% in Germany.

The technologies, machines, electrical equipment, and computer communications that are used in mechanical engineering or in the products of machine-building industries have a decisive influence on the manufacturability and innovativeness of machine-building products (D26–D30). However, it is precisely on these productions that the highest import dependence of Polish engineering lies. The products from the computer, electronic, and optical equipment (D26) sectors that are used in mechanical engineering (D26–D30) in Poland is 85.6% imports; in Germany, this level is 76.4%. The share of imports in the electrical sector equipment (D27) that is used in mechanical engineering in Poland is 71.1% (and 44.3% in Germany). Also, the dependence of Poland's machine-building industry on the import of the intermediate consumption products of the other three machine-building industries is no less high.

The high dependence of the Polish machine-building industry on the import of high-tech products and fossil energy carriers is one of the main reasons for the high dependence of the Polish economy on the import of intermediate consumption machine-building products. The aforementioned dependence on the import of intermediate consumption products is reflected by the authors' *indicator of the share of imports in the intermediate consumption of the sectors of the economy* (Ishchuk, Caputa, & Sozansky, 2020). The following analytical conclusions follow from the results of the conducted assessment. Compared to the German economy, the Polish economy is almost twice as dependent on the import of the machine-building products of intermediate consumption. This is clearly illustrated by the following indicators: the share of imports in the products of intermediate consumption in general *mechanical engineering (D26–D30)* that is consumed by the general economy in Poland is 71.7%, while it is only 38.6% in Germany. Therefore, Polish mechanical engineering provides only 28.3% of the needs of the Polish economy in the machine-building products of intermediate consumption; on the other hand, this figure is 61.4% in Germany. This gives reason to assert that the general level of the dependence of the Polish economy on the import of the machine-building products (D26–D30) of intermediate consumption is critically high and may create risks for the balanced economic functioning and security of Poland under conditions of global instability. The Polish economy is excessively and critically dependent on the intermediate consumption products of all of its machine-building industries.

Separately, it is important to emphasize that the key sectors in which the Polish economy specializes (which are of strategic importance for it) are also critically dependent on the import of the machine-building products of intermediate consumption. In particular, one of the key segments of the Polish economy is undoubtedly the agro-industrial sector; unfortunately, 76.7% of the machine-building products in general (D26–D30) that are used in this sector are imported. At the same time, the corresponding figure in Germany is only 30%. The agro-industrial sector of Poland is excessively dependent on the import of machine-building products of all of its machine-building industries. In particular, machinery and equipment (D28) is a sector that specializes in the production of machines, tools, and agricultural equipment. The share of agriculture, hunting, and forestry (D01T02) in the structure of the consumption of products of the intermediate consumption of the machinery sector and equipment, (D28) is 4.64%. At the same time, 85.6% of the intermediate consumption products of the machinery sector and equipment, (D28) that are used in the agriculture, hunting, and forestry sector (D01T02) of Poland are imported; in Germany, this figure is only 29.8%.

One of the important sectors with which the Polish economy is associated is the food industry (or food sector products, beverages, and tobacco – D10T12). In modern economic conditions, the specificity of this sector largely depends on the depth of the processing of raw materials, the level of technology, and the innovation of products (in addition to the cost of labor and the quality of the agricultural raw materials). In turn, innovation depends on the machines, special industrial equipment, and tools that are produced in the machinery sector and equipment (D28). Thus, it can be argued that the technological competitive advantages of the food industry depend on the products of the machinery sector and equipment (D28). Therefore, the products of the national food industry can be competitive in the markets of highly developed economies for the most part – provided that the technology that is used in this industry is competitive. If the corresponding equipment is imported, it is very difficult to raise the level of the competitiveness of the food industry above the levels of the countries from which this equipment is imported. However, we stated that 71.9% of the production of the intermediate consumption of the machinery sector and equipment (D28) that is used in the food products, beverages, and tobacco sector (D10T12) in Poland is imported; in Germany, the same figure is only 21.7%. In other words, if we take the fact that the machines and equipment that are used in the Polish food industry are mainly imported from Germany into account, then the competitiveness of the technological parameters of the products of the Polish food industry can only be equal to (but not exceed) that of Germany.

Wood processing and paper production are also important segments of the Polish manufacturing industry and economy. The machines, machinery, and equipment for the woodworking industry (as well as for most segments of the processing industry) are also provided by the machinery sector and equipment (D28). Unfortunately, this technique is also almost entirely imported. In particular, 64.9% of the intermediate consumption products of the machinery sector and equipment (D28) that is used in the wood sector and the products of wood and cork (D16) in Poland are imported; and in the paper sector, products, and printing (D17T18), the corresponding indicator is 80.9%. In Germany, the same indicators in the mentioned sectors are 8.2 and 20.5%, respectively.

The high dependence on the imports of the intermediate consumption products of the machinery sector and equipment (D28) and other machine-building industries is typical for the vast majority of manufacturing industries and other important strategic sectors of the Polish economy.

Conclusions and Recommendations

The high dependence of Polish machine-building and key sectors of the Polish economy on the import of high-tech machine-building products is considered – along with the fact that the vast majority of the machine-building products that are produced in this country are controlled by foreign enterprises and transnational corporations under the conditions and influence of global instability, economic and military confrontations, fierce competition for new markets, and economic and political spheres of influence; resources can be considered to be threats to the economic and social development of Poland and, therefore, to the country's security. In this regard, it is quite necessary to review the criteria and benchmarks of the country's economic development in the direction of the import substitution of basic products of intermediate consumption. Let us emphasize that, in addition to the mentioned risks, the high import dependence of machine-building on basic machine-building products as well as fossil energy carriers hold back and do not provide opportunities for innovative breakthroughs and the development of both the economy in general and its main sectors.

The identified and described features and trends of Polish engineering are particularly dangerous under conditions of acute global instability and the full-scale Russian–Ukrainian war and its corresponding consequences for the economic and social sphere of the neighboring countries (in particular, Poland) and the world in general.

It follows from the considered study that, in order to reduce the dependence of the Polish economy and engineering on the import of high-tech products and, thus, increase the innovativeness of the economy and the products of our enterprises, it is necessary to take such measures and actions.

1 *The development and implementation of a state protectionist policy on stimulating the development and protection of domestic engineering.* In particular, it is about utilizing public orders more actively, partnerships between the public and private sectors, fiscal, economic, and organizational incentives for the production of domestic basic machine-building products (engines, semiconductors, and electronics), expansion of value chains within the country, and the substitution of imports in strategic sectors of the economy (in other words, to adhere to Keynes' idea of "National Self-sufficiency"). The adoption of such measures will contribute to reducing the dependence on the import of high-tech products as well as contribute to the growth of the wages and innovative products of Polish enterprises;

2 *The unification of machine-building and the related enterprises in a self-organization for better cooperation among themselves in the direction of creating the most complete production cycle factories within Poland.* To some extent, this study aims to inform small and medium-sized businesses in Poland about the high level of the dependence of the Polish economy and mechanical engineering on imports as well as the economic security risks that arise from this. Perhaps such information will become a signal – an incentive for better cooperation between domestic machine-building enterprises in the direction of developing and realizing national potential. It is clear that a sector such as mechanical engineering cannot be created only by the market itself under the influence of supply and demand. In all of the leading machine-building countries (the USA, Germany, Great Britain, France, Japan, South Korea, and China), this sector is being formed with the help of public-private partnerships, open and hidden protectionist policies, significant public and private investments, etc.; thus, both the enterprises and the state should join in the development of Polish mechanical engineering. In addition to their own business interests, all business entities must also take care of the country's economic security; only such an approach will make it possible to achieve a higher innovative and socio-economic development of the country in general, making it easier to face the modern challenges of global instability;
3 *The control of the activities of transnational corporations.* Transnational corporations have a significant influence on the Polish economy and mechanical engineering. On the one hand, such corporations create a significant number of jobs in the country; on the other hand, transnational corporations cooperate only with their own branches in other countries. The Polish economy interests them only because of the comparatively lower levels of wages; thus, increasing the levels of wages of Poles is disadvantageous to transnational corporations. Given their high presence in the country, they can play a restraining role in the socio-economic growth of the country. In this regard, the state should apply regulatory, fiscal, economic, and informational incentives for the more active cooperation of transnational corporations with domestic enterprises, raising the levels of the wages and working conditions of transnational corporations and increasing the tax burden for and social responsibility of their activities;
4 *The implementation of public and public-private investments in Industry 4.0 technologies.* Modern mechanical engineering and innovative economic progress are impossible without a wide application of Industry 4.0 technologies. Investments in Industry 4.0 technologies are long-term and risky; at the same time, however, future innovative and financial progress depends on them; this is why the main investor and co-organizer of developing and implementing Industry 4.0 technologies should be the state. This will have a direct impact on increasing the implementation and improvement of all types of innovations among the small, medium, and large enterprises in Poland.

References

CSOP. (2021). Official site of the Central Statistical Office of Poland. http://stat.gov.pl

Eurostat. (2022). Official website of Eurostat. https://appsso.eurostat.ec.europa.eu/

Hickiewicz, J. (2021). Początki przemysłu maszyn elektrycznych w polsce do 1939 roku w 100-lecie powstania fabryki w żychlinie. *Maszyny Elektryczne – Zeszyty Problemowe*, Nr 2/126. https://yadda.icm.edu.pl/baztech/element/bwmeta1.element.baztech-b3f3bc6b-1890-4468-8f8b-6c51d366f6e3

OECD. (2022). OECD Statistics.https://stats.oecd.org/

Ostrowski, A. (2021). Industry machine: Better prospects, chance and I will correct results [Report 2021]. https://magazynprzemyslowy.pl/artykuly/przemysl-maszynowy-lepsze-perspektywy-szansa-na-poprawe-wynikow-raport-2021

Ishchuk, S., & Sozanskyy, L. (2021). Problems of mechanical engineering development in Ukraine // Zeszyty Naukowe Politechniki Częstochowskiej Zarządzanie. *Research Reviews of Czestochowa University of Technology – Management*, Nr 44, 10–24. https://zim.pcz.pl/znwz/archiwum.html

Ishchuk, S., Caputa, W., & Sozansky, L. (2020). The industrial sector in Ukraine and EU countries: Competitive advantages and structure optimization models: monograf/Wydawnictwo Wyższej Szkoły Bankowej w Poznaniu. 2020. Poznań. 265 pp. https://www.wydawnictwo.wsb.pl/node/581.

Raporty Specjalne. (2018). Ile yes Polish gene in motorization? https://forsal.pl/artykuly/1179563,ile-jest-polskiego-genu-w-motoryzacji.html

Włodarczyk, M., & Janczewski, J. (2014). Uwarunkowania rozwoju przedsiębiorczości W Polsce w branży motoryzacyjnej. *Przedsiębiorczość – Edukacja*, t. 10, grudzień 2014, s. 94–108. doi:10.24917/20833296.10.7

Zduniuk, K. (2019). Raport Bank Pekao: "*Nowa era motoryzacji*". https://www.pekao.com.pl/dam/jcr:59ba00a1-3940-4bbb-b329f55c25d8e0a7/Nowa%20era%20motoryzacji.%20Jak%20odnajdzie%20si%C4%99%20w%20niej%20polski%20przemys%C5%82.pdf

15 Patent Activity of Biotechnological and Pharmaceutical Companies from the WSE and NewConnect Markets during the COVID-19 Pandemic

Przemysław Sałek

Introduction

Patents have a very long and rich history. The first special legal protection for an invention was given to Filippo Brunelleschi, an architect in 1421, when Florence's City Council granted him a temporary monopoly on transporting heavy stone blocks down the Arno River in boats of his design (Hall, 2020). Since that time, much has changed in the way social and economic processes are conducted. However, one key element of industrial property management that remains unchanged is that patents for inventions allow inventors to commercially exploit their new devices or applications. Ownership of industrial property rights in the form of invention patents, design protection rights, or trademarks significantly translates into an improved financial performance of a company (Strojny, 2021).

By definition, a *patent* confers "the right to the exclusive use of an invention for a specified period of time, in a commercial (industrial) manner in the territory of a given state or states, granted by a competent state, regional or international authority" (UPRP). In Poland, such a right is granted by the Patent Office of the Republic of Poland. For companies seeking to bring innovative products or applications to market, there is most often a significant cost in money and time associated with its R&D. Therefore, the company (or inventor) should be given a "reward" for the financial and labor expenditures incurred. A patent thus provides a guarantee to the innovator that, although the invention has been publicly disclosed, no one will be able to use or copy it without the permission of the rights holder (Adamczak & Gędłek, 2009). In addition, obtaining patent protection allows the company not only to recoup its expenses but also stimulates further innovative work on commercializing new solutions.

Exercising the right to patent an invention is particularly important for biotechnological[1] and pharmaceutical companies. Biotechnology is a combination of two fields, biology and technology. In practice, biotechnology involves the use of living organisms to obtain new products and innovative

DOI: 10.4324/9781003475583-20

manufacturing processes (Polska Federacja Biotechnologii [Polish Federation of Biotechnology]). The pharmaceutical industry, in turn, is responsible for the discovery, development, production, and marketing of drugs and medical devices. In addition to serving an important function in the economy, the pharmaceutical sector secures the population's basic health needs (Polska Agencja Rozwoju Przedsiębiorczości [Polish Agency for Enterprise Development]). The activities of biotechnology and pharmaceutical companies in the area of broader health care contribute to improving people's lives. Biotechnological inventions are making important contributions to the research on many serious diseases, and their research is mainly used for medical purposes (Borowik, 2017). A similar, not inconsiderable, impact on people's lives is being made by new drugs discovered by pharmaceutical companies to help cure or prevent more and more diseases.

The importance of biotech and pharmaceutical companies was further increased when, in March 2020, the World Health Organization (WHO) officially announced that a pandemic of COVID-19, caused by the coronavirus, had begun. As a consequence of the global spread of the disease, as well as the rapid increase in the number of sick people, individual countries began to shut down their economies by implementing lockdowns. Domestic lockdowns had very negative effects on the functioning of individual economies (Goolsbee & Syverson, 2020), including decreased consumer activity, increased unemployment, and decreased investments. At that time, biotechnology and pharmaceutical companies, which were expected to develop vaccines, drugs, texts, and other products to counter COVID-19, began to receive more attention. A sign of greater interest in these companies in Poland was the increase of about 20% in the WIG-leki index from the Warsaw Stock Exchange in the first year of the pandemic (from 11 March 2020, the date on which the WHO recognized the pandemic, to 31 December 2020).

The peculiarities of the biotechnology and pharmaceutical industries, as well as the increased patent activity worldwide during the pandemic period, prompted the author of this paper to analyze patent activity on a national basis and find answers to two research questions: (1) Which biotech and pharmaceutical companies listed on the WSE and NewConnect markets received the most patents (for the most inventions) during the COVID-19 pandemic? (2) Were the patents received by these biotech and pharmaceutical companies related to the COVID-19 pandemic?

Literature Review

According to the literature, there are three basic ways to commercialize an invention: (1) sell the technology license, (2) sell the technology itself, or (3) start a new company and enter the market with a new product (Studziński, 2021). However, in order to get to the point at which one decides to fully pursue the path of commercialization and take full advantage of the opportunities it would offer, biotech and pharmaceutical companies, like all others, must apply for a patent for an invention.

The most important argument in favor of patenting, both internationally and domestically, is that companies working on industrial innovations should have a chance to recoup the costs of their inventions. Because patents grant market exclusivity to a company, they provide such an opportunity and, in addition, encourage the further application of resources to industrial R&D. This, in turn, should increase the level of commercialization of industrial innovations (Moir & Hsu, 2013).

The scientific debate on corporate patent activity began in the second half of the 1980s when it was combined with the topic of intellectual property law. The key topics covered included the impact of intellectual property rights on innovation, the place that intellectual property issues occupy in developed countries, and the need for the international harmonization of laws governing these issues. In the ensuing decades, research on the topic of intellectual property rights and patent activity has been energized by, among other things, a surge in patent filings (Lopez, 2009).

Research on the patent activity of companies operating in Poland and around the world is becoming increasingly popular, and this is influenced by, among other things, the progressive digitization of patent databases. Many patent databases, including those provided by the Patent Office of the Republic of Poland, can be accessed online, and no additional fees are required (Wściubiak, 2018). The increasing availability of patent databases is popularizing research about patent activity. However, patent databases differ in many respects and are classified in many ways. One of these is classification by source: (1) patent information databases of national patent offices, such as UPRP; (2) patent information databases of international organizations, such as World Intellectual Property Organization (WIPO); or (3) patent information databases developed by private entities, such as Clarivate (Strojny, 2021).

Using patent data from multiple patent offices from 2000 to 2008 for Canadian companies, Fan and Zhao (2022) found that companies' propensity to patent was related to their age and size, as well as their R&D spending and profitability, among other factors. In turn, the patent activity of listed companies was important insofar as information about granted patents could positively affect their stock prices in various capital markets. Thus, when a given company receives a patent it strengthens its competitive position and is better perceived by potential investors. It has been proven that for companies listed in the United States, every time a patent is confirmed in rulings, stock prices rise by an average of 1% (Harhoff, 2009).

In their study, Kanesarajah and White (2020) showed that during the first year of the COVID-19 pandemic, the patent activities of most organizations remained high, but some entities (26%) admitted that their patent research activities had undergone some transformations. It was pointed out that in the patent activity, there was, among other things, a change in priorities in terms

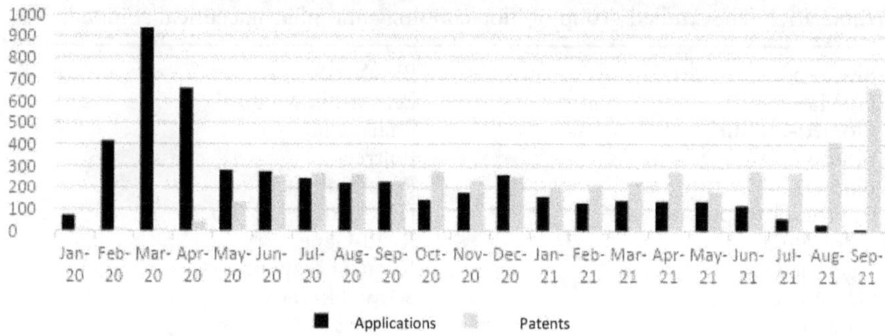

Figure 15.1 Patent applications and granted patents related to COVID-19 (global snapshot)

Source: World Intellectual Property Organization (WIPO) based on data from CAS Content Collection, September 2021.

of patent applications filed, and there were more frequent collaborations with external partners; this increased the scale of operations and expanded the research teams.

The research and innovation efforts undertaken since the beginning of the pandemic to counter COVID-19 were evident in terms of patent activity. Numerous entities were active in terms of both filing patent applications and receiving patents. Globally, the first patent applications were filed and patents were received as early as January 2020 (Figure 15.1), that is, before the WHO officially recognized the COVID-19 pandemic. According to a WIPO survey, patent activity related to COVID-19 included patent applications for inventions in diagnostics, masks and surface disinfectants, and vaccines. The average waiting time to receive a patent was 18 months.

Particularly noteworthy in the WIPO study is the fact that patent decisions were made relatively quickly. The rationale that may have influenced the accelerated decisions of patent offices from various countries may have been the uniqueness of the situation and the many negative consequences that the COVID-19 pandemic had on social and economic life. To encourage the development of inventions to help combat the new virus, many patent offices around the world introduced programs to prioritize COVID-19-related applications (Kanesarajah & White, 2020).

During the pandemic period, the impact that COVID-19 had on the returns of global biotech and pharmaceutical companies was also studied, showing the positive behavior of stock prices in the short term (Ozdurak et al., 2020).

Materials and Research Methodology

The main objective of the research described in the paper was to fill a cognitive gap in the analysis of the patent activity of biotechnology and pharmaceutical companies listed on the WSE and NewConnect markets.

Table 15.1 The studied group of biotechnology and pharmaceutical companies

Bioceltix	PBKM SA[a]
BioMaxima	Perma-Fix Medical
Biomed-Lublin	Pharmena
Bioton	Poltreg
Blirt	Pure Biologics
Captor Therapeutics	PZ Cormay
Celon Pharma	Read-Gene
Genomed	Ryvu Therapeutics
Genomtec	Scope Fluidics
genXone	Selvita
Krka	Sopharma
Mabion	Stem Cells Spin
Medicofarma Biotech	Synektik
NanoGroup	Urteste
Molecure[b]	

Source: Own compilation based on information from the WSE and the InfoStrefa portal.

[a] PBKM was delisted from the WSE in 2022.
[b] Before 2022, the company Molecure operated under the name OncoArendi Therapeutics.

The process of identifying the study group had two steps. The first was the qualification – as representatives of pharmaceutical companies – of companies clustered in the WIG-leki index. It is a sectoral index, which includes listed companies participating in the WIG index and at the same time classified as being in the sector of "drug manufacturing" ("GPW Benchmarkt", n.d.). At the time of the study, the WIG-leki included Celon Pharma, Mabion, Bioton, Krka, Biomed-Lublin, Cormay, Pharmena, and Sopharma. Biotechnology companies, on the other hand, included companies listed on the WSE and NewConnect markets, which the InfoStrefa portal classified as being in the "biotechnology" sector. The study excluded two biotechnology companies whose activities were significantly different from the so-called red biotechnology, which is related to health, medicine, and diagnostics. These companies were Cambridge Chocolate Technologies and Skotan (Table 15.1).

The main method of obtaining information on the patent activity of the biotechnology and pharmaceutical companies that qualified for the study was to analyze the content of current reports of listed companies. Companies on the Polish capital market have numerous disclosure obligations, the primary function of which is to

> ensure that current and future owners of financial instruments have access to relevant information about the public company and serve to eliminate information asymmetry among market participants. Information provided by companies provides investors with the basis for assessing the economic and financial situation of a particular issuer and its growth prospects.

The most important information from the perspective of capital market participants is provided by current reports, which are made available through the ESPI (Electronic System for Information Transmission) and EBI (Electronic Information Base) systems. In the current reports of biotech and pharmaceutical companies, one can also find information on the patent activity of the surveyed entities, including announcements of decisions on granted patents.

Current reports, which companies on the Polish capital market (i.e., companies listed on the WSE and NewConnect) are required to publish, concern events that are incidental in nature (Janowicz & Kędzierska, 2013) but have a significant impact on the company's operations. A content analysis of published current reports is used to identify many phenomena, such as the impairment of assets (Lisicki, 2021), or to obtain information on company mergers (Janowicz & Kędzierska, 2013). Current reports are also a rich source of data on patents, both those received by listed companies from various patent offices and those for which invention applications have been filed.

A content analysis of patent databases was additionally used to verify the data obtained from the content analysis of current reports. In this study, this was mainly the base of the Polish Patent Office. It primarily served to confirm that biotech and pharmaceutical companies for which no patent activity was identified during the period under review actually had no new patents granted.

In order to answer the research questions and achieve the main objective of the study, the following research hypotheses were established: (H1) Companies with the largest capitalization received the most patents during the COVID-19 pandemic period. (H2) Most of the patents received by biotech and pharmaceutical companies were not related to the COVID-19 pandemic.

The starting point of the data analysis period was set for early March 2020. It was in this month that the WHO declared COVID-19 to be a pandemic. The analysis covered a period of more than 2 years, until mid-April 2022.

Results and Discussion

During the period under review, eight biotechnology and pharmaceutical companies in the Polish capital market were identified as having received at least one patent and communicated this fact through a current report. These companies were Genomtec, Celon Pharma, Scope Fluidics, Pharmena, Read-Gene, Pure Biologics, Bioton, and Synektik (Table 15.2). They accounted for 28% of the surveyed sample.

Most of the companies that received patents were listed on the WSE market (63%). However, the largest number of patents received was identified for the NewConnect-listed company Genomtec. It is a company with little seniority in the Polish capital market, and as its debut took place on 17

Table 15.2 Patents received from 1 March 2020 to 15 April 2022

Company	*Number of patents received*	*Stock market*
Genomtec	5	NewConnect
Celon Pharma	4	GPW
Scope Fluidics	4	NewConnect
Pharmena	2	GPW
Read-Gene	2	NewConnect
Pure Biologics	1	GPW
Bioton	1	GPW
Synektik	1	GPW

Source: Own compilation based on information from current reports of listed companies.

March 2021. During the period under review, Genomtec informed investors through a current report five times that it had obtained a patent. Celon Pharma and Scope Fluidics also stand out positively compared with other biotech and pharmaceutical companies; four patents were obtained by each.

Among the identified communications on granted patents, no instances were found where a specific patent related to countering the COVID-19 pandemic. However, it was found that the biotech and pharmaceutical companies surveyed were undertaking pandemic-related activities. This was the case for 41% (12) companies, such as BioMaxima, Biomed-Lublin, Blirt, Celon Pharma, Genomtec, genXone, Mabion, Medicofarma Biotech, NanoGroup, Molecure, Pharmena, and Scope Fluidics. The indicated companies reported on activities related to the COVID-19 pandemic in the following areas in published current reports: (1) sales of tests or diagnostic kits to determine the presence of the coronavirus; (2) ongoing work on a drug for COVID-19; (3) undertaking work on drugs for complications from the coronavirus; and (4) establishing cooperation on the distribution of products related to COVID-19.

Seventeen percent of the surveyed companies reported in current reports on patent applications are filed with the patent office. From the beginning of March 2020 to mid-April 2022, only one such application was related to COVID-19. Pharmena's management filed a patent application for "the use of 1-MNA in the indication of viral infections and allergic diseases". This patent concerned the potential effect of 1-MNA on the effects of COVID-19 infection.

In order to determine whether there was a relationship between the receipt of patents during the period under study and the size of the company, a table was drawn up (Table 15.3) comparing the eight companies that received a minimum of one patent with the eight surveyed companies with the largest capitalization (i.e., market value). The only company that was included on both lists was Celon Pharma. Thus, no link could be established between the company's value and the patents it received during the period from the beginning of March 2020 to 15 April 2022.

Table 15.3 Comparison of companies with the largest number of patents received with companies with the largest capitalization

Company	*Number of patents received*	*Company*	*Capitalization[a] (in million PLN)*
Genomtec	5	Krka	13,740
Celon Pharma	4	Selvita	1,474
Scope Fluidics	4	Sopharma	1,414
Pharmena	2	*Celon Pharma*	1,281
Read-Gene	2	PBKM[b]	842
Pure Biologics	1	Ryvu therapeutics	815
Bioton	1	Captor Therapeutics	623
Synektik	1	Mabion	537

Source: Own compilation based on information from current reports of listed companies and data from the WSE.

[a] Status as of April 15, 2022.
[b] Capitalization at the date of delisting from the WSE.

Summary

The Polish capital market has a large group of biotechnology and pharmaceutical companies (41% of the sample) that communicated through current reports activity related to countering COVID-19, including working on a drug for COVID-19 and drugs for complications related to the transmission of the coronavirus, as well as selling tests to determine the presence of the new disease. However, biotech and pharmaceutical companies listed on the WSE and NewConnect markets showed relatively little inclination to obtain patent protection in this regard. Among the identified patents received by the surveyed companies, no patent related to COVID-19 was found. There was only one company which had filed a patent application (and announced it in the current report) related to COVID-19.

The study also found no relationship between the market value of biotech and pharmaceutical companies and the number of patents they received. Among the companies with the highest market value, only one of them, Celon Pharma, was among the companies that received a patent during the COVID-19 pandemic.

Note

1 This study analyzed companies involved in the so-called red biotechnology, that is, biotechnology related to health, medicine, and diagnostics, because such biotech companies dominate the Polish capital market. Other types of biotechnology pursue white biotechnology, which is related to industrial processes; green biotechnology, which is related to agriculture; blue biotechnology, which is related to bodies of water; or gray biotechnology, which is related to environmental protection. Biotechnology.co.uk, www.biotechnologia.pl/biotechnologia/barwy-biotechnologii, 17179 (02.05.2022).

References

Adamczyk, A., & Gędłek, M. (2009). *Znaki towarowe w działalności małych i średnich przedsiębiorstw.* Warszawa: Krajowa Izba Gospodarcza.

Borowik, M. (2017). Ochrona patentowa wynalazków biotechnologicznych w świetle zdefiniowania pojęcia embrionu ludzkiego w orzecznictwie TSUE. *Internetowy Przegląd Prawniczy TBSP UJ, 2*(32), 7.

Fan, D., & Zhao, L. (2022). Old wine in new bottles: Patenting propensity. *Journal of Industry, Competition And Trade, 22*(2), 207–224. doi: 10.1007/s10842-021-00377-1

Goolsbee, A., & Syverson, C. (2020). Fear, lockdown, and diversion: Comparing drivers of pandemic economic decline 2020. *SSRN Electronic Journal*, 1–7. doi: 10.2139/ssrn.3631180

Hall, B. (2020). Patents, innovation, and development. *SSRN Electronic Journal, 27203*, 3. doi: 10.2139/ssrn.3609655

Harhoff, D. (2009). The role of patents and licenses in securing external finance for innovation. *European Investment Bank (EIB), 14*(2), 80.

Janowicz, M., & Kędzierska, I. (2013). Informacje o połączeniach spółek w raportach bieżących spółek publicznych w latach 2004–2010. *Zeszyty Naukowe Uniwersytetu Szczecińskiego Finanse, Rynki Finansowe, Ubezpieczenia, 58*, 335–336.

Kanesarajah, V., & White, E. (2020). Chasing change: Innovation and patent activity during COVID-19. A report on the pandemic's impact on the global R&D community and innovation lifecycle. *Clarivate*, 7, 15. https://clarivate.com/derwent/blog/chasing-change-innovation-and-patent-activity-during-covid-19/ (accessed on 16 October 2020).

Lisicki, B. (2021). Wpływ skutków ekonomicznych pandemii COVID-19 na raportowanie utraty wartości aktywów na przykładzie spółek notowanych na Giełdzie Papierów Wartościowych w Warszawie. *Zeszyty Teoretyczne Rachunkowości, 113*, 190–191.

Lopez, A. (2009). Innovation and appropriability: Empirical evidence and research agenda. *The Economics of Intellectual Property*, 1–3.

Moir, H., & Hsu, P.-K. (2013). Tailoring patent policy for developing economies. *SSRN Electronic Journal.* doi: 10.2139/ssrn.2365761

Ozdurak, C., Alcan, G., & Guvenbas, S. (2020). The impact of COVID-19 to global pharmaceuticals and biotechnology company stocks returns. *Pressacademia, 9*(2), 68–79. doi: 10.17261/pressacademia.2020.1215

Strojny, M. (2021). Rosnąca rola informacji patentowej w zarządzaniu. *E-mentor, 89*(2), 48–49.

Studziński, A. (2021). *Od bionauki do biobiznesu.* Warszawa: CeDeWu.

WIPO. (2021). *COVID-19-related vaccines and therapeutics Preliminary insights on related patenting activity during the pandemic.* Switzerland: World Intellectual Property Organization, 13. doi: 10.34667/tind.45030

Wściubiak, Ł. (2018). Patent research in the innovation activity of manufacturing companies in Poland. *Studia I Prace Wneiz, 52*, 531–541. doi: 10.18276/sip.2018.52/2-41

Websites

Biotechnologia.pl. Retrieved 22 September 2022, from https://biotechnologia.pl/
Gpw.pl. Retrieved 22 September 2022, from https://www.gpw.pl/
Parkiet.com. Retrieved 22 September 2022, from https://www.parkiet.com/
PARP – Centrum Rozwoju MŚP. Retrieved 22 September 2022, from https://www.parp.gov.pl/
Stooq.pl. Retrieved 22 September 2022, from https://stooq.pl/
Urząd Patentowy RP. Retrieved 22 September 2022, from https://uprp.gov.pl/pl

16 Analysis of Changes in the Productivity of Fuel Companies in Poland during the COVID-19 Pandemic

Adrian Majek

Effective Management of a Business and Its Finances

Every operating economic entity has a set of goals that motivate it to achieve favorable results and provide opportunities for development. These goals may refer to various aspects. Some enterprises may be primarily focused on expansion and building their position in the market, while others strive to be innovation leaders and want to offer potential buyers products and solutions with contemporary properties (Buczkowska, 2012). However, the most common objectives are finance-related. Those responsible for managing a given entity try to manage it so as to maintain financial liquidity, and, in the long-term perspective of their activity, they are oriented toward maximizing their own value (Janik & Paździor, 2011).

All these aspirations can be achieved by fulfilling numerous conditions, which a given individual may or may not be able to influence. One of the aspects that depend on an individual includes how effectively a business is run. Thanks to competent management skills, it is possible for an entity to generate numerous benefits that may bring the company closer to the achievement of its intended goals.

The very concept of efficiency is not understood without ambiguity. From an economic point of view, according to the Pareto principle, it is a combination of goods where the utility of all products on the market is maximized (Wilczyński, 2014). In a general context, it can be defined as the ability to utilize resources efficiently to achieve a goal with the least amount of waste (Szudy, 2014).

Many factors contribute to an organization's effective functioning. According to Jaki (2012), they include:

- material, which is required for the accomplishment of an entity's mission;
- economic, in which the aim is to maximize the effects with given inputs;
- technical and production-related, based on the best use of available resources;
- environmental, relating to the management of the environment;
- qualitative, related to quality management;

DOI: 10.4324/9781003475583-21

- social, which is closely related to corporate social responsibility;
- ethical and cultural, aimed at shaping ethical and cultural norms;
- behavioral, which recognizes a person's interests as a human being.

The economic dimension of efficiency is the most important. In particular, it demonstrates how an enterprise achieved economic benefits from an item of expenditure in a given project (Wilczyński, 2014). Managing an economic entity requires not only ensuring the efficiency of its operations but also ensuring its financial liquidity. Neglecting this element may lead to negative consequences for the entire company, even forcing the company's management to declare bankruptcy.

A company's ability to develop and stay on the market depends on making the right decisions. With every decision comes a certain level of risk and every decision affects the future functioning of the company in some way.

Such scenarios are quite often faced by entrepreneurs who undertake investment activities in order to achieve a certain degree of effectiveness in running a business following the completion of a project. This may be due to an increase in the financial status of the entity, which will be characterized by higher productivity and, consequently, will increase the level of measurable economic benefits obtained by the entity.

Achieving these goals may be more difficult when, in fact, there are too many factors that are not predictable or hard to measure in a quantifiable form. When making investment decisions, risk manifests itself most often in such elements as time, uncertainty, the expected rate of return on investment, or the behavior of the main stakeholders during the implementation of investment activities (Bijańska & Wodarski, 2014).

One of the activities that help a management board in making important decisions is conducting relevant research, of which financial analysis is one of the most popular. It provides information on the basis of which it is possible to determine the financial situation of an entity and identify possible asset management problems. It also provides information for decision-making purposes (Gad, 2015).

The analysis is based on groups of indicators that describe a given phenomenon. Among them, we can distinguish profitability, liquidity, economic output, debt, and the structure of assets and capital. In numerous studies and scientific papers, profitability, economic output, and liquidity are often analyzed and used as measures to answer questions about the efficiency and solvency status of the entity to its creditors. Therefore, these issues are very often chosen to be used when studying the performance of an enterprise, both in terms of investments and its situation (Paździor, 2015).

Factors Influencing the Formation of Raw Material Prices

The competitiveness and development of enterprises from the fuel sector are shaped by determinants which can be divided into two categories: endogenous and exogenous. The first group includes factors that stem from an organization's structure and management style, and are common to all businesses. They include the current economic and financial situation of entities, current and planned investment activities, ownership shares, pay structure, and human capital levels. Exogenous factors include external determinants that impact businesses; for example, price changes in world markets and the demand for raw materials are significant (Firlej, 2014). A company's performance and production-related decisions are also influenced by such things as the pace at which leading economies develop, the growth of oil extraction, oil reserves in OPEC member countries, and changes in legal regulations on gas emissions during energy production and transportation. The growth in oil production from unconventional sources as well as the growing costs of extraction in relation to the market price of raw materials has also had an impact (PKN Orlen, 2016) since mid-2014.

While enterprises can influence their own circumstances with their own actions and management decisions, external factors are beyond their control. An example would be the Coronavirus pandemic. According to Eurostat research, motor fuel consumption decreased by 5% between January and July 2020, with gasoline experiencing the largest decline, dropping almost 10%. In turn, diesel oil demand declined by less than 4%. In fact, the start of the year appeared promising since the demand was higher than in 2019. However, in April there was a decrease in consumption, which was compensated by an increase in margins on raw materials (Araszkiewicz, 2020).

The setting of fuel exchange prices is also not within the control of companies as it is in the case of managing their activities. Fuel raw material prices determine the prices of many goods offered by fuel suppliers (Mazurkiewicz & Nowak, 2018), which in turn may affect the generated economic benefits and marketing effectiveness.

The price of fuel raw materials is also affected by direct factors. The interconnection of raw materials is one reason for the formation of prices. Whenever one changes its price, the other follows suit. This is because crude oil and natural gas are found together in one place. In addition, some commodities are indexed to each other (e.g. the price of crude oil to the price of natural gas). The connection between raw materials occurs because they are used for the same purpose and they can be used interchangeably. Consequently, a shift in demand could occur from one raw material to another. An example of this could be an increase in coal consumption at the expense of a reduction in the use of gas (Gędek et al., 2018).

The prices of crude oil, natural gas, and other fuels are also affected by exchange rates, according to recent studies. According to an analysis of specific exchange rate indicators, the US dollar-Polish zloty exchange rate is influenced by the euro-US dollar exchange rate. In other words, Poland does not have any control over the final consequences related to the conversion of the contracts if they specify the import of raw material purchased in US dollars, and the Polish recipient is dependent on foreign economic processes.

Fuel prices will increase due to the strengthening of the US dollar (Gędek et al., 2018).

Rokicki and Żak (2014) also mention other determinants that affect fuel prices. According to their analysis, this group includes such determinants as the taxation of fuels, which may differ depending on the country and region. It can be observed that smaller countries use a more aggressive fuel taxation strategy than larger countries. This is to help find fuel customers from neighboring countries. Another determinant they observed is fuel prices' seasonality. As a result of increased demand during the summer holidays, fuel distributors raise their prices. The prices are the lowest during the winter.

Fluctuations in fuel prices are caused not only by economic factors but also by the geopolitical situation across the world and in regions affected by destabilization and armed conflicts. In recent years, economic and political crises have affected Venezuela and Libya, and a decline in production has also been reported in other African countries such as Algeria, Angola, and Gabon (Gędek et al., 2018). The situation in Ukraine is also of key importance, where as a result of war, financial markets and exchange rates were adversely affected (Mielus, 2022).

Another major factor is the cost of extracting fuel deposits. These costs and forecasts may vary depending on the location and the timeframe. Research shows that the lowest extraction costs tend to be recorded in Middle Eastern countries, i.e. Saudi Arabia, Kuwait, Iraq, United Arab Emirates, and Iran. Significantly higher prices were observed in countries such as the United States, Kazakhstan, and Russia (Iwaszczuk, Jastrzębski, & Baran, 2021).

Research Methodology

The previous section presented the elements that may influence fuel market prices which, to some extent, determine the economic results achieved by business entities. A problem may arise when the environment of an entity is unstable, as was the case during the Coronavirus pandemic. In such situations, the strength of the influence of determinants on the efficiency of the resources used in the conditions of uncertainty that may also occur in the future is unknown.

The purpose of this chapter was to assess changes in the productivity and in market prices of shares of public companies in the fuel sector in Poland, and to verify whether and to what extent these changes were caused by the COVID-19 pandemic. Accordingly, the hypothesis to be verified was as follows: *fuel prices had a less significant impact on the resource productivity of fuel companies in 2019 and 2021 than they did during the COVID-19 pandemic, i.e. in 2020.*

Coronavirus, a threat in recent years, has changed purchasing habits of consumers and has also affected the financial results and production-related decisions of fuel companies. The analysis presented in this chapter focused on companies listed on the Warsaw Stock Exchange under the WIG-PALIWA index that are involved in the extraction and processing of raw materials such as crude oil and natural gas.

The study was conducted on the basis of quarterly financial reports that were made available by selected companies from the fuel industry, as well as stock quotes from BiznesRadar.pl (n.d.) and Infostrefa (n.d.). The data pertains to the 2019–2021 period.

To study the correlation between productivity and the prices of raw materials or revenues, I used carrying amounts of inventories and indicators that measure economic activity. From among them, the following measures of turnover were used:

- total assets;
- fixed assets;
- current assets;
- inventory;
- trade receivables;
- trade payables.

This is supplemented by the rotation cycles of inventories, trade receivables, and payables, as well as the operating and cash conversion cycles.

To determine the strength of the connections, Pearson's linear correlation coefficient was used. The strength of the relationship depends on the result, which can range from –1 to 1. A negative value indicates that an increase in one feature results in a decrease in another. A positive value means that if the first trait is increased, the latter trait will also be increased.

Findings

Tables 16.1 and 16.2 show the quarterly economic activity indicators and the carrying amount of inventories for the period of 2019–2021. At the start of the pandemic, PKN Orlen had significantly fewer inventories than in the previous year and in 2021. Additionally, in the first two quarters of 2020, turnover ratios were lower than in previous periods. Although debt repayment periods increased over 70 days in the second quarter of 2020, most quarters maintained similar values.

Lotos also held a much lower level of inventories at the time the pandemic broke out. Additionally, turnover measures were lower throughout the year, especially during the second and fourth quarters. This also translated into more time spent on inventory management and operating cycles that exceeded 100 days during these periods. Also, cash conversion cycles took the longest during these quarters, coming to about 80 days.

For PGNiG, 2020 was also the year when the company had a small number of inventories, even though some quarters saw even lower numbers than others. As for activity indicators, the second quarter of 2020 saw one of the lowest turnover figures and some of the longest cycles. This is particularly

Table 16.1 Economic activity of fuel companies from 2019 to 2021 – part 1

		2019				*2020*				*2021*			
PKN Orlen S.A.	**Productivity**	**I**	**II**	**III**	**IV**	**I**	**II**	**III**	**IV**	**I**	**II**	**III**	**IV**
	Inventory (PLN million)	15.33	15.07	14.55	15.32	12.17	12.06	12.28	12.28	14.39	14.8	16.13	18.41
	Total assets turnover	0.38	0.42	0.42	0.39	0.36	0.28	0.3	0.29	0.3	0.33	0.38	0.42
	Fixed assets turnover	0.71	0.76	0.77	0.73	0.64	0.44	0.43	0.41	0.43	0.49	0.6	0.67
	Current asset turnover	0.83	0.94	0.9	0.85	0.83	0.77	0.97	1.01	0.98	0.96	1.07	1.18
	Inventory turnover	1.71	1.94	1.99	1.87	1.84	1.74	2.02	2	1.99	2.1	2.44	2.55
	Trade receivables turnover	2.29	2.73	2.68	2.55	2.72	2.29	2.47	2.44	2.41	2.37	2.59	2.91
	Turnover of trade liabilities	1.69	1.81	1.67	1.64	1.83	1.23	1.61	1.56	1.52	1.52	1.68	1.95
	Rotation cycles	**I**	**II**	**III**	**IV**	**I**	**II**	**III**	**IV**	**I**	**II**	**III**	**IV**
	Inventory rotation cycle	53	47	47	50	50	53	46	46	46	44	38	37
	Receivables turnover cycle	40	34	35	37	34	40	38	38	38	39	36	32
	Liabilities turnover cycle	54	51	56	57	50	74	58	59	60	60	55	48
	Operating cycle	93	81	82	87	84	93	84	84	84	83	74	69
	Cash conversion cycle	39	30	26	30	34	19	26	25	24	23	19	21
Lotos S.A.	**Productivity**	**I**	**II**	**III**	**IV**	**I**	**II**	**III**	**IV**	**I**	**II**	**III**	**IV**
	Inventory (PLN million)	4.53	4.69	4.69	4.85	3.1	3.25	3.5	3.5	4.35	4.6	4.76	5.61
	Total assets turnover	0.29	0.32	0.32	0.32	0.27	0.2	0.3	0.2	0.26	0.33	0.38	0.42
	Fixed assets turnover	0.49	0.54	0.55	0.53	0.43	0.31	0.46	0.31	0.42	0.54	0.65	0.74
	Current asset turnover	0.72	0.78	0.78	0.78	0.73	0.57	0.84	0.55	0.72	0.84	0.9	0.97
	Inventory turnover	1.44	1.67	1.64	1.57	1.54	1.34	1.89	1.22	1.5	1.71	1.96	2.05
	Trade receivables turnover	2.98	2.92	2.95	2.83	2.37	2.07	3.6	2.27	2.66	2.81	2.99	3.59
	Turnover of trade liabilities	2.95	3.29	3.47	3.46	4.26	2.84	2.94	2.77	3.25	3.39	3.34	3.77
	Rotation cycles	**I**	**II**	**III**	**IV**	**I**	**II**	**III**	**IV**	**I**	**II**	**III**	**IV**
	Inventory rotation cycle	63	55	57	59	60	68	49	76	61	54	47	46
	Receivables turnover cycle	31	32	32	33	39	44	26	41	34	33	31	26
	Liabilities turnover cycle	31	28	27	27	22	33	32	34	28	27	28	25
	Operating cycle	94	87	89	92	99	112	75	117	95	87	78	72
	Cash conversion cycle	63	59	62	65	77	79	43	83	67	60	50	47

(*Continued*)

Table 16.1 (Continued)

		2019				2020				2021			
PGNiG S.A.	**Productivity**	**I**	**II**	**III**	**IV**	**I**	**II**	**III**	**IV**	**I**	**II**	**III**	**IV**
	Inventory (PLN million)	2.18	3.18	3.18	4.04	2.23	2.3	2.69	2.69	1.9	3.07	5.44	8.24
	Total assets turnover	0.27	0.15	0.15	0.2	0.24	0.12	0.1	0.19	0.23	0.15	0.16	0.34
	Fixed assets turnover	0.37	0.2	0.2	0.27	0.31	0.17	0.14	0.25	0.32	0.22	0.24	0.57
	Turnover of current assets	1.05	0.61	0.63	0.81	0.96	0.46	0.37	0.71	0.83	0.52	0.47	0.84
	Inventory turnover	5.26	2.99	2.52	3.16	4.39	3.22	2.57	4.38	6.49	4.2	2.94	4.7
	Trade receivables turnover	2.49	1.58	1.91	2.35	2.63	1	0.86	2.23	2.7	1.74	1.58	2.47
	Turnover of trade liabilities	2.94	1.78	1.67	2.88	2.14	0.73	1.72	1.79	2.98	2.01	1.68	2.45
	Rotation cycles	**I**	**II**	**III**	**IV**	**I**	**II**	**III**	**IV**	**I**	**II**	**III**	**IV**
	Inventory rotation cycle	18	31	37	30	21	29	36	21	14	22	32	20
	Receivables turnover cycle	37	58	49	40	35	92	108	42	34	53	59	38
	Liabilities turnover cycle	31	52	56	32	43	126	54	52	31	46	55	38
	Operating cycle	55	89	86	70	56	121	144	63	48	75	91	58
	Cash conversion cycle	24	37	30	38	13	–5	90	11	17	29	36	20

Source: Own study.

Table 16.2 Economic activity of fuel companies from 2019 to 2021 – part 2

		2019				*2020*				*2021*			
MOL Rt.	**Productivity**	**I**	**II**	**III**	**IV**	**I**	**II**	**III**	**IV**	**I**	**II**	**III**	**IV**
	Inventories (PLN million)	7.14	6.86	6.87	6.67	5.35	5.78	5.79	5.81	7.52	7.7	7.79	8.78
	Total assets turnover	0.24	0.28	0.29	0.27	0.2	0.14	0.18	0.18	0.2	0.25	0.27	0.28
	Fixed assets turnover	0.37	0.42	0.43	0.41	0.31	0.21	0.25	0.24	0.26	0.34	0.39	0.4
	Turnover of current assets	0.7	0.81	0.87	0.83	0.59	0.45	0.7	0.75	0.78	0.87	0.92	0.91
	Inventory turnover	2.23	2.51	2.67	2.64	2.36	1.85	2.25	2.21	2.12	2.41	2.75	2.67
	Trade receivables turnover	1.84	1.99	2	2.06	1.82	1.41	1.88	1.89	1.86	2.09	2.26	2.29
	Turnover of trade liabilities	0.93	0.75	0.79	0.77	0.68	0.45	0.6	0.59	0.55	0.67	0.75	0.8
	Rotation cycles	**I**	**II**	**III**	**IV**	**I**	**II**	**III**	**IV**	**I**	**II**	**III**	**IV**
	Inventory rotation cycle	41	37	35	35	39	50	41	42	43	38	34	35
	Receivables turnover cycle	50	46	46	45	51	65	49	49	49	44	41	41
	Liabilities turnover cycle	98	123	117	120	134	201	155	155	164	136	124	117
	Operating cycle	91	83	81	80	90	115	90	91	92	82	75	76
	Cash conversion cycle	–7	–40	–36	–40	–44	–86	–65	–64	–72	–54	–49	–41
Serinus Energy Inc.	**Productivity**	**I**	**II**	**III**	**IV**	**I**	**II**	**III**	**IV**	**I**	**II**	**III**	**IV**
	Inventories (PLN thousand)	0	0	0	0	0	0	0	0	0	0	0	2.66
	Total assets turnover	0.01	0.04	0.07	0.07	0.07	0.06	0.05	0.06	0.08	0.09	0.11	0.15
	Fixed assets turnover	0.01	0.04	0.08	0.08	0.08	0.07	0.06	0.07	0.1	0.1	0.13	0.18
	Turnover of current assets	0.13	0.34	0.64	0.55	0.49	0.4	0.37	0.4	0.51	0.54	0.68	0.92
	Inventory turnover	0	0	0	0	0	0	0	0	0	0	0	43.56
	Trade receivables turnover	0.18	0.52	0.87	0.73	0.69	0.55	0.47	0.6	0.91	0.96	1.34	2.11
	Turnover of trade liabilities	0.11	0.23	0.23	0.31	0.23	0.25	0.22	0.42	0.33	0.34	0.42	0.89
	Rotation cycles	**I**	**II**	**III**	**IV**	**I**	**II**	**III**	**IV**	**I**	**II**	**III**	**IV**
	Inventory rotation cycle	0	0	0	0	0	0	0	0	0	0	0	3
	Receivables turnover cycle	500	177	107	127	133	167	196	153	99	95	69	45
	Liabilities turnover cycle	827	402	392	297	398	359	419	218	274	265	218	105
	Operating cycle	500	177	107	127	133	167	196	153	99	95	69	48
	Cash conversion cycle	–327	–225	–285	–170	–265	–192	–223	–65	–175	–170	–149	–57

(Continued)

Table 16.2 (Continued)

		2019				2020				2021			
Unimot S.A.	**Productivity**	**I**	**II**	**III**	**IV**	**I**	**II**	**III**	**IV**	**I**	**II**	**III**	**IV**
	Inventories (PLN million)	0.21	0.25	0.33	0.24	0.12	0.2	0.17	0.17	0.24	0.36	0.36	0.33
	Total assets turnover	1.4	1.51	1.7	1.76	1.65	1.38	1.9	1.69	1.7	1.52	1.73	2.22
	Fixed assets turnover	11.19	12.62	16.02	16.55	11.41	7.94	8.48	7.47	10.63	10.71	12.48	15.63
	Turnover of current assets	1.6	1.72	1.91	1.97	1.93	1.68	2.45	2.18	2.02	1.78	2	2.59
	Inventory turnover	4.41	4.41	4.39	4.64	6.63	6.36	7.17	7.38	7.77	5.64	5.93	8.28
	Trade receivables turnover	3.31	3.53	4.04	4.06	4.3	3.69	4.67	4.17	3.73	3.51	4.01	4.97
	Turnover of trade liabilities	5.16	5.25	5.11	5.35	5.7	3.99	5.08	4.68	4.46	3.82	4.39	6.14
	Rotation cycles	**I**	**II**	**III**	**IV**	**I**	**II**	**III**	**IV**	**I**	**II**	**III**	**IV**
	Inventory rotation cycle	21	21	21	20	14	15	13	13	12	17	16	12
	Receivables turnover cycle	28	26	23	23	22	25	20	23	25	26	23	19
	Liabilities turnover cycle	18	18	18	18	16	23	19	20	21	24	21	16
	Operating cycle	49	47	44	43	36	40	33	36	37	43	39	31
	Cash conversion cycle	31	29	26	25	20	17	14	16	16	19	18	15

Source: Own study.

apparent in the period of debt collection and repayment of liabilities, both of which have clearly increased compared to the previous periods.

MOL, a Hungarian company, also experienced a decline in the carrying inventory in 2020. In addition to that, turnover ratios decreased as well, and the lowest of them were recorded in the second quarter of 2020. With their decline came longer cycles of managing current assets and repaying liabilities, which automatically lengthened the operating cycle and the period for suppliers to repay receivables.

Most of the analyzed periods showed no inventories for Serinus Energy, with its only inventory appearing in the last quarter of the previous years audited. The turnover results in this entity indicated that the company's activity had not been very productive compared to the other companies in the sector. This is also reflected in rotation cycles, in which individual rotational components take hundreds of days. It is worth noting, however, that management of trade receivables and liabilities has increased in intensity in 2021.

For Unimot, as for most companies in the sector, the lowest levels of inventories were observed in 2020. The lowest productivity values and high rotation cycles could be noticed in 2019, i.e. before the Coronavirus pandemic was announced. The exception was the productivity of fixed assets in 2020, which was analyzed and found to be lower than in previous years.

Tables 16.3 and 16.4 show the coefficients of correlation between fuel raw material prices and inventories as well as the economic activities of companies listed in the WIG-Fuels index from 2019 to 2021.

Increased interdependence of most measures and Ural crude oil can be noticed in the results for PKN Orlen in 2020. Compared to other raw materials, some of the indicators also went up, but the level of inventories was not as dependent on Brent and WTI crude oil compared to 2019 and 2021. A higher correlation can be observed for the turnover of fixed assets, receivables, and trade liabilities for oil products.

A stronger dependence of inventories on Brent and WTI crude oil in 2020 can be seen for Lotos. However, in 2021, the results for turnover ratios and rotation cycles are much higher. Only the turnover of trade liabilities showed a strong, albeit negative correlation with Brent and WTI crude oil. There was a very strong dependence on Ural oil in 2021.

In the case of PGNiG, in 2020 a complete dependence existed only with regard to the carrying amount of inventories and gas prices. The relationships among the rotation ratios were negligible, while the correlations between the rotation and gas cycles were strong, albeit negative, in most cases. Noteworthy is a high correlation between productivity and gas in 2019 and 2021, and for the value rotation cycles in 2021, as well as strong connections between turnover results and Ural crude oil prices in 2020.

Very strong correlations between the productivity indicators and the prices of raw materials in 2021 are observed for the Hungarian company MOL; Ural oil prices correlated closely with almost all turnover ratios and the value of inventories, whereas rotation cycles exhibited the opposite trend.

Table 16.3 Coefficients of correlation of fuel commodity prices and economic activity from 2019 to 2021 – part 1

		2019				*2020*				*2021*			
PKN Orlen S.A.	**Productivity**	**Brent**	**WTI**	**Ural**	**Gas**	**Brent**	**WTI**	**Ural**	**Gas**	**Brent**	**WTI**	**Ural**	**Gas**
	Inventory	0.99	0.99	0.19	0.25	0.38	0.34	0.71	0.87	0.68	0.64	0.94	0.30
	Total assets turnover	–0.75	–0.71	0.47	–0.54	–0.86	–0.90	0.71	–0.48	0.81	0.76	0.16	0.94
	Fixed assets turnover	–0.86	–0.79	0.26	–0.61	–0.94	–0.97	0.49	–0.70	0.84	0.79	0.12	0.94
	Turnover of current assets	–0.62	–0.61	0.62	–0.49	0.60	0.56	0.54	0.95	0.61	0.54	0.39	0.88
	Inventory turnover	–0.85	–0.71	0.12	–0.76	0.48	0.45	0.59	0.94	0.83	0.77	0.18	0.98
	Trade receivables turnover	–0.71	–0.59	0.38	–0.76	–0.73	–0.78	0.87	–0.22	0.58	0.52	0.38	0.84
	Turnover of trade liabilities	0.00	–0.14	0.96	0.05	–0.54	–0.60	0.97	0.06	0.61	0.56	0.30	0.83
	Rotation cycles	**Brent**	**WTI**	**Ural**	**Gas**	**Brent**	**WTI**	**Ural**	**Gas**	**Brent**	**WTI**	**Ural**	**Gas**
	Inventory rotation cycle	0.80	0.70	–0.32	0.68	–0.45	–0.41	–0.65	–0.91	–0.85	–0.79	–0.16	–0.99
	Receivables turnover cycle	0.69	0.59	–0.45	0.71	0.75	0.80	–0.84	0.29	–0.52	–0.46	–0.44	–0.83
	Liabilities turnover cycle	–0.18	0.02	–0.93	–0.29	0.46	0.52	–0.99	–0.14	–0.63	–0.58	–0.32	–0.86
	Operating cycle	0.75	0.65	–0.38	0.70	0.08	0.14	–0.96	–0.53	–0.75	–0.68	–0.28	–0.96
	Cash conversion cycle	0.84	0.64	0.06	0.84	–0.69	–0.74	0.90	–0.15	–0.81	–0.74	–0.11	–0.92
Lotos S.A.	**Productivity**	**Brent**	**WTI**	**Ural**	**Gas**	**Brent**	**WTI**	**Ural**	**Gas**	**Brent**	**WTI**	**Ural**	**Gas**
	Inventory	–0.20	0.12	–0.10	–0.96	0.86	0.86	0.03	0.97	0.66	0.64	0.93	0.18
	Total assets turnover	–0.71	–0.51	0.20	–0.89	–0.56	–0.53	0.53	0.09	0.92	0.88	0.99	0.59
	Fixed assets turnover	–0.78	–0.61	0.16	–0.84	–0.59	–0.57	0.56	0.06	0.90	0.86	0.99	0.57
	Current asset turnover	–0.56	–0.35	0.26	–0.94	–0.47	–0.43	0.45	0.16	0.94	0.92	0.99	0.60
	Inventory turnover	–0.69	–0.56	0.39	–0.77	–0.34	–0.29	0.28	0.22	0.92	0.88	0.97	0.68
	Trade receivables turnover	–0.17	–0.46	0.07	0.81	0.03	0.07	0.33	0.59	0.67	0.64	0.94	0.22
	Turnover of trade liabilities	–0.67	–0.40	–0.21	–0.93	–0.93	–0.96	0.58	–0.61	0.58	0.58	0.87	0.01
	Rotation cycles	**Brent**	**WTI**	**Ural**	**Gas**	**Brent**	**WTI**	**Ural**	**Gas**	**Brent**	**WTI**	**Ural**	**Gas**
	Inventory rotation cycle	0.63	0.52	–0.51	0.72	0.47	0.41	–0.24	–0.07	–0.95	–0.91	–0.96	–0.73
	Receivables turnover cycle	–0.18	0.13	–0.11	–0.95	0.02	–0.01	–0.40	–0.57	–0.67	–0.63	–0.94	–0.24
	Liabilities turnover cycle	0.65	0.38	0.10	0.96	0.94	0.97	–0.56	0.62	–0.47	–0.49	–0.76	0.17
	Operating cycle	0.64	0.61	–0.59	0.54	0.30	0.25	–0.31	–0.28	–0.89	–0.85	–0.99	–0.59
	Cash conversion cycle	0.31	0.46	–0.81	–0.06	0.02	–0.04	–0.15	–0.47	–0.91	–0.86	–0.97	–0.68

PGNiG S.A.	Productivity	Brent	WTI	Ural	Gas	Brent	WTI	Ural	Gas	Brent	WTI	Ural	Gas
	Inventory	–0.22	0.09	–0.09	–0.97	0.78	0.76	0.22	1	0.77	0.73	0.97	0.42
	Total assets turnover	0.78	0.66	–0.31	0.73	–0.48	–0.56	0.64	–0.37	0.03	0.00	0.49	–0.38
	Fixed assets turnover	0.78	0.66	–0.30	0.74	–0.46	–0.54	0.64	–0.35	0.18	0.15	0.61	–0.26
	Current asset turnover	0.77	0.66	–0.34	0.72	–0.54	–0.62	0.62	–0.43	–0.49	–0.52	–0.03	–0.74
	Inventory turnover	0.77	0.57	–0.06	0.88	–0.16	–0.26	0.47	–0.25	–0.88	–0.87	–0.59	–0.94
	Trade receivables turnover	0.59	0.60	–0.66	0.42	–0.35	–0.44	0.68	–0.23	–0.65	–0.67	–0.22	–0.80
	Turnover of trade liabilities	0.84	0.87	–0.34	0.34	–0.34	–0.40	1.00	0.25	–0.81	–0.81	–0.45	–0.89
	Rotation cycles	**Brent**	**WTI**	**Ural**	**Gas**	**Brent**	**WTI**	**Ural**	**Gas**	**Brent**	**WTI**	**Ural**	**Gas**
	Inventory rotation cycle	–0.87	–0.69	–0.05	–0.80	0.16	0.25	–0.38	0.31	0.77	0.73	0.47	0.99
	Receivables turnover cycle	–0.53	–0.55	0.71	–0.41	0.24	0.34	–0.58	0.23	0.63	0.64	0.21	0.84
	Liabilities turnover cycle	–0.87	–0.89	0.29	–0.33	0.18	0.25	–0.99	–0.42	0.75	0.74	0.38	0.93
	Operating cycle	–0.76	–0.68	0.40	–0.65	0.23	0.32	–0.55	0.24	0.70	0.69	0.32	0.92
	Cash conversion cycle	–0.08	0.16	0.39	–0.91	0.07	0.1	0.33	0.63	0.65	0.64	0.24	0.90

Source: Own study.

Table 16.4 Coefficients of correlation of fuel commodity prices and economic activity from 2019 to 2021 – part 2

		2019				*2020*				*2021*			
MOL Rt.	**Productivity**	**Brent**	**WTI**	**Ural**	**Gas**	**Brent**	**WTI**	**Ural**	**Gas**	**Brent**	**WTI**	**Ural**	**Gas**
	Inventory	0.28	–0.03	0.04	0.98	0.92	0.96	–0.53	0.66	0.58	0.56	0.89	0.07
	Total assets turnover	–0.84	–0.67	0.04	–0.81	–0.42	–0.48	0.99	0.17	0.99	0.96	0.93	0.76
	Fixed assets turnover	–0.85	–0.72	0.17	–0.74	–0.74	–0.79	0.86	–0.25	0.98	0.95	0.94	0.75
	Current asset turnover	–0.79	–0.57	–0.14	–0.88	0.43	0.38	0.71	0.87	0.99	0.97	0.87	0.82
	Inventory turnover	–0.70	–0.45	–0.21	–0.92	–0.37	–0.43	0.99	0.26	0.96	0.91	0.89	0.84
	Trade receivables turnover	–0.44	–0.15	–0.03	–1.00	0.05	–0.01	0.92	0.64	0.97	0.94	0.96	0.72
	Trade liabilities turnover	0.46	0.24	–0.35	0.93	–0.48	–0.54	0.98	0.11	0.95	0.92	0.99	0.63
	Rotation cycles	**Brent**	**WTI**	**Ural**	**Gas**	**Brent**	**WTI**	**Ural**	**Gas**	**Brent**	**WTI**	**Ural**	**Gas**
	Inventory rotation cycle	0.65	0.38	0.19	0.94	0.33	0.39	–0.99	–0.30	–0.98	–0.95	–0.89	–0.83
	Receivables turnover cycle	0.48	0.21	–0.06	1.00	–0.03	0.02	–0.92	–0.63	–0.99	–0.96	–0.93	–0.77
	Liabilities turnover cycle	–0.47	–0.25	0.34	–0.93	0.40	0.46	–0.99	–0.20	–0.98	–0.96	–0.96	–0.67
	Operating cycle	0.58	0.31	0.08	0.98	0.11	0.17	–0.96	–0.51	–0.98	–0.96	–0.91	–0.80
	Cash conversion cycle	0.51	0.28	–0.21	0.97	–0.58	–0.64	0.95	–0.04	0.96	0.94	0.98	0.58
Serinus Energy Inc.	**Productivity**	**Brent**	**WTI**	**Ural**	**Gas**	**Brent**	**WTI**	**Ural**	**Gas**	**Brent**	**WTI**	**Ural**	**Gas**
	Inventory	–	–	–	–	–	–	–	–	0.41	0.39	0.78	–0.1
	Total assets turnover	–0.65	–0.38	–0.47	–0.84	–0.55	–0.62	0.52	–0.51	0.63	0.58	0.91	0.22
	Fixed assets turnover	–0.64	–0.37	–0.47	–0.84	–0.48	–0.56	0.53	–0.46	0.62	0.58	0.91	0.20
	Current asset turnover	–0.74	–0.50	–0.40	–0.83	–0.83	–0.87	0.43	–0.73	0.67	0.62	0.93	0.29
	Inventory turnover	–	–	–	–	–	–	–	–	0.41	0.39	0.78	–0.12
	Trade receivables turnover	–0.77	–0.53	–0.33	–0.85	–0.52	–0.60	0.45	–0.55	0.62	0.57	0.91	0.22
	Trade liabilities turnover	–0.32	–0.01	–0.09	–0.98	0.73	0.65	0.11	0.48	0.52	0.48	0.85	0.04
	Rotation cycles	**Brent**	**WTI**	**Ural**	**Gas**	**Brent**	**WTI**	**Ural**	**Gas**	**Brent**	**WTI**	**Ural**	**Gas**
	Inventory rotation cycle	–	–	–	–	–	–	–	–	0.41	0.39	0.78	–0.12
	Receivables turnover cycle	0.67	0.42	0.01	0.95	0.45	0.53	–0.35	0.57	–0.72	–0.66	–0.94	–0.42
	Liabilities turnover cycle	0.50	0.23	–0.05	0.99	–0.71	–0.64	–0.01	–0.38	–0.61	–0.57	–0.91	–0.20
	Operating cycle	0.67	0.42	0.01	0.95	0.45	0.53	–0.35	0.57	–0.73	–0.67	–0.94	–0.45
	Cash conversion cycle	0.08	0.36	0.20	–0.88	0.88	0.84	-0.09	0.58	0.55	0.52	0.87	0.09

	Productivity	Brent	WTI	Ural	Gas	Brent	WTI	Ural	Gas	Brent	WTI	Ural	Gas
Unimot S.A.	Inventory	–0.99	–0.9	–0.3	–0.5	0.67	0.74	–0.87	0.23	0.91	0.94	0.63	0.74
	Total assets turnover	–0.50	–0.21	–0.48	–0.86	0.08	0.07	0.71	0.73	0.34	0.29	0.74	–0.02
	Fixed assets turnover	–0.54	–0.25	–0.54	–0.82	–0.96	–0.98	0.55	–0.60	0.62	0.57	0.91	0.24
	Current asset turnover	–0.49	–0.20	–0.47	–0.87	0.33	0.32	0.57	0.88	0.28	0.23	0.69	–0.07
	Inventory turnover	0.40	0.66	–0.27	–0.56	0.61	0.56	0.55	0.94	–0.33	–0.37	0.15	–0.56
	Trade receivables turnover	–0.59	–0.31	–0.53	–0.82	–0.12	–0.13	0.76	0.57	0.47	0.42	0.82	0.11
	Trade liabilities turnover	0.48	0.71	0.21	–0.61	–0.65	–0.69	0.91	–0.03	0.29	0.24	0.70	–0.09
	Rotation cycles	**Brent**	**WTI**	**Ural**	**Gas**	**Brent**	**WTI**	**Ural**	**Gas**	**Brent**	**WTI**	**Ural**	**Gas**
	Inventory rotation cycle	–0.31	–0.59	0.33	0.60	–0.39	–0.34	–0.71	–0.88	0.45	0.50	–0.01	0.57
	Receivables turnover cycle	0.63	0.35	0.45	0.86	0.18	0.17	–0.71	–0.52	–0.52	–0.46	–0.85	–0.21
	Liabilities turnover cycle	–	–	–	–	0.65	0.70	–0.92	0.06	–0.26	–0.19	–0.66	0.03
	Operating cycle	0.50	0.20	0.46	0.87	0.00	0.01	–0.75	–0.67	–0.09	–0.02	–0.53	0.17
	Cash conversion cycle	0.50	0.20	0.46	0.87	–0.75	–0.79	0.21	–0.84	0.23	0.29	–0.24	0.42

Source: Own study.

They reached their highest level this year, excluding the carrying amount of inventories, which were strongly influenced by Brent and WTI crude oil prices. It can also be seen that in 2020 the productivity measures were very heavily dependent on Ural oil.

For Serinus Energy in 2020, Brent and WTI crude oil showed a strong correlation with the turnover ratios of current assets and trade liabilities and with the cash conversion cycle. Compared to the remaining years, they were the highest. However, before the pandemic very strong links were observed between productivity indicators and natural gas prices. In 2021, a high correlation between the indicators and Ural oil prices was observable, whereas in 2020, there was not so much high interdependence.

When it comes to Unimot, stock exchange prices were influenced by the company's productivity indicators in various ways. The carrying value of inventories was most closely related to Brent and WTI crude oil prices in 2019 and 2021, and in 2020 to the Ural crude oil prices. When the pandemic outbreak in Poland, high levels of correlation existed between Brent or WTI crude oils and the turnover of fixed assets as well as between gas prices with the inventory turnover. In the years before the pandemic, gas prices had a greater impact on productivity than they had during the pandemic. In 2020 and 2021, the Ural oil price influenced economic productivity at a significant level.

Conclusions and Recommendations

Based on the analysis of productivity changes in companies, it has been found that between 2019 and 2021 in most of the companies surveyed, fluctuations in the price of fuel raw materials affected management processes related to the use of current assets. Fuel prices played a larger role in the effective use of assets and their rotation for companies, such as PKN Orlen, MOL, and Unimot during the pandemic. For the remaining companies under study, these impacts in 2020 were comparable to those observed in previous years, or fuel exchange prices had no impact on their positions.

The results of the study cannot confirm the hypothesis formulated earlier, according to which the relations between economic activity and fuel prices were stronger in 2020 than in previous years. However, one should keep in mind that the research sample is not very large and the study spans a relatively short period of time. It was only possible to examine the correlation in four quarterly periods for each year when using quarterly financial data, which may make it difficult to recognize the significance of the variables. In spite of this, certain dependencies may be uncovered by the results.

As a result of the pandemic and existing restrictions, almost every company's asset management was highly dependent on the prices of raw materials used in fuel production and on the problems related to the availability of ordered supplies. Consumers spent most of their time at home as a result of the restrictions and lockdowns, which translated to fewer fuel purchases.

The conclusions and recommendations are as follows:

1 The level of inventories must be increased to achieve even higher productivity results. For MOL and Unimot, carrying amounts of inventories were more closely correlated with WTI and Brent crude oil prices, and for PKN Orlen and PGNiG with Ural crude oil and gas prices. During the pandemic, an increase in raw material prices translated into an increase in inventories but not always an increase in productivity. When determining future inventories, it is recommended to take a cautious approach;
2 In order to purchase a larger batch of supplies and products for their operations earlier, companies in the fuel sector, such as PKN Orlen, Lotos, MOL, and Unimot, need to make adequate investments. As a result, the surveyed business entities would be protected from sudden changes in the environment;
3 In addition to making investments, entities should closely monitor events that could change the business environment rapidly (as was the case with the recent pandemic). Thanks to doing so, businesses have a better chance to avoid possible problems with the supply of necessary inventories (e.g. cash reserves to purchase the necessary supplies and goods);
4 Pandemic-related restrictions and lockdowns resulted in a significant drop in the volume of products and goods sold by the companies in the fuel sector under study, which was reflected in a decrease in revenues. It is recommended that businesses plan to diversify their sales.

References

Araszkiewicz, S. (2020). Petrol stations in Poland and the next stages of the COVID19 pandemic – the fight continues. *At the Petrol Station No. 4/2020* (21), pp. 6–9.

Bijańska, J., & Wodarski, K. (2014). The risk in the investment decisions of enterprises. *Science notebooks. Organization and Management/Silesian University of Technology* No. 70/2014, pp. 53–65.

BiznesRadar.pl. (n.d.). Retrieved 27 September 2022, from https://www.biznesradar.pl

Buczkowska, A. (2012). The goals of the enterprise and the measurement of its achievements. *Scientific Journals of the University of Szczecin. Finance, Financial Markets, Insurance*, 45/2012, pp. 5–19.

Firlej, K. (2014). Quantitative determinants of the competitiveness of selected raw material and fuel companies from the WIG 20 index. In: J. Machaczka (ed.) *Competitiveness determinants of contemporary organizations* (pp. 1–14). Cracow: Publishing House of the Cracow University of Economics.

Gad, J. (2015). Analysis and evaluation of the company's financial situation. In: *Economics, finance, economic law. Handbook for judges and prosecutors* (pp. 69–77). Lodz – Lublin: University of Lodz, Faculty of Management, National School of Judiciary and Public Prosecution.

Gędek, S., Kucharska, A., & Ruszel, M. (2018). Geopolitical and macroeconomic determinants of fuel price growth. *Drives and Controls* 20 (7/8), pp. 102–105.

Infostrefa. (n.d.). Retrieved 27 May 2022, from http://infostrefa.com/infostrefa/pl/index/

Iwaszczuk, A., Jastrzębski, P., & Baran, J. (2021). Analysis of the factors influencing the global crude oil market. In: *Markets, sectors and business models in the age of globalization* (pp. 21–37). Cracow: AGH Publishing Houses.

Jaki, A. (2012). *Mechanisms of the enterprise value management process*. Cracow: Publishing House of the Cracow University of Economics.

Janik, W., & Paździor, A. (2011). *Financial management in the enterprise*. Lublin: Lublin University of Technology.

Mazurkiewicz, J., & Nowak, M. (2018). Fluctuation of fuel prices and the risk zone. *Science Notebooks. Organization and Management / Silesian University of Technology*, 132, pp. 431–438. doi: 10.29119/1641-3466.2018.132.31

Mielus, P. (2022). The reaction of the financial market to the outbreak of the Russian-Ukrainian war compared to the response to the COVID-19 pandemic in Europe. *Safe Bank*, 86 (1), pp. 80–99. https://doi.org/10.26354/bb.5.1.86.2022.

Paździor, A. (2015). *Value management of a modern enterprise*. Lublin: Lublin University of Technology.

PKN Orlen S.A. (2016). Orlen Group Integrated Report 2015. Retrieved 1 June 2022, from https://raportzintegrowany2015.orlen.pl/pl/

Rokicki, T., & Żak, A. (2014). Selected factors differentiating fuel prices in the EU countries. *Logistics*, 6, pp. 13702–13709.

Szudy, M. (2014). Economic efficiency in dynamic terms and the efficiency of the economic system. *Studia Ekonomiczne / University of Economics in Katowice* No. 176/2014, pp. 22–29.

Wilczyński, R. (2014). Measurement of effectiveness and goals of enterprises. *Scientific Journals of the University of Szczecin. Finance, Financial Markets, Insurance* No. 66/2014, pp. 547–558.

Part 5

Financial Implications

17 Effective Methods of Tax Reduction for Organizations in the Era of COVID-19

Agnieszka Wójcik-Czerniawska

Introduction

The COVID-19 pandemic triggered a world health catastrophe and a drop in economic growth of a significance that had never been seen in recent times. The pandemic went from being a health catastrophe to a worldwide economic catastrophe in a few months. It generated a significantly bigger decline in the global gross domestic product (GDP) than the global economic crisis of 2008, approaching over 10% during the first half of 2020 and an estimated 3.4% overall in 2020. The economies of individual nations and of the entire world were affected badly by the COVID-19 pandemic (Hosseini, 2020). International commerce deteriorated, external trade operations were halted, and numerous investments were impeded. Throughout the pandemic, the government provided more funding than in normal times.

However, during the pandemic, taxes declined. Taxes are the largest source of government income and often increase over time, but that did not happen while the pandemic was in full force. A tax is an amount of money charged by a government or state institution that citizens and businesses are obligated to pay. It may be a fixed percentage imposed on goods or services or it may be ephemeral or transitory. The tax amount depends upon the type of products purchased. Taxes are often imposed at the provincial or state level. Taxes on goods and services are taken by the state to finance their activities and organizations. Organizations funded by the government include public hospitals, elementary and secondary schools, colleges and universities, welfare organizations, state offices, and corporations such as Pakistan State Oil. Taxes are also used to build and maintain roads and other parts of a country's infrastructure. When someone buys property, he or she is taxed. Toll plazas on motorways and highways collect taxes that are used to maintain roads and the infrastructure of roads. Food hubs and restaurants charge customers taxes on the goods and services they provide. Electricity and other utilities are taxed, as are Internet and landline services (Arinta et al., 2020).

When looking back on the histories of several economies, we can see that interfering with political aims for economic reasons can result in unrealistic outcomes. The general definition of economic growth is a rise in economic

DOI: 10.4324/9781003475583-23

productivity over time. However, economic growth, long-term transformations, and economic cycles are all different. They are merely short-term economic changes marked by booms and busts that occur over weeks or months. There are few clear reasons for growth or precise numbers because this is a standard social process. Yearly economic growth varies greatly from nation to nation, and so many questions remain about the interactions among diverse sociocultural, economic, and political forces that drive economic growth.

Income tax reduction may increase corporate revenues and substitutions, and this may affect corporate behavior. Decreasing the income tax rate has a positive impact on an economy because it allows laborers to take home a larger portion of their wages and gives investors the opportunity to use a larger portion of their income for investments (Gordana and Biljana, 2021).

Types of Taxes

- **Income tax**

  An income tax is levied on people who own a business. A portion of their income is taken. A tax-varied income leads to varying amounts of taxes taken by the government.
- **Estate tax**

  An estate tax is taken from the owner of property or a corporation that includes land or a definite area in its possession. Different countries charge different percentages of property taxes. It also depends on the value and area where the property is located.
- **Business tax**

  A business tax is directly deducted from the revenues generated by a business. Other analogous bodies also fall under the umbrella of this tax.
- **Goods and services tax**

  A tax on goods and services is an indirect tax levied by a seller and paid by customers. The tax is turned over to the government. Personal products such as lotions, shampoos, and soaps and foods such as biscuits are taxed. The tax is included in the price of the products.
- **Capital gains tax**

  A capital gains tax is levied when a person sells property.
- **Remittance tax**

  Each repentance is tax exempted, but hoping the number of remittances might include taxes, which are charged by the state upon mobility from one country to another.
- **Indirect tax**

  An indirect tax is a tax collected by a third party, who then pays the tax to the state. Service taxes, customs taxes, and excise taxes are indirect taxes.
- **Direct tax**

  A direct tax is paid directly by a person to the state. Income taxes and property taxes are direct taxes.

- **Wealth tax**
  A wealth tax is a tax assessed on the assets of a person, including traveling, jewelry, and cash. Anything a person owns is subject to a wealth tax.
- **Value-added tax**
  A value-added tax is similar to a sales tax in many aspects, but it is different in that it is added to a product at every step in its production, from obtaining its raw materials, its production, and to its sales.
- **Subjective income tax**
  First, the total income of a person is calculated. Then the spent amount is deducted. After deduction, the remaining amount is taxed. This whole process is labeled as subjective income tax.

Benefits of Minimum Taxation on Organizations

Governments all over the world rely on minimum taxes to preserve their tax revenues. This is especially true in developing nations with weaker revenue authorities, which confront significant hurdles in taxing huge multinational corporations effectively. The purpose of this local, or domestic, minimal tax is to prevent revenue base erosion due to the overuse of so-called tax preferences. These tax breaks appear in the form of credits, exclusions, special exemptions and allowances, and they typically result in a lower tax bill for a company. States put a limit on organizations' contributions to government coffers by implementing an organizational minimal tax rate (Popescu & Šebestová, 2022).

The introduction of a minimum tax results in an increase of a little over 1.5% in the median income tax rate, which is the tax rate for firms after accounting for tax breaks for turnover and roughly 1% for profits.

The most efficient tax rates are raised by minimal taxes based on adaptive business income, followed by those firms' assets and turnover. Finally, the revenue effect is determined by the rate used (Osho & Ilori, 2020).

We utilize firm-level statistics to estimate the income that would be generated if a national taxation rate of 5% on circulation and 1% on asset value was implemented. The former may raise an additional 7% in tax income for governments, and the latter could raise nearly a third more for government agencies in the median country.

Effective Methods of Tax Reduction for Organizations during the COVID-19 Pandemic

Taxation is an essential component of every nation's economic structure, as well as a concern of each company. This has been particularly during the COVID-19 pandemic. Modern tax systems are characterized by a certain level of flexibility, which reveals itself in the freedom of taxpayers to plan they're paying taxes and pick tax regimes, notwithstanding the conventional intrinsic essentialness of tax payments. The goal of this essay was to investigate tax returns as a useful technique for reducing the tax burden faced by organizations (Herzfeld, 2021). Several tax reduction tactics are used by organizations to lower their taxable revenues by admitting costs in the latest accounting year rather than neglecting them. As a result, some taxable income is recognized later, along with the resulting income tax burden during the COVID-19 era. The post below explains how to boost your spending expenditures.

Tax Planning

When it comes to the economic productivity of this style of tax planning, it is crucial to remember that even though the economic effect is significantly smaller than with other types of tax planning, the overall number of economic results is quite stable. This is attributable not just to long-term tax benefit programs and the use of special taxation policies but also to the fact that no extra tax amounts will be involved in case of the termination of a particular tax advantage (Ding et al., 2020).

When considering how income taxes can reduce an organization's tax burden, it is crucial to recognize that this approach involves both economic and legal aspects. This research focused on the first and, in our viewpoint, the only permissible type of tax planning. The proper use of favorable taxation regimes in existing legislation is the primary instrument for implementing legal tax planning by corporation.

Limitation on Capitalization

Having a high limit on asset capitalization permits money spent on a fixed asset to grow. It allows for a greater share of expenditures to be allocated in a particular financial year. For instance, suppose a company has set aside $6000 to purchase computer equipment for its employees. They buy the equipment ahead of schedule but do not receive them. The businesses can record the charge in the latest accounting year to enhance the incurred expense account (Alex, 2018).

Donations and Redemptions

Giving money or property to charity is an efficient method for reducing taxes. Donating regularly benefits both the charity and the business by demonstrating a commitment to social responsibility and a brand's ideals, especially during the COVID-19 pandemic. Choose a cause connected with your business and community, and tell your consumers about it. It is a win–win situation that will result in more committed clients for your company. Donating to charity provides inherent benefits as well as current (and future) tax advantages. Instead of sending cash, you may maximize your charitable giving benefits by providing valued stocks. Charities need not pay taxes on stock sales, and thus they receive the full value of the stocks as a contribution. After you have donated the assets, you can buy them back at a higher price than what you first paid for them. If you sell the same shares again in the same year, your capital gains tax base will be significantly larger, and this will lower your capital gains tax burden.

Inventory

Having an inventory allows an organization to include its costs in the costs of goods sold, resulting in more spending and lower payable taxes. It is a form of indirect investment in which investors buy shares and keep them for a long time, independent of the market volatility. Long-term investments are usually taxed more heavily than short-term investments. Mutual funds are required to disperse a certain amount of their net earnings each year, and the revenue distribution is normally borne by the investors. The length of time an investor has had the account is not taken into consideration. Verify the payout date before buying mutual funds to ensure that they are not purchased too close to the payout date.

Accounts Receivable

If a company has any recoverable receivables, it must write them off by the end of each year. It keeps track of the money it gets but does not cash it. It is being reported but not recognized, allowing the company to lower its tax liability.

Debt is needed if the company intends to make an equity stake or acquire debt to satisfy its financial needs. Debt enables firms to incur interest costs, which raises costs. Interest expenditures must always be paid well before the end of the fiscal year.

Expenses for the Family

If a company employs family and friends, it may be possible for the company to make certain expenditures on their behalf. For instance, suppose a corporation decides to buy a car for a family member to use for business. The company can register this as an expense, lowering its taxable revenue. Employing a close relative is one of the most effective strategies with which a small company can save money on taxes (Abínzano et al., 2022). The Internal Revenue Service (IRS) provides several alternatives in this regard. You can employ your children to help you avoid paying taxes on your earnings. The marginal rate on income paid to your children is lower, and in some cases, a tax is completely avoided. Your child's salary is excluded from social welfare and Medicare taxes when your firm is a single partnership. Just make sure the earnings are justified in terms of business.

Work Travel

Businesses can deduct the costs of travel expenditures, enabling them to absorb these expenses. Engaging in travel may result in the accumulation of frequent flyer miles, which can be redeemed for personal trips. Frequent business travel could potentially lead to tax minimization for your company. It is important to note that while expenses for business travel can be fully reimbursed, expenses for personal vacations cannot. However, small business owners have the flexibility to combine travel expenses justified for professional reasons with personal reasons, optimizing their overall business travel costs. Additionally, frequent flyer miles accrued for business purposes can be utilized for personal travel at a later date (Akingbade, 2021).

Consider Harvesting Losses

If you have gotten important taxable profits this year from stock options, the sale of a business, or different valuable assets, contemplate the advantages and disadvantages of financial gain gathering or marketing an investment to come up with a loss for tax purposes. Within the current year, losses may cut back taxable investment returns and even reduce income by up to $4000. The remaining loss (if any) can be carried forward and employed in future years.

You need to initially confirm your foreseen capital losses and gains for the year before considering tax-loss harvesting as a strategy. Begin by adding the capital gains and losses over the constant period; long-run gains are offset by losses, whereas short-run losses cut back on long-term gains. Long-run assets are maintained for a year, whereas short-term assets are controlled for less than a year. To learn about the restrictions on this strategy, see your certified public accountant or tax expert (Yoshino et al., 2021).

They are re-netted as a result of each gain, and simply a loss would be enclosed within the reticulate short-and long-term totals. For example, a payer with $70,000 in web short-term capital gains and $20,000 in net long-term losses can have $50,000 in gross short-term investment income. Once the netting procedure is done, homeowners still have an outsized completed investment return, and they may use tax-loss gathering to lower their liabilities by peddling assets with unrecognized wealth losses (Zhao et al., 2021).

In general, tax-loss harvesting is most useful in specific circumstances, such as when a capitalist needs to rebalance a portfolio or diversify from a familiar concentration situation. Furthermore, since short-run capital gains are taxed at a higher rate than traditional income, this system is most effective when it aims to limit this kind of gain.

Depreciation

Depreciation enables a company to record a large expense for depreciation to avoid paying taxes. For financial statements, though, an entity can still use a standard depreciation.

If an organization's current assets require maintenance or repair, they must purchase assets before they can be required. This has two effects: first, it permits the business to become more efficient. Second, it allows the business to incur significant depreciation costs. Depreciation is recorded as a cost, resulting in a low tax liability.

Consider the Expenses

Spending lowers your overall tax rate, so make sure to include any business-related expenses when submitting your taxes. These costs could include things such as the rent you paid for your office space, which can mount up quickly. You can include the costs of high-speed Internet and other services if they can be directly linked to running your business. Make sure to account for these costs since they might lower your tax liability when you file your taxes.

Invest in an Equity-Oriented Fund

Role-based funds may not be suitable for everyone, but they may save investors a lot of money on taxes, according to Ian Formigle, portfolio manager of the property investment company Crowd Street.

In his view, investing in real estate is perhaps the most free vehicle there is, and there is a road to never paying taxes on (capital invested in real estate) if you choose notto. The Tax Cuts and Jobs Act of 2017 established the suitability of role-based zones as a strategy to reinvigorate specified communities. Eligible profits, such as cash from stock sales, can be transferred to a qualifying opportunity fund, which invests in initiatives in these areas (Barry et al., 2020). This allows you to postpone paying the tax on the capital gains from that gain.

Deferred or Increased Income

In keeping accurate records and tax documents, several firms employ the cash accounting method. It requires a corporation to report income when it is collected and costs when they are paid – in other words, when money is exchanged. As a result, certain novel tax planning tactics emerge. If you anticipate being in a lower tax bracket next year, you may wish to save money by deferring income until next year.

- **When should income be deferred?**

  Assume you completed certain work for a customer in December 2021 and have yet to bill the customer for your services. You can postpone recording the money received until next year if you wait until January to charge your customer for the job you accomplished in December.
- **When should you increase your income?**

  Accelerating income in the current year may make sense at times, especially if you expect tax rates to rise in the coming years. In such an instance, you could issue an invoice and start collecting payments from a customer in the current year so you can pay taxes at the present rate.

The same principle applies to costs. If you are in a higher income bracket in a certain year, you might be able to minimize your tax liability by accelerating spending in that year. A simple chart can help you decide whether to accelerate or delay accruing your income and/or spending it.

Administering Assets as if They Were a Business

Creating a financial structure that includes a limited liability corporation (LLC) to handle numerous investments is one approach to saving on taxes, according to Featherngill. It might be a collection of assets, a parcel of real estate, or a company. Although this approach may be complicated, it should be highlighted that there may be cheaper alternatives while still establishing a governance framework for your assets. Costs incurred by an LLC that functions as a managing firm providing oversight and advice to financial institutions, under specific circumstances, qualify for deduction as business expenses.

Raising Equity Exposure While Reducing Losses

When the time comes to make a trade, the rich prefer to capitalize on stocks; meanwhile the tax rates are often lower than persons on wage revenue – presuming the stock was held for more than a year. They also have the financial means to take higher risks (Yeganeh, 2021).

People with higher total wealth often exhibit greater risk tolerance and have strategies in place to manage it. Therefore, relying solely on deadlines and relatively safe funds may not always be appropriate. In the context of financial decisions, such as tax planning, it is crucial to understand the implications of various tax rates. For 2018, the long-term capital gains tax rates remained zero, 16%, and 22%, depending on a person's income. Wage tax rates in the United States ranged from 10% for the lowest income to 37% for the highest income. Short-term capital gains taxes are based on the federal marginal rate and apply to securities held for less than a year.

According to Featherngill (), the rich strive to manage capital gains and losses for their tax benefit. For instance, near the end of each year, there is a "flurry of activity", with people seeking to offset some of the profits they made earlier in the year. People also engage in low-income neighborhoods through opportunity zone initiatives, according to her.

Change the Way Your Organization Is Structured

If you own a small company, you may not have the advantage of a company paying a percentage of your taxes. You are responsible for paying all Medicare and Social Security taxes. You must pay such taxes if your firm is taxed as an LLC. However, in some cases, you may be able to reduce the employer's two tax liabilities by half. For some small firms, this might be a good decision. Although there are several factors to take into account before taking this step, including paying oneself a decent income, it could be an excellent strategy to lower your taxable liability.

Conclusion

The COVID-19 pandemic has had a severe economic impact on various nations because it has not only affected the economy but also people's health. Because human activities were halted or restricted to stop the spread of the coronavirus and, therefore, an economic crisis ensued. Many groups were successful in implementing strategies for tax reduction, while others failed to do so. Tax reduction is sometimes confused with tax evasion, which is a dirty and nefarious behavior. Tax reduction is legal and legitimate. Tax dodging is an illegal activity (Anup, 2021) in which a company avoids paying taxes, and this affects the government and its infrastructure. Nonpayment of taxes meant to be deposited into a government's account also harms illegal businesses. It hurts a country's economy. Some taxes are expected to come from cross-border commerce and transactions. Corporate owners make a significant contribution to a country's tax system (Otavová et al., 2021).

A tax change's form and finance are crucial to achieving good economic development. Tax cuts may inspire employees to save and invest. If they are not accompanied by rapid spending cutbacks, they will almost surely result in a larger administration budget deficit, which will further reduce savings and increase interest prices in the long run. The net result of growth is unidentified, although many guesstimate that it will be negligible or undesirable. Base-broadening policies can decrease the impact of tax rate discounts on budget deficits while also minimizing their impacts on the stock of labor and levels of saving and investing, which will cause the direct effect on productivity to plummet.

They do, nevertheless, allocate funds across subdivisions for the greatest economic use, which may lead to enhanced competence and increase the frugality's total size. The findings showed that not all tax changes have the same effect on development. Reform efforts that increase inducements and current subsidies, minimize windfall profits, and evade budget deficits will have a more favorable influence on a country's long-term economic status, but they may result in trade-offs between fairness and effectiveness.

References

Abínzano, I., López-Arceiz, F. J., & Zabaleta, I. (2022). Can tax regulations moderate revenue diversification and reduce financial distress in nonprofit organizations? *Annals of Public and Cooperative Economics*. https://onlinelibrary.wiley.com/doi/full/10.1111/apce.12370

Akingbade, W. A. (2021). COVID-19 pandemic challenges to micro, small and medium enterprises in Nigeria: Strategic options for survival. *Acta Economica*, *19*(34), 153–167. http://ae.ef.unibl.org/index.php/ae/article/view/398

Alex, P. C. (2018). 47 Conservative groups & activists urge house action on making individual tax cuts permanent-on behalf of the undersigned organizations, we urge the house of representatives to. https://policycommons.net/artifacts/1757041/47-conservative-groups-activists-urge-house-action-on-making-individual-tax-cuts-permanent/2488960/

Anup, K. C. (2021). Role of policymakers and operators towards tourism revival in the era of COVID-19 in Nepal. *Journal of Tourism Quarterly*, *3*(2), 98–112. http://htmjournals.com/jtq/index.php/jtq/article/view/27

Arinta, Y. N., Nabila, R., Iskandar, I., Irkhamni, N., & Mustofa, U. (2020). Micro small medium enterprises (MSMEs) survival ability in pandemic covid 19 era: Integration of technology, organization, and environment analysis. http://eprints.eudl.eu/id/eprint/2807/

Barry, C. L., Han, H., Presskreischer, R., Anderson, K. E., & McGinty, E. E. (2020). Public support for social safety-net policies for COVID-19 in the United States, April 2020. *American Journal of Public Health*, *110*(12), 1811–1813. https://ajph.aphapublications.org/doi/abs/10.2105/AJPH.2020.305919

Ding, J., Chen, W., & Wang, W. (2020). Production and carbon emission reduction decisions for remanufacturing firms under carbon tax and take-back legislation. *Computers & Industrial Engineering*, *143*, 106419. https://www.sciencedirect.com/science/article/pii/S0360835220301534?casa_token=g8aK31wUx_4AAAAA:EpFs-jpzUQ7nPfUS3ooTWIIWlQUDOwOVJy9CxWbNkScGUpe6wB04eiNOIebEsBQMvmQUIzQ_dzH1

Gordana, D. P., & Biljana, I. S. (2021). Sustaining SME management and innovations in the post-COVID era. In *Handbook of research on strategies and interventions to mitigate COVID-19 impact on SMEs* (pp. 588–608). IGI Global. https://www.igi-global.com/chapter/sustaining-sme-management-and-innovations-in-the-post-covid-era/280695

Herzfeld, M. (2021). The role of professional organizations in practice and policy: How lawyers overtook accountants and economists in the early 20th century tax field. *Tax Lawyer*, *75*(1), 79. https://heinonline.org/HOL/LandingPage?handle=hein.journals/txlr75&div=7&id=&page=

Hosseini, S. E. (2020). An outlook on the global development of renewable and sustainable energy at the time of COVID-19. *Energy Research & Social Science*, *68*, 101633. https://www.sciencedirect.com/science/article/pii/S2214629620302085?casa_token=Qr9-g1QhiVoAAAAA:KQ0po1CglFL15bzPTY_8ZTF61IptyWKiT-YcOrZyuZCcJeO2X1rLVYRjSmCAwsimAMhV_T1iflm3

https://www.tandfonline.com/doi/full/10.1080/0015198X.2021.1963187?casa_token=rH0gsB6EWMUAAAAA%3AqC7kvS7unq866VXVDPxV9418cO0bdSvr4YdOgvIse2uTSrvIyyf10uvzshs_30aY-9Jzjsj4AYMLOEtX

Osho, A. E., & Ilori, F. O. (2020). Influence of transaction transfer pricing policies on corporate organizations tax in Nigeria. *Research Journal of Finance and Accounting*, *4*(3), 34–43. https://core.ac.uk/download/pdf/304991461.pdf

Otavová, M., Semerád, P., Maják, M., & Gláserová, J. (2021). Taxation of non-profit organizations and tax assignments in the Visegrad countries. https://otik.uk.zcu.cz/handle/11025/46997

Popescu, C. R. G., & Šebestová, J. D. (2022). Fiscally responsible businesses as a result of COVID-19 pandemic shock: Taking control of countries' tax systems by putting an end to corporate tax evasion and tax havens. In *Handbook of research on changing dynamics in responsible and sustainable business in the post-COVID-19 era* (pp. 161–192). IGI Global. https://www.igi-global.com/chapter/fiscally-responsible-businesses-as-a-result-of-covid-19-pandemic-shock/294418

Yeganeh, H. (2021). Emerging social and business trends associated with the Covid-19 pandemic. *Critical Perspectives on International Business*. https://www.emerald.com/insight/content/doi/10.1108/cpoib-05-2020-0066/full/html?casa_token=KJWnM7kt3FEAAAAA:5FhOUYZBhXNSqXGTC-tXwZ-ssFSFxQulLmb_D2bwBg9rrXXlOSGSHto1L0RRmFC7k___ndyr1PCD6P33peUrlMuOahUtGUWPo3iti-gq4eS7QhXKe3JJ4w

Yoshino, N., Taghizadeh-Hesary, F., & Otsuka, M. (2021). Covid-19 and optimal portfolio selection for investment in sustainable development goals. *Finance Research Letters*, *38*, 101695. https://www.sciencedirect.com/science/article/pii/S1544612320300854?casa_token=PcEuEx_WcpYAAAAA:ZOEdzb88mHHZluoxedkwsGWRgWz0gL3qI18ZTS7RtwclmWDbPlT5UxaZspBJU2fUdzqPPBbpBFnZ

Zhao, L., Zhang, Y., Sadiq, M., Hieu, V. M., & Ngo, T. Q. (2021). Testing green fiscal policies for green investment, innovation and green productivity amid the COVID-19 era. *Economic Change and Restructuring*, 1–22. https://link.springer.com/article/10.1007/s10644-021-09367-z

18 Consumer Boycott during a Time of Uncertainty

Empty Slogan or Determinant of Customer Capital and Business Value?

Wiesława Caputa

Introduction

In a competitive world dominated by new technologies, the importance of opinion assets, which can be created through the development of customer relationships, is growing. Strengthening customers' bargaining power, increasing their awareness, and sensitizing them to the needs for social programs and environmental protections have made customers active participants in the exchange. This is confirmed by numerous studies that have attributed to customers the roles of designer and co-creator, communicator, and censor of an offered product or the company offering it (Castillo et al., 2022; Krawczyk-Sokołowska, 2018). Thus, the customer has become a source not only of direct, but also of indirect, capital supply to the enterprise, and this is reflected financially in the customer capital (Stüker, 2009). This capital, which determines the value of a company, is built not on the basis of transactional contacts with customers, but on the positive emotions resulting from the establishment, maintenance, and development of relationships with customers. It is based on customer satisfaction, closeness, trust, and commitment (Hughes et al., 2019; Smirnova et al., 2018).

These relationships can be disrupted, or even severed if behavior on the part of the bidder is read by the customer as a threat to the customer's well-being (Chatzidakis & Lee, 2013; Hoffmann, 2011; Yuksel, 2013).

Such a state of emergency was definitely triggered by the Russian invasion of Ukraine. It not only shattered the hitherto established geopolitical order of the world but also violated the value system widely accepted by Western civilizations. It prompted a number of business entities to withdraw from the Russian market. However, some did not make such a decision, and this risked consumer boycotts of their products. This kind of boycott has been the subject of research in the past, but the current boycott is the first one, not only in Poland but also in Europe, in which consumer activism was a reaction to both a violation of a professed value system and also an indirect threat to the general security. This research attempted to elicit answers to the question of whether this boycott was strong enough to force the boycotted companies to change their behavior.

DOI: 10.4324/9781003475583-24

The key objective of this chapter was to analyze the effectiveness and efficiency of the boycott of three retail chains operating in Poland, such as Leroy Merlin, Auchan, and Decathlon, which have not withdrawn from operations in Russia. It was assumed that the acceptance of a boycott would not stop boycotters from making purchases but that by contributing to the entrenchment of negative opinions, the boycott would reduce the value of opinion assets, and this could translate negatively into customer capital and the market value of companies in the long term.

The realization of the goal was based on a literature review and the results of our own pilot studies and studies conducted by others.

Literature Review

The relationship between the bidder and the consumer can be disrupted by a consumer boycott. Many researchers treat consumer boycotts as a form of anticonsumption, stressing, however, that in its essence a boycott is not an expression of a generally negative attitude toward the market and the consumption of goods. Rather, it is a connection to a strictly defined situation caused by the reprehensible behavior (from the perspective of the customer) of a particular entity. As a result, a boycott has a narrower scope and is empowering (Hoffmann, 2011). A boycott is also defined as an attempt by boycotters to persuade consumers to refrain from taking part in certain transactions in the market (Friedman, 1985). Boycotters refrain from purchasing certain products to express their views on environmental, political, ethical, or social issues (Chatzidakis & Lee, 2013; Hoffmann, 2011; Yuksel, 2013). Customer values and ethics, as well as political activism, underlie such behavior (Yuksel & Mryteza, 2009).

A consumer boycott is a form of activity aimed at forcing bidders to behave in accordance with the consumers' value pattern. Many authors stress that consumers, being active participants in the market game, are increasingly using activist strategies to influence the behavior of companies (Tomlin, 2019). By promoting boycotts, they express their dissatisfaction with a company's actions or policies (Shaw et al., 2006). Hence, a boycott can be seen as a planned and collective action aimed at changing a bidder's strategy (Garrett, 1987; Yuksel & Mryteza, 2009). It occurs when a number of people refrain from buying a product at the same time to protest the blatantly offensive behavior of an entity, but not necessarily for the same reason (Andrew & Klein, 2003). However, this does not change the fact that participation in a boycott is based on an independent decision of each customer and that the boycott behavior itself, which is essentially a consumer complaint, is a private reaction of the individual. This makes it much more difficult to clearly identify the causes and motives of a boycott.

The early research aimed at identifying the motives behind boycotts was mainly conducted from a cost–benefit perspective (James, 2010). The change in the customer's bargaining position, increase in the customer's awareness, and, consequently, the customer's expectations have expanded the scope of exploration, which now focuses on the sociopsychological dimension. As a result, the motives for a boycott have become linked to the customer's emotions, and the boycott itself is seen as a way of expressing those emotions (Lindenmeier et al., 2012),

A boycott can also be seen as irrational customer behavior based on a customer's negative emotions. Studies in this area have shown that customer outrage played a key role in an increase in boycott participation (Lindenmeier et al., 2012). The outrage was most often connected to the blatantly offensive act of the boycotted entity, which was a source of unpleasantness for individuals. This emotional state could be triggered directly by an act that was undesirable from the customer's perspective or vicariously through negative emotions that arose from imagining that the company supported countries or entities whose activities threatened others (Andrew & Klein, 2003). The referenced studies showed that participation in boycotts can be motivated not only by prejudice but also by the psychological benefits that consumers might gain. The social component of these benefits generated strategic complementarity, that is, increased participation by others encouraged individual participation. At the same time, the effectiveness of the boycott may depend on the expectations of potential participants regarding the behavior of others.

Undoubtedly, the development of boycott movements has been and is, among other things, driven by increased public attention to corporate social responsibility (Klein et al., 2004). Consequently, the goal of a boycott was not only to influence the company but also to influence the public good and increase the "general good" through organizational modification, government practices, or the building of collective social movements against issues of concern (Yuksel, 2013). Consumer boycotts were strongly linked to consumer well-being, which was created by positive experiences, pleasant emotions, or low levels of negative experiences and moods (Makarem & Jae, 2016).

The source of these experiences or emotions could also be the relationship between the consumer and the offeror. This relationship was based on the dual perceived and correlated customer value assessed from the perspectives of both the customer and the company (Caputa et al., 2021).

Customer value is linked to a product and the process of using it, which must satisfy the basic emotional and social needs of the customer (Kotler & Bliemel, 2005; Sweeney & Soutar, 2001). Regardless of how it was defined, value was a subjective and dynamic category that was linked to the customer's rational and emotional evaluations of a product. Rational evaluation gave way to emotional evaluation as the longevity of the relationship increased, with the longevity of the relationship conditioned by participation in the "heart of the customer" (Storbacka et al., 2001). The share increased as customer satisfaction, closeness, and trust increased, confirming the link to consumer well-being.

Customer value from a company's perspective was reflected in customer capital. This capital is usually boiled down to the sum of the net cash flows that a company acquired over the customer life cycle as a result of delivering customer value (Caputa, 2020; Helm & Günter, 2006; Stüker, 2009). The value of these flows was derived from the customer's willingness and ability to make and develop purchases (i.e., the customer's transactional value) and to trigger such an information transfer (i.e., the customer's resource value), which could determine its contribution to the company's value creation (Caputa, 2020; Helm & Günter, 2006).

Integral to customer value were the brand and relationships – or, in essence, the opinion assets – a company had. These assets were affected by the widespread access to computers, the Internet, and the progressive process of digitization, which facilitated the acquisition and transfer of the information affect. This included, among other things, the visibility, distinction, or authenticity of the company. The "roots of fame" underlying a company's reputation was thus affected (Esa et al., 2022; Fombrun & Riel, 2003; Gaultier-Gaillard & Louisot, 2006).

Regardless of how it was defined, reputation was based on a collective opinion and was the result of how stakeholders, including customers, evaluated a company's past actions through the lens of the values created for them. This clearly indicated that a boycott resulting from a company's violation of a customer's professed values could, on the one hand, negatively affect a customer's willingness to buy and thus, in essence, the customer's transactional value. On the other hand, a boycott could trigger a customer's readiness to launch an information message that negatively affected the roots of fame and, consequently, the market value of a company. Indeed, reputation is considered a key factor in a company's long-term viability and success (Kaur & Sing, 2018; Tangngisalu et al., 2020).

Methodology and Results of Research

The overview presented made it possible to conclude that boycotts are combined with refraining from purchases, with the leading goal of forcing companies to stop practices that negatively affect consumer welfare. Thus, I assumed that the direct effect of a boycott was to reduce a customer's willingness to buy and, thus, reduce customer turnover, which would lead to a reduction in the market value of the customer from the perspective of realizing the interests of the boycotted company. Such an effect gave N. C. Smith insight into the effectiveness of a boycott, which he distinguished from the success of a boycott (Smith, 1990). In his view, success remained linked to achieving the goals of a boycott.

Based on this concept, I linked the effectiveness of a boycott to two effects, the scale of support for the boycott and the actual refraining from buying. The success of a boycott was linked to the abandonment of the decision or behavior that gave rise to the call for the boycott. The path to such an effect may lead to a decline in the value of opinion assets. Consequently, I assumed that a successful boycott, by contributing to the entrenchment of negative opinions about boycotted entities, negatively translated into the value of opinion assets, and thus customer capital and the market value of enterprises in the long term. In light of the review so far, it seemed that positive verification of such an assumption required confirmation that the decision to continue operating in the Russian market was perceived by consumers as blatant (H1). If this was not the case, it could be assumed that the consumer's acceptance of the boycott was not equivalent to refraining from purchasing (H2), although making repeat purchases did not necessarily imply abandonment of the boycott (H3).

Verification of the hypotheses was based on the results of a pilot study conducted among full-time and part-time postgraduate students in April 2022. The research served to validate a survey questionnaire designed to study the strength of the boycott and the factors leading to the boycott during the Russian invasion. The results made it possible to verify the questionnaire. They were also used to analyze support for the boycott of three retail chains operating in Poland that had decided to stay in the Russian market and to assess the actual buying behavior of respondents.

The study population included 345 respondents between the ages of 20 and 49 years, 52% of whom were women. Based on the age of the respondents, the collective was divided into three groups, with the size of each group as follows: those aged 19–26 years (72 people), those aged 27–37 years (159 people), and those aged 38–49 years (113 people). An additional factor differentiating respondents was the income of the respondent's household. Based on their subjective opinions, the dominant group of respondents rated it as average (36%) or good (40%). Only 15% of respondents rated it as very good, and 9% rated it as bad.

The results of the research presented in the study were contrasted with studies conducted by others, such as Neptis, DGP Agency, Spicy Mobile, and PKO Bank.

Four questions in the questionnaire were directly related to the verification of H1: assessment of the acceptance of the companies' decision to stay in the Russian market, the ability to identify companies that made such a decision, the respondent's knowledge of the boycott being undertaken, and the acceptance of a boycott as a form of customer activity.

In general, the results of the survey indicated that the vast majority of the respondents rated decisions to continue operations in Russia as bad (32%) or very bad (39%). More than 71% of respondents agreed with this assessment. Only 12% of respondents rated it as outrageous, while the rest either had no opinion (10%) or considered it rational (15%). It should be emphasized that none of the respondents to the survey chose the answer "absolutely right".

Most of those surveyed were able to name at least one company that made the decision to stay in Russia. The largest number was for the Leroy Merlin chain (336) and Decathlon (267), followed by Auchan (196). Only 15 responses were for other companies, and some of them were not correct. It is worth noting that only one Polish company was included in this group, and it was mentioned by only three people.

Nearly 100% of those surveyed said they knew about the boycott of French retail chains, but only 73% supported it. Most of the other 27% stated that the reason they did not support it was a lack of acceptance of such a form of activity. They lacked faith in the effectiveness of such an action and cited the contribution of boycotted companies to the economy, in particular, their creation of jobs.

Although more than 73% of those surveyed supported the boycott, nearly 69% said they had made a purchase at least once at one of the retail chains listed in the survey between the outbreak of the war and the time of the survey, and more than 26% said they had done so frequently or even regularly. There were mainly two justifications for this behavior: the convenience of shopping at a store (i.e., the proximity to a retail outlet) (92%) and the attractiveness of the offerings of a store, which included a satisfactory price/quality ratio (86%) and the promotions used (88%). It was noteworthy that almost 30% of respondents justified their decisions by pointing to the behavior of others, such as those who stated, "I buy because others also buy". It was noteworthy that those who rated a chain's decision to stay in the Russian market as outrageous were overwhelmingly adamant that they would not purchase any more products from the chain (87%),

Verification of H3 required responses about whether, despite continuing to shop at the surveyed chains, the respondent had participated passively or actively in communicating information that might, in the respondent's opinion, negatively affect others' willingness to shop at the chains or negatively affect the image of the chains. Most of the respondents confirmed their passive or active participation in such a message (Table 18.1).

In general, the information was broadcast and/or received by those who supported the boycott but made a purchase anyway. Only 11% said they had never discussed the problem in face-to-face social conversations. Of the respondents, 66% actively participated in discussions on online forums. Of the respondents who said they were not actively engaged in such activities, more than 87% read posts containing the indicated content.

As can be seen from the above data, those who declared support for a boycott but also used offerings of the boycotted retail chains showed considerable activity in seeking and broadcasting information, the content of which could negatively affect the value of the chains' opinion assets. Such involvement could foster the perpetuation of a negative image of boycotted companies, which in the long term could lead to a reduction in their market value.

Discussion and Conclusions

A boycott is a form of customer activity that can negatively affect customer capital both by reducing the willingness to make purchases and by enhancing the activity to broadcast and receive information containing negative content

Table 18.1 Responses about communicating passive or active information

Despite continuing to shop at the surveyed chains, have you ever participated in the passive or active communication of information that may have negatively affected the use of an offering or the image of the boycotted retail chain? N=198			
	Never	Sometimes	Often
We talk about this decision during direct social conversations	11	67	22
I participate in discussions held on this topic in online forums	34	36	30
I read posts on online forums and other such information available on the web	8	65	25

Source: Own research.

about the offerer or directly calling for a boycott. Thus, the effect of such an action can manifest itself both in the short term (directly) and in the long term (indirectly). Research studies conducted by Lindenmeier et al. (2012) and Andrew and Klein (2003) showed that both the effectiveness and success of boycotts were greater when the boycotted entity blatantly violated the consumer's value system, which was directly related to a reduction in consumer welfare. The presented research results, although indicating a negative evaluation by consumers of the decision to stay in the Russian market, did not confirm H1. Hence, it could be expected that there would be a dissonance between the consumer's stated and actual transactional behavior (H2). This dissonance meant that achieving full effectiveness would be impossible, that is, an outcome in which every person who accepted the boycott refrained from shopping at a boycotted chain. Assuming that the decision to boycott was an individual decision of each consumer, who had a value system that varied and may change the existence of such a condition should be considered hypothetical. Thus, in assessing the effectiveness of the boycott, it was necessary to estimate the degree to which the declarations of customers supporting the boycott were translated into their actual transactional behavior. In light of the research, this effectiveness appeared to be low.

When viewing the scale of the boycott's impact on customer capital, it was important to determine how many customers were lost and what amount of sales was lost by the boycotted companies. The research, which used an application that allowed for cell phone geolocation, showed that for almost a month after the outbreak, the number of visitors to the designated chains increased, in the case of Auchan by up to 11% (Rutkowska, 2022). It was only after this period that declines were noted, and they had varying dynamics across the chains. This could indicate the boycott's progressive effectiveness, especially since the chain that experienced the fastest decline announced its decision to pull out of Russia. In that case, one could even assume that the boycott was effective. In fact, the company's decision was made not due to the influence of the boycott but, rather, to the threat of a collapse of supply chains. It should also be emphasized that the application used only allowed the person's presence near the store to be determined, not the person's actual transactional behavior or even reasons for being near the establishment. It is therefore difficult to estimate the actual customer traffic in the store itself or the scale of purchases made. In addition, the surveys were carried out in only three outlets in Poland's largest cities, so they cannot be considered representative.

The fact that the boycott had an impact on customer capital, however, can be inferred from information released by the PKO Bank (Szutiak, 2022). The bank, in analyzing the dynamics of payments on its credit cards to stores of two of the chains (not mentioned by name) still operating in Russia with their competitors, showed that staying in Russia was associated with a decline in turnover in Poland. This clearly indicated a reduction in the value of the direct capital supply coming from customers. It is noteworthy that among the factors that prompted boycott supporters to make a single purchase, price, and promotions played a primary role, that is, they were the main factors that made up the value proposition. These factors gained importance, especially in a period of uncertainty caused not only by a pandemic and the Russian-Ukrainian war but also by the deteriorating economic situation of households.

Advancing inflation and increasing threats to national security were just some of the factors creating customer uncertainty that may have influenced a shift away from emotional to rational purchasing decisions. The validity of this statement was confirmed by studies conducted in the Polish market (among other indications), which have shown the dominant importance of financial relationships in the creation of customer capital under conditions of deteriorating consumer sentiment. They also showed that factors determining the value of an offer, including the price and promotions, formed the strongest focusing node that explained consumers' purchasing decisions (Caputa, 2014). Observing the behavior of one of the boycotted retail chains, this continuously encouraged purchases through significant price promotions systematically communicated in the mass media, allowed us to assume that this may be an effective strategy for customer retention, and even acquisition.

Previous research, however, indicated that securing a sustainable capital supply that translated into sustained and increased business value remained linked to customer trust and commitment (Fadila et al., 2021; Liang, 2021). This was not served by the customer's commitment shown in the studies to express negative opinions about boycotted entities or even passively assimilate such opinions. Such an effect was observed in the group of customers accepting the boycott but making purchases, and it positively verified H3. In addition, it should be noted that most customers today are members of some kind of virtual community, and this greatly expands the range of information sent and received (Caputa, 2020; SentiOne, 2022). It becomes reasonable to conclude that in the long run, such customer engagement will affect a brand's image, leading to a decrease in reputation and, consequently, company value. This can prove to be an effective motivator to revise original decisions and return to behavior in line with customer expectations. The validity of such a statement was confirmed by the changes in the "brand health" index recorded by one of the boycotted chains after the announcement of its planned withdrawal from the Russian market. The index rose from 0.38 to 0.51, with the number of statements about the company more than doubling (SentiOne, 2022).

It should be recalled that the decision to leave the market was not the result of a boycott. What is certain, however, is that it was noticed precisely because the subject was boycotted. Therefore, this form of customer activity improved visibility. However, there is plenty of evidence showing that negative visibility can serve a company. An example in the Polish market was the boycott of Cisowianka, which not only was not effective but also resulted in an increase in customer interest. However, it seemed that in the case of the retail chains analyzed, such an effect was not to be feared, given not only the historical past of the Poles but also the high degree of the perceived threat from Russia.

Recommendations and Directions for Future Research

The condition for securing the effectiveness of the boycott, and thus forcing a change in a company's decision, was to at least maintain the reach of the boycott and strengthen its impact. The realization of this goal should be based not only on a call to boycott, which in the long term could lead to the effect of "refraining because others refrain", but on the impact on the consciousness of customers to abandon purchasing because "they do not want to do it".

Such an influence must aim at building the conviction of the power of each consumer operating in the relational network and at ruthlessly exposing the negative consequences of the aggressor's spending of funds obtained from companies present in the Russian market. This kind of influence can induce a sense of guilt and responsibility in customers, and this is conducive to abandoning the boycotted companies' offerings.

These recommendations indicate the directions and dimensions for future research.

The international dimension is particularly interesting in terms of comparing the ratio, effectiveness, and efficiency of war-induced boycotts in countries at different distances from the zone of direct hostilities. A study of this dimension should take into account at least two perspectives, that of the customer and that of the company. The limited research perspective adopted for this analysis focused only on three retail chains and elicited responses only from students. It must be expanded.

Another direction is to study the relationship between the consumer's level of empathy and the consumer's actual buying behavior in support of the boycott. The research focused on the expression of consumer emotions in boycott messages, the emotional intensity of these messages, and their relationship to boycott motivations should be expanded. In this context, special attention should be paid to the use of artificial intelligence in research conducted via the Internet and social media platforms.

Attention can also be paid to the quantitative dimension. Creating a list of factors determining the effectiveness of a boycott and the strength of their influence on purchasing decisions could contribute to an attempt to construct a synthetic measure to assess the effectiveness and efficiency of a boycott.

References

Andrew, J., & Klein, J. (2003). The boycott puzzle: Consumer motivations for purchase sacrifice. *Management Science, 49*(9), 1196–1209. https://doi.org/10.1287/mnsc.49.9.1196.16569

Caputa, W. (2014). Kapitał klienta w budowaniu wartości przedsiębiorstwa. Wydawnictwo Warszawa: CeDeWu.

Caputa, W. (2020). Kapitał klienta w środowisku wirtualnym. CeDeWu. ISBN: 9788381022347.

Caputa, W., Krawczyk-Sokolowska, I., & Pierścieniak, A. (2021). The potential of web awareness as a determinant of dually defined customer value. *Technological Forecasting and Social Change*, *163*, 120443. https://doi.org/10.1016/j.techfore.2020.120443

Castillo, H., Grijalvo, M., Martinez-Corral, A., & Palacios, M. (2022). Crowdsourcing ecosystem. The crowd pillars and their implementation process. *Lecture Notes in Management and Industrial Engineering*, 279–291. https://doi.org/10.1007/978-3-030-95967-8_25

Chatzidakis, A., & Lee, M. (2013). Anti-consumption as the study of reasons against. *Journal of Macromarketing*, *33*(3), 190–203. https://doi.org/10.1177/0276146712462892

Esa, E., Mohamad, N. R., Wan Zakaria, W. Z., & Ilias, N. (2022). Do corporate governance and reputation are two sides of the same coins? Empirical evidence from Malaysia. *The Journal of Asian Finance, Economics and Business*, *9*(1), 219–228. https://doi.org/10.13106/jafeb.2022.vol9.no1.0219

Fadila, D., Lupikawaty, M., & Africano, F. (2021). The mediation role of trust on the effect of commitment to religiosity and marketing communication on customer loyalty of Islamic banks. *International Journal of Communication and Society, 4*(1), 137–152. https://doi.org/10.31763/ijcs.v4i1.479

Fombrun, C., & Riel, C. (2003). *Fame and Fortune*. Upper Saddle River, NJ: Pearson Education.

Friedman, M. (1985). Consumer boycotts in the United States, 1970–1980: Contemporary events in historical perspective. *Journal of Consumer Affairs, 19*(1), 96–117. https://doi.org/10.1111/j.1745-6606.1985.tb00346.x

Garrett, D. (1987). The effectiveness of marketing policy boycotts: Environmental opposition to marketing. *Journal of Marketing*, *51*(April), 48–57. https://doi.org/10.1177/002224298705100204

Gaultier-Gaillard, S., & Louisot, J. (2006). Risks to reputation: A global approach. *The Geneva Papers on Risk and Insurance Issues and Practice*, *31*(3), 425–445. https://doi.org/10.1057/ palgrave.gpp.2510090

Helm, S., & Günter, B. (2006). *Kundenwert*. Wiesbaden: Gabler.

Hoffmann, S. (2011). Anti-consumption as a means to save jobs. *European Journal of Marketing*, *45*, 1702–1714. https://doi.org/10.1108/03090561111167342

Hughes, C., Swaminathan, V., & Brooks, G. (2019). Driving brand engagement through online social influencers: An empirical investigation of sponsored blogging campaigns. *Journal of Marketing, 83*(5), 78–96. https://doi.org/10.1177/0022242919854374

James, V. (2010). A socio-cultural approach to exploring consumer boycott intelligence: A commentary essay. *Journal of Business Research*, *63*(4), 363–365. https://doi.org/https://doi.org/10.1016/j.jbusres.2009.04.015

Kaur, A., & Sing, B. (2018). Measuring the immeasurable corporate reputation. *Metamorphosis Journal, 17*(1), 53–64. https://doi.org/10.1177%2F0972622518778210

Klein, J., Smith, N., & John, A. (2004). Why we boycott: Consumer motivations for boycott participation. *Journal of Marketing*, *68*(3), 92–109. https://doi.org/https://doi.org/10.1509/jmkg.68.3.92.34770

Kotler, P., & Bliemel F. (2005). *Marketing-Management: Analyse, Planung und Verwirklichung*. Aufl. Stuttgart: Pearson Studium, 58.

Krawczyk-Sokołowska, I. (2018) Kreatywność stymulatorem postaw proinnowacyjnych w przedsiębiorstwie. *Studia i Prace Kolegium Zarządzania i Finansów, 162*, 5–64.

Liang, B. (2021). How brand experience, satisfaction, trust, and commitment affect loyalty: A reexamination and reconciliation. *Italian Journal of Marketing*, *2022*(2), 203–231. https://doi.org/10.1007/s43039-021-00042-9

Lindenmeier, J., Schleer, C., & Pricl, D. (2012). Consumer outrage: Emotional reactions to unethical corporate behavior. *Journal of Business Research*, *65*(9), 1364–1373. https://doi.org/10.1016/j.jbusres.2011.09.022

Makarem, S., & Jae, H. (2015). Consumer boycott behavior: An exploratory analysis of twitter feeds. *Journal of Consumer Affairs*, *50*(1), 193–223. https://doi.org/10.1111/joca.12080

Rutkowska, E. (2022). Spadł ruch w sieciach nadal handlujących w Rosji. Retrieved 22 September 2022, from https://edgp.gazetaprawna.pl/e-wydanie/58418,13-kwietnia-2022/74425,Dziennik-Gazeta-Prawna/779825,Spadl-ruch-w-sieciach-nadal-handlujacych-w-Rosji.html

SentiOne: Internauci wzywają do bojkotu firm, które nie wycofały się z Rosji [analiza] - NowyMarketing. (2022). Retrieved 22 September 2022, from https://nowymarketing.pl/a/37252,sentione-internauci-wzywaja-do-bojkotu-firm-ktore-nie-wycofaly-sie-z-rosji-analiza

Shaw, D., Newholm T., & Dickinson R. (2006). Consumption as voting: An exploration of consumer empowerment. *European Journal of Marketing*, *40*(9/10), 1049–1067.

Smirnova, M. M., Rebiazina, V. A., & Frösén J. (2018). Customer orientation as a multidimensional construct: Evidence from the Russian markets. *Journal of Business Research*, *86*, 457–467.

Smith, N. (1990). *Morality and the Market*. London: Routledge.

Storbacka, K., Lehtinen, J., & Turnau, P. (2001). *Sztuka budowania trwałych związków z klientami*. Kraków: Oficyna Ekonomiczna.

Stüker, D. (2009). *Evaluierung und Steuerung von Kundenbeziehungen aus Sicht des unternehmenswertorientierten Controlling*. Wiesbaden: Gabler Verlag/GWV Fachverlage GmbH, Wiesbaden.

Swenney, J. C., & Soutar, G. N. (2001). Consumer perceived value: The development of a multiple item scale. *Journal of Reataliling*, *77*, 203–220. https://www.academia.edu/14291355/Consumer_perceived_value_The_development_of_a_multiple_item_scale

Szutiak, M. (2022). PKO BP dowodzi, że z Rosją nie ma żartów. Trzeba ostro. Retrieved 22 September 2022, from https://www.telepolis.pl/fintech/prawo-finanse-statystyki/pko-bank-polski-rosja-platnosci

Tangngisalu, J., Mappamiring, M., Andayani, W., Yusuf, M., & Putra, A. H. P. K. (2020). CSR and firm reputation from employee perspective. *The Journal of Asian Finance, Economics and Business*, 7(10), 171–182. https://doi.org/10.13106/JAFEB.2020.VOL7.NO10.171

Tomlin, K. M. (2019). Assessing the efficacy of consumer boycotts of U.S. target firms: A shareholder wealth analysis. *Southern Economic Journal, 86*(2), 503–529. https://doi.org/10.1002/soej.12389

Yuksel, U. (2013). Non-participation in anti-consumption: Consumer reluctance to boycott. *Journal of Macromarketing, 33*(3), 204–216. https://doi.org/10.1177/0276146713484153

Yuksel, U., & Mryteza, V. (2009). An evaluation of strategic responses to consumer boycotts. *Journal of Business Research*, *62*(2), 248–259. https://doi.org/10.1016/j.jbusres.2022.02.063

19 Value Management Process for Users of Streaming Platforms

Determinants and Developments during and after the COVID-19 Pandemic

Magdalena Sobocińska and Adam Czarnecki

Introduction

New technologies are increasingly applied to the various stages of the customer value management process, which includes creating, delivering, and communicating value to audiences. They expand the possibilities for realizing artistic and marketing visions and goals. For instance, drones allow the production of images that would be difficult to obtain with other techniques. The fundamental change resulting from the digital revolution also applies to visual effects. It is also impossible not to point to the development of streaming platforms, which is causing the perception of time to change. A new category of time has been set up, known as momentary time. This is accompanied by the disappearance of the "culture of waiting" (Urry, 2000, pp. 105–130) and the ability to watch multiple episodes one after another.

The virtualization of cultural participation is mainly linked to the emergence of new business models based on the synergy of human talent and new technologies. These processes were accelerated by the coronavirus pandemic. This was especially true for streaming platforms, which gained many new customers during the pandemic. The aim of this chapter was to show the set of benefits offered to users of streaming platforms as opposed to cinemas and to determine the level of satisfaction of their needs. This chapter in the monograph was based on in-depth literature studies, as well as a semiotic analysis and the results of a survey conducted on a representative sample of Poles aged 18–65 years.

Literature Review

The issue of customer value management is multidimensional in nature and can be analyzed from many perspectives, including the lens of axiology, in which value is defined in terms of what is valuable and the purpose of human action. According to the humanistic perspective, the value is the human being as the subject of an action and the performance of various functions. On the social front, the term refers to the values individuals hold. Value is also identified with objects that satisfy needs and toward which human aspirations are

DOI: 10.4324/9781003475583-25

directed. Taking into account the psychological approach, in turn, it should be noted that value is an element of an individual's belief system and concerns how one should act (Rudawska, 2008, pp. 19–21). As one turns from considering the general notion of value, which is defined in various ways in individual fields, to the category of customer value, it should be noted that it is understood as the subjectively perceived excess of benefits over the equally understood costs of acquiring and using a product (Mruk & Stępień, 2013, pp. 14–21).

The ways in which value is created, delivered, and communicated are being reconfigured by implementing digital technologies in this area and creating new business models based on them (Amit & Zott, 2020, pp. 27–37). Digital technologies are one of the strategic resources necessary for the development of innovations, both disruptive and incremental. The essence of their implementation is that it is possible to identify the needs and expectations of customers, leading to an increase in the value of the market entity by offering customers increasingly better bundles of value (Nowicka, 2019, pp. 17–43; Westerman et al., 2014, p. 30). This is clearly seen in the cultural sphere, in which the emergence of new relationships between art and technology is an important goal. However, it is important to distinguish between digital instruments and digital media; the changes taking place in art are influenced by both digital instruments, that is, digital technologies used as part of creative work within traditional artistic genres and digital media understood in the context of new artistic disciplines and new media art (Kluszczyński, 2010, p. 17). The intensifying relationship between art and technology is expressed through artistic experiments based on human talent and technology, new forms of visual narration, and the virtualization of art promotion processes and digital distribution (Sobocińska, 2019, pp. 74–95), creating a homebody lifestyle and cultural participation model.

It is worth noting that in the discourse on streaming platforms, there are theories that the practice of watching movies at home on demand began when going to the cinema began to be seen as something more than fair entertainment, and wealthy and prominent individuals, wanting to protect their privacy, ordered screenings to be seen in their own homes (Somborski, 2019, pp. 5–8). Although the ability of viewers to watch movies at home has evolved and has been linked to the development of television, VHS, and DVD systems, streaming platforms have, to a greater extent than earlier solutions, made it possible to change the way we perceive time.

The growth of streaming platforms, which occurred even before the COVID-19 pandemic, was due to the attractiveness and uniqueness of the movies and series available on these platforms. The global market leader in streaming platforms is Netflix. In terms of innovation, its business model moved away from the business of renting movies stored on traditional media to creating a streaming platform and then expanding the scope of the business to create original content (Kurti et al., 2021; Mier & Kohli, 2021, pp. 194–205).

The development of streaming platforms has contributed to changes in serial viewing practices, which are expressed in the spread of a phenomenon known as marathon viewing, or binge-watching (Fagerjord & Kueng, 2019, pp. 166–181; Rahman & Arif, 2021, pp. 97–112), which involves watching series in multi-episode blocks and removes the limitations of linear television. Streaming platforms are therefore important players in the digital economy, which is changing not only the mechanisms of how film distribution works but also content consumption (Ulin, 2019, pp. 325–360). They became beneficiaries of the pandemic because there was a significant increase in subscriptions. Indeed, under conditions of fear, uncertainty, and anxiety because of the risk of disease, as well as the closure of cultural institutions such as cinemas, domestic forms of leisure and cultural participation became particularly important. They satisfied many needs, including not only the need for entertainment but also cognitive needs and needs for maintaining family ties (Mróz, 2021, p. 20). In this context, it becomes important to answer the research question about the advantages offered by streaming platforms over cinemas.

Research Methods

The research process, which aimed to find answers to the formulated research questions, was based on the triangulation of qualitative and quantitative research methods, as its application allowed a broader and deeper view of the categories under study and obtained a more complete picture of the recognized market phenomena and processes (Denzin, 2017).

After the literature study, a semiotic analysis was carried out, which fell into the category of qualitative research. It contributed to the field by determining the meaning or sense of a phenomenon occurring in a social space, as well as describing the phenomenon (Glinka & Czakon, 2021, p. 16). At the heart of semiotic analysis is the assumption that the decoding of messages by recipients is a culturally conditioned creative activity. This means that the mental concept of an object (e.g., what the terms *cinema* and *streaming platform* mean to a viewer) is a dynamic category and depends on the cultural experience of the viewer. In semiotic concepts, the sign is arbitrary in nature and the meaning is regulated by convention (Fiske, 1999, p. 62). Following a semiotic approach, a binary opposition analysis was conducted on the differences between watching movies via the Internet on a streaming platform and watching movies in the cinema. It was based on the assumptions that the process of cognition and making sense and meaning of categories involves understanding what something is not, and that there are sets of oppositional values that are highly significant in social processes (Polak & Zurawicka, 2015, pp. 110–120). Conducting the analysis using pairs of binary oppositions, the following criteria were used: context of reception, viewer attention, mood, uniqueness of the event, offering, time, place of reception, screen size, cost of participation, and Internet access.

Another research approach used was a survey. The quantitative survey was conducted of a nationwide representative sample of 1,019 people using a survey questionnaire that was made available to respondents online as part of an online research panel. The choice of the research technique was dictated, on the one hand, by the need to conduct research among Internet users, since the study involved users of streaming platforms, and, on the other hand, by the advantages of research conducted using online research panels, which are defined as large groups of potential respondents who are recruited and agree to participate in various types of research (Roberts, 2003, p. 179). The growing importance of surveys conducted using online panels is related to the fact that these surveys are subject to standardization, have a high response rate, and allow for the preselection of respondents, controlling the sample and minimizing the number of missing data through the use of appropriate formation technology solutions and avoiding errors that could arise at the stage of entering data into the database (Forrest, 2003, pp. 112–115). In addition, the choice of research technique was influenced by the COVID-19 pandemic, which catalyzed virtualization processes in many spheres of socioeconomic life, including in the area of conducting market and marketing research.

The quantitative survey shown was conducted among participants of the ePanel, managed by the ARC Market and Opinion Research Institute. This institute is certified by the Information Security Quality Control Program and Interviewer Quality Control Program for the CAWI technique. ePanel.pl has more than 75,000 registered users and is one of Poland's largest platforms for public opinion research. The results of surveys conducted using the ePanel are representative of the Polish population aged 18–65 in terms of age, gender, region and size of place of residence, and education. The presented study was conducted in April 2022. The study included 507 women and 512 men. The majority of the respondents (42%) in the surveyed population were 45–65 years of age, and the smallest group (12%) were 18–24 years of age. In terms of education, respondents included those with primary, secondary, and higher education. The share of people with primary education in the surveyed population was 40%, with secondary education 35%, and with higher education 25%.

Characterizing the structure of the sample by the size of the locality in which the respondent lived, the largest group lived in rural areas. Their share of the surveyed population was 39%. In contrast, residents of the largest cities, with more than 500,000 residents, accounted for 12% of the surveyed population. The share of those living in cities with up to 20,000 residents was also 12%. Those surveyed came from all 16 provinces in Poland.

Results

Presenting the results of the conducted analysis of binary opposites in the modes of cultural participation involving watching movies, it is important to point out the differences that exist between watching movies at a cinema and via the Internet on a streaming platform. Features of cultural participation involved in watching movies using a streaming platform include the context of reception created by watching a movie individually or in a relatively small group of people sitting near each other. In terms of home-centric cultural participation, there are many distractions for the viewer, whose attention is often divided between several activities simultaneously, while watching a movie online is part of everyday life. New practices of cultural participation, which gained prominence in the era of the pandemic, gave the viewer more choices about what, when, on what device, and in what location he or she could watch. This was accompanied by a sense of independence. This was mainly related to the technological advances taking place. On the other hand, a significant aspect of cultural reception when watching movies at a cinema was the ability to watch a movie with a sometimes large group of people, as well as the enjoyment of leaving home and spending time at a cultural institution. In addition, viewers had an opportunity to increase the uniqueness of a cultural event, especially for premiere screenings of films at which representatives of film crews were present. When watching movies at a cinema, the viewer's attention is focused on the film. However, the viewer must adapt to the cinema's current repertoire, location, and screening time. Figure 19.1 shows pairs of binary opposites delineating ways of thinking about watching movies in the cinema and on a streaming platform.

When combining the results of the semiotic analysis with the results of the quantitative survey, it should be noted that the popularity of streaming platforms in Poland is high. This is evidenced by the fact that they are used by two-thirds of the surveyed population, representing Internet users in Poland aged 18–65. The increasing use of streaming platforms has been accelerated by the coronavirus pandemic and periodic closures of cultural institutions. When determining the profiles of users of streaming platforms, it should be noted that in the youngest age group (18–24 years), almost 9 out of 10 people surveyed used this form of cultural participation. The percentage was much lower in the 45- to 65-year-old group, at 57%. Saturation was highest among men aged 18–24 years and lowest among women aged 45–65 years. This may be related to the fact that people in older age groups are more accustomed to watching traditional television. The most popular streaming platform in Poland is Netflix. It is used by as many as 85% of people who are users of streaming platforms. In second place is the HBO GO platform, which is used by 29% of surveyed users of streaming platforms.

After statistical analyses using Jaccard's similarity coefficient (Leskovec et al., 2014), it was concluded that the phenomenon of co-use of streaming platforms in Poland occurred to a limited extent, as the coefficients reached low values. The vast majority of respondents used only one streaming platform. This is illustrated in Table 19.1.

Among those taking part in a survey conducted during the COVID-19 pandemic, those who used more than one streaming platform dominated those who purchased simultaneous access to Netflix and HBO GO. It seemed

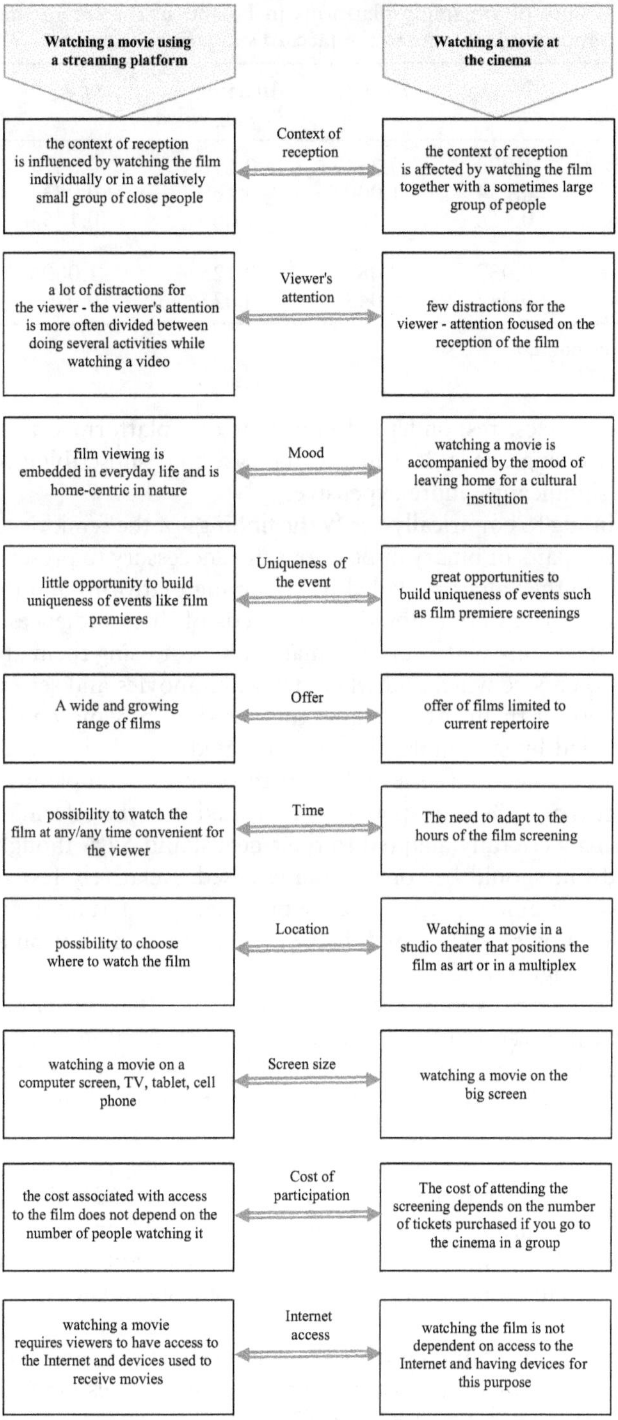

Figure 19.1 Watching movies via the Internet on a streaming platform versus watching movies in the cinema (i.e., pairs of binary opposites).

Source: Own elaboration.

Table 19.1 Co-use of streaming platforms in Poland in the era of the COVID-19 pandemic according to the Jaccard similarity coefficient

	Netflix	*HBO_GO*	*Amazon_ Prime_Video*	*Apple_TV*	*Other_ service*
Netflix	1.000	0.254	0.116	0.037	0.047
HBO_GO	0.254	1.000	0.189	0.083	0.043
Amazon_Prime_ Video	0.116	0.189	1.000	0.125	0.025
Apple_TV	0.037	0.083	0.125	1.000	0.020
Other_service	0.047	0.043	0.025	0.020	1.000

Source: Own elaboration.

that, in most cases, respondents found that one platform was sufficient to meet their viewing needs. It was also the case that subscribing to two platforms was significantly more expensive.

When aiming to empirically verify the findings of the semiotic analysis carried out using pairs of binary oppositions, it is necessary to present the results of a survey on the values provided by streaming platforms and the degree to which their offerings are tailored to the needs of their audiences. According to users of streaming platforms, the main values of using them are related to the ability to choose when and where to watch movies and series, as well as a large variety of them. At the same time, it should be noted that the time utility provided by streaming platforms is rated slightly higher by respondents than the movies and series offerings themselves. Completing the picture was the fact that 36% of respondents indicated that the offerings of streaming platforms were fully adapted to their needs, and 52% thought that they were broad but should be constantly increased. Relatively few respondents thought that streaming platforms only provided m entertainment, as well as that the best movies were shown first in the cinema and not on a streaming platform (see Figure 19.2).

In analyzing the responses regarding the values that were mostly created by cinemas, the respondents stated that these cultural institutions primarily provided the opportunity to watch a film on a big screen and presented the best films. The latter issue, however, was not so clearly perceived by respondents, as the average rating on a 7-point rating scale was 4.62. Users' perceptions of the value created by streaming platforms, as well as by movie theaters, may have been affected by the COVID-19 pandemic, which caused many movie premieres to be delayed or even moved to an online venue. A 7-point scale was used, where 1 meant that the respondent agreed to a small extent and 7 meant that the respondent agreed to a large extent.

Another important finding from the completed survey was that streaming platforms were more of a substitute for watching movies on TV than at the cinema (average ratings of 4.83 vs 4.63).

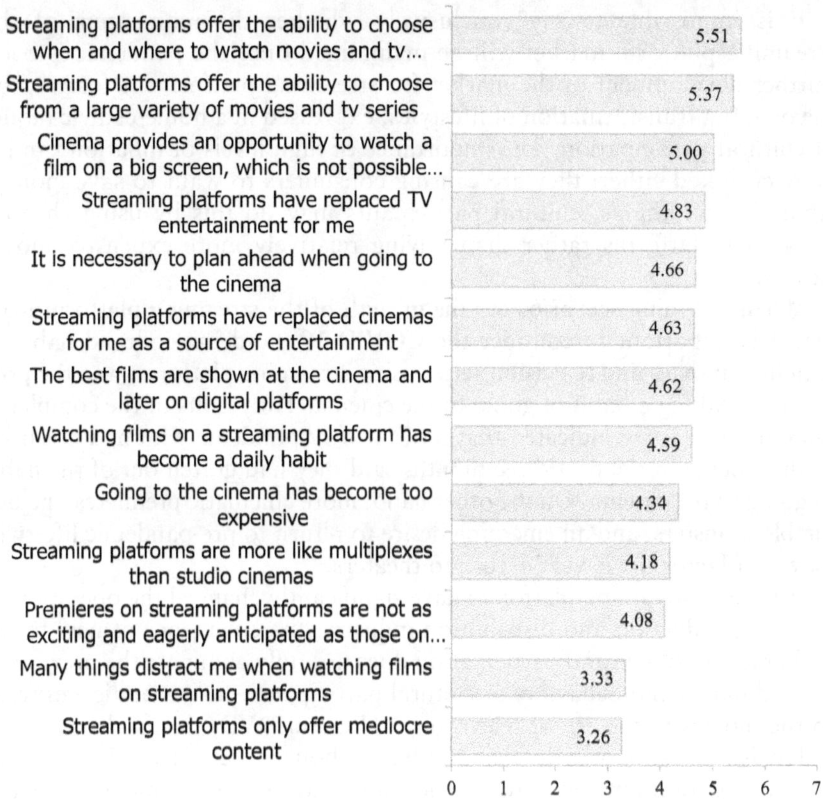

Figure 19.2 Perception of the value offered by streaming platforms by their users (N=676).

Source: Own elaboration.

Summary

Turning to the formulation of conclusions resulting from the considerations carried out in this chapter, it should be emphasized that adaptive responses could be observed in consumer behavior during the COVID-19 pandemic, including the accelerated virtualization of cultural participation. The analyses conducted allowed managerial implications to be formulated, but at the same time, they pointed to the need for and directions of further research on the issue addressed. They could identify to what extent the increasing use of streaming platforms was a reaction to the closing of movie theaters or to what extent it was a long-term change in the behavior of cultural participants. Subsequent research on the issues addressed in the current study could be repeated in a year's time. The next major direction for quantitative research in this area is to complete it among cultural participants in the U.S. market and other European markets.

It is impossible to say conclusively whether the momentum of the streaming platform market will be maintained once the pandemic is over. Further development of the market for streaming platforms is fostered by the ongoing transformation of lifestyles, expressed in a home-centric model of cultural participation. The importance of high levels of inflation cannot be overlooked either; they are causing consumers to want to save money. Among other things, cultural participants may do this by using cheaper streaming platforms rather than buying relatively more expensive movie tickets.

When outlining scenarios for the growth of the streaming platform market, it is important to consider the COVID-19 pandemic-induced habit of watching movies and television series using streaming platforms and the process of breaking a habit of going to the cinema. The results of the completed quantitative survey indicated that 34.7% of respondents who had not been to the cinema in the past three months said they had gotten out of the habit of going to the cinema. On the other hand, more cinematic premieres, including blockbusters, and an emerging desire to return to pre-pandemic lifestyles may be a factor in viewers' return to theaters.

Although streaming platforms have significantly changed the operation of the film production and distribution industry, the emergence of new forms and practices of cultural participation does not fully eliminate the previously formed habits and behaviors of cultural participants. Just as audiences went to the movies in the era of television, VHS, and DVD, this is also the case today. It is also noteworthy that Netflix has bought a cinema in Los Angeles with a long tradition and history, where it intends to hold premieres, and that Martin Scorsese has forced Netflix to premiere screenings of *The Irishman* in New York cinemas concurrently with the online premiere (Rogowski & Wróblewska, 2020a).

An attribute that favors cinemas is that access to original content often requires that viewers subscribe to several streaming platforms, although as the completed research indicated, the phenomenon of co-use of several streaming platforms in the Polish market currently is occurring to a limited extent.

Recommendations for Practice

The managerial implications of the completed study relate to the customer value enhancement of marketing activities carried out by streaming platforms, on the one hand, and by movie theaters, on the other. The development of the market for streaming platforms will depend on the extent to which their offerings are tailored to the needs of different market segments. This is all the more important as new players enter the market for streaming platforms in Poland, as Disney+ is currently doing. Given the intensifying relationship between new technologies and customer value creation, it is recommended to further increase the scope of individualization of marketing activities and improve the solutions used so far based on SEO data, SEM data, big data, data mining, and artificial intelligence. Also of great importance is social listening, which is an automated study of trends in social networks (Saura, 2020).

Further investment in advanced Internet marketing should not involve a move away from classic forms of marketing communications. The proper communication of films and series, including new ones based on unique features and technological innovations and a strong brand should also rely on classic forms of communication, including television and outdoor advertising. This is especially important from the point of view of new customers. At the same time, it should be emphasized that the thoughtful shaping of consumer experiences and sensations is becoming increasingly important, as the modern consumer is overstimulated.

From the point of view of cinemas, it is important to ensure a unique range of films and premieres. This is all the more important because the COVID-19 pandemic–induced changes in the film industry are linked to the fact that the pandemic has contributed to the development of the production of films for online exploitation as a first field. Online exploitation, however, has its limitations in terms of financial effects, as it does not replace cinema revenues for producers and distributors, which to date have accounted for a significant portion of revenues and enabled relatively quick repayment of liabilities (Rogowski & Wróblewska, 2020b, p. 15). Another recommended measure for cinemas is to introduce various types of price promotions that can offset the perception of the relatively high cost of attending cinema screenings. It is also reasonable to consider increasing the scope of cooperation between individual cinema chains, as well as studio cinemas, in order to join forces and organize promotions that remind viewers of the magic of the big screen in cinemas, which orchestrates a specific broadcasting and viewing situation, different from that created by streaming platforms.

References

Amit, R., and Zott, C. (2020). *Business Model Innovation Strategy: Transformational Concepts and Tools for Entrepreneurial Leaders*. Hoboken: Wiley.

Denzin, N.K. (2017). *The Research Act. A Theoretical Introduction to Sociological Methods*. New York: Routledge.

Fagerjord, A., and Kueng, L. (2019). Mapping the core actors and flows in streaming video services: What Netflix can tell us about these new media networks. *J. Media Bus. Stud.*, 16. https://doi.org/10.1080/16522354.2019.1684717.

Fiske, J. (1999). *Wprowadzenie do badań nad komunikowaniem*. Wrocław: Wydawnictwo Astrum.

Forrest, E. (2003). *Internet Marketing Intelligence. Research Tools, Techniques, and Resources*. New York: McGraw-Hill.

Glinka, B., and Czakon, W. (2021). *Podstawy badań jakościowych*. Warszawa: PWE.

Kluszczyński, R.W. (2010). *Sztuka interaktywna. Od dzieła-instrumentu do interaktywnego spektaklu*. Warszawa: Wydawnictwa Akademickie i Profesjonalne.

Kurti, E., Salavati, S., and Mirijamdotter, A. (2021). Using systems thinking to illustrate digital business model innovation. *Systems*, 9(86). https://doi.org/10.3390/systems9040086.

Leskovec, J., Rajaraman, A., and Ullman, J. (2014). *Mining of Massive Datasets*. Cambridge: Cambridge University Press.

Mier, J., and Kohli, A.K. (2021). Netflix: Reinvention across multiple time periods, reflections and directions for future research. *AMS Rev.*, 11. https://doi.org/10.1007/s13162-021-00197-w.

Mróz, B. (2021). *Zachowania konsumentów w czasie pandemii COVID-19*. Warszawa: Szkoła Główna Handlowa w Warszawie.

Mruk, H., and Stępień, B. (2013). *Tworzenie wartości dla klienta z perspektywy konsumentów i przedsiębiorstw*. Warszawa: PWE.

Nowicka, K. (2019). Biznes cyfrowy w optyce innowacji. W: K. Nowicka (red.), *Biznes cyfrowy. Perspektywa innowacji cyfrowych*. Warszawa: Oficyna Wydawnicza SGH.

Polak, K., and Żurawicka, M. (2015). Badania semiotyczne i ich praktyczne wykorzystanie. W: A. Dąbrowska, A. Wódkowski (red.), *Badania marketingowe. Praktyka nauce – Nauka praktyce*. Warszawa: Instytut Badań Rynku, Konsumpcji i Koniunktur.

Rahman, K.T., and Arif, M.Z.U. (2021). Impacts of Binge-Watching on Netflix during the COVID-19 pandemic. *South Asian J. Market.*, 2(1). https://doi.org/10.1108/SAJM-05-2021-0070.

Roberts, M.L. (2003). *Internet Marketing: Integrating Online and Offline Strategies* (International Edition). New York: McGraw-Hill.

Rogowski, S., and Wróblewska, A. (2020a). Film artystyczny na rynku kinowym (rozmowa z Romanem Gutkiem i Maciejem Zabojszczem). W: S. Rogowski, A. Wróblewska (red.), *Dystrybucja filmowa. Od kina do streaming*. Warszawa: Wydawnictwo Naukowe Semper.

Rogowski, S., and Wróblewska, A. (2020b). Wstęp. W: S. Rogowski, A. Wróblewska (red.), *Dystrybucja filmowa. Od kina do streamingu*. Warszawa: Wydawnictwo Naukowe Semper.

Rudawska, E. (2008). *Znaczenie relacji z klientami w procesie kształtowania wartości przedsiębiorstwa*. Szczecin: Wydawnictwo Naukowe Uniwersytetu Szczecińskiego.

Saura, J.R. (2020). Using Data Sciences in Digital Marketing: Framework, Methods, and Performance Metrics. *J. Innovat. Knowledge*, 1. https://doi.org/10.1016/j.jik.2020.08.001.

Sobocińska, M. (2019). Talent i nowe technologie jako stymulanty rozwoju rynku filmowego. W: A. Majer, T. Szczepański (red.), *Kultura produkcji filmowej: teorie, badania, praktyki*. Łódź: Wydawnictwo Biblioteki Państwowej Wyższej Szkoły Filmowej, Telewizyjnej i Teatralnej im. Leona Schillera w Łodzi.

Somborski, J. (2019). VOD: Więcej i od razu. *FilmPro*, 1(37).

Ulin, J.C. (2019). *The Business of Media Distribution. Monetizing Film, TV, and Video Content in an Online World*. New York: Routledge.

Urry, J. (2000). *Sociology Beyond Societies: Mobilities for the Twenty-First Century*. London: Routledge.

Westerman, G., Bonnet, D., and McAfee, A. (2014). *Leading Digital: Turning Technology into Business Transformation Hardcover*. Boston, MA: Harvard Business Review Press.

20 Enterprise Investment Activity during the COVID-19 Pandemic

Kinga Ociesa

Introduction

A key aspect of the development of the economy and enterprises is investment activity. Economically efficient investments are tools that stimulate structural changes in the economy. In addition, the implementation of the right investment decisions allows, inter alia, for the building of a competitive advantage, which increases the market share and maximizes the value of enterprises, which is the main goal of business entities (Mandziuk et al., 2016). Investing is closely related to the process of raising capital. The investment possibilities of enterprises depend on the ability to finance capital expenditures. Investment projects that do not take into account financial constraints may adversely affect the financial liquidity of a company, which may lead to the bankruptcy of the entity (Michalak, 2007).

Investing is a complex process that depends on many different factors. Among the determinants of investment activity, there are both external factors reflecting the environmental conditions and internal factors related to the investment needs of enterprises (Janik & Paździor, 2011). The macroeconomic environment may create opportunities and threats affecting the investment potential of enterprises. However, investment decisions regarding the use of emerging opportunities are also conditioned by the internal situation of a given economic entity. The indicated groups of factors are closely related to each other and affect the course of investment processes of enterprises. The internal determinants of investing activities depend on the decisions made in the entity. They include, among others, the size of the enterprise, the economic and financial conditions, the specificity of the company's operations, the financial capabilities of the entity, and the propensity for risk and propensity to invest (Kokot-Stępień, 2016). In turn, the external determinants of the implementation of investment projects include, among others, the general economic situation of the country, the sociopolitical stabilization of the country, the cost of obtaining foreign capital and the availability of external funds, the expected economic growth, and the investment climate in a given country. The specified determinants played a special role in the time of the COVID-19 pandemic. The crisis caused by the SARS-CoV-2 virus had

DOI: 10.4324/9781003475583-26

a negative impact on the functioning of many areas of the economy, posing numerous challenges for business entities, including investment activities.

Macroeconomic Environment as a Determinant of Investment Activity

As a result of the pandemic crisis, enterprises were forced to operate in an unstable environment. The consequences of restrictions on running a business were, inter alia, the instability of financial markets and the uncertainty of current and future revenues and cash flows, as well as the reduced ability of enterprises to settle current liabilities in a timely manner. The emerging financial problems of enterprises had a negative impact on their creditworthiness. Based on experiences during the initial phase of the pandemic, the banks developed new models of credit risk management, taking into account the division into sectors and subsectors in the assessment of creditworthiness (Jedynak & Bąk, 2021).

Stringent isolation measures were put in place to contain the spread of the coronavirus. The restrictions imposed on socio-economic activity had a negative impact on economic activity, as a result of which the world economy slowed down (Nowosad et al., 2021). According to the estimates of the Central Statistical Office, the gross domestic product (GDP) in Poland in 2020 decreased by 2.2% in real terms compared with the previous year. The largest decrease in the GDP was recorded in the second quarter of 2020 (–7.9% y/y). On the other hand, in 2021, the GDP grew in real terms by 5.9% (Główny Urząd Statystyczny [GUS], 2022). The pandemic constraints also resulted in a reduction in investment activity. In 2020, the gross fixed capital formation in Poland dropped in real terms by 9% y/y, while the investment rate (the ratio of gross fixed capital formation to GDP) fell to 16.6%. A decline in investment outlays was also recorded in the enterprise sector (by 6.1% y/y). In the wake of the pandemic, companies concentrated their spending on maintenance activities, reducing capital expenditures. The largest decreases in corporate investment expenditure occurred in the second and third quarters of 2020 (–13.6% y/y; –9.8% y/y). Already at the beginning of 2021, as a result of the improved conditions for running a business, there was a marked increase in investment expenditures in the enterprise sector (Q1 5.4% y/y; Q2 14.3% y/y) (Departament Strategii Rozwoju, 2022).

The negative effects of the crisis caused by the COVID-19 pandemic would be much more felt if not for the numerous actions taken by the government and the central bank. The Polish government implemented an aid program consisting of six anti-crisis shields and a financial shield. Support was provided through various institutions, including PFR, BGK, ZUS, MRPiT, and ARP. The aid offered to enterprises included loan subsidies, other subsidies, loans, guarantees, exemptions from contributions, and salary subsidies. The Government Fund for Local Investments was established to support investments worth more than PLN 400,000. Eighty-six percent of companies were financially supported by the anti-crisis shield. Entities from the SME sector received 70% exempt loans from the Polish Development Fund, with a total value of PLN 100 billion (Dębkowska et al., 2021). In order to mitigate the effects of the pandemic, corrective measures were also implemented in the area of monetary policy. In March 2020, the National Bank of Poland decided to lower the reference rate to 1% (from 1.5%). In April 2020, it reduced the rate to 0.5%. However, in May, the MPC lowered the reference rate again, and as a result, it reached the level of 0.1%. The central bank also lowered the required reserve ratio from 3.5% to 0.5%. Another activity stimulating the Polish economy was the lifting of the systemic risk buffer amounting to 3%. The introduced changes translated into a reduction in the average interest rate on loans and the release of funds in banks for granting loans (NBP, Internetowy Serwis Informacyjny).

The COVID-19 Pandemic in the Chemical Sector and the Sector of Computer Game Producers

The economic slowdown also translated into deterioration of the financial results of many enterprises. One of the sectors that was adversely affected by the pandemic was the chemical sector. Problems in this sector resulted, inter alia, from obstructed transport due to border closures, supply chain disruptions, and reduced demands for certain products. The COVID-19 pandemic forced changes in the business profiles of chemical companies. Some companies, in order to adapt to the prevailing environmental conditions and take advantage of the opportunities of increased demand in the area of personal protective equipment, expanded the scope of their offerings to add disinfectants or protective shields. According to the data of the GUS (2020), the value of the sold production of Polish Chemistry in the first half of 2020 decreased by as much as PLN 16 billion. The worst situation in the Polish chemical industry took place in April 2020, when the value of sold production decreased by about 30% compared with the previous year. In a survey conducted by PARP, almost half (49%) of enterprises in the chemical industry assessed the impact of the pandemic on their entities as negative. On the other hand, 39% of companies noted both positive and negative impacts of the COVID-19 pandemic on their operations (PARP Grupa PFR, 2021). In turn, according to the European Chemical Industry Council, the Polish chemical industry was the best in coping with the effects of the pandemic lockdown compared with Europe. The pandemic highlighted the importance of the chemical sector for the entire economy. The chemical industry is essential for the production of medical products, medicines, personal care products, and detergents by supplying raw materials and additives (Ullmann, 2021).

Despite its many negative effects, the COVID-19 pandemic had an indirect positive impact on the activities of certain sectors. A consequence of the increase in demand for certain products and services during the pandemic was the improvement of the financial results of selected enterprises. These entities included mainly companies from the information technology, media, entertainment, and consulting sectors. Due to pandemic constraints, the demand for services from online entertainment and media companies increased significantly, including the producers of computer games (Jedynak & Bąk, 2021). According to the PARP report, in 2020, 73% of companies listed on the Warsaw Stock Exchange producing computer games recorded an increase in revenues. Despite the pandemic's difficulties, the sector grew in many ways. Confirmation that the pandemic period was a "golden period" for producers of and investments in games was the estimated 30% increase in revenues in this sector in 2020 (PARP PFR Group, 2021).

Based on the above analysis of statistical data and a literature review, it can be concluded that at the time of the COVID-19 pandemic, one of the important factors influencing the investment decisions of enterprises was the uncertainty of the macroeconomic environment. During the pandemic crisis, there was social and economic destabilization and negative investment moods. However, at the same time, the costs of financing with floating-rate loans decreased and the availability of external funds increased. Therefore, it is reasonable to pose the following research question: *Does a reduction in investment financing costs translate into an increase in investment intensity in an unstable environment?*

In order to try to answer the above question, this chapter analyzed the investment activity of companies listed on the Warsaw Stock Exchange in the WIG-CHEMIA and WIG.GAMES5 indexes in the years from 2019 to 2021.

Research Methodology

The research published so far showed that companies limited their investment activities in the time of the pandemic. However, the analyses performed did not distinguish companies listed in the WIG.CHEMIA and WIG.GAMES5 indices. In order to fill the indicated research gap, empirical research was carried out through a review of the data contained in the financial reports of the indicated companies. The research sample was divided into two groups: the chemical sector and the sector of computer game producers. The following entities are currently listed in the WIG-CHEMIA index: PCC Rokita, Polwax, CIECH, Zakłady Chemiczne Police, and Grupa Azoty. Those listed in the WIG.GAMES5 index are: 11 bit studios, CD Projekt, CI Games, Huuuge Inc., and Ten Square Games. The selection of the research sample also resulted from the different sensitivities of the chemical sector and the sector of computer game producers to economic fluctuations and pandemic restrictions. The audit covered the financial statements of the listed companies for the years from 2019 to 2021. Thus, the time range covered the pre-pandemic period and the pandemic mitigation period.

Findings

In the analyzed years, there were significant fluctuations in the levels of net profits and sales revenues, both in chemical companies and companies producing computer games. The worst period in the year of pandemic restrictions in the chemical industry was the second quarter of 2020. All companies recorded a decrease in sales revenues and net profits compared with the previous quarter. The lowest rate of changes in sales revenues, amounting to –27% q/q, was achieved by CIECH, while the lowest rate of changes in the net financial result, at –420% q/q, was achieved by Polwax. In the gaming sector, greater variations in the shaping of the indicated financial data were observed. In 2020, the lowest average rate of changes in sales revenues, –12%, was recorded in the first quarter of 2020 and the lowest average rate of changes in net profits, at –8%, was recorded in the third quarter of 2020 (BiznesRadar.pl).

In the analyzed period, the average level of the investment intensity ratio, measured as the relation of CAPEX to sales revenues, was also subject to significant fluctuations and varied depending on the sector. Chemical industry companies showed a relative stabilization in terms of the implemented investment policy in individual quarters in the period before the pandemic and during the expiration of the pandemic restrictions. On the other hand, in 2020, despite the unstable environmental conditions, there was a marked increase in the investment activity of the analyzed group of entities. It is surprising that the investment intensity ratio was at its highest (between 19% and 34%) during the pandemic crisis. In turn, gaming companies were much more active in making investments before the outbreak of the pandemic. In addition, from the first quarter of 2020, sinusoidal fluctuations in the average investment intensity of companies listed in the WIG.GAMES5 index can be observed (Figure 20.1).

The large diversification of the financial situation and investment activity of the surveyed entities required in-depth analysis. For this purpose, the investment activities of individual companies were reviewed.

PCC Rokita Capital Group

The PCC Rokita Group is an international capital group consisting of 80 companies operating in the chemical, energy, and logistics sectors. In the face of the pandemic, in order to adapt to the market demand, the PCC Group started producing disinfectants, detergents, and cleaning agents. The COVID-19 pandemic also forced the company to partially limit the implemented investment projects. In 2019, the companies that made up the PCC Group incurred capital expenditures in the total amount of EUR 163.5 million. In the following year, as a result of the unstable conditions caused by the pandemic crisis, the Group invested only EUR 66.6 million. In 2021, investments amounted to EUR 110.9 million. The carrying amount of investment projects disclosed as fixed assets under construction as of 31 December 2020, was PLN 114,963,000, which meant a 29% decrease compared with the previous year (2019: PLN 162,580,000). The Group's key investments included the construction of the Process Innovation and Scaling Center, the modernization and optimization of the propylene oxide plant, the expansion

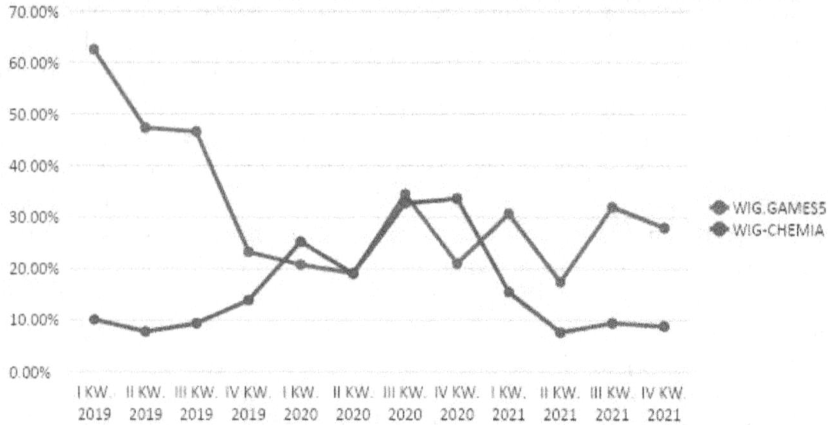

Figure 20.1 Average investment intensity of companies listed in the WIG-CHEMIA and WIG.GAMES5 indices in individual quarters in the years 2019 to 2021

Source: Own study based on the financial statements of the companies surveyed.

and modernization of power grids, and the expansion of the ethylene oxide storage base. In 2020, the parent company obtained government aid in the form of cash grants and grants in the form of loans on preferential terms for investment projects in the amount of PLN 56,046,000. In the published reports, the PCC Group emphasized the significant impact of investment decisions made on the competitive position, profitability, and development of companies operating within the Group. At the same time, the Group emphasized that investment activity depended on the situation related to the pandemic crisis. In addition, the management board was analyzing the possibilities of changing the financing structure, regardless of the drop in interest rates caused by the pandemic.

Polwax

Polwax SA is the largest Polish producer and distributor of refined and deodorized paraffins, waxes, and products based on paraffins. The November pandemic restrictions affected the company's financial results because the demand for paraffin masses used in the production of candles was reduced. The total investment expenditures for the purchase of intangible assets and tangible fixed assets presented in the cash flow statement in 2019 amounted to PLN 14,860,000, PLN 31,865,000 in 2020, and PLN 2,221,000 in 2021 (the amounts do not include cash flows from forward transactions). The capital expenditures on fixed assets in the analyzed period were as follows: PLN 10,357,200 (2019); PLN 4,894,000 (2020); and PLN 2,312,800 (2021). The decrease in investment outlays in the following years was mainly due to the suspension of the construction of the solvent de-oiling installation, but the decision was made in 2019, that is, before the outbreak of the COVID-19 pandemic.

CIECH Capital Group

CIECH is an international capital group that produces soda ash, baking soda, and evaporated soda, as well as pesticides and polyurethane foams, and is a supplier of sodium silicates. After the outbreak of the COVID-19 pandemic, the Group expanded the scope of its activities to the production of specialized protective masks. The CIECH Group also took steps to minimize the risk of failure in implementing the assumed investment plans, focusing on key projects and adjusting investment expenditures to the current economic situation and the possibility of obtaining capital. In 2020, capital expenditures incurred by the entities forming the Group oscillated at the level of PLN 757 million, which meant an 84% increase compared with the previous year (2019, PLN 412 million). In 2021, the upward trend continued, and investments in the amount of PLN 899 million were implemented. In pandemic conditions, the main investment project for the construction of a salt works in Germany was finalized. In the analyzed years, numerous investment projects were implemented with the use of public funds.

Grupa Azoty Capital Group

The Grupa Azoty Group is one of the key companies in the fertilizer and chemical industry in Europe. According to the Group's reports, the pandemic crisis did not affect the timeliness of the implemented strategic investment projects. The level of capital expenditure on property, plants and equipment, and intangible assets in 2019 was approximately PLN 1 billion, in 2020 approximately PLN 3 billion, and in 2021 approximately PLN 2.5 billion. The increase in investment outlays resulted from the implementation of key investments in recent years. In the structure of completed investment projects, the dominant role was played by investments related to business development (in 2019, they accounted for 48.2% of investment expenditures, in 2020 for 63.3%, and in 2021 for 50%). On the other hand, the share of investment expenditures related to maintaining a business in total investment expenditures amounted to 17.8% in 2019, 11.8% in 2020, and 11.3% in 2021.

Grupa Azoty Zakłady Chemiczne Police

The Zakłady Chemiczne Police SA Capital Group is part of the Grupa Azoty SA Capital Group. During the pandemic period, the Group continued its investment programs. In 2019, the expenditures of the Police Group on property, plants and equipment, and intangible assets amounted to PLN

198,715,000. PLN (47% were investments related to business development). In the following year, despite the pandemic crisis, the value of investment outlays increased to the level of PLN 1,639,046,000. PLN, of which 93% were investments related to business development. On the other hand, in 2021, investment expenditures were PLN 179,637,000. PLN (43% were investments related to business development).

11 Bit Studios

11 bit studios is a joint stock company operating in the field of the production, publishing, and distribution of computer games. The company's management board in the published reports emphasized that the COVID-19 pandemic did not affect the company's current operations, and therefore, in the face of the pandemic crisis, it continued its development plans in terms of investments. In 2020, the total investment expenditures amounted to approximately PLN 34.4 million, compared with approximately PLN 49.3 million in 2019. In 2021, the company spent over PLN 37.4 million on investments. Most of the investments were financial investments (i.e., bank deposits and financial instruments). However, expenditures on tangible fixed assets and intangible assets (in particular for the production of games) were also significant. In 2019, they amounted to PLN 14,436,630, in 2020 they increased to PLN 29,754,426, and in 2021 they slightly decreased to PLN 28,878,349.

CD Projekt Capital Group

CD Projekt is a capital group operating in the video game industry. Before the pandemic, during the pandemic, and in the period of pandemic mitigation, the Group implemented numerous investment projects. In the analyzed years, the dominant share for the structure of CD Projekt investments were expenditures on development, that is, the production of games and technologies (in 2019 approximately PLN 165 million, in 2020 approximately PLN 203 million, and in 2021 PLN 155 million). The Group also allocated a large part of its capital expenditures to the acquisition of intangible assets and tangible fixed assets (in 2019 approximately PLN 92 million, in 2020 PLN 19 million, and in 2021 PLN 30 million). In 2020, CD Projekt invested its cash surplus in treasury bonds and bank deposits for a total amount of PLN 405,156,000.

CI Games Capital Group

CI Games is a capital group engaged in the production, publishing, and distribution of computer games. In the area of the Group's investment activities, expenditures on development work (i.e., game production) dominated; in 2019 they amounted to almost PLN 18.3 million, while in 2020 they increased to approximately PLN 19.9 million. The Group also incurred expenses for the purchase of intangible assets and tangible fixed assets. In 2019, they amounted to PLN 2.1 million, and in 2020 they reached the value of almost PLN 2.6 million. In 2021, as part of cash flows from investing activities, CI Games listed the total amount of expenses for the purchase of property, plants and equipment, intangible assets other than goodwill, investment properties, and other non-current assets as over PLN 44.4 million.

Huuuge Inc. Capital Group

Huuuge is an international capital group whose main activity is the production and distribution of mobile games. Despite the pandemic crisis, the Group's capital expenditures on the acquisition of property, plants, and equipment showed an upward trend. In 2019, they amounted to PLN 1,085,000 USD, in 2020 to 2,140,000 USD, and in 2021 to 2,595,000 USD. In the years from 2020 to 2021, the Huuuge Group also incurred expenses for the purchase of software (in 2020, USD 1,297,000, and in 2021, USD 3,860,000). However, the largest share of the capital expenditures in 2021 was for the acquisition of intellectual property rights, in the amount of USD 9.5 million. In addition, in 2020, the analyzed entity acquired subsidiaries, investing the amount of PLN 2,088,000 USD.

Grupa Kapitałowa Ten Square Games

Ten Square Games is a producer and publisher of mobile games available in the Free to Play model. In the analyzed years, the Group's investment activity developed dynamically, and this was confirmed by the growing investment expenditures incurred for the purchase of intangible assets and tangible fixed assets (in 2019 PLN 3,463,000, in 2020 PLN 3,792,000, and in 2021 PLN 24,386,000). In addition, in 2021, the Group acquired the company's shares, incurring expenditures of almost PLN 218,161,000.

Conclusions and Recommendations

Projects undertaken as part of investment activities are conditioned by many factors. A review of the activities of selected companies confirmed the complexity of the investment process, especially in the face of a pandemic. The analysis showed that most of the surveyed entities continued their strategic investment plans despite the pandemic crisis. The dominant percentage of enterprises used available public funds to finance their investments, as well as loans with variable interest rates, which decreased significantly during the pandemic. Moreover, a large differentiation of the dynamics and the amount of investment outlays can be observed in both groups of companies. Undoubtedly, enterprises saw the necessity to implement investments in order to maximize the value of their units. At the same time, they analyzed the macroeconomic environment and estimated the risks associated with the unstable environment in order to minimize the possible negative effects of the pandemic. However, due to the large variation in investment decisions of the surveyed enterprises and the dependence of investment activities on many different factors, it is not possible to clearly define the impact of lowering financing costs and increasing the availability of external funds on investment activities.

The above considerations allowed for the development of the following conclusions and recommendations:

1 The implementation of optimal investment projects is of key importance for the development of business entities. Investments are the foundation for building a competitive advantage and enterprise value. Entities focused on maximizing the company's value should pay great attention to the preparation of strategic investment plans that take into account all risk areas. This is particularly important in the chemical sector, which is much more capital-intensive than the sector of computer game producers. Investment projects are created well in advance, and due to numerous procedures and strictly defined budget plans, they are characterized by low flexibility. Therefore, already at the stage of planning investment projects, enterprises should prepare multi-variant strategic scenarios that take into account crisis situations. The prepared strategies could protect the companies from having to abandon their investment plans (in particular, the PCC Rokita Group and Polwax). However, in the absence of investment potential for the implementation of all the assumed projects, one should focus on key undertakings for the development of the company in order to prevent loss of liquidity caused by the failure of implemented investments.
2 Investment activity is conditioned by external factors and the situation of a given entity. Enterprises, when undertaking investment projects, should identify their strengths and weaknesses as well as opportunities and threats from the environment. In the face of the crisis, numerous aid programs appear to support investment activities (the CIECH Capital Group has implemented many investment projects based on public funds). It is recommended that all entities review the possibilities of financing with public funds and take advantage of the emerging new perspectives. At the same time, it should be borne in mind that the situation may change, for instance, interest rates may be raised, and this would negatively affect the financial risk of enterprises that are financing their investment activities with floating-rate loans.
3 The flexibility of an entity has a significant impact on its operations, especially in unstable conditions. Enterprises should constantly analyze the environment and adapt to the dynamically changing situation. A review of the activities of the surveyed companies showed that even in times of crisis, numerous opportunities emerge, but they should be noticed and properly used. It is recommended to adapt the offered products and services to the

market demand. Sometimes it is associated with the diversification of the conducted activities and the targeting of investment plans to other areas of activity (in the pandemic period, only the PCC Rokita Group and the CIECH Group decided to produce personal protective equipment). Taking risks can turn out to be the key to success.

4 Enterprises for which a crisis is a "golden period" (in the pandemic era they included, among others, the producers of computer games) should take full advantage of the increased investment potential. Mergers and acquisitions may be a chance for business development. In the face of the crisis, entities with a stronger market position should consider the possibility of acquiring other units (in the analyzed period only GK Huuuge Inc. and GK Ten Square Games acquired shares of other units). On the other hand, entities with a weakened position should observe the competitive environment in order to protect themselves against a possible hostile takeover.

To sum up, the outbreak of the COVID-19 pandemic undoubtedly influenced many areas of the economy, including companies' decisions regarding investment activities. For some sectors, the pandemic was a golden age and an opportunity to implement key investment projects, while others had to abandon investments in order to maintain their current operations.

References

Dębkowska, K., Kłosiewicz-Górecka, U., Szymańska, A., Ważniewski, P., Zybertowicz, K. (2021). *Tarcza Antykryzysowa. Koło ratunkowe dla firm i gospodarki?* Warszawa: Polski Instytut Ekonomiczny.

Departament Strategii Rozwoju. (2022). *Raport – Inwestycje w Polsce. Okres: I kw. 2020 r. – III kw. 2021 r.*

Główny Urząd Statystyczny. (2020). *Biuletyn Statystyczny GUS nr 6/2020.*

Główny Urząd Statystyczny. (2022). *Informacja Głównego Urzędu Statystycznego w sprawie zaktualizowanego szacunku PKB według kwartałów za lata 2020–2021.*

Janik, W., & Paździor, A. (2011). *Zarządzanie finansowe w przedsiębiorstwie.* Lublin: Politechnika Lubelska.

Jedynak, P., & Bąk, S. (2021). *Risk Management in Crisis: Winners and Losers during the COVID-19 Pandemic.* New York: Routledge. doi: 10.4324/9781003131366.

Kokot-Stępień, P. (2016). Uwarunkowania decyzji inwestycyjnych w przedsiębiorstwach branży hutniczej. *Finanse, Rynki Finansowe, Ubezpieczenia, 82*(1), pp. 89–97. doi: 10.18276/frfu.2016.4.82/1-07.

Mandziuk, R., Nawra, P., & Ossowska, J. (2016). Inwestycje rzeczowe przedsiębiorstw. *Finanse, Rynki Finansowe, Ubezpieczenia, 1*(79), pp. 545–553. doi: 10.18276/frfu.2016.79-43.

Michalak, A. (2007). *Finansowanie inwestycji w teorii i praktyce.* Warszawa: PWN.

Narodowy Bank Polski. (n.d.). Internetowy Serwis Informacyjny. https://www.nbp.pl/ (Accessed: 20.6.2022).

Nowosad, A., Turanli, Ü., & Lorenc, K. (2021). The coronavirus SARS-CoV-2 and its impact on the world. In P. Dykas & R. Wisła (Eds.), *The socioeconomic impact of*

COVID-19 on Eastern European countries. New York: Routledge. doi: 10.4324/9781003211891.

PARP Grupa PFR. (2021). *Branżowy Bilans Kapitału Ludzkiego II – branża chemiczna*. Raport podsumowujący I edycję badań realizowanych w latach 2020–2021.

PARP PFR Group (2021). *The game industry of Poland* [Report 2021].

Ullmann, M. (2021). Bez innowacyjności chemia nie jest w stanie się rozwijać - rozmowa z dr inż. Tomaszem Zielińskim. *Laboratorium – Przegląd Ogólnopolski, 1*, pp.10–13. https://laboratorium.elamed.pl/archiwum[wydanie,53939,1,2021,53941]#53941 (Accessed: 20.6.2022).

Index

Note: **Bold** page numbers refer to tables; *italic* page numbers refer to figures and page numbers followed by "n" denote endnotes.

For Product Safety Concerns and Information please contact our EU representative GPSR@taylorandfrancis.com
Taylor & Francis Verlag GmbH, Kaufingerstraße 24, 80331 München, Germany

www.ingramcontent.com/pod-product-compliance
Lightning Source LLC
LaVergne TN
LVHW021121300926
849160LV00010B/806